THE EARLY MARRIED LIFE OF MARIA JOSEPHA LADY STANLEY, WITH EXTRACTS FROM SIR JOHN STANLEY'S 'PRÆTERITA.' Edited by one of their Grandchildren, JANE H. ADEANE

ALDERLEY OLD HALL
Burnt down 1779

The grace of God and a quiet life,
A mind content and an honest wife;
A good report and a friend in store,
What need a man to wish for more?

Favourite lines of Sir James Stanley, d. 1746

LONGMANS, GREEN, AND CO.
39 PATERNOSTER ROW, LONDON
NEW YORK AND BOMBAY
1899

TO THE MEMORY OF

LOUISA DOROTHEA STANLEY

THROUGH WHOSE TENDER CARE OF PAST RECORDS

IT HAS BEEN POSSIBLE FOR HER

TO WHOSE CHARGE SHE COMMITTED THEM

TO GIVE SOME IMPRESSION OF

TWO CHARACTERS OF MARKED INDIVIDUALITY

'I am the first Antiquary of my race. People don't know how entertaining a study it is. "Who begot whom?" is a most amusing kind of Hunting. One recovers a Grandfather instead of breaking one's own neck, and then one grows so pious to the memory of a thousand persons one never heard of before! One finds how a Christian name came into a Family, with a world of other delectable erudition'

HORACE WALPOLE to REV. W. COLE,
June 5th, 1775

PREFACE.

MANY of the readers of the 'Girlhood of Maria Josepha Holroyd' have asked whether there are no letters of her married life equally worthy of being preserved; and have suggested that, if such be the case, a selection from them would form a welcome companion to the bright letters of her earlier days.

To this question the present volume is an answer. It consists of extracts from Sir J. T. Stanley's MSS. up to the time of his marriage, and afterwards of selections from the correspondence of his wife, Maria Josepha, which tell the story of the early years of a married life that lasted over half a century (1796 to 1850).

To picture that life it seems needful first to give some account of her husband. He was the elder son of Sir John Thomas Stanley, Bart., of Alderley, Cheshire, and of his wife, Margaret Owen, a Welsh heiress, who brought the estate of Penrhos into the family. He was born in 1766, succeeded to the baronetcy 1807, and was created Lord Stanley of Alderley in 1839.

His early training and associations were very different from those of his wife. Both were brought up among the makers of History, but while she had been accustomed to the notice and conversation of the remarkable men who frequented the house of her father, Lord Sheffield, Sir John as a boy was, in the more common fashion of that day, kept very much out of sight and hearing, and was entrusted by his parents to the care of others. His mother had decided opinions about her son's education, and, according to her wishes, he was taken early from school to travel under the care of a tutor, Mr. Six. From that time forward he never again had the companionship of boys of his own age.

It was a peculiar training, very desultory and incomplete as to intellectual discipline, but not without value in the experience of life and society.

Before he was twenty, he had mixed in the Court circles of three European capitals, Brunswick, Turin and Rome. French he spoke fluently, German and Italian with facility, and his love of German literature never left him.

In 1789 he sailed with a few companions for Iceland in his own ship, the 'John,' an enterprise then almost unprecedented. His Journals and his drawings remain to tell the story of his adventures in the North.

Sir John in politics was a strong Liberal, and stood alone among the Cheshire squires of the time. Fox-hunting, their chief occupation and topic, had no attraction for him, and consequently, beyond cultivating friendly intercourse, he had but little in common with his county neighbours.

As time went on, a tendency to gout inclined him to lead a sedentary life, so that the active management of his estate devolved on his wife, who ruled with remarkable ability.

Sir John's turn of mind inclined him to think and write much on metaphysical subjects. The fiery spirit of his youth was not inconsistent with a dreamy and introspective cast of mind. He was essentially dignified, high-minded and intellectual. His chief characteristics were the hatred of injustice and the love of truth.

His relations with his tenants and dependents were ideal, and the words which were said a hundred years ago over the grave of Beaumarchais might be applied to him : ' His domestics grew grey in his service and the companions of his youth were the friends of his more advanced age.'

The old people round Holyhead Mountain used to tell how, when confined to the house, Sir John would send for their fathers to talk over the local folk-lore, and over traditions and customs that are now fast dying out.

His children, who adored him, grew up among the associations of their beautiful homes in Cheshire and Anglesey, and found congenial society in Alderley Rectory, where lived his younger brother, Edward, afterwards Bishop of Norwich, with his gifted wife and children, one of whom, Arthur Stanley, became Dean of Westminster.

Among Sir John's children his chosen companion was his daughter Louisa Dorothea, who, with kindred tastes, helped him in all his literary researches, and after his death preserved with reverent care his every written word.

This volume may in part fulfil her long-cherished wish, that the materials she collected might be put together, so that the memories of her parents' life should not pass entirely away unheeded by the succeeding generations.

JANE H. ADEANE

LLANFAWR, HOLYHEAD.

CONTENTS.

———

SIR JOHN THOMAS STANLEY.

CHAPTER I.

CHILDHOOD AND SCHOOL LIFE.

1766–1780.

CHAPTER II.

BOYHOOD AT THE COURT OF BRUNSWICK.

1781–1783.

CHAPTER III.

FOREIGN SOCIETY AND SARDINIAN ROYALTY.

1783–1786.

MARRIAGE BELLS, 1796.

MARIA JOSEPHA STANLEY.

CHAPTER I.

FOLLOWS THE DRUM.

1797.

CHAPTER II.

AT HER OWN FIRESIDE.

1798-1799.

CHAPTER III.

' SO WISE AND MATRONLY.'

1800.

LIST OF PLATES

The design on the cover, drawn by MR. HAROLD HUGHES, is an adaptation of that on an ivory fan which was among the wedding gifts of M. J. Stanley.

SIR JOHN THOMAS STANLEY.

CHAPTER I.

CHILDHOOD AND SCHOOL LIFE.

1766–1780.

School memories—Death of Thrale—Mount Clare—Fête at Hoylake—First ride—Driving his first team—Raising the devil—Love of flowers—School at Greenwich—Visit to Cambridge—Last days at the Old Hall—Treasure trove—Winnington—Storm and fire at Greenwich—Burning of old home—The Park House—'Four and twenty fiddlers'—Dinner at Hoo Green—Tunbridge Wells—Sir H. F. Campbell—Gordon riots and Lord Sheffield's services.

Extracts from Sir J. T. Stanley's Præterita.[1]

A MAN's life previous to his third year is an absolute blank. Sir William Jones[2] calls the fourth year the period of recollection, but it will be found that most of us retain some faint reminiscences of things which have been felt or noticed previous to our fourth year. A few recollections remain with me, as vividly impressed on my mind as those of the events of yesterday. I can remember the gathering of a flower of Veronica in a garden near Bath; my grandmother (Lady Stanley) making wine of mulberries; a fallen tree lying across the road; all which circumstances I cannot connect with a later date than the summer or autumn previous to the commencement of my fourth year. I have in mind a grass walk under a cut hedge, and a mound at the end of it where stood the mulberry tree, and the parlour looking into the garden, and the place in it where my grandmother sat with the mulberries on a table before her; and the lane leading down to the house where lay the elm. After her husband's death in 1755, she purchased a house in

---

[1] His early memories were so called by Sir John half a century before the recollections of Mr. Ruskin were published under that title.

[2] Sir W. Jones, English orientalist, jurist, and littérateur, 1746–1794.

Gay Street, Bath, where she lived, excepting a few months each summer spent in a villa near Bath, called Larkhall.

She was the only child of Thomas Ward, Esq., of St. Clement Danes, a banker; the house in which he was a partner is the same as that of the present Messrs. Goslings and Sharpe. She lived with her husband, Sir Edward Stanley, for many years in Essex Street, near the Temple. Sir Edward had only two children by her: James, who died when about eight years old, and my father, born 1735. She survived her husband about fifteen years, living at Alderley till her son's marriage, and at Bath till her death in 1774.

I remember seeing my grandmother in her coffin, and mourning clothes being brought to me and my sister; and when the winter was past my being taken to Loughborough House School, and left there in the midst of seventy or eighty boys, all older than myself. Loughborough House had been a nobleman's mansion in the manor of Lambeth Wick. It stands a few yards off the high road leading from Westminster Bridge to Streatham, about three miles from the bridge. It had been let by Lord Holland a few years only before I went there to a French Protestant clergyman, M. Perney, who had recently come to England. He was appointed one of the preachers of the chapel near St. James's Palace, and was induced to attempt to establish a school for very young children on a scale of show and expense exceeding any others then existing.[1] The occupation of a nobleman's villa for the purpose, the purchase of a service of plate for the use of the scholars, the providing beds for each of them separately, with the conversion of an extensive walled garden into a playground had their effect, and he soon had eighty or ninety boys of the higher classes of society placed under his care.

The unparalleled scale of expense is shown by the following:

	£	s.	d.
Master Stanley, for one year's board, tuition and masters, etc., from March 1774	52	10	0
5 Pair of shoes	1	1	0

The average expenses of good education may perhaps be judged by Rev. Dr. Young having in 1751 paid £15 for one year's board etc. at school for his son Arthur (the Author and Agriculturist.)

The playground retained the vines and fruit-trees which
had been planted against the walls when a garden, and it
was a singular proof of the good discipline in which the boys
were kept that grapes, apricots, peaches, and cherries were
allowed to remain ungathered. Rose trees, which had
grown to the size of large bushes, blossomed unmolested.
It was a great treat when on some holiday each boy was
permitted to gather one.

The master to whom I am most indebted for any advantage I gained during the time I was at the school was the
Rev. Reynolds Davies. He was engaged to teach the boys
Latin, History, Geography, and English. I remember his
singling me out, perhaps because I was the youngest, to sit
on his knees, and tell me stories. Of my schoolfellows I
can name the following:—the Duke of Bedford and his
brothers—Lords John and William Russell, the Duke of
Hamilton,[1] the present Lord Clancarty, Eastwick, Anger-
stein, three Edmonstones, Augustus Hervey—a son of Lord
Bristol, Stanhope, Clive, Lord Garlies,[2] a son of Sir Robert
MacAlister, Gibbs, Nield, Gideon, afterwards Mr. Eardley
Palmer.

The one I was most intimate with was Hervey, named
after his father, Augustus. He was a warm-hearted, passionate, intrepid boy, a little older than myself. Hervey
left the school at the time I did, and was sent to sea under
the care of his uncle, Constantine Phipps, Lord Mulgrave.[3]
He was killed by a cannon-ball, standing close to his uncle
on the deck of the 'Courageux,' one of the fleet which,
under Lord Howe, was relieving Gibraltar.

[1] 10th Duke of Hamilton, born 1767, died 1852.
[2] 8th Earl of Galloway, born 1768.
[3] In the spring of 1778 Lord M. commissioned the 'Courageux,' a 4-gun
ship which had been captured from the French in 1761. In the action of
July 27, off Ushant, the 'Courageux' had a distinguished part. The French
three-decker 'Ville de Paris' had fallen to leeward of their line, and lay right
in the line of the English ship's advance. The look-out on the forecastle
called out that they would be foul of the three-decker. 'No matter,' answered
Mulgrave; 'the oak of old England is as well able to bear a blow as that of
France.' The 'Courageux,' however, just cleared the jibboom of the 'Ville de
Paris,' and passed to windward of her, pouring in a destructive broadside.
Dict. Naval Biog. vol. xlv.

Clive and Edmonstone were also my friends, and Thrale my partner in a garden, whose share of it, and a box-myrtle, I inherited by his death. He died in March 1776, an event to which Dr. Johnson has given a classical notoriety, and I never see a box-myrtle without a thought of past times.

Clive's father and mother were much attached to our family. Mr. Clive was a partner in Gosling's bank, and the friendship might have arisen from my grandmother's father having been also a partner. I often went with Clive on Saturdays to his father's villa at Roehampton, called Claremount (now Mount Clare). They were happy days: freedom in full scope, pleasure grounds, gardens, fields, and Richmond Park open to us, and no fear of a scolding on returning to the house; and then the getting crabs, bulrushes, &c. &c.

In the spring of 1775 I had a serious illness and was carried home to my father's house in Grosvenor Place. I remember sitting at a window looking out over the fields between the house and Sloane Street, not then built, however.

In the summer of 1776 my father and mother took me with them to Alderley; we travelled in a coach with two outriders, and reached Alderley the evening of the third day. I date from this time my accurate remembrance of the houses, rooms, moat, mill and gardens &c. at Alderley, the stone entrance gates, the stone terrace, the bridge, the hall, the parlour and its pictures, the dining room, the great stairs, and the chiming clock on them; the whole house as it surrounded its inner court with all outbuildings; the beech wood, the mere, the adjacent country of the Edge being a common, and of Sossmoss with only three clumps of firs; and of prison bars played in the open spaces between them.

From Alderley I was taken to Chester, and from thence to Hoylake, where we passed a night in a hovel called a public-house, and there I first found by chance 'Robinson Crusoe,' which I devoured. My father gave a fête to all the country round Hoylake. We had cockfighting, men running races in sacks for hats, and girls, almost without anything on them, for smocks. Large West-Indiamen could then ride at anchor in the lake. I recollect the deep sands and rabbits in Delamere Forest, a night spent at St. Asaph, a visit to Bodelwyddan, and seeing bullocks drove across the Conway river near the castle.

I was put upon a pony for the first time when at Alderley, 1776, a vicious little animal which ran away with me near Sossmoss, and I was not allowed to ride again for a year or two—a great mortification, as a pair of boots had been made for me in London.

My first ride, was, I believe, on the day of my mother's last ride, for I do not remember ever seeing her on a horse after; but till her death she never kept her bed, and her power of encountering fatigue till she was past seventy was astonishing. When near this age she walked with me from Penrhos to the top of Holyhead Mountain and back again, with the spirit and activity of a young girl.

I well remember being at Baron Hill in 1777 with my father and mother when the fêtes were given on the occasion of the marriage of Lord Bulkeley to Miss Warren.

I have a full recollection of my amusements at Penrhos : of bathing in the little bay, of building castles under the sycamore trees, my swimming a vessel in the brickfield holes near Beddmynych, my driving four labourers harnessed to a little phaeton, made for my mother when a child, and many wanderings over the fields with my uncle Robert Owen, and his giving me a guinea.

Before I left Loughborough House I had got through the Latin Grammar, and had translated and learned by heart a part of Ovid. I had picked up a little French, and drew tolerably for my age. M. Perney left it to his ushers to make religion a part of education as they pleased. I remember Mr. Davies often speaking to us of God as a Being who saw everything everywhere, but more as of One who was watching to see our faults than to guide us to good and protect us from evil. It is possible that, fear being a passion more easy to excite than love, and more powerful in its

immediate operation, Mr. Davies succeeded in making us
tell fewer lies, and keep our hands off M. Perney's fruit.
I do not know that I was more credulous than other boys
of my age, but I certainly was very credulous. I remember
once looking in earnest for the Dog and the Bush in the
moon through a spying-glass, and at another time believing
that some of our wickedest boys, who said they would raise
the devil by forming themselves into a ring and saying the
Lord's Prayer backwards, would absolutely succeed in
bringing him out of the ground. . . . How I gained it I
know not, but a love of Nature had grown up with me to be
a passion, and I cannot but think that a sense of the beautiful
in the natural is by some inexplicable law united in the
human mind with a sense of the beautiful in the moral
world. The confinement within walls in which I passed so
many of my early years was perhaps rather a stimulant than
otherwise of my love of Nature. I knew every flower that
blossomed in our playground, and the impression they made
on me was so strong that I have them all now before me,
each in its respective place. Whenever I see polyanthuses,
crocuses, snowdrops, wallflowers, lilies, the fellows of my
old fellow-prisoners, I think of Loughborough House. Our
walk to church (Stockwell Chapel) was across fields and a
little common ; no fear of punishment could keep me in my
ranks. I darted out of them to get branches of blackthorn
and gorse bushes, and I well remember having a long task
set me, for making a dash at a weed when I saw it in blossom,
after having watched it for two Sundays growing near a
hedge above a hundred yards' distance from our path.

The boys were seldom allowed to take walks in the
country; indeed, I remember only two excursions, one
towards Kennington Common, and another to Denmark
Hill, near Camberwell. I was sent to Mr. James's school
at Greenwich after the Christmas holidays, 1777. Mr.
James was a scholar, and so far was a better master than
M. Perney ; he, for some reason or other, took me under
his special protection, and I was given a garden in partner-
ship with his son, in the garden of the house, no other

boys being admitted into it. When tired of solitude I joined my schoolfellows; when tired of them I flew to my retreat. The garden within the garden certainly did lead me to put thoughts together much more than I should have done, had I had to pass the whole of the time I was not at my lessons with the other boys. In truth, I learned little during the three years I was at Greenwich. All the difference in my classical knowledge was in Virgil becoming as easy to me as Ovid. A Greek Grammar had been put into my hands, but before I had got well through the alphabet, an order came from my father, at the suggestion of my mother, that I was to proceed no further.

The summer after this inexplicable interference with my studies, I went to Alderley with my father and mother, taking Cambridge in our way. Dr. Postlethwaite, who had been my father's tutor at Trinity College, did the honours of the place, and I remember his asking me if I was learning Greek, and on my saying I was not to learn it, his observing I should then never read Demosthenes, and my mother replying, it would be sufficient for me to be able to speak as well as Cicero. We dined with Dr. Hinchcliffe,[1] the Bishop of Peterborough, then Master of Trinity; and with Mr. Stephenson at the King's College, who was a manager of Lord Derby's estates, as my grandfather, Sir Edward, had been, I believe, of the estates of Lord Derby's grandfather, Lord Strange. Of my days at Alderley, the last I spent at the old Hall, I have many reminiscences:—of Oswald Leycester,[2] at the time curate of the parish, his playing with me, and calling me Pickle, and of a visit from the Toft family, and their coach standing with four bobtail black horses at the grand entrance, and of the then young Ralph Leycester running with me up to the Beacon after our

---

[1] Extract from a letter to J. T. S. in 1781, from his tutor, Mr. Six. 'Trinity College: Our Master (Bishop of Peterborough) is now at college. I saw his eldest daughter, a beautiful little girl, playing in the court with a tame kid, and drawn about on a wooden horse by her sister. How such a sight is pleasing to the eye fatigued by a dull repetition of black gowns and mathematical faces . . .'

[2] Maternal grandfather of Dean Stanley.

dinner, between the services one Sunday, and our both being severely scolded for not appearing at church till the end of the first lesson.

My father was a frequent visitor to Lord and Lady Penrhyn at Winnington, and I remember a day or two spent there, and Lord and Lady Buckinghamshire dining in the Hall on their way to Ireland, of which Lord B. was then Lord Lieutenant, 1777–78.

I think it was in 1778 that my father and mother, rambling through the old hall, opened a closet in one of the rooms, which they found locked, and while examining it, the ceiling fell in, disclosing a case of silver-handled knives and forks, having a crest engraved on them of a dove with an olive-branch in its mouth, being that of the Irelands of Bewsey, one of whom, Thomas, married Margaret, a daughter of Sir Thomas Stanley, Kt., who died in 1607.

In 1778 I was left at school during the Christmas holidays, and my brother Edward [1] was born on January 1, 1779. On that day there was a storm in which 300 trees were blown down in Greenwich Park. The day after the storm a fire broke out in the hospital. The dome in a blaze was a magnificent sight from our play-yard; it maintained its form for a long time in the midst of flames bursting out from between its columns, and before the wood work under the cupola gave way, it showed itself as a dark skeleton set off by the light within it. My father rode up to the school gate when the worst was over, and took me down with him to the waterside. We there saw gutted walls, blackened columns and embers, and half burnt beams of wood, now and then throwing out a few flames.

Alderley Hall was burnt in the month of March 1779. I read the account of it in a newspaper while at my French lessons, and burst into tears.

. . . It was never known what caused the fire; it began in the kitchen chimney, and it was supposed a beam reached the flue of the fireplace in the library, where my father, some evenings before, had been burning papers. All the

---

[1] Bishop of Norwich, and father of Dean Stanley.

books and papers in the house were burnt. No lives were
lost, but the gardener, Mackay, had a narrow escape; he
slept in a room over the library, and did not wake till all
the staircases were in flames, and had to let himself down
from his attic window. My father had gone to Chester,
and was on his return the night of the fire; he was first
told of it at the Allerton toll-bar. . . . The house stood on
a rock (a breaking-out of the sandstone of Alderley Edge)
surrounded by a moat, to complete which the rock was in
part cut through, and from some of the windows a view of
the extended plain of Cheshire was magnificent. . . . I
mourn over its destruction, and never pass by what were
once its accompaniments, the mill, the Glastonbury thorn,
the pillars, the stone walls of the terraces, without a regret
that my father, instead of occupying the Park House, had
not laid out the same sum he did there in rebuilding, and so
keep what had been for many centuries the home of the
family. . . . The hall was nearly a square of between
forty and fifty feet, with an immense fireplace. There was
a closet parted off from one corner, above which was what
was called a Chapel, having been perhaps used as such in
the time of Sir Thomas and his son, Sir James Stanley,[1]
who were Catholics.[2] I remember pouncing into it one day
to my surprise, from a kind of long saloon near it, never
occupied. It was handsomely panelled, with gilt sprigs on
each panel. The way to it from the gallery was down some
steps through a concealed door, and the gallery had much
carved work in it of arms and crests. There were a few
family pictures in the hall, which were saved, one of the
first baronet, and one of his son, Sir Peter. A full-length
picture of my father, by Gainsborough, was too large to be
thrown out of the window when the house was burning; the

---

[1] ' A fair man was Sir James, and of remarkably mild and placid character.
He drove up to the Edge almost daily in his carriage, drawn by four black
long-tailed mares, always accompanied by a running footman, named Critchley '
(Family records).

[2] Sir Edward, who succeeded his brother Sir James in 1746, was brought up
a Protestant by his godfather, Sir John Stanley of Knightsbridge.

people did not think of cutting or tearing it out of the frame, so it perished.

In 1748 Sir Edward Stanley had given his sister, Mary Stanley, a lease of the Park House [1] for her life. After her death, in 1766, Mr. Stockton, the steward, became the occupier of it. My first sight of the Park House was in 1778, on being driven to take shelter in it from a shower when fishing in the Verdon meadows. Mr. and Mrs. Stockton and the maids dried my clothes, and the cows were in the yard, brought up for milking, and a syllabub was made. There was little thought that in a year it would be the family mansion house. . . . The Park House was a fair specimen of the dwellings of rich yeomen or small squires of Cheshire. The boarded parlour, with its fireplace in the corner, was not uncomfortable, and neither my father nor mother seemed to regret the loss of their old home. Indeed, I have no recollection of their ever having been more apparently happy. My father determined on staying permanently where he was, and my mother employed herself in drawing plans for adding to the Park House. They had very few servants, and Mr. Stockton carried on his farming business as usual, his niece Jenny Street cooking for the double establishment, and superintending the making of a cheese 30 or 40 lbs. weight every day. The priest, Mr. Mackay, who had for many years lived with Mr. and Mrs. Stockton, had died the preceding year. He had made a little Paradise of the front garden, an area of about a quarter or half an acre, filling it with a profusion of flowers. A high clipped yew hedge screened it in part, hiding the outbuildings.

I had freedom to roam as I pleased, and was allowed to have at my service exclusively a labourer's son, James Dean, little older than myself. He helped me in building a house for myself in the yard, in making bows and arrows, and fishing rods. It was in this year that Mr. Davenport, being of age, came to live at Capesthorn. He accompanied my father and myself to the races. It was then that the

[1] See Appendix.

coming of age of Mr. Jonas Brook was also celebrated at Mere. I remember there was a ball, and that I danced. Mr. Leche of Knutsford sang 'The Four and Twenty Fiddlers,' and there were tents and drinking in the park.

I may place in this year my going to dinner at Hoo Green. The meetings of the club were weekly, the dinner hour 2, the dining-room the upper story of the house, the roofs sloping over the heads of the members present, 50 or 60 gentlemen yeomen. The adjournment to the Bowling Green took place about 4 o'clock, a party (Lord Stamford, Sir H. Mainwaring, Mr. G. Leycester, Mr. Booth Grey, always of it) settling themselves in the alcove at the corner of the Green, to drink punch and ale, and eat plum buns. I always met Lord Grey, the present Lord Stamford, at these dinners. We were the same age, and visits to Dunham had made us intimate.

In the summer of 1778 I remember the Chester Militia passing through Greenwich on their way to Coxheath. My father came from London to dine with the officers, and I was of the party. We dined at an inn close to our school, then called the 'Star and Garter;' it was afterwards occupied as a school by Dr. Burney,[1] on his old one being burnt at the foot of Combe Hill. Sir Robert Cotton was commanding officer. . . .

My father had some farms near Croydon (sold 1786), amongst them that called Purley, held by Mr. Tooke, and where Horne Tooke wrote his book called the 'Diversions of Purley.' I was sometimes taken by my father to a house he had on his Surrey estate in the hamlet of Wallington. The beautiful stream of the Wandle river made an impression on me. Water seemed to be running everywhere, by the side of every road and through every field. The roadsides at Wallington were full of a pretty little blue flower. I remember the spot where I first discovered it, and gathering some. No one at home had ever noticed it; I could not find out that it had a name. At Brunswick every one knew it: it was the 'Vergiss-mein-nicht.' I have the long parlour

---

[1] Charles Burney, Greek scholar, brother of Madame D'Arblay.

at Wallington before me, associated with all the stories of
the 'Arabian Nights' and Persian tales which my mother
made my sisters read out loud. . . .

My father and mother took me from the villa at
Wallington on a tour through Tunbridge Wells to Coxheath.
I have Tunbridge Wells in my memory as a fairy scene, the
houses scattered amongst trees, the Pantiles, the Common,
a circulating library in the Pantile walk, where on a bench
at the door I sat for a couple of hours devouring 'The
Peruvian Tales.' . . .

. . . I must name a few of my companions at Greenwich.
Niel B. Edmonstone, my schoolfellow at Loughborough
House, was there. Henry F. Campbell[1] I must name next,
for I have had in him an intimate friend through life. We
passed a year together in the same house at Neuchâtel soon
after we had both left school. He got a commission in the
Guards, and was with his regiment at Talavera, where he
received a severe wound, a ball entering his mouth, and
passing out a little below his ear. He is now Lieutenant-
General and Sir H. F. Campbell. I recall, besides these,
Legge, a son of Lord Dartmouth, Moneypenny, Thompson,
Sutton, son of a gentleman of Nottinghamshire, Warren,
now Dean of Bangor, Stephenson, Reynolds, two little boys
of the name of Shaw, Warner, a West Indian, Lyttelton, son
of Lord Lyttelton, Firmin, a son of the Button Maker near
Somerset House, Terrason a French boy, Baynton, son of
Admiral Baynton, Cockburne, son of General Cockburne,
Turnour, son of Lord Winterton, Birch, son of the inn-
keeper of 'Ye Green Man,' Blackheath, Gosling, son of the
banker, Powney, a merchant's son, MacAlister, Monson,
Brincoe, Waring, Spooner.

We had two half-holidays a week, and in summer they
were frequently spent in Greenwich Park or on Blackheath.
The Park, with its long avenues of chestnut trees, the deer,
the slopes from the Observatory, the giant steps, the old
thorns, the One Tree Hill, the dells full of fern, formed a rich

---

[1] 1st Foot Guards, and was Colonel-in-Chief of the 25th regiment at the
time of his death in 1856.

and beautiful picture for imagination to keep hold of through
life. Blackheath had, however, more charms for us than
the Park. The whole heath was given up to us for our
playground; we had our cricket matches when we pleased,
and we might ramble about till absolutely tired with our
liberty. We got brown bread and butter at the Windmills,
fished for newts, and swam our little ships in the ponds. A
wild place called the Hanging Wood, on the Woolwich side,
was the scene of a few mischievous exploits, for there were
gardens and orchards on the borders of it, and out of sight
of the ushers an apple-tree was sure to be invaded. I was
detected one day in an oak-tree, whose branches overhung
an orchard, and notwithstanding the apparent absurdity of
being in an oak-tree gathering apples, I could not plead
'not guilty,' and got flogged.

1780. Our school at Greenwich was not so shut out
from the world as to keep us from taking interest in Lord
George Gordon's riots. We heard that London was burning
and that the mob was in full march to burn all the places
round London against which they had any spite; and we
looked in all directions from our windows and playground
for flames. What we knew was that Lord Dartmouth's
house on Blackheath was garrisoned by a party of soldiers.
I remember our seeing them in our walks. This, of course,
couples itself on to the year when I saw the Guards
encamped in Hyde Park and St. James's Park.

[To Colonel Holroyd, afterwards Lord Sheffield, and father-in-
law of J. T. S., with his regiment of Militia, the country was
eminently indebted for repelling the fury of the mob at the Bank,
where they had nearly forced an entrance. He also prevented
Lord G. Gordon from addressing the infuriated mob that besieged
the House of Commons, by threatening that if 'any of the mob
made an entrance into the House he would inflict summary vengeance on his Lordship as the instigator.' His regiment of
militia was led by Colonel Holroyd into the thick of the riot at
High Holborn to protect, if possible, Mr. Langdale's distillery.
Mr. Cokayne, Clarencieux King of Arms, writes: 'I have often
heard my father (William Adams) speak of the sacking of the

distillery of Marmaduke Langdale (a Papist), and the horrible
sight of men and women, mostly drunk, perishing in the flames
and in the burning spirits with which the streets were flooded.
It made a great impression on him, though he was only nine
years old, being home from school and at his father's house in the
neighbouring street of Hatton Garden. . . . When you come to
think of the panic throughout London and its vicinity (the Lord
Mayor Kennet having actually run away), I think the honours to
Holroyd were well deserved.'

The Privy Seal for the Irish barony of Sheffield was dated six
months after the Gordon riots, December 10, 1780.

See 'Dict. Nat. Biog.' and Lodge's 'Irish Peerage.']

James Six   *J. T. Stanley*

CHAPTER II.

BOYHOOD AT THE COURT OF BRUNSWICK.

1781–1783.

School life ended—Abroad with tutor—Sir Joshua Reynolds at Düsseldorf—An English boy at Brunswick—Presentation to the Duchess—The royal circle —The Abbess—The hero of Minden—The Dowager Duchess—The Princess of Wurtemburg—The three brothers—'Brunswick's fated Chieftain '—The Star out of reach—Society in winter—Baron Munchausen—Spring and singing birds—Shooting competition—Lady Derby's visit—Gathering clouds—Perils at Calais—On English ground again.

Extracts from Præterita.

I WAS taken away from my school in Greenwich when the Christmas holidays began in 1780, and a tutor was provided for me.

Mr. Six had but a short time before taken his degree of M.A. at Cambridge, and obtained a fellowship at Trinity College, having been a sizar there, and distinguished himself as a scholar and mathematician. My father allowed him 200*l.* a year, and he was to accompany me when I went abroad. It was first intended I should go to Westminster School; but my mother was not fond of the routine of an English education. Mr. Six was the only son of a Canterbury manufacturer, whose father had emigrated from Holland. He was a man of a philosophic turn, and had invented the registering thermometer called Six's Thermometer.

My home must have been a dull one after Greenwich, for I had no companions to play with but my two eldest

sisters, and no exercise but walks with them and their
governess in the parks and the five fields behind our house
in Grosvenor Place, and an hour's walk in the streets with
Mr. Six. . . . I had a French master, M. Perrin, and was
made to take lessons on the harpsichord. My chief occupation was getting up puppet-shows. I drew things, wrote a
play, and contrived a stage, and the dressing of puppets was
set about by my mother and sisters as a matter of life and
death, and my governor was called in to take an active part
in the business. My mind was, however, getting in a few
stores, by reading a great many of our poets. Some of
Richardson's and other novels, which had belonged to my
grandmother, fell into my hands, and some voyages; but
what was of more real value to me, I attended a course of
philosophic lectures given by Mr. Walker in Hanover
Square, and got a taste for natural philosophy. I made
electrical phials, and watched the stars at night to give
them their names. I never see Orion now, but I think of
him as shining over the laundry in Grosvenor Place.

My father sent me to the theatres with Mr. Six whenever
a Shakespeare play was acted, and this gave me food for
thought. The peculiarity of my life all this while, from
Christmas to August, was that I had no intercourse with
boys of my own age. My father would have let things take
their course if I could have found companions, but not so
my mother. The least chance offered of emancipation from
her sway would have alarmed her. I remember going out
one morning early, and bringing home a currant tree from
Covent Garden. The going out was a mere outburst for
freedom's sake, when I thought I should not be missed; but
when the currant tree, which somehow or other was discovered, betrayed the deed, I had a day's gloom to pay for it.

In August 1781 Mr. Six and I set out from Grosvenor
Place for the Continent.

. . . We were at Margate on the 14th, and after a fair
passage we landed at Ostend. . . . It was war time, and we
sailed under Austrian colours. A splendid barge of fifty or
sixty tons burthen carried us from Ostend to Bruges, on a

canal wide and deep enough for sea brigs to navigate. At
Bruges oleanders in full blossom in the open air were a new
sight to me.   We were carried on from Bruges to Ghent in
a much more splendid barge than our first one.   The state
cabin was a richly furnished room, capable of holding sixty
or seventy persons, and in the middle and forepart of the
vessel hundreds of passengers were comfortably provided
for.   We had no servant, and had to watch ourselves the
'plumbing,' as it is called, of our trunks at the custom
house at Ghent.   Diligence travelling brought us to Brussels
and Aix la Chapelle.

Düsseldorf was our next stage.   We crossed the Rhine
on the Pont Volant, an immense vessel capable of holding
on its deck a village full of human beings, horses, cattle,
carts, and produce of every kind.   It swung across the
stream, retained from falling down it by ropes sliding along
a main rope fastened on both sides of the river.   We gave
the best part of a day to seeing the gallery of pictures at
Düsseldorf, and I remember meeting in it Sir Joshua
Reynolds [1] with Mr. Metcalfe, a friend of my father's, and
Sir Joshua sitting close to a window, pointing out a picture
for Mr. Metcalfe to look at.

We started in the evening for Münster, and stopping at a
village we found an assembly of peasants drinking, singing
and dancing in an immense Westphalian barn, covering a
quarter of an acre, and made not only to hold the produce of
a farm, but all the live stock on it, including the farmer and
his family.   We had a perfect Teniers picture before us,
with all the lights and shades of a profusion of candles and
lanthorns.   We were pressed to take part in the revels, and
it was a merry scene bursting on us in the midst of a slow
journey in the dark.   We were shown at Münster a splendid
palace lately built at the expense of the town for its sovereign
bishop, a voluntary tribute of love and respect.   It was to be

---

[1] Sir Joshua had painted in 1761 a picture of Sir John Stanley's mother ;
Margaret Owen, heiress of Penrhos, and one of the 'Seven lovely Peggies of
Anglesey.' See portrait facing p. 31.

night travelling again with us, but our conveyances were
now to be appropriately called 'waggons.' Waggon there
was indeed waiting for us, a long open carriage made of
boards, with boards slung between them for seats; we had,
however, the comforts provided for us of cross bars to lean
against, and straw to put our feet on. In this vehicle we
were jolted on till sunrise, and glad was I then to get out.
I date from this walk my first observations of the variety of
colours and tints produced by the refraction of the sun's
rays upon dewdrops. I have never seen dewdrops so
perfectly resembling gems, but the resemblance is always to
be found if looked for, and frequently I do look for it, and
then I think of my walk near Osnaburg.

At Hanover we hired a kind of phaeton or barouche to
take us on to Brunswick, being quite disgusted with our
waggon conveyances, and we travelled to our journey's end
with more comfort.

Our first quarters in Brunswick were at the Hôtel d'Angleterre. I remember carrying our letter of recommendation to
Mr. Zimmerman, professor at the college of natural history,
and the eagerness with which he instantly set to work to
render us all the service in his power. He got an *abonne-
ment* for us for *entrée* into the parquet of the opera house,
the only theatre the duke kept up, and prepared matters for
our presentation at court. He brought us in contact with
several professors and masters by whom I was to be taught
German, French, dancing, fencing, riding, and music, for
my father had made it a point that this last should be
brought into the course of my education. 'Mind and don't
forget your notes' was his last if not his only admonition
when I was leaving home. Mr. Eschenberg, one of my
German teachers, was famous for an admirable translation
of Shakespeare, and Mr. Ebert, the other, as famous for a
translation of Young's 'Night Thoughts.'

M. Dupré, the dancing master, began with teaching Mr.
Six and me how to make our approaches and bows to the
duke and duchess when we were presented—a low bow
first, then two measured paces forward with one hand on

our swords and the other in our breasts, then another bow,
then more paces, and then a third bow; and all this we
practised formally for a week.

The riding school was an appurtenance of the palace,
and the duke was liberal in his supply of horses and attendants for it.   The mode of riding taught was anything but
English; high, demi-piqued saddles kept us upright in our
seats, and rising in the stirrups was not to be thought
of.   Great formality was to be observed in going up to
the horse and getting on him, and a whip or stick was only
to be held in a certain position.   Of the fencing-master
I remember that he was a hard-featured, good-natured
German, receiving our pokes on his *plastron* with great
unconcern.

I was, a few days after our arrival, at the opera, with
my hair about my ears and my shirt collar open like an
English boy, when Mr. Six was told the duchess [1] wished to
see me in her private box.   I was, of course, presented to
Her Royal Highness, who immediately, in a torrent of
English, expressed delight in seeing what she had been
accustomed to see in her own country, and insisted that I
should come to court as I was, in the teeth of etiquette;
and so it was, excepting that I rigged myself out with a
dress coat and ruffles and a sword, instead of wearing
common English clothes.   I forget how long our presentation was delayed, and the circumstances of it, except an
attempt to follow M. Dupré's instructions unsuccessfully,
for neither the duke nor duchess would stand at a sufficient
distance, nor be quiet enough to be approached with Dupré's
number of bows and paces.

I do not remember feeling awe or nervousness on the
occasion, though the court was at that time particularly
brilliant and imposing from a reunion of the ducal family
in honour of the duke's eldest daughter's (Charlotte Augusta)
marriage with the Prince of Würtemberg.   I have a recollection of having seen her the first day I was at court,

---

[1] Princess Augusta, sister of George III.

before she set out on her journey to Russia, where a melancholy fate awaited the young bride.[1]

The duke's two sisters, the margravine and the abbess of Quedlinburg, a Protestant establishment, were both at court. The duke's uncle, Prince Ferdinand, the hero of Minden, was also present, as well as the duke's mother, a sister of the king of Prussia, in the court room. The duke's children always made their appearance : namely, the hereditary prince, his two brothers, and the Princess Caroline, afterwards Queen of England, then a beautiful girl of about fourteen.

[1] Augusta, eldest daughter of the Duke of Brunswick-Wolfenbüttel, perished in a mysterious manner. She was born in 1764, and before the age of sixteen (about 1780) was married to the King—then Prince—of Würtemberg. She was very fair, with light hair, and had an interesting figure. She accompanied her husband into Russia, where he entered the military service. They resided at St. Petersburg and other parts, till the Prince left the dominions, having, as he asserted, cause to complain of his wife's conduct, which induced him to leave her behind. They had then three children ; these were permitted to accompany him, but the care of the Princess was entrusted to the Empress (Catherine II.) herself, who took her under her immediate protection.

At the end of two years it was made known to the Prince, as well as to the Duke of Brunswick, that she was *no more*. The duke demanded that her body should be given up to him. The request was not complied with, nor did he ever receive authentic proofs of her decease or the circumstances attending it. Doubts were entertained whether she was not still living in Siberia with other victims of the Empress.—*Extract from the Memoirs of Lady Craven, Margravine of Anspach.*

Under Peter the Great, Castle Lode became Crown property, being appropriated as a prison for state offences. The last inmate in this capacity was a Princess of Würtemberg, whose fate has given a horrible interest to its walls. She was confined here by Catherine II.; some say for having divulged a State secret, others for having attracted the notice of her son Paul. Be this as it may, she was young and very beautiful, ... was at first lodged here with the retinue and distinction befitting her rank, and is still remembered by some of the oldest noblemen in the province, as having entertained them with much grace, and condescended to join in the waltz, where her personal charms and womanly coquetry joined to rank, gained her many manly hearts.

Gradually her attendants were diminished, her liberty curtailed, and the sequel to this was her death under most heartrending circumstances. Her corpse was put into a cellar of the castle, all enquiries stifled upon the spot, and being obnoxious to Catherine no appeal to her justice was made. Nothing was done in Paul's time nor in Alexander's, nor, in short, till years after, when the Prince of Oldenburg, nearly related to the deceased, came expressly to Castle Lode. Owing to the quality of the atmosphere the body was found in a state of preservation which left no doubt of identity, and was decently interred in the church of Goldenbeck.—*Letters from the Baltic,* by Miss Rigby.

The duke was a sensible man of highly polished manners, the model of a well-bred gentleman, courteous with dignity, conversing with everybody freely, without inviting familiarity, and so generally well-informed as to always render his conversation agreeable. His government of the duchy was judicious and mild, but he was forced to be economical in order to pay his father's debts, which amounted to a large sum from a foolish vanity of drawing to his court by its splendour and amusements the gentry and nobles of neighbouring states.

The duke had distinguished himself early in life when hereditary prince, as a commander in the field, and nursed an ambition of some day or other commanding in chief the forces of Northern Germany. Could he have been content with his own little sovereignty, and persevered in accomplishing what he had begun to do for the good of his subjects, he would have been a happier man, and left behind him a name really more glorious than he could have acquired, even by a victory, instead of a defeat, at Jena.

The duke's sister, the abbess, I remember as a lively and apparently amiable woman. She was always one at the duke's card table. I heard him one evening say, when she had revoked or played some wrong card, seated as he was, opposite the abbess (and close to Madame de Hartfeldt, who always had her place at his card table), ' Les erreurs sont toujours à côté de l'Eglise.'

The duchess of Brunswick was, with her brother, our king (George III.), brought up in a cloister-like manner, under the auspices of Lord Bute. As has been said, she was not a wise woman, but she was good-natured and forbearing. . . .

Mirabeau says of the Duchess: ' A la vérité, elle est toute Anglaise, par les goûts, par les principes, et par les manières, au point que son indépendance presque cynique fait, avec l'étiquette des cours allemandes, le contraste le plus singulier que je connaisse.' . . .

Her mode of living was simple, her behaviour decorous to all, and no attention was wanting on her part to acquit herself faithfully of her duties as a mother or a wife. I have some right to speak as I do, for I saw much of her when misfortunes sent her to her own country in old age. The last time I saw her was about ten days before her death, in her armchair, dying of a broken heart; enquired after, perhaps, for form's sake, by a few of her own family, but rarely visited, except by her daughter, who, I would willingly persuade myself, in the midst of all her follies and giddiness loved her to the last. I have little to say of the duke's uncle. He was an ornament to the court, but apart from Minden, I have him in my memory only as a cypher, with his cards in his hand, his hair dressed in a close formal fashion. He had a palace in the town, where he held a levee now and then in the midst of clocks playing tunes, of all which he had stories to tell as presents made to him by great personages. He was never married. He was a favourite at Berlin; he was not likely to have enemies anywhere. The dowager-duchess often had evening drawing-rooms of her own, which the whole court made a point of attending. She was in features like her brother, the Great Frederick, and as dignified as a low stature would allow in address and manner.

The Prince héréditaire was a very young man. All I can connect with him is a broad orange riband. His next brother was a boy of about twelve years old. These elder brothers both died young, and made way for the third to be a duke of Brunswick.[1] Napoleon prevented him from having anything but the title for years, but he won a name in history amidst many great names in Napoleon's time. He fought for Germany inch by inch with his 'Owls,' as the English newspapers named his followers. He was that 'Brunswick's fated Chieftain,' who 'Rushed into the field, and, foremost fighting, fell.'

I know not when I first noticed the Princess Caroline, but she is now in my memory as I saw her at Brunswick . . . which gives it the strongest and most delightful hold of me. . . . It has been said that love in its first dim and imperfect

[1] Frederick W., Duke of Brunswick, commander of the Corps Noir. Killed at Quatre Bras, June 1815.

shape is but imagination concentrated on one object, and if so, I might almost give the name of love to what I felt for her before I left.   She awakened feelings which certainly were new to me, as associated with any one definite beautiful and lovely form.   What she was when I had nearly reached my sixteenth birthday, and she her fifteenth, need not make me shrink from the confession of a first love, if love it was. Changed indeed she was from what I remembered her in her early days, when I met her in after times; but the picture I have before me as I write is the one I saw in the court circles, at the opera, or in the gardens of the palace at Brunswick. . . . Four years after this time Mirabeau called her ' tout à fait aimable, spirituelle, jolie, vive, sémillante.'

On the eve of womanhood, all that he saw was what the rosebud is to the rose, but the bud just becoming the flower was the more likely to excite a passion in a heart but little older than her own : a passion which if reciprocal would have in both hearts the same youthful colouring and charms. But I must not lose myself in poetry, I wish only to state the facts in the plainest style.   I did think and dream of her day and night at Brunswick, and for a year afterwards. . . . I saw her for hours three or four times a week, but as a star out of my reach. . . . She was so different from what she was, or at least from what she had become in my mind, when she was next seen by me; I could not find a feature or look reminding me of former times.   I saw her as a stranger, as a being I had never seen before.   One day only when dining with her and her mother at Blackheath, she smiled at something which had pleased her, and for an instant, an instant only, I could have fancied she had been the Caroline of fourteen years old, the lively, pretty Caroline, the girl my eyes had so often rested on, with light and powdered hair hanging in curls on her neck, the lips from which only sweet words seemed as if they could flow, with looks animated, and always simply and modestly dressed. How well I remember her in a pale blue gown, with scarcely a trick of ornament !

We found none of our own countrymen at Brunswick on

our arrival, only an Irish gentleman, Sir George Montgomery, brother of the Marchioness Townshend, and his governor, Mr. Johnson, an artillery officer; but a Greenwich school-fellow of mine, Mr. Sutton, of Nottinghamshire, came and took up his abode at the college. Lord Downe,[1] with a governor, and Mr. Carey, afterwards Lord Falkland, soon joined us, so that at last we formed a numerous English colony. The winter was severe. The sledge-driving of the court and gentry in the streets was brilliant, from the fantastic shapes of the sledges, the dresses of the ladies, the caparison of the horses, and lively by the continual 'hoch! hoch! hoch!' of the gentlemen drivers, and the horses' bells. The great theatre was open for balls and masquerades; extra balls were occasionally given at court, and dinners and suppers now and then by the duke's ministers, Monsieur Ferron, the finance minister, and Baron Munchausen, grand maître de la cour, &c.

Prince Henri, the King of Prussia's brother, came to Brunswick during our stay, and his visits were always the cause of doings more than usually gay at the court. In the winter we joined skating parties at a place called 'Les Étangs,' about a mile and a half out of town, and Mr. Six and I became tolerable proficients in the art. The exchange of visits all through the town on New Year's Day was a singularity to us Englishmen. We hired a coach for our rounds;[2] it was cold work, the thermometer below zero, the glasses caked with ice.

---

[1] Fifth viscount.

[2] Verses by Mr. Six on a card figured like playing cards at Brunswick, left at houses on the New Year's visits.

'Wünschet Glück zum neuen Jahre.'

The Old Year ended and the Rubber done,
See with the New the Game anew begun;
Dealt to your hand, no honour I can show:
It was in quest of honours here I flew;
Yet deign on me to cast one kind regard:
I, tho' no Court, may prove a lucky Card.
And this, indeed, I cannot fail to do,
If the sincerest wishes make 'à tout.' *

* A trump.

We all went to Court regularly twice a week in winter, and after making our bows at each of the card tables in an inner room, launched ourselves in the throng in the outer room, to find amusement as we could with the *noblesse* and gentry of the country, who had the privilege of being at the court, the line between the privileged and non-privileged being very strictly drawn.

French was spoken in our hearing more than German; very few spoke English.

In spring and summer the court was sometimes held in the garden. The duke had built a beautiful pavilion for the purpose. The gardens had been lately laid out according to English taste, in patches of shrubberies, with winding walks, but one straight, long, broad path between high horn-beam clipped hedges was preserved as a chief feature of its old character. I might almost say I lived in these gardens in fine weather. This has made my remembrance of Brunswick one of green and leaves, and flowers and birds, as well as of a court and operas.

The gardens were an aviary, but so were the streets. I caught the mania, and my room was filled with birds. The Duchess had a villa called Little Richmond, about three miles from Brunswick. Our English party were allowed to ramble over the grounds, and had the use of a boat belonging to the place.

Six or seven miles further than Little Richmond was Wolfenbüttel. We spent a day there, Sir George Montgomery and I on hired horses riding races half the way. I remember our return by moonlight through forests filled with nightingales singing their hearts out.

The ditches of the fortifications of Brunswick were filled with water. One evening, paddling about in a fisherman's boat with either Montgomery or Sutton, I heard a great shouting and firing of guns at a little distance from us. It was an annual meeting of the burgesses of Brunswick, with their mayor and aldermen, or their heads, by whatever name they were called, for the shooting at a gilt eagle on a high post; and prizes were distributed to those who knocked off pieces, according to their weight. There was a great crowd all in high glee, with the Hereditary Prince in the midst of them. We saw a gun put into his hand, which he fired, and down came part of the eagle. The piece which fell·was weighed with great scrupulousness, and he received his money. Then there was drinking and shaking of hands and shouting, and more guns fired.

1782. Lady Derby [1] came to Brunswick in the course of this summer. She had no companion. . . . She stayed, I think, near a fortnight, and was paid all sorts of attention by the court, and fêtes were given on purpose for her. The duke was too gallant not to be in high spirits, and the duchess too much pleased with seeing a countrywoman to be jealous, or to seem to think of the circumstances in which poor Lady Derby was then placed. She claimed me as a relation. I had powdered at last my brown locks, but she heard my name, and called me to her, and said, 'Why will you not come and speak to your cousin?' I knew little of her story, but I think she had a feeling of my keeping aloof from her purposely. She was beautiful, and I have her contour and engaging smiles and manner vividly in my memory at this moment; but young as I was, I could observe her unhappiness in the midst of the flatteries she received, and the attempts to please and make her happy. The opera of Pyramus and Thisbe had been got up at Brunswick, and I was near enough to Lady Derby to see her shed tears when one of the songs was sung. I was quite a child when I saw her first, soon after her marriage, about the time of the fête at the Oaks. I saw her at Brunswick as fascinating as she had been in her full glory, and I saw her again afterwards on a sofa, retired from the world at Richmond, and palsied in all her limbs. Her death, early in his life, left her husband free, and he married an actress without a heart, and who, nevertheless, was a good wife.

The sky seemed blue, clear, and serene over the court of Brunswick, but black clouds were gathering together below

[1] Married 1774, Edward, 12th Earl of Derby. She was only daughter of the 6th Duke of Hamilton, who married the beautiful Elizabeth Gunning in 1752.

the horizon. Four years after I left, Mirabeau, one of the demons who was to let loose the tempest (unconscious of the part he was to act), passed a few days at Brunswick, and describes all there to have been then nearly as I left it. In another four years the Duke of Brunswick [1] was at the head of armies, and a few years afterwards, stripped of his dominions, he was for three days a sufferer of excruciating agony on his deathbed, far from his home and family. His duchess, driven with insult from her palace, had to throw herself penniless on the generosity of her native country, which cared little for her, and of the court succeeding that of which she had been the Princess Royal, but in which she had not a friend except a daughter who at the time was hated and disgraced. I almost witnessed her death, certainly embittered, if not hastened, by grief, mortification and neglect; and who could have foreseen from any usual course of human affairs that her daughter, the first blossom of the court of Brunswick of my early days, the then innocent and lovely maiden, whom the wind was not allowed to touch too rudely, should have had, before her untimely death, to go through such scenes as her trial before the House of Lords, and her repulse by soldiery at the door of Westminster Abbey? Then the mysterious death of her sister, the Princess of Würtemberg, the death of her eldest brother in the prime of life, and of her youngest in the field near Brussels after all his wanderings. And the very palace in which I saw the Brunswick court assembled in its prosperity is burnt to the ground.

What a black curtain has fallen as a drop-scene before my eyes when I think of Brunswick between my early and my latter days! . . . .

We went regularly on Sundays to a chapel in which the Church of England service was read in French, and in which the duchess had a large glazed pew or gallery.

I have but faint recollections of any conversations with Mr. Six on religious or moral subjects, excepting his per-

---

[1] Charles William Ferdinand, Duke of Brunswick, served under his uncle Ferdinand in the Seven Years' War, 1756–1763; married Princess Augusta of England. Killed at the Battle of Auerstadt, October 1806.

severingly maintaining that neither in words nor actions
a departure from the truth could in any case be justified.[1]
Neither Mr. Six nor I were thrown into the way of
religious conversations at Brunswick by any acquaintance
with clergymen. Mr. Zimmerman introduced us to one,
the Abbé of Jerusalem, the father of Goethe's ' Werther.' I
saw him but once.

Our excellent friend Professor Zimmerman, planned an expedition for us to the Hartz mountains, in the month of May.

A letter from J. T. S. to Lady Stanley belongs to this time.

June 1782: Brunswick.

Dear Mother,—I returned three weeks ago from a
journey to the Hartz mountains where I have been above and
below the earth. We have seen mines and mountain tops ;
in the first we were 600 feet deep in the earth, and on the
last 3,000 feet above the plain. These mountains look from
Brunswick as the Snowdon range from Holyhead. The
Hartz mountains are covered with wood, except one which is
higher than the rest, and has snow on it. . . . It appears from
letters that the influenza, which here killed some old people
and forced almost everybody to keep their beds, has spread
itself over London. It has not, I hope, visited Grosvenor
Place, but left you to enjoy uninterruptedly the season of
strawberries and peas. . . . In return for your present of
the Profile of the King, I send you a Profile cut in the Brunswick Mint.[2] Poor Loo's death gave me great concern. He
kept alive, it would seem, till I was gone, that I might not
see him die, but Loo lived a long and happy life.

Your dutiful son,
J. T. S.

My father summoned us home after a year's stay at
Brunswick. I was happy and begged for another year, but

---

[1] J. T. S.'s favourite virtue through life. ' Truth' was engraved on his
private seal, and in later years he adopted from the Greek the word Alethea
(ἀλήθεια) as a name for one of his daughters.

[2] See Profiles, p. 15.

we left in September, taking with us our servant Keller, an honest, faithful creature, from whom I learnt more German than from my professors.

It was still war, but hostilities between England and France were so far relaxed that packet-boats under a neutral flag plied for passengers as in peace time between Dover and Calais, and a passport was easily obtained for our safe entry in France. Sauntering out of the town of Calais the morning after our arrival, Mr. Six and I found ourselves on the sands at a little distance from the pier. It was warm, and we pulled off our clothes to give ourselves a good washing, but had scarcely got into the water when we heard a shot, and soon after a second, which made us look about us. We saw a sentinel on the pier end waving his hand as much as to say, 'Be off!' which we were, as soon as we could pick up our clothes, which we were allowed to put on without a third shot. Thus, after all our travels, we came in personally for a share in the great contest between our country and its colonies and their allies. Our passage was a stormy one: our vessel could not make Dover and ran into the Downs, almost grounding on a tail of the Goodwin Sands. After our anchor was dropped, a Deal boat came alongside, into which I leapt instantly. Mr. Six and the other passengers soon completed her lading, and dashing through a heavy surf, we stood on English ground on October 2, 1782. We arrived at Alderley, where we found my father, on October 10. Mr. Six soon took his leave of my father and myself, and left alone together, a month or two passed away pleasantly in exchange of visits with our neighbours and a trip to Buxton. My mother and sisters were in Wales. We had only the old parlour of Mrs. Mary Stanley to live in at the Park House, with the hall for our dining-room, where neighbours were invited. I remember very merry dining-parties in the old Park House hall. The party gathered round the fireplace in the corner: Mr. Leycester, Mrs. and the Misses Parker of Astle, Mr. Brook of Chilford, Mr. and Mrs. Jodrell of Henbury, old Mrs. Leigh of Bootle, of the number. My father seemed delighted with

having me back all to himself. He was busy putting down
fences at the house and turning roads, with a crew of
labourers—the standard ones, old Peter Hinshall, Will
Worthington, &c., and an old man who had been at the
Battle of Fontenoy (1745). The year after the burning of
the Hall all the land round the Park House was let by my
father to one Stephen Penncroft. It was a favourite
expression of his that he hated the occupation of a field,
even to having a cow. To be without a care of any kind
was his elysium, and he has said in my hearing often, that
if he could have his choice of life, it would be living in
a hotel.

At Buxton the Crescent was not yet built, it was hardly
rising out of the ground, and we found a numerous company
squeezed together at the Hall. Among the people we met
was an American loyalist family of the name of Phillips.
They had been forced to abandon, by the failure of our cause,
large estates and a beautiful mansion on the banks of
Hudson's River. The sister of the Phillips was married to Sir
W. Pepperell, who distinguished himself in the war ending
with the peace of 1780. We found Lady Warburton at
Buxton, but just married, and another Cheshire bride, Lady
Brooke of Norton, both in the full bloom of beauty and high
spirits, and bright in scarlet riding habits. Time passes:
Lady Warburton, the beautiful and gay bride I am describing,
died last year, gay almost to the last, but seventy-five.

Short days came on, the place thinned, and we returned
to Alderley from Buxton, and before winter well set in my
father took me to Bath. I have a remembrance of balls,
concerts and plays, and meeting Lady Hesketh, Mr. Palmer
of Ireland, Miss Parker, since Mrs. Glegg, Miss Hunt, since
Mrs. Agar. I saw Bath as one who had once belonged to
it, and I recalled as old acquaintances Gay Street, Marlborough Buildings, the Abbey, the Parades, the Circus, and
the Pump Room.

only eighteen months old. Ladies attending him. Decorated with the *cordon bleu*, half covering his body. An area
on the outside of his room covered with canvas for his play-
yard. Seemed lively and happy.

The next evening the opera ' Personne Sauvée.' Amongst
the dancers young Vestris, Niveton, and Mad. Guimard.

June 14.—We got up early in the morning to walk
across the country to Melun on the Seine, twelve miles or
more, to be in time for the passage boat on its return to
Paris. We lost our way in a wood, and came unexpectedly
to a cluster of cottages, a kind of oasis. An invitation to
rest ourselves was welcome. The woman into whose house
we went gave us some milk and brown bread. She had
four or five children, one of which she hung by a string
against the wall to keep it from being troublesome. It was
the only thing we saw against the wall, for except a chair or
two and a table there was no furniture ; neither cupboard,
nor chest, nor shelf. I have seen Scotch and Irish hovels,
but never one so empty of everything but its inmates. However, the woman and her children were not ill clad and
seemed healthy, and the house itself was not a bad one. . . .

We reached Paris about seven. We continued by degrees
to get into every quarter of the town. Well do I remember
our first sight of the Bastille, with its dark-coloured frown-
ing towers and deep ditches and drawbridges. It was in
the year 1783 I saw it as I have described. In 1789, only
six years afterwards, I was in Paris, and found workmen de-
molishing the last few courses of the towers which were
above the level of the ground. All was light and airy and
thronged with people where the Bastille had stood. I
could not resist the temptation of having a share in the
work of demolition ; I borrowed a pickaxe and brought down
a few fragments of what remained, which I put into my
pocket, and which I still have. . . . The Bastille had, from
its first date, for several hundreds of years, been so much
more frequently filled with innocent victims of tyranny
than with offenders deserving punishment, that I never
have reproached myself for my youthful enthusiasm in doing

what I did.   'Vox populi, vox Dei' is a proverb too often
misapplied, but it is not always so.   Hatred of the Bastille
was the 'vox populi.' . . .   And the King and Queen of
France I saw at Paris, how secure I thought they were upon
their thrones! and the poor Dauphin, eighteen months old,
whose every look was met by the blandishments and smiles
of the first ladies of the land, and shown by them to us
strangers as the hope of France, for whom all that Fate
could have in reserve of blessing, greatness, and human
happiness was preparing.   How little could I foresee that
the song of Malbrook, then sung in every street of Paris,
caught from the lullabies of the Dauphin's nurse by the
Queen, caught from her singing it by the court, and from
the court by common people, was so soon to be succeeded
by 'Ça ira,' and the 'Marseillaise'! . . .   I was one of the first
Englishmen who had visited Paris after the peace which
gave Independence to the Americans.

We arrived at Dijon on June 27.   My father and mother
had spent some weeks there in 1768, and I had often heard
them talk about a villa near the town belonging to a
president of parliament, in which they had witnessed great
feasting and merriment. Remembering the name M. Mossard,
I walked to it.   I was shown a dining-room with trap doors
in the floor, through which the tables, with their succession
of courses, rose and sank again, to save the diners from the
annoyance of removal and replacement of dishes by servants; [1]
but the house and gardens were in ruins.   The president
had died; a merchant had bought the place; corn was growing where there had been bosquets and lawns, flowers and
festivity.   We made a bargain with the voiturier to carry us
on to Neuchâtel.   After a few miles' travelling, with the
Mount Jura hills before us, we entered the principality.   We
travelled on till the lake and country round Neuchâtel burst
upon us, but a dense haze [2] hid from us the grand ninety

---

[1] A fashion set by Louis XV. at Petit Trianon.

[2] This haze, which had annoyed and perplexed people at the time, was
afterwards discovered to have been carried by a violent volcanic eruption which
took place in Iceland, and continued great part of the summer of 1783.   It
was remarked that this haze had not the effect of a common fog: it had no

D

miles of Alps. . . . We were set down at the ' François,' about
10 A.M., and proceeded immediately to the dwelling of
M. le Ministre Meuron, who had agreed with my father to
receive us as boarders (*en pension*) at the rate, I believe, of
100*l.* a year each.   He occupied the upper story of a large
house belonging to the President Sandoz, at the entrance to
the eastern Faubourg.   I had a good room, from the windows
of which I had a view of the lake.   M. le Ministre's family
consisted of himself, his wife,[1] a sister of hers, two sons, and
one pensionnaire, M. Henri, a young man of about twenty.
The party was increased after our arrival by two young
German noblemen, the sons of Count Witgenstein, and their
governor, pensionnaires like ourselves.   Ministre Meuron
was about thirty years old, lively, good-humoured, much
beloved and esteemed by everybody.   The Ministre took us
to a soirée at Madame de Peyron's, the best house in the
place, almost a palace, situated in the Faubourg, and built
by M. de Peyron (Rousseau's friend and executor) at an
expense, it is said, of 20,000*l.*

As this was our first introduction to société Neuchâteloise,
and as almost all those present were afterwards friends with
whom I have spent the happiest of my young days, I shall
here give their names.   We found the party assembled in
the garden, with the beautiful lake in full view, and we were
soon set down in a long bosquet, in which, after tea, we
played at vingt-et-un till about half-past nine.   The gentlemen were ourselves, the Marquis of Blandford, Sir John
Sebright, both *en pension* with M. Trytorius, M. Munro,
and Comte de Tott ; and the ladies, Madame de Peyron herself, a handsome-looking woman ; Madame de Portalès, two
Mdlles. de Montmollin, two Mdlles. Delor, Émilie and Adelaide, and their mother ; Madame de Bord, and her daughter ;

moisture.   The lava thrown out from the volcano covered more than seventy
miles of country, and the pumice stones which fell into the sea kept afloat in
such a mass as to make it believed that an island had risen out of the sea, so
as to cause vessels to be sent by the Danish government to ascertain the fact.
I, who in 1789 visited Iceland, little thought in 1783 that I was then breathing
air laden with particles blown from that island.—J. T. S.
    [1] Sister of Sir John Blaquier.

Madame de Trytorius; two Mdlles. Godot; Mdlle. Julie, the daughter of the President Sandoz, and Mdlle. Chaillot. We met nearly the same party at one house or another almost every evening we remained at Neuchâtel. It was the custom of the place for those classed in it as ' la société' to meet alternately at each other's houses; married women seldom mixing with the unmarried, they set themselves down to whist and left the young to their own fancies and games of ' vaurien ' &c.

About a mile from Neuchâtel was a wood of about forty acres, with an area of greensward in the midst of it. It took its name from being a place at which the inhabitants played a game called ' Jeu de Maille,' something like our cricket or golf. As it was the only shady place near the town, picnic parties were often made for passing a day in it, and many pleasant mornings and evenings I spent rambling through its wood with the young and beautiful Neuchâteloises of our coterie, playing at games with them or listening to their singing, while their mothers were playing at cards.

At Neuchâtel we found the Abbé Reynal and M. Mercier,[1] self-banished for a time from France, from fear of prosecution for a freer use of their pens than was agreeable to the arbitrary government of their country. M. Mercier had just published his ' Tableau de Paris.' They were sometimes guests at M. Meuron's table. The Abbé was a short, Frenchman-like looking man, about sixty years old, an incessant talker. It was said that he had once been invited to dinner by a gentleman who had maliciously invited another, as great a talker as himself; and on the latter contriving to be first in getting the ear of the company, the host whispered to the Abbé, ' Que je vous plaigne;' the answer to which was ' Attendez; s'il crache ou se mouche, il est perdu.' As his anecdotes entertained me, he found I listened to him; I became a favourite; but he bored me at last, and I fell into disgrace by falling asleep one day when we were in a carriage together, while he indulged himself with a discourse on the British constitution. He roused me up by violent abuse of our House of Commons, adding, on my staring a little, ' Ah !

---

[1] Louis Sébastien Mercier, French political littérateur, 1740-1814.

je vois, vous ne serez jamais un grand homme!' His prognostication has proved true. . . . I have since been a member of the one House, and now I am a member of the other, and have witnessed enough to make me prefer a private to a public life.

Time flew rapidly at Neuchâtel.[1] Three months of summer in new and delightful scenery, and in the midst of gay young companions were sure of passing as sweetly as rapidly. No change was dreamt of, and the weeks passed uncounted. A letter came, and Mr. Six and I were ordered to join my mother at Lyons, and to proceed with her from thence to some warm climate in the south, for the winter. My mother joined us a few days after our arrival at Lyons. Valencia in Spain was talked of as the place we were to winter in, but we spent two months at Lyons.

My mother had one acquaintance there, Madame de Rochambeau, who had known her when at Lyons with my father in 1768, at the time my sister Louisa was born.

All the society we had was passing a few evenings at her house playing at Lotte, and an evening now and then with Lord and Lady Bulkeley, then at Lyons, and we were invited to dinner by M. de Flesselle, at his country house (the unfortunate M. de Flesselle of the Revolution).[2] What a difference I found between these two Lyons months and any two of my three months at Neuchâtel! For I had not a single young companion to speak to.

[1] The principality of Neuchâtel had passed from the House of Châlons in 1694 to William III., King of Great Britain, as heir of that family, and he transferred his interest in it and Vallingen to Frederick, King of Prussia. The Jura Mountains fall so rapidly towards the lake that a very narrow slip is left for the houses to be built upon. The entrance of the River Seyon into the lake forms a little port. The old King of Prussia, whenever he had to speak a word to one of his Neuchâtelois subjects for something to say, used to ask them if the torrent of the Seyon had done any mischief in his capital.

'On peut regarder,' says a Swiss author, ' the Neuchâtelois as the happiest and freest people of Europe.' Even if they could purchase their total independence, they would be fools if they did it. Their king receives from them a revenue of only 5,000*l.* a year, which he mostly spends for the benefit of the country, and he can only recruit his army in it as his subjects of their own accord enlist, and they may serve against him if they please in any foreign service.—J. T S.

[2] Provost Flesselle, murdered July 1789.

We descended the river in a great passage boat, my mother's carriage being placed on board of it, in which we sat unmolested by our fellow-travellers. Of the river I have clear ideas remaining as the wildest I had ever seen, and of a mountain said to be the retreat in his old age of Pontius Pilate, and of my first sight of olive trees. We shot the rapids at Pont St-Esprit, scarcely aware of them. After leaving Avignon we travelled over miles and miles of country, a great deal of it waste, and covered with wild, sweet-smelling plants, such as sage, thymes, sweet marjoram, and mints. We passed over the Pont de Gard by moonlight, and arrived at Montpellier, set down at a bad inn, so filled that we had to sleep on straw beds spread out on a floor. And here we stopped. Money was wanting to carry us further. My mother, it appeared, had expected remittances at Montpellier and none had come. She had so very nearly emptied her purse on the road, that she was under the necessity of depositing her diamonds a few days after her arrival with a jeweller or banker in the town, for a supply to enable her to pay even her daily expenses. All this put out of her head her intention of crossing the Pyrenees. She resolved that we should stay where we were. We had the whole second floor of a tolerably sized house, with a garden behind it, not far from the town gate. . . . Economy, I soon found was to be the order of the day. We were never to receive a visitor, and this was literally the case. I cannot recollect having seen within our doors more than five or six persons, including a drawing-master, a music-master, and a fencing-master. In short it was my mother's intention to exclude herself from the world. It was on account of her health that she came abroad; but at my age, sent as I was to see the world, I cannot look back without some wonder at my Montpellier life. My mother might have been introduced to the best society of the place; for the Lyonese Baroness de Rochambeau sent her a letter of introduction to the Intendant of Languedoc, who lived at Montpellier. And we were invited to an assembly at his hôtel, where we met many persons who were inclined to be civil to us. In particular

the Bishop of St. Pol de Léon, whom, many years afterwards,
I became intimate with, when in London he acted as one of
the committee of French refugees to which I was the
deputy from the committee of subscribers for the relief of
French emigrants in the third year of the Revolution.

I read a great deal at Montpellier . . . the books were
all French. I became intimate with the bookseller, his wife,
and daughter, a handsome, sweetly mannered girl of about
twenty. She had dark eyes and dark hair, but it was
softened by her wearing powder. The acquaintance would
have been undoubtedly dangerous, as acquaintance grew
into intimacy; but I discovered she had her lover, a rich
merchant's son, who was offering to marry her, notwithstanding his father's opposition to his wishes. . . . I was
soon master of their secret, if secret a love could be called
which all the intimate friends of both parties knew. . . . It
was a fortunate chance that threw Rose Tournelle in my
way. She was modest, beautiful, and cheerful, and it was a
pleasure to me to be often in company with such a woman.
I sat by her while she was preparing books for her father's
binding, talking to her a little, now and then, of her family
affairs, or making her listen to my confessions, my opinions,
and short stories of my past days; or telling her what
castles in the air I was building for myself for days to come.
Had she been a coquette, vain, artful, or not already in love,
what mischief to me she might have been the cause of! As
it was, she perhaps kept me from mischief. I was longing
for female society. I am not sure that I did not now and
then envy her lover, but it was well that things were as they
were. Her parents were sensible, honest, and industrious,
and loved and valued her as she deserved. It was a virtuous,
happy ménage altogether. Her lover, M. Abut, was older
than her by ten or fifteen years, well-looking, sensible, and
tolerably well-informed. He attached himself to me for the
purpose of practising his English. He did not seem to be
under any apprehension of my stealing the heart of his
mistress. M. Abut was a Protestant; there were many
Protestant families at Montpellier, descendants of the perse-

cuted Huguenots, and they were but barely tolerated till the
Revolution put an end to all predominance of religion in
France. My mother, Mr. Six and I attended a Protestant
meeting held under an open shed every Sunday in a field about
two miles from the town. The congregation consisted of about
150 well-dressed people, some of the wealthiest merchants of
Montpellier. The meetings were in defiance of the law, and we
might have been arrested at any time, and sent to the galleys.

In June or July an order came for us from my father to
join him and my sisters at Paris, and I left Montpellier as
far as I can recollect without regret. My Montpellier hours
are in my memory on the whole hours of disappointment
at having been deprived of the enjoyments of society, and of
vexation at the insignificance of the life I was made to lead.

A voiturier took us to Paris. My mother, Mr. Six, and
myself in our chariot, and Dubois, our *valet de place*, and
Suzette in a cabriolet. Suzette was a faithful, honest
creature. My mother hired her to be her maid at Montpellier,
and kept her till her death (1816), three months after which
Suzette herself died. On reaching Paris we took up our
quarters in the Hôtel de la Grande Bretagne, in the Faubourg
St-Germain; my father, with my two eldest sisters and
Mr. Oswald Leycester, arrived a few days after us. My
father stayed about a month at Paris, leaving us to take our
departure from it to Turin as soon as my mother had gone
through the course of mesmerism, under the famous Mesmer
himself, which she thought would relieve her from a numb-
ness of the left side. I saw her one day at the doctor's
'bacquet,' as he called it. It was a round decked tub, five or
six feet in diameter, from the midst of which several iron
rods issued, each bent at a right angle a foot or six inches
from the bacquet, and sharpened to blunt points, which the
patients sitting round the tub could direct to what part of
their bodies they pleased. Ropes were twisted round the
irons connecting them, which the patients laid hold of. The
doctor was sometimes in and sometimes out of the room,
but government ordered a report of all this charlatanism to
be made by commissioners, of whom Franklin was one; for

many persons fell into swoons at the bacquet, or went mad, as it were, for a time, and the public called out for an inquiry. As for my mother, it did her neither good nor harm.

My father found a few English friends in Paris: the Duke of Dorset, then our ambassador; Lord Chesterfield, on his way to Spain as ambassador; Mr. Palmer, &c. Except my once going alone with him to a dinner with the Duke of Dorset, making a quartette with him and Madame Banelli, the opera dancer, I do not remember dining out of our hotel. . . . I went to what plays I pleased, sometimes with, sometimes without Mr. Six, read books of all kinds to myself, and practised on my fiddle. At last the word was given, and off we set for Turin.

At Turin we took up our quarters at the best hotel in the town, 'La Bonne Femme'; over the entrance a woman without a head very ungallantly represented what was meant by female goodness.

I was nearly a year older when we entered Turin than when we were stopped on our way to Spain at Montpellier, and our minister, Mr. Trevor, was requested to present us to the king and queen, the Prince and Princess of Piedmont, and the Duke and Duchess of Chablais; to bring us acquainted with the diplomatic corps; and procure for us the *entrée* to the casino, and invitations to such of the nobility of the place as were in the habit of opening their houses to strangers. Mr. Frederick North, afterwards Lord Guilford, Lord Dungannon, Lady Clarges, Mrs. Carter, Mr. Sykes, the eldest son of Sir Francis Sykes of Basildon, Berks, Mrs. Parsons, and Mr. Pettiward came to Turin to pass some weeks of the autumn, so that I soon found myself one of a numerous English party. Where one was, all were, and the opportunities for our meetings became frequent as winter approached.

Mr. Trevor was a perfect gentleman, well bred and kind-hearted, and did the honours handsomely.

My mother and I soon after our arrival were invited by him to dine at a villa he had hired from the Archbishop of Turin, not far from the Superga (the royal cemetery), which stands 800 feet high, a landmark for the whole of Piedmont.

Lord Hampden, the elder brother of Mr. Trevor, with his lady, old friends of our family, were of the party.

The many representatives of courts formed of themselves a pleasant society.   They were all men of the world, well informed and of polished manners.   M. Choisant was the French ambassador; Prince Jousyeouf from Russia, a magnificent seigneur, whose house was furnished like an Oriental palace; the Marquis de Jouga[1] from Portugal. These all gave dinners and balls in their turn.   They were intimate, however, with few of the Piedmontese nobility, so that the company we met consisted chiefly of foreigners, of which two-thirds were English.   At the Marchioness St. Giles' we had always a rendezvous twice a week with the corps diplomatique; and then there were the great balls at court and at the casino.

The court was not gay.   Victor Amadeus was old and stupid, and allowed his Spanish bigoted wife to have her own way, which was to spread as much solemnity and gloom as she could over everything.   Though she consented, for policy's sake, to have a ball now and then, she would not let anyone stir from their seats, but to get up and dance before her; and all was dulness and form, excepting in the outer rooms, where the pages played all manner of tricks, and where a few gentlemen, stealing away from the royal presence, could talk at their ease.   The king never stirred from his seat, any more than the queen, and the Prince and Princess of Piedmont, the Duke and Duchess of Chablais, and 'les petits princes' as they were called, though all more than twenty years old, sat the whole evening motionless. The noblesse were, however, fond of their sovereigns, for they never interfered with their pleasures, except when their extravagance threatened them with a ruin of their fortunes; the government then for a time sequestered their

[1] An old man who took it into his head to be in love with one of the most beautiful women of the court, Comtesse de la Lance, the *adorée* of our countryman, Mr. Foylane, whom she persuaded to turn a Catholic.   Her uncle, a cardinal, wrote to her on this occasion, 'Faites toujours les amours comme cela, ma nièce.'   Mr. Foylane was a Yorkshire gentleman of great fortune, and his conversion to catholicism made a great noise.—J. T. S.

estates. The Prince of Piedmont, the eldest son, was as bigoted as they were, and never troubled himself with politics, and his wife, a grand-daughter of Louis XV., was an unoffending, amiable woman, very ready to sacrifice any love of gaiety she might have brought with her from France, for the sake of peace. The Duke and Duchess of Chablais, an uncle and niece married by a papal dispensation, were content to be quiet in their station, and 'les petits princes' were like little boys still in their nursery. I became very intimate with Chevalier Salmon,[1] son of their governor.

[Lady Stanley's impressions of the court of Turin are given in the following letter to her mother, Madam Owen, in Anglesey, to whom she wrote regularly.]

Turin : February 2, 1785.

My dearest mama's kind and entertaining letter from Chester, I had the pleasure of receiving in due time. I am very much pleased to find you stopped there, and revived yourself with seeing and conversing awhile with your old friends and acquaintances. So Miss Molly Hesketh is married at last ; as to H. Hesketh I make no doubt but he will marry himself again, for he can never exist without a governess, and if he takes one of the Kenricks he is likely to have a pretty tight one. I am grieved to hear that an entire good understanding does not subsist between the Judge[2] and his son and daughter-in-law [Miss Hesketh], for I thought the last conciliation was a complete one. What would the old gentleman be at? Can't he learn to know his own mind, and determine what he means to bestow, and what not ?

The number of new American families must be a great addition to the society of Chester. I am very glad you have been prevailed upon to comply with your kind host's invita-

---

[1] Our friendship was kept up by letters for many years. He changed his name to that of Comte d' Andizeno, and was appointed Governor of Chambery. He lived to 1836.—J. T. S.

[2] Judge Williams, of Bodelwyddan, who showed his tenacity of character to the end. He died sitting up in his coach on circuit.—ED.

tion to prolong your stay there, for I own I am always delighted to hear of your gadding about a little, you have too much time to pass in dulness and loneliness at Penrhos. As to us on this side the Alps, we go on tolerably well, though we have not failed of experiencing exceeding cold weather. In a former letter I remember I promised you an account of the royal family. To begin then: The king is aged about sixty, is a well-looking man, and a very worthy well-meaning one, a very good king, and well beloved by his subjects. The queen, who is a Spaniard (sister to the present King of Spain), is not, I believe, as old as the king her husband, but looks at least twenty years older; in short, she looks a little, dry, shrivelled old woman, and puts one always in mind of some descriptions one has read in fairy tales which begin with 'There lived formerly a queen, and she was so old, so very very old . . .' &c. &c. However, she is not so old; but so it is she contrives to look. Her manner, as far as I have seen of it, and experienced with regard to myself, is very affable and obliging, but she is reckoned formal and a little (Spaniard-like) proud and austere in general. The king's eldest son, and heir apparent, is styled the Prince of Piedmont; his age may be about thirty. With respect to his person, it is very plain; but nevertheless his countenance is very agreeable and his manner extremely pleasing. His princess is sister to the present King of France,[1] and she is one of (without exception) the most pleasing women one ever saw. She is rather handsome; but it is not as a beauty one admires her, but for an amiable countenance; indeed, I never saw one that expressed more goodness of heart and affability of mind, and altogether natural, unassuming and unaffected; and she is accordingly adored here by everybody. The king has besides, here, four other sons, all unmarried; indeed they are by no means as yet in any respect their own masters, having been educated and being still kept up very strictly, though the oldest of the four is five or six and twenty, and the youngest nineteen or twenty; two of this king's daughters, you know,

[1] Louis XVI.

are married to the King of France's two brothers; a third
remains here, and is, poor girl, married to her uncle, the
king's brother.   I would as lief, says Lady Hampden, be
married to my father, and indeed I am of the same mind.
But so it is, and I hope she herself thinks differently of the
matter; for here she is, looking pretty enough, lively and
good-humoured, loves dancing, amusement, and a little
gaiety, methinks, if she could meet with it; but under the
eyes of the queen but very sparing measures of that com-
modity can be dealt out.   This said princess, niece and
daughter, is styled Duchess of Chablais.   And so much
for the royal family, of whom I think I have given you
a pretty full account.   I wish it may amuse you a bit; but
they have taken up so much of my paper that I must now
bid you a hasty good-bye.

I am very happy to find that Sir John and the damsels
are at Bath, as I hope and trust the latter will be well
amused there.   Stanley is very well, and desires his best
duty.   Be assured his youthful days are much more wisely
and profitably spent than those of most English lads are;
he sees good company, and hears talk of reason, principle,
and morals, which few others do.   One may hope, therefore,
that he will turn out better than the generality, and I trust
he may chance to do so.

Adieu, my dearest mama,
Ever yours,
M. STANLEY.

To Mrs. Owen,
    at Penrhos, Holyhead, Anglesey, Angleterre.

[Her son's education seems, however, to have been carried on
in an erratic manner, each master enlarging his mind in directions
remote from the subject he was engaged to impart.   He says:]

I had a violin master, and Italian master, and a drawing
master.   My Italian master was an abbé, by name Bussani.
I read little with him, but I made him teach me chess.   Of
my music master I remember little, but that he was always
talking to me about shooting and sporting dogs.   My drawing

master, instead of teaching me much, made a miniature of me, which I gave my friend Chevalier Salmon. Of my dancing master I can say no more than that on Ash Wednesday he came to me from mass, with his forehead covered with ashes, which he had taken care to plaster on from fear of their falling off. . . .

Mr. Trevor had a chaplain who read prayers every Sunday for the benefit of Protestant families in the hall of our minister's house, which service we attended.

The ceremonies of the Roman Catholic Church are performed at Turin with great pomp—the washing of the poor people's feet by the king and queen, and the waiting on them at dinner by the high officers and ladies of the court. The Fête Dieu is kept with a display of tapestry from every window, and endless processions of priests and monks. . . . I witnessed at a Turin church darkened, hundreds of men baring their shoulders and flogging themselves with whips; and fathers and mothers force their daughters to become nuns. I was present when a beautiful young lady of seventeen took the veil, a sister of my friend the Comte de Salmon. The poor girl had no vocation for it. The court assisted; she was led to the altar dressed out in finery. Her tresses were then cut off, and she was taken away to the interior of the convent. . . . Few of the nobles are rich enough to be hospitable, but they assemble together often in a subscription suite of rooms, and at the theatre. In spring, summer, and autumn the ladies parade most evenings with the court, in brilliant equipages, moving at a foot pace, so that the gentlemen walking near may keep conversing with them, much in the same way as in Charles II.'s time the fashionable world of London had its meetings at the ring in Hyde Park. . . .

I got intimate with a few families before I left the place, and had I stayed a few months longer I should have been like an *enfant de famille* in many houses, and my services accepted as a *cavaliere servente* occasionally, with as much innocency as if I had been a relation or a husband's friend.

The king had two or three foreign regiments in his service. One of them, the Regiment de Chablais, formed part of his garrison on my arrival, and I became acquainted with some of its officers. One was an Englishman, a Catholic, Mr. Shirley. . . . They had concerts, and often assembled in a coffee-house to eat ices. My friend Salmon fought a duel with one of them. He was in fault, giving too much importance to a few ugly words said without any meaning to affront. He had, however, the best of it, for his sword ran through his adversary's leg as it was parried downwards. The consequence was to the officer a lying in bed for a month; to Salmon a contrition, which made him a better man. We both spent many hours by the bedside of the sufferer.

The king was absolute, and I never heard, when at Turin, a word said about politics. An immense army was kept on foot, all the officers being of aristocratic birth. The soldiers received low pay, and discipline being severely maintained, desertions were frequent. An order was issued for the immediate execution of every deserter who could be caught, and many were the volleys of death fired off in the fosses of the citadel, which I heard echoing from one end of the town to the other, and which, strange to say, seemed not to excite pity for the sufferers in any breast, high or low. . . . The strong feeling which is caused in England by the shedding of blood seems to be wanting in an Italian constitution. In the course of a few months, I was informed, there had been fourteen assassinations in the town, on very slender provocation; and I, one night, saw a woman lying dead on the esplanade, near the citadel, with her throat cut, surrounded by a crowd expressing little surprise, and very indifferent about any search being made for the murderer.

I might almost say that at Turin I first digested into any form my love for liberty, and hatred of an arbitrary power. . . . In my own country I had heard of public rights being attended to and preserved, as if they were as inherent to the soil as the grass which grew on it; in Switzerland they were everything, and in France even I had heard the system of government called tyranny; but in Piedmont the words ' public rights ' and ' freedom ' seemed to form no part of the common language spoken. The king and court stood aloof from the population as if in no point belonging to it. It was little foreseen that in a few years the royal family would be forced to quit their palaces and take refuge on the rocks of Cagliari in Sardinia.

I trace back to my alcove, and my wanderings on the Colline, the commencement of far deeper thoughts than those suggesting themselves at the time. I feel assured my being is not to be ended here, and that whatever I am to be in a future state will depend on what I have been in great measure. I recollect that I prayed often, not from fear of God or wishes for anything, but from my love of a Power on which I felt myself dependent. The love of goodness, that is the love of justice, kindness, mercy, and all the attributes which we give to God, seem to me to constitute religion. . . . As we grow up, the Angel of God who was with us in our childhood leaves us to our faults and the consequences of all our acts. I cannot say to what extent my Turin rêveries influenced my life, but they sowed seeds which, though lying dormant, have in my later years been vegetating, for I have returned to them.

The Valentine Palace was my favourite resort on the evenings of hot days. It stood on the banks of the Po, in the midst of shady gardens which few people ever entered, and getting acquainted with the housekeeper, a friendly, humble old woman, I could get my cup of coffee from her when I pleased, placed on a table on a lawn between the house and the water, where for an hour I could forget all troubles and build castles in the air.

Occasionally, however, the quiet of the Valentine Palace was broken in upon by the court. A fête, before I left Turin, was given in it to the King and Queen of Naples. They were a week at Turin. It was full of fêtes, balls, drawing-rooms, dinners, and reviews, to the great disturbance of the court's peace. The King of Naples was not very kingly, always making a great noise, and now and then catching hold of the head of his chamberlain and lugging him about the room.

In the summer months the Palace of La Vénerie, on the

banks of the Douro, is the favourite residence of the court. The royal apartments had a grand appearance when I saw them lighted up and filled by the noblesse of Turin, at a ball to which I was invited with my mother and Mr. Six. I remember well our drive there between flaming cauldrons full of pitch oil, fixed on poles, bordering the road its whole length of three miles from the town to the palace; while myriads of the ' lucciole ' (fire-flies) were crossing it in all directions, sparkling like diamonds, sapphires, topazes, or rubies, as the eye caught a sight of them in their variety of flights.

After nearly a year at Turin, orders came from England for our return. After passing the gates, ' Happy people,' said my mother, as we met some people returning to Turin from a walk, ' they are returning home, and we are leaving what has been our home, for the last time.' We were carried up the Mont Cenis on chairs on men's shoulders, and spring flowers were yet in blossom on its plain, varieties of ranunculuses among the number. We spent a day at Chambéry, and paid a visit to ' Charmettes,' Rousseau's home for some of his early years. He has contrived in his ' Confessions ' to render his ' Charmettes ' interesting classic ground, connecting itself with the development of his deep mind into thoughts which have worked great changes in the world. The ' Charmettes ' was an ordinary farmhouse, close to the road; nothing could be less romantic than its appearance and situation. I had not then read the little ' pervenche ' anecdote, or I should certainly have looked out with a keen eye for a periwinkle plant. Who has not been charmed with the ' Voilà de la pervenche ' bursting from Rousseau's lips, on seeing a flower of it by the roadside, when walking with his friend, M. Peyron, to revisit his old abode after forty years' interval? ' It brought suddenly,' he says, ' to my recollection my first walk with Madame de Warens to Les Charmettes.'

It is not so much of Rousseau and Madame de Warens that we think when his ' Voilà de la pervenche ' meets our eyes, as of ourselves. We have each a ' voilà de la pervenche ' of

our own to apply to some ' Charmette' of our own, with its
own recalled lane, or bank, or wood, or fields.

My father was at Alderley, and I went with Mr. Six to
join him there. In a week's time Mr. Six told me we were
to part, and I never saw him afterwards. He went abroad,
and died at Rome in the winter of the same year, 1786, aged
twenty-nine.

In December my father took me with him to Bath,
spending a day on the road with Lord Stamford at Enville,
and stopping to see ' The Leasowes.' Shenstone was living,
but not at home. He had converted a few acres of uneven
pasture-lands and wooded glens into a little paradise. I saw
a seat in a wooded recess opening to the western sun, and
the half of Staffordshire spread out like a map below it; and
the urn he dedicated to the memory of one he had loved,
William Somerville, with its sweet line—

Debita spargens lacrima favillam Vatis amici.[1]

'The Leasowes' have passed into other hands. Shenstone, with all his sentiment and pleasing verses, had not a
mind full and deep enough for his retreats and haunts to
say much of him, and few now visit the classic ' Leasowes'
as they would Stratford-on-Avon, the island of St. Pierre,
the Twickenham villa, Burns's cottage, &c., not to see what
is to be seen, but to live, as it were, for a moment with the
spirits associated with their names, and dreamt of as still
hovering over them.

At Bath we lodged not far from the Pump Room. I
was introduced to the famous Mr. Wilkes,[2] and danced a
minuet with his daughter at the lower rooms. Strange
enough, the 45 Minuet was called out by the master of

[1] ' Sprinkling the ashes of a friendly Bard with tributary tears.'

[2] 'John Wilkes, M.P., blamed the King's speech in No. 45 of the *North
Briton.* A warrant was issued for his apprehension, and Wilkes was arrested
and sent to the Tower, 1763. At the Middlesex election No. 45 was freely
chalked upon the houses, in allusion to the condemned number of the *North
Briton.* Noblemen most hostile to Wilkes were compelled to illuminate their
houses in honour of his success at the poll, and the grave Austrian ambassador
was pulled out of his carriage, and 45 chalked on the soles of his boots.'—
History of England, by S. R. Gardiner.

E

the ceremonies, Captain King.[1] I became soon acquainted
with Lord Howe[2] (and was constantly in a quadrille with
his daughter), also with Miss Heywood, afterwards Mrs.
Montaulien, and Lord Valletort; and with Sir Philip Gibbs
and his daughter, afterwards Lady Colchester.

It was arranged that early in the spring of 1786 I should
return to my former quarters at Neuchâtel with my old
friend Oswald Leycester, and I was very impatient for my
departure.

[A letter of J. T. S. to his sister Isabella gives an incident
occurring on one of his Alpine expeditions.]

1786.

We were joined upon the glaciers by some countrymen,
one of whom struck me by his choosing to come upon it
with his spurs on. Before we set out on our journey,
conversing one evening with M. Meuron concerning the
'ridicules' that young Englishmen often gave themselves,
I offered in jest to lay him a wager that we met with one
of them upon the ice with spurs on. I little thought really
that I should find one. I did, however, and at the same
time had the mortification of seeing a French nobleman
who had set out with us for the glacier, dressed in trousers,
and good thick shoes with nails in their soles.

The glaciers of 'La Tour,' of 'Argentière' and 'Les
Boissons' seemed rolling down from the Aiguilles that hung
over them. Mont Blanc appeared much higher than from
the plain, although we were on a level with the Montan-
vert. . . . We discovered beyond all these mountains the
valley of Le Valais. The Rhone flowed through it, no
broader than a riband, and shone like silver amid the gloomy
shades of the mountains. While Campbell and myself were
contemplating the view, Oswald Leycester had entered into
conversation with a Valais shepherd. We joined them. The
shepherd had chosen a spot to sit down under the wind. He
was covered with a cow skin, the hair turned outwards, and
scarcely sewed into the form of a coat. He had a goitre;

---

[1] Captain King, married to Margaret Bulkeley of Presadfad, Anglesey.
[2] 4th Viscount, Admiral Howe.

but his features were remarkably handsome. Two piercing black eyes and a Roman nose such as Raphael or Rubens represent under a helmet. He had the most graceful attitude I have seen, grace in the manner in which he held his stick, grace in the manner in which he held his head. On our asking him why he did not choose rather to go into the town where he could treble the money that he earned in tending the flocks of the parish on these heights, ' C'est vrai,' he said. ' Mais que ferois-je dans la plaine, moi qui ait toujours vécu sur les hauteurs? Je deviendrois malade.' We asked him how much he was given for watching the parish flocks through the summer. ' Three louis.' Also something to his son who assisted him. ' Le voilà,' said he, pointing to a young lad perched on a point of rock where he seemed no bigger than a crow. The shepherd had a cottage lower down where he lived with his wife in winter, and occupied himself then in cutting wood and making baskets or little knick-knacks.

Oswald Leycester gave him a crown. He looked at it, then at Leycester, then at the crown again. He never thought it was Leycester's intention to give him so much. At last, without getting up, but in the noblest manner, he said :

' Vous ne savez pas combien vous m'avez obligé, monsieur. J'en avois grand besoin '—and bowed, not servilely ; it was a gentle bend of the neck accompanied with a smile, more expressive of gratitude than all the bows of a courtier. . . .

J. T. S. to Isa Stanley.

February, 1787.

Thursday or Friday we leave Neuchâtel, not, as I expected, for England, but to make a tour during six or seven months through Italy. . . .

Four of us leave the same day—Mr. Campbell, Mr. Hüger[1] the American, Oswald Leycester, and myself. We are every one of us like children going to school. I am at a loss to find out what this place has so attracting ; for the regrets we

[1] Benjamin Hüger of South Carolina.

E 2

each feel could hardly be more poignant if we were preparing
to leave our homes for a voyage round the world. Mr.
Campbell sets out for England, Hüger for Mayence. Thus
acquaintances who have never for months passed a day
without seeing each other, and to whom every little circumstance that has been interesting to one has concerned the
whole, will be scattered up and down the world. . . .

I shall be glad to see Rome and Naples ; but I wish to
God it was over!

Rome : April 1787.

I have been pleased with meeting my friends at Turin ;
and here I am in Rome, where I am to spend a month in
continual hurry. We have arrived here for the Holy Week.
We have seen the Pope officiate, and mixed with the crowd
that received the general Benediction.

I have been presented to the Count of Albany, styled
still by his servants King of England. He wore the Order
of the Garter, but permitted himself to be addressed as
Count, and as to such I was presented to him. The old
man receives a great deal of company in his house since he
had his daughter with him. It is one of the gayest in Rome.
This daughter is acknowledged by the name of Duchess of
Albany, which the world gives her. It was in consequence
of a quarrel with his wife that he has sent for this girl who
was in a convent at Paris, and he has settled all his fortune
on her head.

The Pretender, for so we English still call him, received
me with civility, made me sit aside of him, and spoke to me
in English. Poor old man ! he is interesting from what he
was : but he is now in a second childhood.

I was presented last night to the Duke and Duchess of
Gloucester, and to-night we are invited to a ball there.
There will be the Duke of Buccleugh, Lord and Lady
Clive, Sir Abraham Hume and his lady, and many more
English.

According to my mother's request I am in mourning for
my Uncle Robert Owen, and shall be so all the time I am in
Rome. . . .

[After leaving Rome, J. T. S. and Oswald Leycester extended their tour to Sicily and Naples. He describes their ascent of Mount Etna, which occupied ten hours, ' two of which, though it was June 10, were through snow ; ' and a month seems to have been spent exploring the island. ' To complete our good fortune,' he adds, ' we saw a fine stream of lava running down Mount Vesuvius as we entered the Bay of Naples.' The friends returned to England through Neuchâtel. In a letter home J. T. S. refers to their ' intention of staying a fortnight with our friends there. We promised when we set out to Italy, and have too great pleasure in perspective there not to keep our word.' The charm of Neuchâtel to him consisted in his friendship for the beautiful Adelaide, who remained throughout life his ideal of perfect womanhood.

.   .   .   .

Thirty years later the daughters of Sir J. T. Stanley and Oswald Leycester found themselves at Neuchâtel and made the personal acquaintance of the Neuchâtelaise lady of whom they had heard all their lives, and whom they had grown up to regard with the deepest interest. One of the travellers [1] writes as follows to Lady Maria Josepha Stanley :

' We have seen " Adelaide." She is still strikingly handsome ; hers is that kind of sterling beauty that time cannot entirely fade. She is more like Miss Berry than anything else of womankind I ever saw. I never saw eyes in which intelligence and warmth of heart sparkle so clearly, and you read in them at once all the spirit and highmindedness which marked her letters and her conduct, and without having heard a word about her I should have been struck by her among a thousand. . . . When one thinks of her as an Englishman's wife, Corinne comes into one's mind instantly. . . . Certainly, as " Adelaide" says, there is something romantic and dreamlike in the two young men of whose gaiety and gallantry Neuchâtel still talks, revisiting it again in their united families.'

After her death J. T. S. received back his own letters to her with a packet of her journals, and he thus records the revival of old impressions.]

. . . I dare not write down all that occurs to my memory

---

[1] Catherine, daughter of Oswald Leycester, married to Rev. E. Stanley, brother of J. T. S.

of my twentieth year, spent at Neuchâtel. Love would be the chief theme which I could dwell upon. . . .

Let it suffice for me to say, I loved, and was in return, at last, beloved ; that it was all in purity and sympathy of character ; that not even a kiss was exchanged when there was separation and last looks met each other. Obstacles to marriage intervened, and the object of my love, aged only eighteen at the time, the daughter of an old officer, died many years ago, unmarried.

*   *   *   *   *   *

[So ends the Præterita.

But the extracts that have been given here form only a small part of a record which fills many volumes of manuscript.]

CHAPTER IV.

NORTHWARD BOUND—THE FAROE ISLANDS.

1788-1789.

Dreams of Iceland—Preparations in Edinburgh—Fellow-voyagers—The good
ship 'John,' and rules on board—Hair powder obligatory—Stromness
Harbour—Dauntless young American—Ferryland affronted—Suspicions of
Faroe natives—Invitation from the Chief Justice—Hospitable Mrs. Wang—
Nolsoe—'A few rubbs'—Ostroe—Eider ducks—Supper at the Provost's—
Waited on by fair hands—Danish crowns—The moving stones—A Faroe
Island bride—The pastor of Suderoe—The 'Angelica.'

[THE next event in the life of J. T. S. was his visit to the Faroe
Islands and Iceland.

The opening words of the chapter were written many years
after by his daughter, Louisa Dorothea.]

'In Edinburgh none are probably now living who can
remember the day when the "John" sailed from Leith
Harbour, with Mr. Stanley and his small band of adventu-
rous gentlemen, bound for Iceland ; yet there must be some
who have heard their fathers speak of an expedition which
in those days—1789—was certainly no common or everyday
occurrence ; and even now, when yacht voyages to distant
lands are become more frequent, such an enterprise as this
would be considered among the remarkable events of the
day. It is now indeed a tale of long ago.

There was doubtless much talk in the old town of
Edinburgh about this voyage then. For a young gentleman
of twenty-three of family and fortune to undertake such an
enterprise as a voyage to Iceland, quite alone, was in itself a
subject to excite the public talk, and must have been viewed
with interest by the many eminent men of science and
learning who formed at that time the society of Edinburgh,

for Mr. Stanley's object was not mere curiosity or pleasure. He was a devoted lover of science, and at an age when most young men think of little beyond amusement, his mind was ardently and eagerly bent upon the pursuit of knowledge, whilst his heart was warmly alive to the wonders and beauties of Nature.'

Journal, J. T. S., 1788.

About a year ago, when I returned from the Continent, where I had spent many of my young days, I was often on the Thames with two of my Neuchâtel companions in boating on the lake, Campbell and Beaufoy; and in a boat, we felt, as it were, at Neuchâtel again. One day we fell into a talk of extending our excursions seawards, and a voyage to Iceland was spoken of by Beaufoy, as a jest rather than a thought in any earnestness. 'When we go to Iceland' became at last a proverb with us, and we talked of the geysers. Dr. Johnson says that men will 'talk themselves into the doing of anything,' and so we talked on about visiting Iceland; of how it could best be done; of what there might be in the voyage to afford pleasure and gratify curiosity. Beaufoy urged me on.. My father gave his consent; he had been familiarised with my talking about a visit to Iceland when we were in London, and thought no more seriously of it than a yacht trip to one of the Hebrides. When he found I was in earnest, he made some objections, but I soon wrung from him his not very slow leave. Beaufoy advised me as to preparations, and the following May was fixed on for our sailing. I was to hire a vessel at Leith early in the spring, with good accommodation, and with a careful captain and sufficient crew; to have her victualled for six months, and to secure, if I could, a doctor and one or two men of science. I resolved to pass the winter at Edinburgh, that I might be in the better readiness for my spring task, which I found a much more troublesome and expensive one than I expected; for a ship and full crew, including a good captain and a six months' provision for a cruise, are not to be had for a few hundreds of pounds; and I had to suffer much disappointment from persons, who at first were all eagerness to go with us, changing their minds.

When all was nearly ready for the excursion, Beaufoy found himself, for family reasons, unable to go with me. Beaufoy's desertion would have made me abandon all thoughts of the voyage; but I had now gone too far not to feel that my character and my honour were involved in the prosecution of the design. My other partner in the scheme— Campbell—failed me also, finding that he could not obtain a whole summer's leave of absence from his regiment. Dr. Hume, a physician recommended by Dr. Robertson the historian, and who was to have been my head philosopher, deserted me because I would not allow him the full direction of everything. He had been indefatigable in providing everything that could render the voyage pleasant as well as useful. I take some reproach to myself under the circumstances for not having estimated high enough the advantages I would have derived from Dr. Hume's companionship on the voyage. My quarrel with him was brought on and kept up by faults in both our characters, and I was very young and very captious.

Dr. Hume had engaged for me a Mr. Pierie, a retired lieutenant of the Navy, to take the command of the vessel, having under him a Mr. Crawford, together with a mate, six picked sailors, two well-grown lads and a cook, and two extra men. The vessel was to be paid for, with the victualling of her crew, exclusive of my party, at the rate of 70l. a month, and I was to provide a spare anchor and cable, as well as a spare boat (a six-oared cutter) for her. She was a brig called the ' John ' of Leith, just launched, and her fitting up inside was to be left to me. I added to my party three other persons previous to sailing. . . . I was near having another companion who might have added to our cheerfulness. A few days before we sailed, Mr. Watkin Williams Wynn, the son of the baronet of the same name, who had been sent by his father to attend some lectures at Edinburgh, asked his father's permission to accompany me on my voyage if I had no objection. The permission was obtained, but

Sir W. W. Wynn's sudden death intervened while his son was preparing for the voyage.

The 'John' had been in the Roads, under the lee of Inchcolm and near the king's ships, for some weeks. I frequently visited her, and gave dinners and breakfasts on board to my friends. I gave the final order for departure and embarked myself on the 26th of May, 1789.

[The party consisted of

Mr. Stanley.

James Fosbury (his servant).

Lieutenant Pierie, R.N., Commander, and his son.

Mr. F. Crawford, owner of the brig, and captain under Lieutenant Pierie.

Mr. Baine, a teacher of mathematics at Edinburgh, who was to make scientific observations and drawings during the voyage.

Mr. Wright, student of medicine at Edinburgh, acting as surgeon and botanist.

Mr. Benners, of Santa Croce, belonging to Denmark. Son of a Danish merchant or planter; a student at Edinburgh; kept the accounts during the voyage.

Mr. Calden, a North American, about fifteen years old; a ward of the Earl of Selkirk.

Master Brown.

Taylor, a collector and setter of minerals at Edinburgh.

Twelve seamen and a boy.

Garrick and Tom, sailors.

Ferryland and 'Crab,' two dogs.

Some regulations were proposed by Mr. Stanley, and signed by all, as recorded by one of the party.

1. That everybody should be out of bed by 7 A.M.
2. That breakfast should be at 8, and a fine of sixpence paid by every person not attending ready dressed. (Mr. Stanley wishes us to be all dressed with our powder in our hair every day before breakfast.)
3. Dinner to be at 1 P.M.   Same fine for absence.
4. Tea, when weather permitting it, at 5 P.M.
5. Supper at 8 o'clock.
6. No candle to be burning in your cabin after 11.]

J. T. S. to Dr. Scot.

Stromness Harbour, in the Isle of Pomona, Orkneys:
June 1, 1789.

We cast anchor here this evening. Our passage has
been varied, and we have experienced all the vicissitudes of
a sea life, excepting the extremes of danger. We sailed
from the Forth on the evening of the 28th. The next day I
went with Wright and Benners to Inchcolm: they picked
up plants and shot birds; I sat myself down on a little grass
plot, sprinkled with daisies and violets, and drew the castle.
In returning to the ship the tide was against us and it
rained very hard. On board I found Calden and Crab. . . .
You must know that Calden had come on board in a
Newhaven boat, and had sent it inshore; and as none of
ours could be spared, and we had not time to make a signal
and wait for a boat to come for him, we decided to set him
ashore in Largo Bay, and he was to return to Leith in a King
Gordon boat.

I was awoke early next morning by Pierie, who told me
the wind had tacked suddenly to the southward in the night-
time, and the ship was fairly out at sea, on the outside of
the Isle of May. 'And Calden?' said I. 'Why, Calden is
on board, and we can't get back unless you have a mind to
lose another week waiting for a wind.' I thought a little
within myself, and called Calden. He was d——d glad of
it. 'But what will Cullen say?' He did not care. 'And you
have no shirt, or any one thing but what you have on your
back.' It was all one to him; in short, the consequence
might be too serious to me if I returned, so I resolved to
keep on my course for the Orkneys; and here we are, with
Calden along with us. The young fellow has been laughing
and sick all the way. But now the difficulty is, how to
send him back. He cares little how it is; he has but half
a crown in his pocket, and, I do believe, would set out for
Edinburgh with no better supply if I was to let him.
I intend consigning him to the care of a friend of

Mr. Pierie and getting him shipped on board the packet for Leith.[1]

[On the passage to Faroe from Orkney Mr. Baine gives an anecdote of the Newfoundland dog. 'I was told, this morning,' he says, ' that Ferryland, the proudest dog on board, on receiving a cuff from Mr. Crawford, walked to the ship's side with the greatest composure and jumped into the sea. This is not the first time they have differed ; we should have lost the dog, had not the weather been easy.'

Of the Faroe Islands Mr. Stanley says :]

I have the recollection of our approach to the Faroe Islands as one of a vision of fairyland. Towards evening, the sun, which was sinking behind the land, filled the whole air with purple of various tints ; masses of dark purple clouds, and a long range of high mountains of romantic forms, their summits, as well as the edges of the clouds, brightened up here and there with gold and red. The Faroese have a better climate than the Icelanders, and can grow a few oats in small patches round their houses. Their chief dependence is on their sheep. They dry their mutton in the air, and though without salt, they can keep it almost from year's end to year's end. It is most probable that the islands were named from the number of sheep kept on them, ' faar ' being the Danish word for sheep.

The first questions asked us by the Faroese when they came aboard were, whether ours was a king's ship, a privateer, or a merchantman ; and when told we were none of these things, but a yacht coming to these islands merely for the pleasure of seeing them, they seemed to think we were

[1] Further details as to young Calden's story may be given here. By a general contrivance, Mr. Calden was concealed from Mr. Stanley till the pilot was gone, and when it was impossible to return, the vessel going before the wind at the rate of six knots an hour, the young fellow showed himself and jumped about frantic with joy. 'I think,' says Mr. Wright, in his journal, ' Mr. Stanley himself was not much disappointed.' A note from the latter says : ' Our young American had no mind to leave us, and so by a combination formed to carry him off, in which he was a hearty concurrent and promoter, we found him on board when the pilot had left the ship, and we were in the midst of a strong tide.'

making fools of them. Some years afterwards these good people had cause given them to mistrust any vessel with guns visiting them, for Baron Hombesh, having a letter of marque from our Admiralty, landed and plundered them; the value of what he took was, however, paid afterwards by Government to the Faroese; the occurrence would have been disgraceful to England if it had not been so.

Wright's Journal.

June 16.—. . . A boat with the Danish flag astern came alongside with a message from Mr. Lund, the Chief Justice of the Islands, or law-man as he is called, inviting Mr. Stanley to his house, in the Island of Waggoe, distant eighteen or twenty miles. Mr. Stanley was not able to go himself, but wished that I would go in his place, which I did, Mr. Groote favouring me with his company. We set off at 3.40 P.M. When we were near Mr. Lund's house, I was surprised to hear an old man, one of our rowers, begin to sing, having previously taken off his cap, with a very solemn countenance. He was joined in a chorus by his companions. This lasted ten minutes, and Mr. Groote told me it was a psalm of thanksgiving; on leaving home and returning to it a psalm is always sung.

[By the desire of Mr. Stanley, Mr. Wright and Mr. Baine made an expedition to Skellingsfell, the highest hill in the Faroe Islands. The party, which included Mr. Groote, acting as interpreter, were hospitably entertained at a farmhouse by Mrs. Wang, a minister's widow, and her beautiful daughter. The dress of Mrs. Wang rather surprised them at first. She wore a little close cap; above this was tied a black silk handkerchief folded triangularly. Mr. Wright began to express his sorrow at her having a headache, when Mr. Groote informed him it was the usual female headdress. She had on a coarse spotted woollen jacket, which is wrought upon wires, above this a black petticoat reaching to her heels, and sheep's leather shoes. Such was the dress of Mrs. Wang the first day, but on the second she was much finer.]

Wright's Journal.

Mrs. Wang was dressed in black, and the form of it is what was worn in Britain a few years ago, under the name of skirt and jacket; on her head was a very small white cap, barely covering her ears, with a large spreading-out border of muslin; fixed to the cap was a tapering piece of muslin, a piece of which came down over her face to the eyes. The daughter was dressed in a cap of the same kind without the triangular appendage; the rest of her dress differed little from her mother's of yesterday. A fine shawl covered one of the whitest necks I ever beheld; a red jacket, striped petticoat, and black apron.

June 15.—Mr. Stanley, Benners, Calden, and I set off for the Island of Nolsoe in a Faroe boat rowed by six natives. We were accompanied by the rest of the party in the cutter rowed by our own sailors, who were completely beaten by the Faroese, to their great mortification—afterwards, however, they passed us hoisting their sails.

We landed at Nolsoe (*Anglice*, Needle-eye), from the extremity of it being perforated with a hole through which a boat can be rowed. . . . We went in to a farmhouse where we got milk, cheese, &c. The farmer pays an annual rent to the king, of 250 sheep skins, one barrel of butter, and some dozens of coarse stockings for the use of the army. For this he has a comfortable house to live in, and as much mountain land as will feed 600 or 700 sheep, a number of cows, &c. Mr. Stanley played a game of chess with him. The Faroese are very fond of chess and are very expert at it.

J. T. S. to Dr. Scot.

Frederick's Waag, Stromva, Faroe Islands : June 18, 1789.

. . . We are at anchor before the capital of the Faroe Islands, which is a village consisting of a few huts. It contains, however, as much hospitality as I ever desire to meet with, and every attention has been shown us. . . . We agree pretty well together at this moment, but I have had a few

rubbs with every one in his turn. I have been obliged to affect
being very passionate and imperious, and, God knows, though
there is a little of both these two characters in my composition, how often I have shammed them when I have been
as willing to waive authority as the most passive being, and
as cool as the most negative. But I have thought it incumbent on me to behave otherwise than I felt, to preserve
something like order. . . .

J. T. S. to his Sister, Isa Stanley.

Stromva, Faroe Islands : June 18, 1789.

As the ship which is to carry my letters to Copenhagen
is not yet sailed, I will send you an account, my dear
Isabella, of our yesterday evening excursion. We were
rowed to an island called Ostroe, some five or six miles
distant, and landed in a village near which the provost or
chief clergyman of the Faroe Islands resides. We paid him
a visit, and we were received with the greatest attention.
The first thing offered to us on entering was a dram. This
is the constant custom whenever you enter and whenever
you leave a house in these northern countries. We were
next presented with pipes and tobacco, and for the first
time in my life, for the sake of being sociable, I smoked a
pipe quite full. I thought it would have made me sick, but
however, I escaped. We were next given coffee, and we
then left the house to see some nests of eider ducks, belonging
to the clergyman. We came to a freshwater lake on which
were a couple of small islands. The one the provost had
made himself by sinking stones and covering them with
soil, and had planted it with angelica, or quanden, as the
Faroe people call it, a plant much resembling hemlock. . . .
Under this the ducks had their nests. . . . By never having
been molested or shot at, they had become remarkably tame;
they were swimming in numbers quite close to us all the
time we remained on the island, and some landed again
while we stood there.

We returned to the provost's house, and had intended
to just thank him for his politeness and reimbark; but he

insisted on our walking in, and there we found a table covered for supper. . . . We had on the table dried lamb and mutton. I must own I could not relish this dish, for the meat had been neither smoked nor dressed in any manner. It had been only hung up to dry, and was to all intents and purposes as raw as when killed. This is the only meat the people of these islands eat during winter. We had besides, on the table, most excellent cheese and butter and very good barley bread. On this I made a good supper. We had to drink malmsey, madeira, and claret. It was with some difficulty I got a little water to mix with my wine, and it was with still more difficulty I got leave from the provost to put anything into my glass but wine, and it was but seldom I had occasion to put any of this into my glass, for the provost kept continually filling it up to the brim. It grieved me much I could not talk to our hospitable landlord, but he could only converse in Danish. Every other gentleman in company spoke English, and I must here observe that I have been surprised at meeting with so many intelligent and well-informed men as are here at Faroe.

One custom we were witness to could not fail of striking us very much : the minister's lady and her sister would not sit down to table, and though they had maidservants, they stood behind our chairs and served us with what we wanted at supper. It was in vain that we remonstrated and expressed our reluctance to see them thus troubling themselves ; in vain we got up to assist them ; we were told such was the custom, and we must submit.

On going away, which was not till midnight, the provost made me a present of the model of a Faroe boat, and accompanied us to the waterside.

There is one ancient custom still practised in these islands which I must mention. Wright, our surgeon, is just returned from visiting a gentleman to whom I had a letter on the island of Mygennes, the most remote of the Faroe Islands. On taking leave of a farmer at whose house they dined, the host took out of a box a large handful of Danish crowns and asked whether they would be accepted by Mr. Wright, which being answered in the negative, he seemed much disappointed, as he said he was the first Englishman who had been on the island within the memory of man.

A thick fog surrounded us as we were going home, but yet it was daylight. I had the 'Castle of Otranto' in my pocket, and none of us being sleepy or in a humour to talk, upon their request I read it to them all the way. The scene was suitable to the subject. The fog just let us see the high rocks by which we rowed, and against which the sea broke into foam. We reached our ship a little past two o'clock, glad to find ourselves in our home, and yet sorry to leave off the story before we knew to whom the great enchanted helmet belonged. Adieu, my dearest sister,

Your most affectionate brother,

J. T. STANLEY.

P.S.—I send enclosed a little of the eiderdown which I took out of one of the nests.

Wright's Journal.

THE MOVING STONES.

June 21.—We could not get off yesterday morning sooner than seven, on account of a heavy rain. We were attended by our pilot and another guide. We began our journey by ascending a mountain 1,800 feet at least in height. Having ascended this hill, we had to ascend another not quite so high as the first, and then our way lay through a valley in which we sunk ankle-deep almost every step. The sheep on the hills looked very miserable from the wool having been lately torn from their bodies, for in Faroe the sheep are never sheared, but their wool is plucked off in a most barbarous manner by hand, and many die in consequence. We got to a farmer's house near the stones by the seaside about twelve, as wet as it was possible for water to make us, for it had rained incessantly the whole way. We stripped and dried ourselves the best way we could,

F

while a dinner was preparing. The landlord sold us stockings at 10*d.* a pair. Our dinner consisted of fish, pancakes, eggs, &c., after which we went in a boat and landed near the stones. We found two of them standing about six feet from the shore, but could only observe one of them in a state of motion. It was a mass of basalt 75 ft. 4 in. in circumference and 23 feet in height, on the side next the shore. We could clearly see its motion, but to put the matter out of doubt we had a fishing-rod which we placed so that one end rested on the stone and the other on the shore, and it moved backward and forward on the latter full two inches. The rock seems to be placed in a socket, balancing on its base. Its motion is more or less according to the sea's motion ; in a high running one Captain Flore has seen the end of the rod move more than six inches. The sea at present was calm. We set off on our way home at five, the rain as heavy as ever, and had not gone far before Mr. Stanley and Mr. Calden began to complain of weariness. This increased when we began to ascend the last high mountain, and now Crawford and Taylor began likewise to flag, as well from a sensation of hunger as fatigue, the first of which was very pressing on us all, for our biscuit, of which we had taken with us only a very small quantity, had been finished at the farmhouse. Mr. Stanley was at last so overcome[1] that for the last thirty yards of ascent he was dragged up by the guide ; we had now got to the top of the hill, when Mr. Stanley threw himself down and instantly fell asleep. The guide covered him up with great-coats. I was aware of the bad effects which sometimes proceed from great cold, therefore I insisted upon Mr. Stanley's getting up, which, though very unwillingly, he at last did, and began the descent with one of the guides. Mr. Calden and Mr. Taylor now came up, the latter informing us that he had been seized with a violent

---

[1] I began to suffer from hunger, and it increased so that I cut a slice off the body of one of the curlews we had shot, but the rawness of it disgusted me and a sudden faintness came on, and with it a drowsiness which at last I could resist no longer. . . . But Wright woke me and talked of Sir Joseph Banks and Solander.—J. T. S. (See Appendix).

inclination to sleep, but had resisted it; we sent back our
other guide to see what had detained Crawford, who was the
only one now missing. He found him fast asleep upon a
stone, and with difficulty waked him and brought him
forward. We crossed the snow again and were descending
the best way we could, when Mr. Calden called out to Mr.
Stanley and myself, who with the guides had got on some
way before, that Crawford was again missing. We were
alarmed, and despatched the guides to look for him. I also
went, but neither Mr. Stanley nor Taylor had strength to
accompany me. The guides who got to Crawford sooner
than I did, found him asleep as before, and on being
awakened he absolutely refused to move till he had taken
out his nap. When I came up he was pale and ghastly,
and was disputing with the guides as to remaining where he
was. He talked incoherently and seemed in some measure
to have lost his recollection. I first took his gun from him,
with which I was afraid he would do some mischief, and
then ordered the guides to force him along if he would not
move himself. The poor fellow was very sick, and proceeded with the greatest difficulty, notwithstanding all the
assistance which I and the guides could afford him. Mr.
Stanley (who by this time had forgot his own situation from
his apprehensions for Crawford) and Calden made all the
haste they could home to send some more assistance and some
refreshment for Crawford. We got on with him very slowly;
he often begged hard to be allowed to rest a little, in which he
was no sooner indulged than he instantly fell asleep. When
we had got near home we were met by a man with a bottle
of rum and some pancakes which were sent by Mr. Stanley;
the latter were no sooner presented than devoured, and after
them Crawford found a glass of grog an admirable restorative. On reaching the house we found Mr. Stanley and
Calden eating sage soup, in which we lost no time in joining
them; this, qualified with a little wine, completely restored
Crawford. All those who had been affected with the inclination to sleep, say it was preceded by a most violent
craving for food. The hunger was followed by sickness,

languor, and sleep, which, if indulged, might possibly have been eternal. After supper we went to bed, and it was 10 A.M. before any of us waked. We were joined by the commandant and his party at two o'clock; they would have come sooner, but could not without having a heavy fine imposed on them for travelling before sermon was over. We bade adieu to these good people, who saluted us with a discharge of three muskets, which we returned by as many shots from the boat. We called at Mrs. Wang's on our way back and got coffee, tea, sweet biscuits, &c. After Mr. Stanley had taken a drawing of the house and the mountain of Skellingsfell, we took a final farewell of the widow and her daughter. The sea was very rough, but we diverted ourselves the best we could in our way home, except Mr. Baine, who was excessively hippish and ill-natured all the way.

[Mr. Baine gives his own account of his ill-humour. He had, it appears, very much admired Miss Wang, and mentioned her so often that some of his companions took the liberty of joking and bantering him about her, carrying the joke rather too far, and he lost his temper, which was not mended by his having caught cold, and being in a state of great suffering from rheumatism in his leg and a hurt to his great toe. He pleads these in excuse for a quarrel he had the following morning with Mr. Stanley, he having used harsh language to Mr. Calden, upon which Mr. Stanley expostulated with him. It ended in a violent quarrel, and Mr. Baine went ashore determined to inquire for a passage to Copenhagen; but instead of doing so, he took a walk, made a sketch of a farmhouse and the town of Frederickswaag, felt very unwell, returned, and went to bed. Mr. Baine on the following day seems to have regained his tranquillity after the late storm, and said nothing more about it; but made it up with Mr. Stanley.]

A FAROE ISLAND BRIDE.

June 24.—There is a pretty servant girl who is to be married in a week or two; and in Thorshaven the dress of a bride is very peculiar, and never worn again. The sheriff accordingly wrote to Mr. Stanley, mentioning this, and

inviting us all to call on him at six in the evening to see a
Faroe bride and have a dance. My messmates were on
tiptoe at the news; we all got dressed in our uniforms, but
before seven Mr. Stanley received a second note expressing
surprise why an Englishman should make a lady wait for
him, for the bride had been dressed two hours. We set out
in the barge and went to the sheriff. The table was
immediately set for coffee; it was poured out by his
youngest daughter, a pleasing girl about eighteen or nineteen, performing her office very well, though speaking no
English. Their coffee is the best in the world. Tea, or, as
they call it, tea-water, came afterwards. The table being
cleared, the bride and bridegroom were introduced. She was
a pretty little fair girl, and her intended husband is a soldier
of the garrison, a good-looking young fellow. He was in
his uniform, with the black cloth peaked cap resembling
a cardinal's hat. The bride's appearance was striking.
Mr. Stanley has got as a present the handkerchief, the handsomest part of the costume. Her gown was a dark claret-
coloured stuff, a striped lawn apron, a lawn handkerchief
with a rich border of glass or crystal. Mr. Benners says it
was mother-of-pearl disposed into artificial flowers. Round
her waist was buckled a girdle of crimson velvet about two
inches broad; that part round the waist was covered with a
number of plates of silver-gilt jointed into one another, forming
oblong compartments ornamented with bas-reliefs, executed
in a tolerably good style, representing Scripture histories
and hieroglyphics; that part of the belt which hangs down
reached the bottom of the apron, and is ornamented with
about nine or ten studs of silver-gilt of a square pyramidal
form, prettily chased, and terminated by a plate of the same
metal about four inches long, ornamented like those on the
other end. From her bosom hung a lozenge plate of silver-
gilt about three or four inches in diameter, and in the plate
were fixed nine studs, to which small medals were suspended,
decorated with hieroglyphic figures of marriage &c. The
plate was hung by a chain of the same metal fixed to a large
pin with a round head about three-quarters of an inch in

diameter, hollow, and ornamented with handsome filigree work. . . . Her hair was combed back close to the head—the fashion of the country—powdered, and the cap reached halfway forward ; it was of an exceeding fine piece of net-work, decorated with pieces of gold lace prettily disposed, three or four of them reaching forwarder than the rest, terminating in tassels of gold fringe ; round a small knob from each side of the cap hung two pieces of gold lace about an inch broad, one over each shoulder, down to the girdle, and terminating in tassels. Round her neck was a chain consisting of three smaller ones, whether gold or silver-gilt I do not know. She wore Faroe shoes; no other can be worn on any account on such an occasion. . . . Lieutenant Pierie walked up to her and put something into her hand (which we afterwards found was a biscuit, and a piece of cheese inscribed ' May you never want what you wish for ') and saluted her. He was followed by Mr. Stanley and the rest of us. Mr. Stanley gave her a pocket-book and some ribbons, and each of us gave her something which we had received from Mr. Stanley for the purpose before we left the ship. Mr. Stanley tied a ribbon round her waist and another round her arm, and the girl seemed to be made very happy. When we had fully gratified our curiosity, the company—consisting of the sheriff and his two daughters, two young ladies, his friends, the provost, Mr. Quellin, Mr. Lund, and Mr. Groote —led up a Faroe dance, which, from its simplicity, I suppose was very ancient. The parties draw themselves up in a ring (if the room is too small to admit all in one ring it is doubled), they join hands and dance round from the right to the left, four short steps forward and two back, when they make a pause, and again advance ; this is the whole of the dance. They dance to their own singing ; the song is short, and is repeated twice or thrice till the dancers tire of it, then they stop and agree upon another song, and then dance again till they have had enough. Stewart, Benners' servant, who plays decently on the fiddle, had been ordered to attend, and we now showed the company our English and Scotch dances. They enjoyed them much. Mr. Lund, who plays pretty well on the fiddle, struck up some strathspeys, but not with the spirit of Niel Gow or my friend Scot.

The Faroese [1] next entertained us with a different kind of dance. They place themselves as if going to lead down a country dance, the partners holding the ends of a handkerchief or two tied together by the corners, elevated about the height of the eye. One sings—in this dance it was the bride who happened to be the best singer in the room—while they run under the handkerchief, and then dance down the outside of those going up.

From Baine's Journal.

June 27.—There was much mirth at dinner to-day. Mr. Stanley was sitting in a brown study, his fish and sauce cooling on his plate. 'A penny for your thoughts, sir,' said I. 'Sir,' he replied, 'I am thinking that our cutter ought to have a name, and that if each of us were to give the initial letter of his mistress's name we might see what name or word we could make of the whole together.' It was agreed to do so. I paid my penny for the thought, and from the contributed initials out came 'Angelica' at last as our cutter's appellation.

[1] One of those present wrote sixty years later:

'Thorshaven : January 22, 1850.

'I see that you have talked to Sir John Stanley about his visit here in 1789. It was a pleasant time to my brother and me. Along with him was an American student, his name Calden, from the Academy in Edinburgh; he was of my age, perhaps half a year younger, so we were soon heartily acquainted, and made many excursions on the heights, sometimes on the hills, sometimes in boats to the cavern in Nolsoe and other places. He was a droll fellow, and the time when our ancient bridal dress was presented to the company, he questioned about the reason why it was so. It is now not used; the bridal dresses are all sold, so I believe there are none left : the last in Suderoe was burnt with the house, so it is now only a tale of the times.'—*Extract from letter written by Schroter, ex-Pastor of Suderoe, Faroe, to Sir Walter C. Trevelyan, and forwarded to J. T. S.*

CHAPTER V.

ICELAND.

1789.

Arrival—The governor and his silent associate—Invitation to dinner—The learned footman—Snæfell Jokul—Black and white foxes—Crab's courage—Ascent to the region of fire and snow—Heckla—The American boy and the Union Jack—The geysers—Enthusiastic welcome—Monument erected—Witchcraft—Indreholme—Mr. Stephenson—Iceland dinner at Ness—Off Copenhagen—Strange conjectures—The Princess Royal—*De flamme en flamme*—Wild weather—Adam Smith and the customs—Oyster Club feast.

Wright's Journal.

ARRIVAL IN ICELAND.

July 4.—About eleven, a breeze sprung up bearing for the harbour of Häfinsfiord. . . . When we approached, it being high water, we signalled for a pilot. One soon came off, and we dropped our anchor at 9 P.M. The jolly-boat was hoisted out, and Mr. Stanley, Benners, Crawford, and I went ashore. Having hammered at the rocks for specimens and wandered about the cliffs, where we found abundance of flowers, we returned to the ship at 12 P.M. About half-past twelve at night,while after supper we were drinking a hearty welcome to each other on our arrival in Iceland, two men entered the cabin, one dressed like a gentleman in the usual fashion, and the other in a spotted, coarse woollen coat with black velvet cuffs, who we afterwards found was the provost or clergyman of Bersested. The first, on entering, asked if any of us could speak French. He was immediately answered by Mr. Stanley, who speaks it well. The stranger then said he was sent by Count Levitzau, the governor, to inquire who we were. Count Bernstorff had written to the Governor informing him that a Mr. Mackenzie was soon to

visit Iceland, but a second letter had stated that the visit
was delayed. Mr. Stanley then told him who he was and
expressed surprise that the Count had not mentioned him
likewise. Soon after this the stranger rose and told Mr.
Stanley that he was himself Count Levitzau, the governor,
and begged pardon for not letting him know sooner. He
had been under the necessity of acting as he had done as
expresses had arrived from merchants in Häfinsfiord saying
that an armed English vessel had entered the harbour. . . .

Reports of the probability of war between England and
Denmark had so frightened his domestics that not one could
be persuaded to come on board. So he determined to come
himself.

After drinking some punch he departed with his silent
associate, inviting us to dine with him to-morrow.

July 5.—The count stood at his door to welcome us; he
conducted us to a very handsome room, and presented us to
his countess, a fine agreeable woman, who was dressed in
white satin, and otherwise in very good fashion. . . . We
sat down to dinner a little after four. The countess did the
honours, and there was another lady present. The dinner
was elegant and abundant, consisting of soup, both roast
and boiled mutton, a pudding made of common sorrel,
smoked salmon, potatoes, a lettuce salad, cresses, and a
fresh salmon, turnips, tarts, sweetmeats, &c. &c., and lastly
a large vessel full of raspberry jam with fine cream. Along
with these we drank claret and malaga, all served in a very
orderly manner by a boy and footman, the latter of whom I
was surprised to find could speak good Latin.

July 7.—About three the cutter, with the St. George's
ensign at her stern, was sent on shore, and came off with the
governor and his lady; when within a certain distance of
us the sailors rested on their oars, and a salute of seven
guns was fired. When all were collected we sat down to
dinner. We had our coffee on deck, prepared by the fair
hands of the amiable countess; after which our sailors
were called upon to dance Scotch reels, and the count,
Mr. Stanley, Benners, Calden, and I danced on the quarter

deck. The governor and his lady left us at ten, accompanied by Mr. Baine and Calden, who steered the boat.
They were saluted with seven guns at parting, which they
returned with three cheers.[1]

July 13.—At three o'clock the ' John ' was under way for
Rekjavik, or rather for Snæfel's Jokul, for as the horses for
the expedition to Heckla could not arrive before Friday, Mr.
Stanley determined to fill up the time by visiting Snæfel,
said to be the highest mountain in Iceland. . . .

. . . The natives told us that we should meet with im-
passable rents and chasms on the snow, and that no person
had succeeded in getting to the top since Olaffer and his
companions were on the mountain, about thirty years ago.

We were not, however, to be frightened from our purpose,
and off we set, 8.5 P.M., attended by one of our sailors and by
the Danish carpenter. At half-past ten we got to the place
where snow is perpetual. The thermometer was at freezing
point. . . . A consultation was held, and Mr. Stanley resolved
to go on as far as we could. Each put on a coarse pair of
woollen stockings over his shoes. The snow became harder;
wide rents crossed our way—some of them 7 feet in width,
and, by a piece of lava attached to a string, I found to be
50 feet deep. In these we could see the layers of snow of
every year to a great depth, assuming vivid blue and green
tints. After much labour we arrived within 500 feet of the
summit. Mr. Stanley and I then began to ascend the

---

[1] NOTE BY J. T. S.—Count Levitzau and his countess were both young,
and brought up at the court of Denmark. He was sent to Iceland as governor
soon after his marriage. The countess was a beautiful woman, and might
well have pined for the admiration and enjoyments of society, but she bore her
privations and the cruel Iceland winters with the most inflexible good-temper.
In a conversation I had with her, she expressed herself content. They had
three children, and with these and her husband, and his secretary and his
wife, her home could not be called a solitude. . . . Alas ! who shall say what
is before them ? About ten years after my voyage I asked the Danish minister
in London if he could give me any account of my friends. 'A melancholy
one,' he said. 'Last summer the Countess Levitzau was with all her children
crossing the Little Belt from one island to another, and was shut up in her
carriage on the deck of the ferryboat, when, by a gibe of the boom, the carriage
with all in it was dashed overboard. The count saw the carriage sink.'

remaining part on all fours—the steepness and slipperiness
had so increased, we could not get on by other means. Near
the summit we were stopped by a chasm, with a bridge of
snow. . . . Mr. Stanley was in much danger when about
to cross over. Fortunately he stuck his pole into the
surface before venturing, when it immediately gave way,
being only a bridge of snow less than a foot of thickness
over a deep rent. . . . We remained in suspense some
minutes. Those below called on us to desist, and on the
carpenter's being desired to fetch the barometer up to us, his
answer was that he had more regard for his soul and body
than willingly to throw away both. In the meantime I was
trying the depth of the snow, and in one place, at the depth
of 6 feet, I found rock or hard ice resist my pole. Accordingly
Mr. Stanley and I set about digging holes in the snow for
our feet, and raising ourselves gradually and bearing as
lightly as possible over the mouth of the cavern, we got to
the top and endeavoured to persuade those below to follow,
but to no purpose; and as for the carpenter, neither threats
nor promises had any effect on him. He swore he would
not budge an inch for all the world.

It was 1.5 of July 15 when we reached the summit, from
which we could see the sun just about to rise.

On exposing the thermometer, the mercury fell to 27°.
There being no chance of the carpenter coming up with the
barometer, we began to descend, after writing our mistresses'
names on the top of a mountain, on the whitest snow,
emblematic of their innocence and purity.

After we had rejoined our party, I proposed to carry up
the barometer to the summit, since the carpenter refused.
This was agreed to, and Mr. Stanley and I found it much
easier getting to the top than the first time, by reason of the
steps we had made. . . .

The sun had now got up in all his glory, and the shadow
of Snæfel's Jokul was thrown on the sea's surface so finely
towards the south-west that it was some time before we
could convince ourselves that it was not another mountain, before concealed from us in a fog. To the south we

saw the harbour, in which our brig, the 'John,' and another
vessel appeared like two small specks.

July 17, *Rekjavik.*—On going ashore I found Benedict,
the governor's servant, with a present of two foxes, one
black and one white, from his master to Mr. Stanley. We
saw the king's falcons, thirty-nine in number, all hooded;
not perfect till eight years old; 15 rix dollars each. . . . The
horses are come. . . .

July 30.—At length we set off for Heckla. The party
consists of Mr. Stanley, Messrs. Crawford, Calden, Baine,
Benners and Wright, attended by Taylor, James Garrick,
Tom, the Shuster,[1] and three guides, twenty-two horses and
two dogs, Ferryland and Crab.

August 5.—Several smart earthquakes were felt last
night. At half-past seven we arrived at the banks of the
largest river I ever saw, called the Elf. Two boats came to
us from the opposite side. While this was doing, Mr.
Stanley's little dog Crab swam across, though the stream is
rapid, and on not finding his master on the other side,
plunged in again, and was returning when one of the boats
took him up. His courage was the more remarkable, as the
Newfoundland dog, who seems never to wish to be out of
the water, feared to swim over, and was at last forced to do
it against his will.

August 8.—The foot of Mount Heckla is reached.

J. T. S. to Dr. Scot.

Rekjavik, Iceland : August 21, 1789.

My dear Scot,—We have seen the famous springs of
Geyser, and have reached the summit of the more famous
Heckla.

Our journey to Heckla was a very slow and uncomfortable
one; it was as bad as bad roads and bad weather could make
it. Our cavalcade consisted of twenty-three or more horses,

---

[1] The Shuster was a shoemaker who had learned his trade in Germany, and
was hired as an interpreter during our stay in Iceland; a very mild honest
fellow.—J. T. S.

and we were in all fourteen persons. We slept in our tents, and had nearly all our provisions with us. We rode over streams of lava, some no less than ten miles broad. We traversed several marshes, and had great trouble in getting through, for the horses were for hours together up to their knees at every step. Some part of the country was, to make us amends, laid out in extensive pastures. The herbage was of a fine colour, intermingled with wild flowers—the butter-flower and wild thyme, forget-me-not and candied turf,[1] and a thousand others. We crossed several rivers. One measured by Mr. Baine was about 900 feet in breadth : the horses were forced to swim over, and we followed ourselves with our baggage in a small boat.

The country near the bottom of Mount Heckla is fine for Iceland, but it assumes a dreary appearance when you begin to ascend the mountain. We rode up five miles, and then were forced to leave our horses. We began by scaling the sides of a rough stream of lava; then the ascent became steeper, and we found the hill covered with loose stones and dust, thrown out from the crater.

The wind became fiercer and the gusts so violent, as to force us, notwithstanding our long poles, against the rocks of lava. Little Crab, my favourite terrier, was blown off his legs to the distance of a pace or two, and old Ferryland had need of all his strength to preserve him from a similar disaster.

A thick fog surrounded us, and at one moment I despaired of ever arriving at the top of Mount Heckla. An instantaneous break in the clouds relieved us from our anxiety. . . . The fog separating, had shown us a crater on my left hand. It was only 60 to 100 feet deep, and mostly lined with snow. I slid down to the bottom of it in an instant, and, now screened partly from the wind, I climbed up the last remaining height, where I found to my great joy a good many of my companions, among whom was little Calden with an English Jack tied to his pole, which he was waving with great exultation.

[1] Candytuft ?

You will wish to know what I saw and what I found on the top of Heckla. Nothing. The clouds concealed even the view of the hill itself from us. Fifty paces covered with black pumice stone, and of lava burnt to cinders, were all we could discover. At the same instant a thin smoke rose from one of the craters, and the thermometer, when in the air at 34°, rose, when laid on the ground whence issued the smoke, to 144°.

But, with the Doge of Genoa, I might tell you one thing surprised me very much on the top of Heckla, and that was to find myself there. The Doge of Genoa made this answer to the courtiers of Louis XIV., who had obliged him to come to Versailles, contrary to the laws of his republic, when they asked him what he thought most surprising in the place.

We travelled back from Heckla to the boiling spring called Geyser.

Imagine a spring of water five or six feet in diameter gushing out of the earth to the height of 130 feet. Imagine this column breaking into foam as white as snow, and, when it first gushes out in one collected mass, reflecting the purest blue. Add to this picture the volumes of steam ascending on all sides, the noise, and stones thrown up by the water to a much greater height than itself.

We spent more than three days in the neighbourhood of the springs, and then directed our march towards the ship, after having been absent three weeks. Everybody on board is in perfect health, and, believe me, in much better humour with each other than when the ship first sailed from the Firth. . . . Yours, J. T. S.

Wright's Journal.

. We reached a farmhouse, Mossfell, built upon a tumulus .n a pleasant valley. Shuster told us there was a good church and a clergyman of great merit and hospitality. We were met by his son who politely offered us the use of the church for the night, which we thankfully accepted. The parson spoke Latin fluently, and presented Mr. Stanley with some Icelandic books. He accompanied us himself towards Rekjavik. He told us his name was John, and on asking his surname he said he had none. His father's name was Hanna. He was called John, son of Hanna, or Han's son. After riding a few miles he took an affectionate leave, repeating two or three times, with tears in his eyes, ' Salvete, Salvete Brittanici.'

On our return to Rekjavik, August 19, all the inhabitants turned out to meet us. The crew on landing gave three cheers, after which the honest fellows ran up and welcomed us most heartily ; some of them even shed tears. The poor dogs were sadly tired ; as for the Newfoundland, poor Ferryland, he had hardly strength to drag himself along the last day of the journey, lying down repeatedly. Mr. Baine says his last effort to come to the boat, about a hundred yards, was so painful, that though the most patient creature living, he could not do it without repining ; and when he reached the quarter deck, he laid himself down and would allow no one to touch him. His feet were rubbed with butter, and Mr. Baine wrapped him in two boat-cloaks and left him to repose. A monument had been erected by Captain Pierie and his crew on the small island at the mouth of the harbour of Rekjavik, to commemorate this visit to Iceland. It was 14 feet high, with a square base of 4 feet, and ending in a square of 8 inches, with the following inscription cut out by Captain Pierie on a plate of copper in the middle of it :

> JOHN THOMAS STANLEY
> Lieut. JOHN PIERIE
> Messrs. WRIGHT
> BAINE
> BENNERS and
> CALDEN. Visited Iceland, 1789.

It was built by the masons employed at the new church in Rekjavik, the captain and crew laying the first stone, under which some British coins were placed.

' When I went with Pierie to the island,' says Mr. Stanley,
' to obtain a promise from the people that the monument
should be taken care of, some of our sailors prevailed on the
captain to ask me to give a present of a few shillings to an
old woman living there, to prevent her by witchcraft bringing
some mischief on our vessel during our voyage. I do not
recollect that the request was absolutely for my buying from
her a fair wind; but it was evident they thought, if
unpropitiated, she could raise up a foul one against us. I
thought it most prudent to comply with their wishes, to keep
their imaginations free from any prospects of danger. The old
woman seemed very poor and harmless, but in all probability
she had made the people of Rekjavik believe that she possessed some supernatural powers. She wished us a prosperous voyage in return for my present, which perfectly satisfied
the sailors. Had I not given anything to the old woman,
and our ship had been subsequently in any danger, I am
confident it would have been attributed to my want of a
proper faith in Scandinavian witchcraft.'

Wright's Journal.

August 23.—At 1.35, after prayers, Mr. Stanley, Crawford,
who steered, and I set off for Indreholme, which we reached
in less than two hours. We were received by Mr. Stephenson,
superbly dressed in scarlet, and his two youngest sons. Mr.
Stephenson had got together a great many presents for Mr.
Stanley; the most valuable was an elegant silver vase, on
the top of which was an ornament of several figures, with
the names of himself, his wife and children; he has also
got some specimens of natural history for us. Mr. Stanley
made him, his charming daughter, and his sons, presents.
When we were in the boat, we were saluted by a discharge of
seven small cannons and three cheers, to which we made a
suitable return. We left at 6.40 P.M. A fine breeze at first,
but it gradually freshened into a storm. We close-reefed
our sails, and a great sea washed over us. After supper Mr.

Stanley got Mr. Stephenson's present—which holds three-quarters of a bottle—filled with wine, and proposed his father's health. We pledged him, and did honour to the baronet and his lady and daughters.

Mr. Stanley also gives an account of this day:

The reception we met with at Indreholme was very gratifying. The establishment has a village-like appearance; the outbuildings very numerous, and the house, divided into gable ends, covering a large space. We were welcomed into what in Iceland may be called a large room, but low, and having small windows. Coffee, sweetmeats, cakes, and a large bowl of crowberries were set on the table. Mr. Stephenson's behaviour was that of a most perfectly well-bred gentleman. He is indeed, next to the governor, the first man of consequence on the island, and he has an ample fortune to give him, and make him feel, his consequence; he has increased his wealth considerably by the employment of a great many boats in the cod fishery. Count Levitzau told me he might be considered as having realised at least 20,000*l*. On the way from his door to the boat he was not satisfied with having made me the present of the silver cup &c., for, seeing me with only a strong oaken cudgel in my hand, he insisted on my changing it with him for a handsome cane with a silver-gilt head. I wished we could have seen more of him and his family while in the island.

Wright's Journal.

ICELAND DINNER AT NESS.

August 25.—About five o'clock Mr. Stanley, Benners, and myself, attended by Shuster, set off for Ness to eat an Icelandic dinner which Mr. Stanley had requested to be prepared for us; we reached the house (the apothecary's) in less than an hour, and found it was the handsomest we had seen in the island, the governor's not excepted. I was surprised to find the shop stored with a great variety of medicines in good order; they are supplied by the king.

We had the company of the physician at dinner. He lives next door. He explained to me in Latin the nature of the dishes, and by his example encouraged me to taste them. Before each person a dried cut piece of cod, a round cake of rye bread, and a knife were placed. In the middle of the table was set a vessel full of sour butter, and a plate full of smoked shark; there was also salt and fresh butter. Of the latter, bread and dried fish, we ate a little, but though I made three violent attempts I could not swallow a particle of the shark or the sour butter, which are, without exception, the most nauseous, villainous, and diabolic substances that I ever tasted. The physician eat of everything, even of the shark, which, however, he seasoned well with pepper, saying it otherwise felt rather heavy on the stomach.

We preferred wine mixed with water to the syre, or sour whey, and the apothecary, out of compassion, at last brought some to us. There was likewise on the table a dried head of a large fish, the skin of which, though tougher than parchment, the doctor ate with some butter, as pleasantly as he would have done a pancake. After these were removed, two large vessels were placed on the table, one full of curds and cream made from sheep's milk, and the other with rye bread mashed down with cream. After dinner we visited the church, built about four years ago. We bade our host adieu about eight, and rode back to Rekjavik.

August 27.— . . . After dinner, set off to the provost's at Häfinsfiord; his wife is procuring a female Iceland dress for Mr. Stanley, who intends to call at Bessested for two dolls which the countess is preparing. . . . The Iceland dress is come; it is very rich, as indeed it ought to be, having cost twenty guineas.

August 29.—When we were getting up this morning, the apothecary's son and another young man came on board with the necessary constituents of an Iceland dinner, with which Mr. Stanley means to treat some of his philosophical friends at Edinburgh. The feast of the ancients in ' Peregrine Pickle ' will be nothing to it. While Mr. Stanley was taking an observation of the sun's altitude at noon, his

hat fell overboard. Ferryland immediately leapt overboard and brought it, the ship lying to for him. . . . Mr.
Stanley finished this evening two drawings of the Great
and Small Geysers. . . . As soon as the wind changes we
sail for Denmark, without visiting Norway as was once
intended.

September 27.—At half-past one, anchored in the Roads of
Copenhagen, in which the Danish fleet, consisting of more
than twenty line of battleships, is lying. A salute of nine
guns was fired by us while anchoring. After dinner and
prayers, Messrs. Stanley, Baine, Benners, Crawford, and I
went ashore in the cutter, manned by the crew with ribands
round their hats, with ' *Sans changer*,' Mr. Stanley's motto,
painted on them in gold letters. On returning to our ship
we found that an officer had been on board inquiring what
we were, on account of our salute, and the St. George's
ensign we had hoisted on anchoring. Some time after an
officer came from the admiral, and asked how many guns
we had fired yesterday, and in about half an hour five
guns were fired from the admiral's ship.[1] The ' John ' is to
come within the Booms to have her bottom cleaned, if leave
can be got; but this is not certain, for there are strange
doubts about us. Some say that Mr. Stanley is the Duke
of Clarence in disguise; others, that he is the Duke of
Sudermania; and it is said that Count Bernstoff himself
has great suspicions that we had some more important
purpose in view in visiting Iceland than natural history.

October 1.—Went with Mr. Stanley to see the porcelain
manufactory; the intendent, Mr. Mohr, is the same who
wrote the Natural History of Iceland. Mr. Stanley has be-
spoken some tea and coffee cups and vases with the geysers
and Heckla painted on them.

October 4.—Mr. Von Bhelen accompanied Mr. Baine and

---

[1] We were given to understand that our salute of the day before was not
returned, from ignorance of what we were. The fact was, that according to the
then practice of gentlemen's yachts we wore a pennant, a rather saucy
display when in the sight of men-of-war. From our appearance the admiral
could not be satisfied that our vessel was not only a merchantman. A
merchantman would have had no salute.—September 28, J. T. S.

myself to the Chapel Royal, where we saw the Prince and Princess Royal—a most heavenly creature.

'This princess,' writes Mr. Stanley, 'was the daughter of the unfortunate Matilda.[1] I was presented to the princess, and agree with the doctor that she was a heavenly creature, and I was surprised by the peculiar amiability of her manner, and the few words she said in her interesting tone of voice.'

October 11.—Found the ship cleaned and new painted. In the evening went with some gentlemen to the King's garden. Mr. Stanley was introduced to Count Bernstoff. . . . During dinner Mr. Stanley received a message intimating that Prince Frederick wished to see him in the evening. He was presented to the Prince Royal yesterday, and received very graciously.

J. T. S. writes: 'I received a note from the king's chamberlain, M. Berloff, saying he would present me himself, which he did to all the royal family excepting the king. Mr. Elliott honoured me with his company on board after my presentation, introduced me to some members of the diplomatic corps, and took me to an assembly at the Austrian minister's, saying to his lady, as he presented me, " Mons. Stanley vole de flamme en flamme," alluding to my visitations of Etna, Heckla, and Vesuvius.'

The 'John' encountered a tremendous gale on her way home. Mr. Stanley says: 'The storm we encountered between Norway and Leith was by far the most formidable we had met with during the whole of our voyage. . . . In passing the 'Thorn' man-of-war we saluted her with eleven guns, which were returned by nine. On approaching the harbour we saluted Leith with another eleven. The report brought out a great number of people, amidst whose acclama-

---

[1] Caroline Matilda, sister of George III., married Christian VII., King of Denmark. In a sudden fit of jealousy, 1772, he imprisoned her in the Castle of Zell, and beheaded Count Struensee and Brandt. The Queen died 1775, aged 24. In 1784 the King was pronounced deranged, and his brother Frederick became Regent.

tions we landed. I found an order at the Custom House at Leith, from Mr. Adam Smith, the first commissioner, that my ship was not to be visited by the officer, and that everything brought home by me was to be allowed to land free of duty. The collection of dried plants made by Dr. Wright [1] during the voyage to Iceland and elsewhere was presented to Sir Joseph Banks.

[An interesting account of the hot springs of Rykum and Hankadal was communicated by Mr. Stanley to the Royal Society of Edinburgh, and, with an analysis of the waters by Dr. Black, appears—No. IV., V., and VI.—among the papers of the Physical Class in the third volume of the Society's Transactions. On page 95 we read :

'Sir Joseph Banks made a voyage to Iceland, 1772, and brought from thence many incrustations formed by the waters of the boiling springs. . . . It raised a strong desire for an opportunity of examining the water and learn by what means this silicious matter was dissolved in it.

'This opportunity was at last given us by J. T. Stanley, Esq., who, excited by motives similar to those of Sir Joseph Banks, equipped likewise a vessel and made a voyage to Iceland in the summer of 1789. He brought from thence and from the Faroe Islands a number of specimens of volcanic and fossil productions and a quantity of water of the two most remarkable boiling and exploding springs of Iceland, called by the natives Geyzer and Rykum.']

Note by J. T. S. on Iceland Dinner given at Edinburgh on his return, 1789.

My friends of the Oyster Club had expressed a wish I would bring the materials for an Iceland feast back with me, that they might have some idea of the luxuries of the island. Accordingly I had packed up a specimen of each article the apothecary had placed before us, and each had promised

---

[1] Soon after his return Dr. Wright was given a medical appointment in India. He was highly thought of and prospering, but riding out one day, the horse, making a sudden plunge, threw him, and he died from the effects of the fall.—J. T. S.

he would do his best to make a meal. Everything was
spread out soon after my return in the room next our club-
room, but my philosophers left everything almost untouched.
It was like a *Festin de Pierre*, but the display afforded much
amusement, and added not a little to the pleasure with
which the oysters and apple tarts, the usual club fare, were
afterwards assailed.   Of the party, amongst others, were
Adam Smith, Dr. Hutton, Dr. Black, Sir James Hall, Henry
Mackenzie, Professor Robinson, and Dugald Stewart.
What a constellation!   With such guests at table, who would
not sit down to try to eat even an Iceland dinner?   But in
truth an Iceland dinner might, if I had not requested it
should be strictly an Iceland dinner, have been rendered
much more palatable and savoury; and if good beef and mutton
and fresh salmon, cod, ptarmigan, and plovers could make
out a good dinner, the apothecary, who was a very liberal
man, would have given the company no reason to complain.

CHAPTER VI.

POLITICS, DIPLOMACY, AND SOLDIERING.

1790–1795.

Mrs. Nesbitt—Pocket boroughs—Assembly at Mr. Pitt's—Lord Lonsdale and docile M.P.s—Dinner at the Coal Exchange—Father and son—Icelandic fox —Sir Joseph Banks—Plants from Iceland—'Sçavoir Vivre' Club—Lord Auckland—J. T. S. and Lord Downe—M.P.s for Wootton Bassett—The Hague—Death of Adam Smith—Through Flanders to France—Caps of Liberty everywhere—The prince and the miller—Paris—Flame and fury— A peaceful English home—Helping hands to old French friends—Death of Dr. Scot—Translation of Bürger's ' Leonore '—Cheshire Militia song—Bexhill Camp.

J. T. S. to Dr. Scot.

Grosvenor Place: January 3, 1790.

. . . I have only stirred from home since my arrival to see my mother and sisters. I was received with open arms, as a mother and sisters would receive a son returned from an expedition to Iceland and the Northern Sea. . . . My father was very glad to see me, he has a strong claim on my gratitude. I believe I could command his fortune at this moment if I wanted it; he complied with every wish I expressed. Much as I owe to him, I hope he will not think me at any time deficient. . . .

P.S.—Ask of Pierie or Crawford if they know where the goat is which went with me to Iceland. I wish her to be sent to London, for I think she deserves to have her liberty and a good field to run in for the remainder of her days. Nasmyth will send me the sketch he made of the Iceland dog for me, and I wish at the same time he would make a similar drawing of Ferryland.

Grosvenor Place: February 6, 1790.

. . . The two paintings of the hot springs came in safety, and have been much admired by everybody who has seen them. *À propos* the poor little Iceland dog, which I called Geyzer, is dead. He died of the distemper. We regretted him, poor fellow, on account of his having come from so distant a land and escaped so many perils in his voyage. The white fox, however, that I may blend good with bad tidings, is arrived safe; he is as tame as ever, and more beautiful. We have given him a court to himself, in which he runs, without any chain, and somehow or other he has ingratiated himself into great favour with everybody in the house. Mr. Crab often pays his respects to him, and they romp and sit together for whole hours. We take it for granted they talk of Iceland. . . . The white fox was given to me when he was not more than two months old, and the governor, Levitzau, had him at least a month before. He was brought up with the children, who were constantly feeding him with milk. Since I have had him he has scarce ever been left to himself. The seamen used to romp with him every hour of the day, and he was never fed but by the hand. He should, of course, be as tame as any domestic animal. He is far from it; . . . he bit his friend, Billy Pierie, through the hand once without any provocation. His bark is so similar to that of a dog that we have been mistaken on hearing him, and fancied that one of the dogs was shut out. He has, besides this, a whining noise, peculiar to his species. . . . A sailor boy came yesterday from the ship and went to him, and the fox jumped about him, showing great marks of pleasure.

Grosvenor Place: January 13, 1790.

. . . I have given very little time to society as yet, as I must give a good deal to my father and mother. . . . And now let me tell you that my hopes are most flattering. A friend [Mrs. Nesbitt] with whom I was acquainted in my earliest days, and of whom I have spoken to you, has served me most essentially. Mr. Rose[1] behaved most cordially when I first saw him since my return. . . . The advice which both he and Mrs. N. have given me coincides in one thing, which is, that I should begin by coming into Parliament, and I have

[1] Statesman and political writer, 1744-1818.

acquiesced. I come in, therefore, for a borough on the side
of Government, and Rose takes me by the hand. Had I
arrived in London and communicated my views to him a
few weeks sooner, I might have been at no greater expense
than 1,200*l*. It will now be some thousands. . . . I shall
have to stem the torrents of politics alone till you join me in
June. I hope, however, to make good my course, as the
wind comes from so fair a quarter. I was at court yesterday. . . . Sir Joseph Banks has been very civil with visits,
messages, and invitations, and I dine with him next week.

Memorandum by J. T. S.

My first visit to Norwood House was in 1789. I was at
Streatham, where my brother was at a school kept by the Rev.
Reynolds Davies. 'Do you remember,' he said to me, 'a lady
who, with Lord Bristol, whenever his son, Augustus Hervey, was
sent for out of school, used always to send for you at the same
time? A Mrs. Nesbitt [1]—she is living not far from here.'

I remembered her well, for, besides seeing her at Loughborough
House, I was often invited to pass a day at Lord Bristol's house
in St. James's Square; and when I was at school at Greenwich,
she and Lord B., when paying a visit to an old friend of hers at
the hospital, begged a holiday for me. Poor Augustus Hervey!
he was a noble-spirited lad, warm in his youthful friendship for
me, for the few years it lasted. He had the character of a Hervey:
impetuous, eager, clever, and fascinating. He went to sea when he
was twelve. On an exchange of very few shots with the French
fleet besieging Gibraltar, one struck him on the chest.

The day after my conversation with Mr. Davies, I mounted my
horse, and was soon at Mrs. Nesbitt's door. I found her in a
long boudoir, working at a tambour frame—her best-looking days
all passed by, and her grey hair tucked up under a close French cap.
The moment she heard my name she got up and threw her arms
round me, crying out, 'Can it be you, the friend of Augustus?' [2]
After this I visited her often, dining, and sometimes passing two
or three days at Norwood.

[1] Her picture as Circe, by Sir Joshua Reynolds, was given to J. T. S., and
is still in possession of the family.

[2] Augustus Hervey, placed under Mrs. Nesbitt's care by Lord Bristol. See
Dictionary of National Biography.

It was at her house that I made acquaintance with George Rose, Lord Mulgrave, Mr. Townshend, an East India director, the daughters of Lord Chancellor Thurlow, and Mr. Crespigny, a relation of her husband, Mr. Nesbitt, dead long before, and some few others.

The house had swelled itself out from a cottage, by additions to it by Lord Bristol, and after his death by Mrs. Nesbitt, into a comfortable and spacious villa, with stables &c. Lord Bristol in his rides had been struck with the picturesque and peaceful character of the woody recess in which the cottage stood, divided by a space of cleared land, enclosed from Norwood Common. He purchased the place, and obtained from the Archbishop of Canterbury a grant of several acres, at that time covered with wood, so that there were meadows and pasture fields, a garden and pleasure ground of nearly half a mile in length, all within a ring fence. The common was covered with gorse, and extended from the crown of Norwood hill towards the west, to the Dulwich Road on the south, crossing a valley to cultivated lands, with only here and there a dwelling on them.

Journal of J. T. S., 1790.

Tuesday, February 7— . . . Norwood is a pleasant retreat, and Mrs. Nesbitt's house is situated at the entrance of the wood. . . . Gipsies have frequented this wood from time immemorial. Everybody has heard of Norwood gipsies.

Had I told Mrs. Nesbitt a fortnight earlier of my wish to come into Parliament, I should have been named with Mr. Townson for the borough of Okehampton, in Devonshire. It has belonged to the Duke of Bedford and Lord Spencer; Lord Spencer gave 22,000*l.* for the half of it. There are 250 voters, or thereabouts, in the town; these are chiefly tradesmen, and will vote for whoever holds out encouragement to them. Mrs. Nesbitt has this moment received information that the canvass goes on most favourably for Townson and Anderson. Colonel St. Leger and the other candidate on his side have left the town, disgusted with the little popularity they seemed to have. I saw Mr.

Townson yesterday for the first time.   We dined at Mrs.
Nesbitt's ; he is an East India director, a quiet, sensible man.

Everything Mr. Rose says of me is in my favour; if I
have a friend on whom I may depend, it is him. . . . It is
most probable that the Parliament will be dissolved in May ;
it must be soon decided, therefore, whether I get a seat or
no. . . .

My father and myself dined with Palmer in Oxford
Road.   He has a very great estate in Ireland, is unmarried,
and has travelled over the Continent all his lifetime, and is
acquainted with people of all ranks and characters.   He
is cheerful and witty.   Palmer's house is pleasantly
situated at the end of Oxford Road, facing the park, and
furnished with good pictures.   We had at table Mr.
Parsons, Mr. Seward, Dr. Ash, Mr. Piozzi, Mr. Dumbleton,
a Mr. Stewart, who has walked all over Europe, Mr. Boswell,
and some foreigners.   I went in the evening to an assembly
at Mr. Pitt's, in Wimpole Street.   I met Mrs. Walker and
her daughters, Mr. Morgan, Mr. R. Leycester, Mr. Hamilton,
Lady and Miss Cunliffe (cousins of my American friend,
Hüger), Mr. Chetwynd, Mr. Pettiward, Mr. and Mrs. Blackburne, and Lord and Lady Howe, whom I have known since
I was a schoolboy.

Wednesday, February 17.— . . . I breakfasted this
morning with Rose at his house in Old Palace Yard.   He
knows many people, and he gives their characters. . . . Lord
Lonsdale has enough interest to bring ten members into
Parliament, and some of them are so much his dependents,
that they ask him which way he would wish them to vote, as a
servant comes for orders.   He makes them feel their dependence as much as possible, and will not tell them which way
he has determined they shall vote till late in the debate.
He will not let them help themselves at his table ; and
then, no one knows from whence come these people who sit
in the House of Commons as representatives of the nation.
One of them offered to hold the Bible for Mr. Banks to kiss
when they were taking their oaths on first coming into
Parliament.   Lord Barnard, the son of Lord Darlington,

will have, some day or other, at least 100,000*l.* a year.
No subject of England should have so much. I admire the
laws of one of the republics of Switzerland, by which the
citizens assume the right of diminishing the fortune of any
individual when it becomes so disproportionate to the
rest as to be dangerous.

After breakfast Mr. Rose told me that Lord Auckland
had consented to my being with him at the Hague during
the summer. . . . Mr. Rose had been employed with Mr.
Pitt in looking over the list of boroughs which were to be
disposed of, and the persons who wished to come into
Parliament. He believed Mr. Pitt's engagements were not
so numerous but that I might succeed. . . . For himself,
he promised me all his influence could do, and that if there
should be no opening at the beginning of Parliament,
I should be named to fill up the first that happened afterwards. I dined with the officers quartered at the Tower,
at the Coal Exchange. Harry Campbell, my old school-
fellow, had invited me to meet Mr. Raddock, whom he told
me I should like, and I did so. There were only Campbell,
Mr. Raddock, and Mr. Hervey, second son of Lord Bristol.

February 18.— . . . Mr. Forbes and Mr. T. Wilbraham
called here in the morning. I begin to be tired of showing
my Icelandic curiosities to every visitor. A visit to the
Cotterels, and a lounging walk with Lord Archibald
Hamilton, filled up the remainder of the morning. . . .

February 19.—I dined quietly with my father, *tête-à-
tête*. He talked of my grandfather, Sir Edward, who was
a younger brother, and brought up to the law. He had
considerable practice, and bought estates in Somersetshire.
He made alterations in his house and park at Alderley, and
cut down trees which he thought less beautiful than
an open space. Previous to this, the fine beech wood
stretched quite down to the moat. The same silent thanks
will not be paid to him which are frequently felt by me,
when I walk under the shade of the trees still standing,
for Sir Thomas who planted them. Sir Edward has
some thanks, however, from his grandson for the clumps of

firs he has planted on the edge.   Did anybody ever repent
the expense he had been at in planting?   Their successors,
when in future days they walk under the shade of the trees,
thinking of the times when they were planted, will ask who
planted them; and the name will not be forgotten by
them or their children.

J. T. S. to Dr. Scot.

Grosvenor Place: February 21, 1790.

. . . It is now determined that I accompany Lord
Auckland.   But I am not the only one who is going to learn
the routine of business under him.   Lord Hawkesbury sends
a son, and the Marquis of Blandford may be there.   I have
told Rose I would go at any time—next week, if Lord
Auckland would allow me.   The ship from Leith with the
remainder of my things is arrived.   Bistella[1] and the goat
are both in Grosvenor Place.   This last I shall send down
to Alderley with the waggon, and she shall enjoy her liberty
in the park for the remainder of her days.   The fox, I
believe, is turning red.   This would be a most curious
circumstance, as in Iceland they never become that colour.[2]
Every Saturday evening I spend at Sir Joseph Banks'.
His house is constantly open on this day for all his friends.
These are chiefly men who are engaged directly or indirectly
in the literary world.   Three rooms, filled with books &c.,
are thrown open.   The company assembled generally may
amount to thirty or more; all scientific foreigners are there.

[1] Bistella was brought from Iceland.   The farmer, Johan Erickson, who
lives at the cottage near which we pitched our tents at the foot of Mount
Heckla, gave her to me.   Here she is in London.   What a contrast for her,
if she had ideas to discern it !   Bistella was her name in Iceland—the man
told me it was the name of an old witch or enchantress, talked of in their songs
and traditions.   She is white, excepting a liver-coloured spot on the right side
of her face, and her ears, which are pricked as those of a Pomeranian dog,
are slightly tinged with the same colour.   Her size that of a spaniel, and
her tail curled, rather bushy.   Most of the Iceland dogs are of this kind.
Shakespeare speaks of a ' prick-eared cur of Iceland.'   They are only fit to run
after the sheep.   The breed came originally from Norway.—J. T. S.

[2] This fox, at the time of his death, had on his Iceland suit of pure white,
in which he could be seen in a glass case till 1882.—ED.

The conversations are interesting, and the manners of the landlord most hospitable. Such a society, you will allow, must be agreeable. My name is on the list of candidates for a seat in the Royal Society, and likewise for becoming member of a club composed of Sir Joseph Banks and other people in the philosophical world, who dine together every Thursday at the Crown and Anchor in the Strand. . . .

Journal of J. T. S.

February 20.—Last evening I went to Sir Joseph Banks, and gave him the seeds and plants I had brought with me from Iceland, which he promised to give to the gardener at Kew, that they might have a fair trial. . . . I saw there Dr. Blagden, Mr. Cavendish, Mr. Dalrymple, Count Roden, Mr. W. Beaufoy, Mr. Frederick North, Mr. Thorkelin, and several others.

Sir Joseph has devoted his life and fortune in a noble manner to science. When he was twenty he made a voyage to Newfoundland for the sole purpose of looking for plants on that coast. He took a passion for botany in a most violent degree when very young, and during the time he was at the University of Oxford he would saunter up and down the country with a sack or box on his back, and has been taken up on suspicion of bad intentions by those who could not conceive what he was about.

Sunday, February 21.—I dined at Norwood. I found my little brother Edward there, who came running out to shake me by the hand. . . . Mrs. Nesbitt interests herself about my seat in Parliament as much as I can myself. . . . Lord Hawkesbury sends his son with Lord Auckland to the Hague. Lord A. has not his equal in knowledge of treaties and negotiations, and the state of trade of every nation. He has been sent with full powers of negotiation to Paris, when there was an ambassador there; he has been sent, though only the younger brother of a baronet, to Madrid as ambassador. He is now ambassador at the Hague, and has been created an Irish peer. All this has happened within the

space of very few years.   The Duchess of Marlborough has
recommended her second son to Pitt as the hope of her
family.   Mr. Pitt gives him the highest character for sense
and disposition.   He is appointed secretary to the ambassador.   I dined with Mr. Hippesley in Grosvenor Street.
Hippesley was secretary to the ' Sçavoir Vivre ' Club.   He
went to the East Indies, and returned with a fortune.   We
had present, Mrs. Hippesley and her sister, Miss Stewart,
Lord Herbert, Sir Francis Standish, Mr. Harrison, and Mr.
Morant.   I went afterwards to Clifford Street, stayed till
ten, and then went to Lady Mary Duncan.   Her favourite
Pacchierotti was there, and her nieces.   She introduced me
to Lady Caroline Tufton.   Mrs. Abington, the actress, with
all the behaviour of a woman of fashion, without her airs,
was in the room, and Lady Boyne came and claimed my
acquaintance.   I am really obliged when those who do know
me will do this, for my short-sightedness forces me to be so
reserved.

February 23, 1790.—Davies dined with me.   I love
Davies.   I have not an older friend, for I was under his care
when he was usher at Loughborough House, when only eight
years old.   He took as much pains to teach us to be good
men as to teach us our school exercises.   Passionate in his
manner, strict, sometimes unjust, he had the art to make
himself loved by most of the boys under his care.   Augustus
Hervey and myself both loved him exceedingly.   There is a
simplicity in his manner, and an adherence to truth and
honesty, sometimes against his interests, which is singular.
Mr. Six only that I ever knew, equalled him in his love of
veracity.   I was six years under the care of Mr. Davies.
Edward has been two, and if I am permitted to direct
his education, shall remain two years more.   He has made
astonishing progress in Latin, history, and geography
already, both at Macclesfield and under Mr. Inglis at
Loughborough House.

February 24.— . . . I breakfasted with Rose ; he invited
me to dine with him, and said he expected Lord Auckland to
spend the evening with him, and would take this the only

opportunity of introducing me to him, as he was to set out for the Continent to-morrow. Rose had no company but his own family. Lord Auckland came in the evening, and took me by the hand, saying he was very glad to have my company at the Hague. He left it to me to join him when I pleased, and I made a kind of promise I should be there in the beginning of April. Sir John is extremely pleased at my successful prospects. He has written a note thanking Rose for his kindness in warm terms.

March 2.—This morning my great bookcase has been fixed in my room. Now I shall feel comfortable. Oh, how I love to be surrounded with a library ! Solitude surely is when one is left without other resources than one's own brain ; and now I am in a numerous company. Every author whose book is on my shelves is my companion ; he tells me his thoughts : I compare them with mine. Perhaps I follow some traveller through his adventures, and fancy myself a partaker in them. I traverse the desert, or am exposed to the storm, or rest with him in his hut. Perhaps Weiss instils into me his ' Principles of Philosophy,' often bold, often true. Voltaire captivates my understanding ; Rousseau sinks into my heart. I shall now stray from book to book, steal a thought from each, or pick out some beauty to admire. . . .

My sisters dined here. Campbell came after they were gone. He stayed with me till past twelve. We talked of little else than of Neuchâtel.

J. T. S. to Dr. Scot.

Grosvenor Place : May 10, 1790.

When I wrote to you last, I seriously expected to be on the Continent before a week was at an end. My things were packed up, and I went to take farewell of Mr. Rose, when he spoke to me of a borough for which I might come into Parliament under favourable circumstances in every way. The borough is Wootton Bassett, in Wiltshire. Two peers, whose estates are situated in the neighbourhood, had con-

contended with each other repeatedly who should name the member for the place. Their interests were so nearly balanced, however, that for once they thought it advisable to unite, and bring in each one member for the place, as it has a right of electing two. Lord Bolingbroke, or more properly his uncle, one of the parties, has named Lord Downe, a strong partisan of the Opposition. Lord Clarendon, the other chief, has given me his interest. Thus, like the two kings of Brentford, Lord Downe and myself come hand in hand. Mr. Rose, who promises nothing, but gives me great encouragement, has introduced me to Mr. Pitt, who has said everything that was flattering in my favour; and has gone so far as to say, what can be done for me shall be done. . .

J. T. S. to Dr. Scot at Edinburgh.

Grosvenor Place : June 21, 1790.

. . . But, before I proceed any further in my letter, let me inform you of my being at this moment a representative in Parliament of the people of England. Last Friday Lord Downe and myself were elected members for Wootton Bassett, in Wiltshire. In your next letter you will wish me joy on this event. On Thursday I set out for Holland. Lord Auckland has written to me renewing his invitation to be with him at the Hague.

. . . To Mackenzie[1] and Playfair, and Dugald Stewart and Professor Robinson likewise, give my remembrance. Happy shall I be whenever Fate brings me into company with any one of them again. They have not many equals in the world, and I value much the acquaintance they have permitted me to form with them. In the literal sense of the word, bid them from me 'farewell.'

J. T. S. to Dr. Scot.

The Hague : July 9, 1790.

. . . Lord Auckland invites me often to dine with him. I meet at his table Lady Auckland, three or four of his

---

[1] Henry Mackenzie, author of 'Man of Feeling,' 1745-1831.

H

children, Mr. Robertson (his physician), Lord Henry Spencer
(secretary to the embassy), Mr. Garlick (his under-secretary),
sometimes Lord Dalkeith your cousin, and his governor;
and Mr. Jenkinson, son of Lord Hawkesbury. I have been
presented at court, and introduced to some societies. I read
a great deal, and my greatest pleasure is to walk for hours in
a most beautiful and romantic wood which is close to the
town.

I wish only that a friend like yourself, dear Scot, might
be at hand, with whom I might now and then discourse on
the disappointments of life, or reason on the occurrences of
the day, with the power of making happy those around me.
Such is the ultimate of my wishes.

Hague : August 20, 1790.

. . . I heard of the death of Adam Smith a few days
before I received your letter. His end was that of a good
man, and he practised to the last the philosophy he had
taught. Very few men are held in so much estimation by
their friends as Mr. Smith was. Gentle and unassuming in
the society which I so diligently attended every Friday evening at Edinburgh, and which, if you remember, was called
Mr. Smith's Club, I have heard him listened to with the
greatest respect and deference whenever he delivered his
sentiments on any serious subject. He never argued ; indeed,
I never heard any dispute on a speculative subject in that
society ; discussion alone took place there. Mr. Smith more
frequently listened than spoke ; his calm composed manner
when he did take a part contrasted well with Dr. Hutton's
vivacity, Playfair's diffidence, or Mackenzie's sprightliness
and wit. We must regret the loss of the sixteen volumes
of manuscript which Mr. Smith ordered to be thrown into
the fire some few days previous to his death ; but this regret
is diminished by the discovery in his cabinet of others that
may be published.

[J. T. S. left the Hague and passed through France in the early
days of the Revolution. From Paris he wrote to Dr. Scot,
October 25, 1790.]

. . . I arrived here last Tuesday, and came through
Brussels. I was told at Aix that I should find it very
disagreeable, if not dangerous, to travel through countries in
which such revolutions are taking place as in Flanders and
France; but I have found a perfect tranquillity, to all appearance, reigning in both. In Flanders I was made to
produce my passport with great exactitude at the gate of
every town I passed through, and this was the only inter-
ruption I met with. A high pole was generally fixed in
every marketplace with a cap of Liberty on the top, and
this was the only sign we saw of the revolution. Near
Namur things have not, however, the same tranquil appearance. The two armies are there drawn up in sight of each
other, on either side of the Meuse. The Austrian army, by
all the accounts I could gather, must have consisted a
fortnight ago of 18,000 men, without including the garrison
of Luxembourg. The Flemish army I should not think so
numerous, that is to say, the disciplined part of it, for Mr.
Vandernoot, the agent plenipotentiary of the States, has
lately enlisted a great number of peasants. He has mixed
them with the regulars in part, and a great number of priests,
carrying crucifixes in one hand and sabres in the other, lead
these poor fellows against the enemy. In every skirmish
which has yet taken place these raw troops have been
thrown into confusion and great numbers killed; and the
Austrian soldiers, when they can lay hands on one of the
friars, exercise every kind of cruelty on him. This happened,
at least, at first. . . . The regular regiments of the Brabanters
have stood firm. The army is well commanded and the
artillery well served; but what an army it must be to stand
for any length of time against the whole force of the
Emperor, when once he is at liberty to bring it against
Flanders! . . . I came through France without any inter-
ruption. I was not even required to show my passport, and
travellers are now no longer molested by those insulting and
impertinent excisemen who were stationed on the frontiers
of every different province. At Chantilly we were shown the
gardens of the Prince de Condé, and a miller now refuses to

supply the gardens with the water which used to come from a reservoir above his mill. At Paris all is quiet, save the tongues of the politicians in the coffee-houses of the Palais Royal, and the galleries in the National Assembly, which applaud what is said or done, as at a theatre.

J. T. S. to Dr. Scot.

Paris: October 28, 1790.

. . . Everything is at present quiet, but there is a spirit of jealousy, of discontent, of fury I may almost call it, apparent in the public. Every individual seems so ready for action, and the people for riot, that many are the probabilities that a flame will burst out soon. The question which irritates the minds of the democratic party at this moment is that of the *Renvoi des Ministres*, which the Assembly has declared can only be done constitutionally by the king; but the people think—and pains are taken to keep the people in such opinion—that where the ministers do not possess the confidence of the nation, which they say is now the case, the king should be forced to dismiss them. The battle is, whether they shall stay or resign; and the ministers do not seem inclined to comply with the wishes of the democrats.

[In 1791 J. T. S. revisited Alderley after three years' absence, and writes to Dr. Scot:]

'Here was I returned to the same spot of earth in which life had begun. I yesterday paid my first visit to my favourite walk. . . . On the other side this mere the eye rests on a thick venerable wood of beech trees above 140 years old, planted by one of our great grandfathers on his marriage. There are no trees so large in the county—that is, in beech—for the oaks, alas! are gone. The finest gloom is caused by the blended branches of the wood, and the silence that reigns there is only broken by the shrieks of the large kites which constantly build their nests in the neighbourhood, and the calls of the teal and the wild ducks to each other in the

mere.   At the further end of the park stands the small
remaining part of the old house; now converted into a
farmhouse.   A garden is made where the chief part of the
building stood, and potatoes and onions are flourishing where
once was the old hall, in which our predecessors often regaled
their tenants, or mustered perhaps the forces of the village
in times of danger.   The moat, in some places still very
broad, surrounds the farm and its garden. . . .

[In this same year a too transient gleam of happiness fell
across the life of J. T. S.   This time his father's approval confirmed
his own inclinations, and he became engaged to a lovely Irish
girl, Maria, the only daughter of Mr. Jones of Cork Abbey, whose
acquaintance had been made in Italy.   Their prospects were of
the brightest, when a neglected chill brought on the fatal illness
which robbed him of his bride at the very time the marriage was
to have taken place, leaving, as he said, the world all dark
to him.   To Dr. Scot he afterwards wrote] :

'I cherished belief in Revealed Religion, to remain convinced that a superior Being interfered with the concerns of
this world, as the only source of Comfort remaining to me
within it; driven as I had been almost to Despair.'

[His letters during the next three years to his old friend show
that he was actively engaged in helping the French refugees, in
militia duties, and in literary work, but his own words prove that
public life was uncongenial to him.]

J. T. S. to Dr. Scot.

Chester : June 24.

I arrived here on Wednesday evening to join the Cheshire
Militia, and am now reinstated in all the duties of my military
character.   I have been lucky in escaping the most tiresome
part of the business, which is the getting the men into order
when they first muster.   They have now a really very
respectable appearance, and they went through their
exercises &c. this morning with almost the regularity of a
regiment of the line.   I shall be here a week, the regiment
will be then disembodied, and I shall go to Alderley.

November 1792.

This letter will introduce to you the Count de Botherell,
a French nobleman, who is come to solicit from our
committee some relief for his countrymen now at Jersey.
They are too numerous for an efficacious relief to be given,
but I think they have the same claim on our fund that French
distressed families in this country have. This gentleman is
recommended to me by the Bishop [1] of St. Pol de Léon in
very strong terms, and his application should, in my opinion,
be treated with respect by our committees. A considerable
portion of our fund should be given towards relieving the
French at Jersey. They are refugees in the British
dominions.

March 13, 1794.

My dearest Scot,—I am sorry that from illness you have
been prevented attending the committee in Bishopsgate
Street. We have heard there of the care with which you
have treated the emigrants who have applied to you for
relief. Your behaviour towards them has deservedly acquired
for you their love and gratitude. It has been with great
comfort that I have heard from your mother of your having
rather gained than lost ground since I left you.[2] . . .

You have read the report of Mr. Adams's speech on the
Scotch trials. I waited in the House after he had sat down,
to hear what the Lord Advocate would say in reply; but
when he said that the proceedings of a court of justiciary
could not be inquired into by members of the House of
Commons without their being guilty of great indiscretion, I
went away lest I should be put in a passion and tempted to
speak. If I had stayed I should certainly have voted with
the minority, as I hitherto have done whenever these Scotch
trials have been the cause of divisions. . . . So much for
politics, in which I am not so interested as I used to be.

[1] The Bishop who, in 1784, had shown great hospitality at Montpellier to
J. T. S. and his mother.
[2] Charles Scot, M.D., died March 25, 1794, age 35. (*See* Appendix.)

[J. T. S. was one of the earliest English students of German literature, and his translation of Bürger's ' Leonore ' first introduced that poem to English readers.   The literal version of it was followed later by another,[1] which was illustrated by Blake; but while Blake's pencil revels in the horrors of that ghostly ride, Sir John's English instincts revolting against spectral impossibilities, he abandoned the original and gave the ballad a happy ending.

The foaming courser forward flew
Fire and stones his heels pursue,
Like whirlwinds dashed around.

On right and left, on left and right,
Trees, hills, and towns flew past their sight
     As on they breathless prest.
' With the bright moon like death we speed,
Does Leonora fear the dead ? '
     ' Ah ! leave the dead at rest.'

Behold where in the moon's pale beam
As wheels and gibbets faintly gleam,
     Joined hand in hand a crowd
Of imps and spectres hover nigh,
Or round a wasted wretch they fly,
     When William calls aloud.

' Hither ye airy rabble come,
And follow till I reach my home.
We want a marriage dance.'

     .   .   .   .   .

Wild, snorting fire, the courser rear'd,
As wrapt in smoke he disappear'd.
Poor Leonora fell.

     .   .   .   .   .

Wake, Leonora ! Wake to Love !
For thee his choicest wreath he wore.
     Death vainly aimed his dart.
The past was all a dream; she woke.
He lives—'twas William's self who spoke
     And clasped her to his heart.

[1] British Museum, containing three illustrations by Blake.   London, S. Goswell, 1796. Press-mark 1347 m 48.

[His duties with the Cheshire Militia took J. T. S. ultimately to Sussex, where the regiment was encamped at Bexhill in the neighbourhood of Sheffield Place, and where a friendship sprang up with Lord Sheffield and his family, which led him to hope that domestic happiness might still be within his reach. . . .

A spirited song was composed by him for the men of his regiment, which was illustrated with views of Pevensey Bay and Beachy Head, drawn by himself and engraved by T. Bewick.]

I

Awhile, brother soldiers, attend ;
   Of the life that we lead I will sing:
We're militia men, called to defend
   The cause of our country and king.
From the plains of lov'd Cheshire we come,
   O'er England we wander away ;
We follow the beat of the drum,
   And, as ordered, we love to obey.

CHORUS.

For Cheshire men still are the same
   Their fathers were, loyal and bold ;
Chief of men they were called—and the name
   May we long be deserving to hold.

.   .   .   .   .

V

If England but breathes the same soul
   Which of old called her sons to the field,
When they sought haughty France to control,
   Again to our arms she must yield.
We remember the name that we bear,
   What our fathers have been in their day ;
When they march'd against France, what they were
   Let Cressy and Agincourt say !

CHORUS.

VI

With sense of our duty, like theirs,
   May we still their example pursue ;
And may Cheshire, as years follow years,
   Possess hearts as honest and true.
To UNION then fill the glass high,
   Victorious we long will remain ;
To conquest or death we will fly,
   Our King and our Laws to maintain.

CHORUS.

JOHN THOMAS STANLEY,
Major, Cheshire Militia.

Lord Sheffield to his Daughter M. J. S.

Sheffield Place: November 4, 1796.

In addition to the distress of the family, poor aunt tumbled plump, and was found with her head in contact with the candlestick, at the bottom of the staircase, at eight last night. When I took her up she knew not how she happened to fall. I supported her to a warm bed; she was blistered. The effect has been great, and Dr. Tenant says she will soon be much better. The very dear lady has had a quiet night. She seems rather better than the last two or three days.

M. J. S. to Serena.

November 5, 1796.

I shall be much obliged to you not to be so careless another time, Mrs. Holroyd, but to mind how you walk down stairs, as it does not give me any particular appetite for my breakfast when I receive a letter with the account of this morning; but I hope by the time you receive this that all traces of your frolic will have disappeared. . . . I am sure I wish it was in my power, by writing or anything else, to afford you and your partners in attending a sick room any amusement. . . . Why am I to be so supremely happy, while the home I have left is filled with those most dear to me in an anxious and unhappy state of mind? The last accounts of the dear lady do not raise my hopes. . . . I fear the anxiety and melancholy of the scene hurting both your spirits and health. I cannot describe the pleasure it is to me to see William Clinton[1] in his trips to town. I do love so dearly to ask a thousand questions about you all and listen to his accounts.

. . . We have been this morning very busy in writing descriptions of the geyser to be placed under the Views. To be concise, clear and sufficient, is very difficult, and takes a good deal of time.

Adieu, dear old aunt.

[1] Son of General Sir Henry Clinton, engaged to Louisa D. Holroyd.

From Margaret (Owen) Lady Stanley to Maria Josepha
Holroyd, on her marriage to her son, Mr. Stanley.

Clifford Street: Wednesday.

May the happiness of my dear daughter Maria, so well deserved, prove everlasting, and may her fortunate husband ever find his felicity in her affection, and remain as sensible of her merit as he is this day, and may her new mother ever appear to her deserving of friendship and confidence and be assured that mother has a heart most sensible to every sentiment of friendship and tenderness and which can never change when kindly dealt with. May then truth, ease and confidence ever reign between us, and on such basis friendship will always stand secure.

You flatter me by expressing your liking of my little gift. I would it were a richer one, with greater wealth it would have been so, but as it is, it is just a token of goodwill and inclination.

Adieu, my dear Maria. Welcome to us again and again. Sister Emma [1] bids you the same and joins me in esteem and love. To grandmama [2] I will be sure to say all that is right; and believe me ever affectionately yours, &c. &c.

MARGARET STANLEY.

Do pray ask your *sposo* and yourself whether we may go colours flying to-morrow—that is to say, whether any objection lies to our bedecking our folks with favours, namely, cockades of white riband in their hats, for we think it would look mighty pretty along the High Road and announce to the people that we are a joyful train, and make them stare and say ‘ Who’s that ? ’

Isa and Lou Stanley (sisters of J. T. S.) to M. J. S.

Alderley Park: October 20, 1796.

Dear Maria,—At length I have the pleasure of addressing you by the name of dear sister, and I wish I could express as I feel all the tenderness connected with that appellation.

As my sister wrote last, I now take up the pen to tell

[1] Youngest sister of J. T. S.   [2] Madam Owen of Penrhos.

you how extremely pleased we were with your affectionate letter received yesterday. . . . Be it known to you that Sir John Stanley has no better fun than reading tittle tattle letters from our correspondents, and I think he will like his new daughter all the more for affording him the entertainment he may receive from cheerful letters such as we shrewdly guess, by the sample she has given us, she can write.

I will set the example by telling you that last night we were at a Knutsford assembly. As ere long you will become an inhabitant in this neighbourhood, it is necessary you should in some measure be acquainted with the county. You must learn then that all our beaux and belles trip it gaily on a nice spring floor in this same town of Knutsford, and many a tender flirtation goes forward and many a preliminary of marriage is settled therein; of course you will think it a charming place for those damsels who are disposed to follow your example. . . . Last Monday the Toft family (remember these are your good friends the Leycesters) dined here, and it may literally be said kept the wedding. After a decent little concert, so disposed were we for merriment that we danced, six jolly couples. Even the old squire, George Leycester, footed it as lightly as the youngest part of the company. My father would have joined the dance had he not been gouty. 'Come! Haste to the Wedding' was the favourite dance, but observed to be rather out of date. . . . After supper we drank the bride and bridegroom's health with three cheers, and did not part till twelve o'clock. When you know the sobriety of the Toftites you will take this as a great compliment.

Take as many loves as I have room for, and believe us affectionately,

ISA and LOU STANLEY.

The bells rang three days. Some say there is danger of their being worn out.

[The marriage took place at a time of great anxiety concerning the health of Lady Sheffield,[1] the bride's stepmother. The aunt

---

[1] Lucy, daughter of Lord Pelham.

Serena, who had always been a second mother to Maria Josepha and Louise Holroyd, remained at Sheffield Place with her brother to share his anxieties, and three days after the wedding received the following letter from the Bride.]

M. J. S. to Serena Holroyd.

Bolton Row : October 14, 1796.

I have sat down to my writing desk the instant that the dearest of all dears is gone out, that I may not run the chance of being tempted by any of the delights around me to let time run away and prevent you hearing from me. You owe some thanks to a cold that has taken the liberty of catching me, or else I should probably have gone out with him ; but I am as stupid as Old Nick, and only fit to write to you. . . . Thanks for your dear letter a thousand and a thousand times. Your prophecies and wishes will all come to pass. They must ; and, barring unforeseen misfortunes, such as human beings must inevitably meet with, we shall be one of the happiest pairs in England. As to the degree of happiness which I am now feeling continuing, I should be very sorry if it could, for it is certain ' Joy goes but to a certain bound, beyond 'tis agony,' since we are both at this moment the most uncomfortably happy people you can imagine. . . . I only feel it is not a dream when he is out of the house, which is a difficult matter to get him to be. . . . Indeed, you none of you know half the value of his inestimable heart, much as you love him. I must not write any more upon this subject, because I cannot satisfy myself with any possible expressions to tell you what I am feeling. Can it last ? If it does, how have I deserved such blessings ? Adieu. Love us and think of us. You are not forgotten by us, believe me, in this tumult of felicity, dearest of all dear aunts. Yours ever and ever,

M. J. STANLEY.

I cannot help thinking it still a joke when I am called by my name, and want to see some people that I may get accustomed to it.

Lord Sheffield to his Daughter M. J. S.

Sheffield Place: November 4, 1796.

In addition to the distress of the family, poor aunt tumbled plump, and was found with her head in contact with the candlestick, at the bottom of the staircase, at eight last night. When I took her up she knew not how she happened to fall. I supported her to a warm bed; she was blistered. The effect has been great, and Dr. Tenant says she will soon be much better. The very dear lady has had a quiet night. She seems rather better than the last two or three days.

M. J. S. to Serena.

November 5, 1796.

I shall be much obliged to you not to be so careless another time, Mrs. Holroyd, but to mind how you walk down stairs, as it does not give me any particular appetite for my breakfast when I receive a letter with the account of this morning; but I hope by the time you receive this that all traces of your frolic will have disappeared. . . . I am sure I wish it was in my power, by writing or anything else, to afford you and your partners in attending a sick room any amusement. . . . Why am I to be so supremely happy, while the home I have left is filled with those most dear to me in an anxious and unhappy state of mind? The last accounts of the dear lady do not raise my hopes. . . . I fear the anxiety and melancholy of the scene hurting both your spirits and health. I cannot describe the pleasure it is to me to see William Clinton[1] in his trips to town. I do love so dearly to ask a thousand questions about you all and listen to his accounts.

. . . We have been this morning very busy in writing descriptions of the geyser to be placed under the Views. To be concise, clear and sufficient, is very difficult, and takes a good deal of time.

Adieu, dear old aunt.

[1] Son of General Sir Henry Clinton, engaged to Louisa D. Holroyd.

J.T. Stanley (afterwards Lord Stanley of Alderley)
and Crab his favourite Terrier.
n. 1766. ob. 1850.

thaw seems to agree with the dear lady . . . she feels more languor and feebleness lately. . . . Tell the man that the apparent torpor of the Admiralty has, during the last four or five weeks, when I could think of anything but the dear lady, greatly increased my expectoration. Every Gazette in Europe has for a long time announced the Brest armament, and there was reason to believe Ireland was the object. Yet Lord Bridport was at Portsmouth the day before yesterday, and the French are in Bantry Bay. We have had only a very inferior fleet at sea under Colpoys,[1] and even that is now come in. The superiority of our navy has not prevented any one French expedition that I can recollect, nor protected our Quebec, Labrador, Newfoundland, or Mediterranean trade; but if we do not now annihilate the French Bantry fleet, I shall expectorate with a vengeance.

Theresa Parker to M. J. S.

My brother went to dine with Lord Gower at Wimbledon on Sunday between four and five, and was stopped *en chemin* by a highwayman who took his watch which was not gold, and his servant's which was, and eight guineas. My brother had ten guineas in his pocket which he could not find, and consequently saved them; fortunately he was by chance without firearms, else I dare say he would have been foolish enough to have used them, and as the man held a pistol to him all the time he might not have escaped so well. He was in a chaise and four without a servant behind, and I am convinced the postillions were concerned in it.

Adieu. I shall write from Stanmer; but alas! from there my letters must be melancholy. I believe all his family were prepared for poor Harry Pelham's death. Lady Betty Cobbe is with Mrs. Pelham.[2]

I wish the major at Old Nick for carrying you off. I

---

[1] John Colpoys, English Lord of the Admiralty, and Governor of Greenwich Hospital. Died 1821.

[2] Catherine, daughter of Thomas Cobbe, Esq., who married Lady Elizabeth Beresford, sister of 1st Marquis of Waterford.

have a great mind never to take a fancy to anything but my own sweet self, which I cannot be parted from ; for it is so tiresome to get very much attached to a person and then comes a nasty great man and carries away all one's comfort to the Antipodes. I am sure it is a piteous case, and I want you for ever.

Ever affectionately yours,

THERESA PARKER.

M. J. S. to her Sister Louisa.

January 21, 1797.

Your letters that we received from William [Clinton] on Monday, prepared us for yours of yesterday. . . . Since I have been destitute of all hope, my anxiety has been for poor papa, aunt, and you, and I have wished the awful moment over, that her eternal happiness might begin and your fatigues and anxieties end. Dear woman, except by her illness she never gave a relation or a friend a moment's pain ; and how much happiness she gave all of us by her amiable cheerfulness and sweet temper ! Why she was taken from us, when to some so necessary, perhaps some future day we shall know, when all events are explained. At present it does indeed seem hard. . . . Do tell dearest papa how our hearts are with him at this moment, and we both most ardently wish we were within reach to assist by-and-by to comfort him. God preserve his health and yours, and give you all strength of mind and body to support each other. If it is ever so few lines, write as often as possible ; I am hungry for one of your letters ; and do not ask him for franks if it worries him. I shall not think much of a few shillings spent for letters. My love complains that he is sure I never say anything kind from him to you, and that he feels for you and loves you more than he can say.

Serena to M. J. S.

Sheffield Place : February 1797.

I do not believe our dear woman knew her state at last though I believe she thought herself in a bad way. It was but a very few hours before her death that she said, ' My

dear aunt, it is a bad business.' She was perfectly sensible
to the last moment, and though I have gone through scenes
near to my heart, none could be more affecting.   For the
last twenty-four hours my brother supported her, his tears
running down, and kissing her hands and forehead in
silence.   The dear soul trying to pat his face, calling him
'Naughty boy,' saying she 'did not suffer' and was 'quite
comfortable.' . . . The concern is very general.   However,
none but us can know in how many ways she is a loss to
my brother; it is a total break-up of the greatest domestic happiness a man at his time of life could feel.   In
proportion to the uncommon blessing so is the loss.   It is
so impossible to write a hundredth part of what one wants
to say.   I sit down in despair, with the wish that I have
had, God knows, often since we parted, that we could meet
even for half a day!   A letter yesterday from poor Lord
Pelham, written with a trembling hand, was beyond what you
can conceive affectionate to my brother. . . . Dear Sheff has
tried to convince me I could live better in London, but were
I to give up every wish of my heart and merely consider the
point as relative to them, I should never consent to the
trial. . . . I listen, therefore, but am unshaken. . . .

[The Cheshire Militia having been ordered to the north, Newcastle became the headquarters of the regiment, with its major
and his bride.]

M. J. S. to Louisa.

Newcastle: January 1797.

I wish you may find three months' marriage increase a
husband's love and admiration as much as I have found
they have, and then you will comprehend why the poor
Crow [1] liked to find a merit in my making no difficulties in
such a new situation, separated from all my relations and
friends, and a most comfortable prospect of an uncomfortable
home, the only one to be had.   You was a very impertinent
jackanapes, and I was indignant; but I will acknowledge
that, except in his partial eyes, I was not deserving of

[1] One of her quaint names for J. T. S., in reference to his strongly marked
eyebrows.

i 2

praise for finding no grievances, since if I had, things would only have been more uncomfortable, even to myself. . . . I hope you continue my village children at school and keep account what I owe you.

My rogue came home at eight. He gave the mess claret when he was there the first time upon his becoming major, and they drank him eight pounds' worth.

These nasty He dinners are shocking bores, for he cannot excuse himself if inclined, and I have very little of his company now with one vile duty or another. He is drilling with Major Atherton every morning, learning six ways of cutting down a man, and not having yet made himself an adept in one cut of three motions, I suppose many days will be required to make him perfect in all. Has William heard of Major Le Marchant? I understand he learnt this method of using the broadsword from the Hungarians, and they had it from the Turks. As far as my judgement can reach it appears obviously a great improvement in the use of the sword, as you wound and with a blessing on your honest endeavour may probably kill your adversary, and never leave yourself unguarded for a moment. So now the French may come as soon as they choose. Our cavalry will be able to cut them all off.

My man has laid hold of a famous abuse in the regiment, which he has undertaken to correct, merely because he does not like to put his name to an untruth to cheat Government. (Poor man ! to be an old Roman in the days of the emperors !) . . . He has discerned that 'whoso signeth or doth sign a return of effective men, as effective men able to carry arms, if they are not so, shall be cashiered, according to the exact terms of the Articles of War.' Now it so happens that this is very fine hunting weather. Different sportsmen pursue different game, and the major of the Royal Cheshire Militia is very keen to be in at the death of certain and sundry abuses, a particular beast of the Hydra genus, born of Indolence and Inattention, and fostered by a careful nurse, false Good Nature. The head, which at present his massy club is raised to extirpate, is eleven boys from the age of seven to fourteen, returned and mustered as effective men, and who receive pay as such, though they are not even drummers or fifers. Yesterday was the day for signing a weekly return, and accordingly he insisted on the eleven young gentlemen being removed from the list before his name should make its respectable appearance at the bottom of the paper. And he wrote to Lord Grey upon the subject, who I expect will be wonderfully astounded and (perhaps internally only) shockingly indignant, for he was instrumental in part of the business. . . . But the major most innocently supposes him ignorant of the whole affair, and represents it accordingly. Pray inquire of the learned gentlemen, profound in military practices, milord and William, whether this is a very common occurrence in militia regiments. Not that it will make any difference to my old Cato, for I cannot, with all my eloquence, persuade him either that cheating Government is not like cheating between man and man, or that if others do wrong, one may as well do likewise. He is very thick-skulled on some topics. I believe I told you Sir W. Howe is gone. Sir W. Meadows is appointed in his place. We are now under the command of Sir G. Osborne. It is expected he will order the troops here to meet those under his command at Durham halfway, and exercise them once a week . . . and yet it is customary to flatter him here by the appellation of Old Woman! Sir W. Howe, then, who never gave the soldiers any trouble, was an old—what? An old man I suppose; for I am sure it is a far more helpless thing than an old woman! the former cannot do without the latter—that is, woman—young or old, and I do not recollect hearing of men being useful or necessary to old women in any way.

Newcastle: Friday, February 1797.

Mrs. Atherton is a pleasing good-humoured little woman, but very delicate. . . . I like her, and therefore will not have her die this spring; seeing as there are very few young women or pleasant old ones in the town, those there are had better live while I am here. . . . Pray tell William in answer to his inquiry concerning musters, that the little gentlemen are always reported sick on these occasions. There was a letter from Lord Grey yesterday, more quiescent than I expected, but he has not taken the matter quite right yet, and only talks of discharging the two youngest; consequently the major is at this moment looking as wise as an owl in an ivy bush, writing a second letter to make him sensible. His lordship will in all probability think him a d—ear troublesome fellow. The depôt of the artillery in this district, their guns, all the powder &c. for the troops, is at Tynemouth, at the mouth of the river, where, if the French do come, they can with ease take possession of all, since it would be impossible to move it with expedition for the want of horses. . . . Colonel Lawson has repeatedly represented this to Sir W. H., and likewise that other generals of districts have removed their depôts ten or twelve miles inland; but he will not take any steps, saying he was limited in his powers. They hope to make more impression on Sir W. Meadows.

M. J. S. to Serena.

Newcastle: February 17, 1797.

If I could, I would tell you with what greedy appetite I sat down to read your letter and Louisa's yesterday, and with what pleasure I devoured them. . . . Though I lately gave Louisa a long lecture about her propensity to look forward not to blue skies but to black, to which she gives way so unhappily for her comfort, yet who shall say they possess any hold on happiness in this world? Think, when you came to us in the summer, how we congratulated one another that you would find Sheffield Place in a state of such domestic comfort, cheerfulness, and felicity such as you had scarce ever known it to be, and the prospects were so fair that you would know nothing but happiness there. . . . What a reverse! and now how have you left it?

I suppose by this time you have seen the prints of the Geyser. I have desired Miller to get a coloured copy of the large print framed for your own self to hang up in your own

room at Bath to make the dowagers stare. . . . Pocock and
Miller, who are publishing at their own expense, agree to let
the Man have so many copies for himself and family. . . .
We like you should have the best copy that is to be had.
I long to hear papa has got his before he set off; possibly
he would like to take it with him to show the Irish folk. . . .
I am just come home from an old lady's card party. My
poor Man has had such a headache all day, he really was not
able to go. I would not send an excuse, as the good people
might have thought it all a sham; but having played two
rubbers of whist and drank my tea, I thought it a downright
kindness to the company as well as myself to come home;
because of course I furnished conversation to the three card
tables and all the sitters for the rest of the evening.

Adieu, dearest old aunt.

M. J. S. to Louisa.

Newcastle: Sunday, 19th, 1797.

I cannot sit down quietly to write to you without from
time to time looking round to see if the French are behind
me, for really the alarm here is so great, and I am afraid so
just, that I hear of nothing else. The apathy displayed in
this part of the kingdom cannot be exceeded, though it may
be equalled by all orders and degrees of persons in all places
and in all situations. Not a step is taken towards raising
the supplementary militia. . . . It is very doubtful whether the
keelmen and pitmen will assist the French or us in case of
a landing; yet none of the pit owners or gentlemen of the
county have spirit enough to assemble them and represent
that to defend the country is to defend themselves, as the
object of the enemy will be to destroy the collieries, which
must deprive them of bread. To gain them would be to
gain the assistance of 9,000 able men. One would think
the whole nation had taken a soporific draught or were
desirous rather than fearful of the success of our enemies!

. . . What is said in London of India affairs? They
will supply excellent food for the croakers, with much
apparent reason too. The West Indies also; what dreadful

accounts of mortality from there! These are not humdrum
times, it must be acknowledged, but replete with most important and serious events affecting every individual, however
exalted or however obscure, in every part of Europe.

Newcastle: February 22, 1797.

Several vessels are near the shore ; amongst others a
50-gun ship to protect the colliers. She has brought in a
French frigate which had long infested the coast. I am sorry
to say, out of thirty men which composed the crew of the
French vessel, twenty-five were English or Irish. I think it
will be a pity if they are not severely punished. Lady Liddell
called on me a few days ago. I have that visit to return whenever my Man will cease exercising his men. Miss Roddam
and I walked to the moor to see them. The cavalry were
likewise out, working hard at broadsword half a mile from
the Cheshire, but in sight, and a pack of hounds, with forty
or fifty horsemen following in full pace, passed between the
two.

Lord Sheffield to M. J. S.

Dublin : March 1797.

I was glad to receive the very dear Poll's long letter,
and intended a long answer, but I must forthwith go to
the House of Commons. The major is doing so much good
to the regiment and also to himself, that I shall be sorry
when another commanding officer reaches the Cheshire. As
I am now a complete vagabond, I think it likely I shall find
you wherever you may be. . . .

Pelham,[1] who bears his life of worry better than I
expected, will go soon with me to Cork &c. There will be a
recess when the money bills go to England. In respect to
money, Great Britain and Ireland seem in a woeful case.
Ireland, however, is not in bad train as to pecuniary matters.
I wish her defence had been better provided. I have seen a
great many of the yeomanry. Many are very tolerable,
some of them very good. I suppose you know they amount

[1] His brother-in-law, Right Hon. T. Pelham.

to 33,000. It was generally believed the French meant to attack this country. I shall enclose a letter from William giving a curious account of the French expedition to Wales.

M. J. S. to Louisa.

I delight in the spirit of the Taffys,[1] and hope that this little attempt at invasion, thus ended, will raise the spirits of John Bull without whisking him round to the other extreme of thinking himself out of danger. What honour for the supplementary and yeomanry of Pembrokeshire! Surely the French behaved like cowards. . . . In coming home last night we had a most beautiful spectacle, the finest aurora borealis I ever saw; there is not a bit of moon now, and the northern hemisphere was as light as if the full moon was only behind a cloud. The darting of the bright rays of light —coruscations, as my learned friend in the ' Post ' called them —were extremely beautiful, and I dare say very portentous.

M. J. S. to Lord Sheffield.

Lord Grey has spoken to the Duke of York respecting the drummer boys, with the Man's reasons for not returning them on the effective strength of the regiment—namely, that they were not capable of bearing arms. I give you Lord Grey's words : ' The Duke of York perfectly approves of the regulations I had adopted relating to the boys, as he conceives it was not possible to keep up the establishment of drummers and fifers in a regiment unless some boys were taken and instructed in order to replace vacancies that might happen. He said, though this was not strictly conformable to the King's regulations, that it was customary and adopted by most regiments in the Service and was always allowed as far as one company. I therefore desire all the boys may be replaced and returned as privates, as formerly, which the Duke of York has directed me to inform you of.'

[1] A muster of Welsh women in their red cloaks at Fishguard caused the invaders to retire.

You may imagine my Man was very indignant; he talked of refusing his signature to such a return. I was desirous he should not attempt measures of resistance which he could not carry through. . . . After much consideration and growling, he answered as follows:

'Though in perfect strictness a private order might not supersede a general regulation, such as that of 93, and an Act of Parliament, I shall not oppose my judgment to the Duke of York's authority, but comply with his desire as communicated to me through you; and for the future I shall return ten of our supernumerary drummers, however young, as effective soldiers. If the circumstance should occasion any difficulties to the muster master or the civil magistrate when the regiment happens to be mustered, you will allow me, I trust, to produce your letter in justification of my conduct.'

. . . Strict orders arrived yesterday for all officers to join before the 10th. So we shall have Colonel Barmeston again. It is very public-spirited in me to be vexed, for I shall get much more of my beloved's company.

[Louisa Holroyd married Captain William Clinton, March 12.]

Serena to M. J. S.

Privy Gardens: March 16, 1797.

. . . You will easily conceive that it was great relief to me when at last this long-intended union took place, having in some degree lost my faith in blue skies from all I have seen and suffered since last June. . . . Louisa looked uncommonly well, and as easy and unaffected as possible. I expected her to be nervous; but she seemed only serious and attentive. William looked quite handsome, with happiness and affection in his eyes. Thoughts of my poor brother and other circumstances came across us all, as well as poor Henry Clinton being a prisoner, and yet I was glad to know he was alive and well, and not at the West Indies. We had a very nice breakfast and cold collation, and then, at one o'clock, the bride and bridegroom set out for Bush Hill.

. . . So much for my history. . . . I heard from my brother yesterday. He was going to Lord Waterford's, and afterwards to Bantry Bay. There was a letter yesterday from Sévéry[1] to Louisa, doubtful if he could come this year, but said nothing of marriage. Much lamenting our misfortune &c. . . . To be sure I have at this moment my beautiful Geyser glazed and framed, just brought in.

M. J. S. to Serena.

Newcastle: March 17, 1797.

My dearest Aunt,—You now see both your children disposed of in such a way as few mothers can dare flatter themselves to hope for their darlings. My happiness can hardly admit of addition, except from once again being within distance of the few near and dear friends I am for a time taken from. This is a prospect I can indulge in with certainty if we live, which I hope to God we all shall for many years; for I should not like to spare anybody for some time, and I don't think you would approve of my taking myself off yet awhile. Louisa's prospects are as fair as mine, with the exception of not having all the income we could wish her.

. . . The Man makes such a clatter of ' Pray go to bed ! ' that I must leave off, as it is late, or I could write much more. Adieu.

Most affectionately yours,

M. J. S.

Serena to M. J. S.

Bush Hill: March 21, 1797.

Just as I was setting out with Harriet Clinton for this place, I received your dear welcome lines, and you have been a nice thing for writing just as you do. True it is I feel like a mother that has disposed of her two darling girls to my heart's content, and every observation you make on the subject is perfectly just. . . . The longer I live the more convinced I am that all our best happiness consists in family love. . . . Would that you could fly to us for the

[1] Gibbon's friend and heir.

few days even that we are to stay here! The weather is so
fine; the place so beautifully neat and cheerful, with the
good humour of the servants, make all so very pleasant that
we shall go to gloomy Privy Gardens with great regret.
Lady Pelham asked me if my brother would now give the
diamonds to Louisa, and I said I believed not, though he
had offered them to Miss Pelham. 'Then,' says Lady P.,
'why can't he sell them while they are modern?' Was it not
a curious idea? . . .   Yours ever,
                                              S. H.

M. J. S. to Serena.

Newcastle: March 25, 1797.

. . . I believe I should infinitely prefer his [J. T. S.]
insisting on seeing every letter I wrote or received, rather
than that he should be indifferent and uninterested in them;
but he takes great pleasure in reading all I show him. Those
I do not show, he never expresses or implies the smallest
curiosity to see, and I believe nothing would make him open
or read a letter of mine first, though it were from his own
sister. . . . In this way he preserves the medium, for with
regard to his own letters he goes far beyond it on the indulgent side. Since we have been married he has never
received one and scarcely written one which he has not
shown me. Those few which he has not given me were
those in which I was convinced he had spoken the most
affectionately of me. The ease of my style would be lost
were I to write with the idea of showing it to any person
with whom I lived. I could never mention him in the
manner I wished, least it should seem written for his eye. . . .

You must forgive my saying so much on one subject,
but trifles are the sum of human life, you know, and certainly
they make up the sum of domestic happiness or misery. . . .
Indeed, I have done dancing, so don't swear; but if you could
see how well I am, you would think I could do anything.

M. J. S. to Louisa.

Newcastle: April 1, 1797.

Aunt desired me to answer about Mrs. Foley[1] to you, and that you would communicate to her. I will certainly take her, and give her 16*l.* per annum, which aunt mentions as what she will be satisfied with. I think it quite enough to begin with, since if she suits me, which I hope she will, I should wish to have it in my power with ease to make an addition to her wages.

You cannot think how funny it is to walk the streets between eleven and twelve with a lanthorn before one, which we have done one or two fine nights from our cousins the Roddams' house, being but a little distance. I should have expected such a curioso, philosopher, mythologist, antiquarian, historian, &c. &c. as you are, would have discovered the head with which your letter was sealed could be no other than Esculapius, from the emblem of the serpent, and no more like a Roman emperor than your great grandmother. I pronounced the gentleman's name and title, and so did my Crow, as soon as we saw it.

Tell William I forgive his impertinence in compassion to his ignorance; when he has been married a little longer, he will be convinced of the important and undoubted truth that a woman is always in the right; therefore, when he found the two crows were not in the same story [this refers to contradictory orders about a commission], he should have supposed for certain the she crow could not be the one to blame; therefore, though he did right to delay any purchase, with such contrary directions, he ought to have taken it for granted the old cock crow was a fool, and did not know his own mind. He is to purchase 'a belt to go over the shoulders.'

M. J. S.

'A belt to go over the shoulders,' but never let *your* wife

---

[1] Serena's late maid, 'Bull,' now entered the service of M. J. S.; her marriage to W. Foley, Serena's footman, 'who insisted on wearing rouge,' having turned out disastrously.

write such naughty things about crows. I shall find more uses than one for the belt when it comes.   J. T. S.

He is a rascal to write this addition, but I hope William will be satisfied about the belt, and be ashamed of himself.

M. J. S. to Louisa.

Newcastle: April 8, 1797.

A propos of boys, the drummer business is not at an end. The muster master arrived a few days ago, and the muster of the regiment took place yesterday.   He hummed and hawed a little about them at the time (for the major was not so accommodating as to report them sick, though he had consented to return them in consequence of the duke's order).   This morning the Man was to sign the truth of the muster, stating particularly that no persons under age, or boys, were mustered as effective.   He was to sign upon honour; but three oaths were to be taken to the truth of the assertion by others.   He begged to be excused signing, unless a parenthesis was inserted after the words 'no boys' 'except those allowed,' in which case his signature was ready.   This made Mr. Muster Master think, and ask again to see Lord Grey's letter, which he said was no authority for him, and he thought it was his duty to respite them. After some pro and con, it has ended with the muster master's respiting the ten boys, which, unless the War Office gives an order to take it off, will conclude the affair triumphantly for us.

Harriet Clinton to M. J. S.

April 13, 1797.

We have got a letter from my dear brother Henry,[1] at Nantes.   It is the greatest comfort to know he is safely landed, though it is in France.   I am now rather wild with joy, for I own to you, dear Poll, I have had ten thousand fears about him. . . . Thanks for your letter, and also for the yellow gown, which appears more beautiful than ever.   Lady Louisa Gordon's wedding gown is to come to

---

[1] Taken prisoner of war.

the trifling sum of 500*l.*, a much higher price than the Princess Royal's; but her Royal Highness's nightcap cost 500*l.* I am anxious to see the Prince of Würtemberg; he is so terribly big, I hear. . . . Last night I went to Baroness Nolchens, and there I met the Chief Justice. He asked a thousand questions about the ' Crow,' if he was handsome, and what sort of man. I told him, a very pleasant, charming man, with a very sensible intelligent countenance. He said he understood you were very much in love, and asked if it was true, and talked a great deal of nonsense. At this moment up came the Miss Stanleys, who I was very glad to see, and he took himself off.

Mr. Moreton (Lady Ducie's son) is to marry Lady Frances Herbert, Lady Carnarvon's daughter; Mr. George Byng, Miss Montgomery, Lady Townshend's sister. Only think of Sir William Homan's choice, that long-chinned Lady C. Stuart, Lord Bute's daughter! Nobody knows where they are gone. She went off with him, after Mrs. Beaumont's ball, last Friday. When Lord Bute was waked to be informed of it, he said, ' It is more her business than mine. Shut the door!' Poor foolish girl! I am sorry for her, and astonished at him.

Isa Stanley to M. J. S.

1797.

Dear Maria,—I had intended to write as soon as we came to town, with an account of the state of affairs at Alderley, but many things contributed to put me in a constant bustle, and made me leave undone things I ought to have done, We left two she servants there, one by name Betty Holt, who takes charge of the linen and stores, and can make preserves and pickles, and is not above cleaning the rooms. Her wages are 12*l.* 12*s.* ; Fanny's, 6*l.* 6*s.* With the additional furniture you will bring, you will add greatly to the comfort of the house, which is not well furnished either in regard to elegance or plenty, which made me fear you would find many inconveniences, being accustomed to so elegant and complete a mansion as Sheffield Place. With all its imperfections, I could not leave it without a selfish regret, though I felt glad it was to belong to those who would take interest in it and improve it.   If ever you are rich enough, it may be made very beautiful.   I dare say I forgot many things, though I took pains to recollect what came within the verge of my power.   The house linen is neither very fine nor plentiful, but sufficient for the present.   You have two good cows and a cow calf.   You are commanded by us to have a spaniel called ' Bounce,' who is a great favourite of ours ; and there is a gentleman spaniel called ' Punch,' who is a fine fellow but not an especial favourite.   What is most wanted in the furniture line is a comfortable sofa.   There is an old one, but it has not the pillows and cushions of modern days.   My brother knows the sofa by the names of the ' Graces,' and the 'Trojan Horse.'   As we were never confined to our beds, there are many things requisite for a sick room wanted.   You will find a tolerable piano of Broadwood's, the joint property of Isa and Lou, who leave it for your use till you suit yourself with one to your fancy.

Lord Sheffield to M. J. S.

Whitehall : May 18, 1797.

The very dear Pol's account of things is very satisfactory indeed, and I am now quite convinced that you both should be privy councillors, and that the Man should be a major-general.   It is a great advantage that you have so good and so sensible a general as at present.   I suppose you know that the same attempts have been made in most parts to seduce the soldiers, and nearly at the same time ; and I also suppose William has given you some accounts of proceedings respecting the Guards.   Louisa should detail the disastrous stories of Ireland, of which she hears enough. . . . The last ship of the fleet was out of sight yesterday at one o'clock. Lord Howe deserves to be keel-hauled for yielding to the proposition of dismissing such officers as the sailors required. There must be an end of all subordination.   Nothing now can do but a peace, which will dismiss the greater part of them.   The Man will have great pleasure in recollecting hereafter the essential service of his late attention to the Cheshire. I am the Man's and the Woman's ever, S.

Serena to M. J. S.

Clifton : May 22, 1797.

. . . I came here on Saturday, and if you knew Lady Hesketh[1] you would comprehend her countenance *rayonnant* with the sweetest welcome. . . . I found Lady Jane Stanley[2] with her. . . . I have my poor Tuft[3] with me, and though it is melancholy, poor fellow, to have him blind, you can't think how quiet and content he seems. I take him into the garden and he follows my voice. The rest of the day he lies on the sofa, sleeps, and eats as usual, and says he likes to live, and that he dotes on the mistress who nurses him. Lady Hesketh takes to him sentimentally, and thinks his blindness makes him so interesting. I think this is a good opportunity of telling you that one day lately I had so fagged myself in the morning that I was unable to go in the evening where I had promised, so as soon as I had dined I lay down on my sofa till ten. I literally thought it scarce any time, having taken out a certain box of letters of Maria's and read without intermission, save to meditate on the past, the present, and to come. In good sooth they beguiled me of some tears, but they were of pleasure, and concluding with reflections on your present situation after all. that was or might be, I raised my thoughts in sincere praise to Heaven with grateful satisfaction.

M. J. S. to Louisa.

Blyth : June 4, 1797.

Religion is not the thing most attended to in respect to the soldiers here. One clergyman is appointed to read prayers to the whole brigade at three this afternoon : they

[1] Lady Hesketh, widow of Sir Thomas Hesketh, and daughter and heir of Ashley Cowper. She was cousin and favourite correspondent of the poet Cowper, and niece of 1st Earl Cowper.

[2] Lady Jane Stanley, daughter of 11th Earl of Derby, who married (1714) Elizabeth, only daughter and heir of Robert Hesketh of Rufford, co. Lancaster.

[3] Lady Sheffield's pet dog, which by special invitation had been included in the party that visited Gibbon at Lausanne in 1791.

are to be drawn out upon the sands, and, as there are 25,000 of them and the wind whistles and howls famously, I recommend for a text, ' He that hath ears to hear, let him hear.' ' A rushing, mighty noise,' which might be very *à propos* for Whit Sunday, is all I should think that can be heard by any without a miracle. It is really making a farce of the business, and in these times of profusion, it is a very paltry saving to take away the chaplains from the regiments. . . . We have had the most narrow escape from thieves at Newcastle that I suppose anybody ever had. A man was concealed in the house for four hours on Saturday evening. The maid and another person with her were sitting in the kitchen between ten and eleven when they were alarmed by hearing footsteps above and noises. They called in a neighbour and went upstairs. When they got to the garret door a man said, ' Ha! ha! are you there?' and whistled, which proved he expected a companion. The whole reconnoitring party trundled downstairs, one atop of t'other, as fast as possible, though a man was of the party, and ran into the street to call assistance. Meantime the thief made his escape, and was fortunately too much alarmed to carry anything off with him. He must have been a great fool, for had he kept quiet an hour longer, the whole house might have been stripped with the greatest ease, and very pretty pickings there were of one kind or another. My jewel box, a large silver dish, Madam Owen's gift, some more plate, and about thirty-five guineas in my writing-box, all these things were locked up in drawers in my room. I no more thought of the chance of the house being robbed than I did their being conjured away. We have had a narrow escape and have learnt wisdom by it, and removed my box to Mrs. Roddam's.

Theresa Parker to M. J. S.

Parliament Street : June 15, 1797.

Oh, bonté, est-il possible ! No, never was anything so stupid. One of my principal reasons for writing was to tell you the best story that ever was heard, and I am glad I kept it for the *bonne bouche.* You may perhaps remember having seen a lady who is called by some people Miss and by others Mrs. Dolly Stainforth. You may also perhaps have some recollection of her usual style of dress, of her beautiful black arched eyebrows, of the fine bloom of her cheeks and the agreeable shaking of her head. I must then inform you that on the king's birthday she decked her face with more than usual splendour and ornamented her person with a robe of beautiful lilac colour.

Thus equipped she entered the apartment to pay her compliments on the day. Hither also went the little Princess Charlotte (the Prince of Wales's daughter), who can just speak, and is a remarkably sensible little child. The first object that struck her eyes was the beauteous Miss Stainforth, and she expressed her joy at so fine a sight by smiling and laughing and nodding to her, and saying, 'Dolly, Dolly, pretty Dolly!' and appearing delighted to see her; for which flattering mark of distinction Miss S. thought proper to return due thanks, and made a low curtsey, nodding her head with its tall feathers all the time, and the child, who is very stout on her legs, repeated the same, mimicking her exactly. Dolly then began to articulate, but no sooner did the sound of her voice reach the poor little child's ears than she began to cry and roar to such a degree that nothing could pacify her, and she would say nothing but 'What! Dolly speak?' And so great was her alarm that it was long before she recovered. The princesses, who knew what the child meant, were almost dead with laughing, and everybody was in a roar except the Prince of Wales, who, I suppose out of contradiction, looked grave.

I have not heard whether Miss S. penetrated the cause of the fright, which was that the Queen had the day before made the little princess a present of a large doll dressed exactly in the same sort of lilac-coloured gown, and, being made to go by clockwork, shook its head precisely in the same way. From the striking resemblance between her eyebrows and cheeks and those of the aforementioned wooden machine, the child naturally imagined it was her own doll brought from Carlton House. You need not doubt the veracity of

K 2

the fact, for my authority is no less than that of the five princesses, who with great delight related it to Lady Mary Osborne. The next day Princess Elizabeth told Lady Holdernesse of it, who was so much delighted thereat that she went to Stratton Street to tell it to Lord Pelham.

Lady Pelham was somewhat shocked, and made a few attempts to persuade us not to spread the story; but that would be an effort far beyond me. The word is that Dolly Stainforth dines in Stratton Street to-day, and I make no doubt in honour of the day will be habited in the same lilac vestment. I am also persuaded that she will begin talking of the dear little princess who took so much notice of her. If she does we must all die, that's certain. I am not famous for behaving well on any occasion where risibility is in question. This epistle is much too long for you probably, and certainly for my eyes, which have hurt me abominably lately; your sister is, I believe, the cause of it, by prophesying that it would happen to make the likeness to the Duchess of Devonshire more striking.

Serena to M. J. S.

Clifton: Monday, June 19, 1797.

I think my brother's going to you the very best scheme to amuse and interest him. I would not wish your advising him to go again to Ireland, which he talks of; for as sure as he does, some Irish girl will try to take him in, and I would not answer for anybody.

You must have heard me mention Lady de Vesci [1] with the highest regard, for a more charming woman never existed. She was a blessing miles round her, with everything in herself sensible, pleasing, elegant, and amiable. I passed a fortnight at Lord de Vesci's, at their delightful Abbeyleix, when I was last in Ireland, and I shall never forget her kindness and all I then had an opportunity of knowing of her. I went in very low spirits, and she soothed me in a thousand ways, led me to her schools, and all her improve-

[1] Selina, daughter of Sir Arthur Brooke, Bart., of Colebrooke, married 1st Viscount de Vesci.

ments &c., which Lord de Vesci assured me were all her own. How I do pity him, her friends, her poor, and in short all that were within her reach!

Lady Hesketh has gained strength since I came to her, and seems in many respects better. She likes you much for inquiring about Mr. Cowper, who is but indifferent. He has not written lately.

We have found a jaunting car on springs, which we sometimes prefer to the postchaise upon the Downs. The Irish call it a *vis à vis* because we sit back to back. So scandal says.

Theresa Parker to M. J. S.

Parliament Street : Monday, July 10, 1797.

I think everybody we care about has already departed, except Lady Mary Osborne, who is now, however, one of the happiest of beings. Lord Carmarthen's[1] marriage with Lady Charlotte Townshend is declared ; and it really would make anybody who did not know them happy to look at Lady Mary, for I never saw so much joy in anybody's face in my life. We dined at Lady Grantham's at Putney yesterday. Dolly was there and inquired tenderly about the state of your health ; she was habited in a muslin robe . worked by Miss Stanley. Lord Holland and Lady Webster were married a few days ago, and are now living at Holland House. As to news touching peace or war people's hopes are a little damped by the king's message the other day, about supplying the Queen of Portugal. The Watch Tax 'discomgrumbles' me a good deal, and I think it a very hard one upon servants and tradesmen, who really wear them for use, not for ornament.

T. P.

Serena to M. J. S.

Clifton : Monday, July 24, 1797.

Blessings on the dear little Crow![2] This moment *almost* I received dear Mrs. Firth's[3] glad tiding which missed me at

[1] 6th Duke of Leeds.　　[2] Rianette Stanley was born July 11, 1797.
[3] Ann Firth, the faithful friend at Sheffield Place, who had been present at the birth of M. J. S., and whose help was found indispensable at every family crisis.

Bath. I confess I am not recovered from the agitation, but I must write because we leave this early to-morrow morn for Cheltenham, where I hope to hear immediately how the dear nursery goes on. I feel the distance we are from each other, and yet I have nothing to apprehend, and am as happy as any granny in Christendom, but shall be more so when I am composed. Joy to dear Mr. Stanley! What would I give to see you all at this moment! My dearest Maria, you have indeed every warm wish of my heart that it may please God to preserve to you your present blessings, and that every hour of your life may find comforts increasing. This dear little Crow shall be endowed with every virtue to bless you both. If I have not the fairy powers, I will at least pray for them, and Heaven will grant it. . . . Tell me, what could make dear Firth send me black wax? It gave me a momentary terror that was frightful, though reason would have prevented any alarm. . . . With a million of loves and blessings,

I am most sincerely yours,

S. HOLROYD.

M. J. S. to Serena.

Newcastle: August 4, 1797.

If I did not see and hear the animal all day long, it would be impossible to persuade myself that anything more had passed than a dream of about an hour and a half, somewhat unpleasant; and indeed, if I did not in the Louisa style coax myself not to indulge in feelings too happy lest it should not continue, I must imagine that my dream had lasted ever since, though changed into one of perfect happiness. . . . I wish you could look at us, were it but for a quarter of an hour. Were you an entirely indifferent person to me, and had you but an inch of heart, I think you would find it a gratifying spectacle to see me so loved by such a being as him, who does love me so. And as you are not at all indifferent and have a pretty large portion of heart, methinks you would be in an ecstasy of pleasure. Do tell me how I can possibly have deserved to have such a lot, as to be united to the man in the world most calculated to make me happy

and good for something; which might not have been the
case, perhaps, had I less entirely loved, esteemed, and respected
the partner of my life. Get out of my head, Man! for I want
to write of other matters, not entirely foreign to be sure, but
a little different. . . . I have not yet come to the intent of
this letter, which was to ask you to answer for our child's
sins. Lady Stanley is one godmother, and we are going to
write to papa to-day to beg him to be the godpapa. I
would rather have reserved him for a he thing, but as Sir
J. S. has declined, we cannot help 'axing papa.' I think it
would not be an objection to you, that you could not get over,
were the usual tax to be levied on you; but I must mention
that my beloved dislikes as much as myself the custom, and
that we do not intend to take any money from the gossips.
It would be bad policy, as we mean to have a dozen or two
and may sometimes wish to have sponsors who cannot so
well afford their five guineas. Foley really seems all I could
wish. Both nurse and doctor approve of her manner with
the child. Mrs. Bigge has gone to town and is so good as to
promise to get me some caps, the only part of the young
animal's apparel in which I feel a wish to be smart and
coxcombical. Adieu.

Serena to M. J. S.

Cheltenham: August 8, 1797.

. . . Need I say how affectionately I feel the pleasure
of the additional tie of godmother to your little babe?
Though were I endowed with powers to bless her, she
needed no more interest with me than she has as my dear
grandchild; but I do really *like* to be all that I can to connect me more and more, since you are kind enough to wish
it. I hope she is to be *Maria*. . . .

M. J. S. to Louisa.

Newcastle: August 9, 1797.

Lady Ridley gives a breakfast next week (Tuesday), and
though longing to go of all things, and as able as ever I was

or can be, I sacrifice my inclinations to a sense of propriety
and fear of old grimalkins, inasmuch as it is within two
days before the expiration of the month. All the gossiping
old women in Christendom shall not prevent my doing like
other folks after Thursday; but I found that unless I would
be wondered at by all the town (and perhaps it might have
reached the judges and gone the circuit with the lawyers) I
must not stir out into the haunts of men before that time.
The general drank tea and played at chess with me some
days ago, which was contrary to all etiquette, but it would
have been too ridiculous not to have admitted him. . . .

M. J. S. to Louisa.

Newcastle: August 19, 1797.

Yesterday Mrs. Bigge and General Musgrave went
with us to St. Andrew's church, and, with Mrs. Firth,
answered for the sins of Maria Margaret Stanley,[1] as the
representatives of Lady Stanley, Mrs. Holroyd, and Lord
Sheffield. They dined here afterwards, with the addition of
Miss Roddam and Captain Trollope. I thought I was as
tough-nerved as Samson; but nevertheless found myself
mistaken, being so overset with the attentions and cere-
monials, and more people at dinner than I had associated
with for a long time, that I could have cried if anybody
had encouraged me to it, and felt so bewildered that I
hardly knew what I said or what anybody said to me, all
dinner time. However, I perked up, beat the general at a game
of chess in the evening, and am very well at your service.

Letter from Serena to her Godchild and Great-Niece,
aged six weeks.

Cheltenham : August 24, 1797.

As I cannot look at your blue eyes, my little love, nor
kiss your little white hand, I am determined to be the first
to begin this distant correspondence, in hope that when you
can know what it is to feel affection you will let me have a

---

[1] Called Rianette as a diminutive of Maria.

share in your young heart, and if it is half as warm and as large as those of your happy parents, you will have room for me, as one to whom you were born dear, and to whom your birth has given many sweet sensations. What blessings can I wish you, my child, my grandchild, my godchild, and above all my Maria's child? What but to be as happy as your dear parents are at this moment—a happiness that includes every virtue, durable, rational, and springing from their hearts and mutual attachment, which I prophesy will only end with their lives. Happy child! They will dote on you as a part of each other, and while they unite in forming your mind and guarding you from every evil, you will insensibly partake their happiness. . . .

Theresa Parker to M. J. S.

Saltram: Sunday, August 1797.

. . . I should like a long volume from you, just to tell me how you are, how the brat thrives, when it is to be made a Christian, and who is to answer for its sins, with any other 'nanny goats' you may think proper to relate. The Lennoxs come here next week, and also a person who I have a great curiosity to see in company, viz. Mrs. Siddons. She has been acting at Plymouth for some time, and my brother being acquainted with her, has invited her here, and she arrives for one day with her husband and two daughters. We have not seen her act as we did not think it worth while to go so far into an immense crowd, as we can see her in London.

M. J. S. to Louisa on her twenty-first birthday.

Blyth: September 1, 1797.

Now I wish you joy of being arrived at years of discretion. May you see many many more birthdays in increased and increasing happiness. I will not wish you any happier than I am, because that would only be by taking you into t'other world, and I had rather see you again once more first; but I do wish circumstances and events would allow you to be as happy, by allowing dear Bill to be more with you. . . .

This house is certainly the best in the place, as to size, but that is all. In the room where I am writing, and in my bedchamber over it, there have been four windows, but Mr. Pitt caused three to be bunged up. Hurrah! In the midst of my militia distresses, my Man comes from the camp and brings an account of the 'Sun' saying preliminaries of peace are agreed on. May it be true! and I really believe the whole of the kingdom will be distracted for joy when finally signed, and till then I shall not believe them least I should be disappointed. The disturbance in Scotland continues, for part of the Essex regiment marched this morn from Newcastle, and the rest are to follow to-morrow, towards Scotland.

The Cheshire song was printed on purpose to give away to the soldiers, and they are very pleased.[1]

Blyth : September 2, 1797.

I think we shall find enough employment and amusement at home for all the winter and spring, and those who want to see us must come to us. Do you hear? I will not answer for the proceedings of a future year; it is a long way off, and sufficient to the present day is the happiness thereof. I wished for you exceedingly the evening before last. Just as it grew dusk we walked out by the seaside for above an hour. The sun had set most brilliantly, after a tempestuous day, leaving a beautiful variety of tints in the western sky. The wind had sunk. Near where we walked the sea was calm, but on the opposite side of the river, where the waves were broken by dashing among the rocks, we could hear the roar of mighty waters. As the daylight vanished the moon shone in full splendour upon the sea; it was low water; consequently, when we gained the water's edge we had traversed a considerable tract of sand, and could just distinguish the ragged line of the sand hills behind us, which gained consequence and height from the gloom which

[1] See Militia song by J. T. S., page 103.

surrounded them. In such scenes—which a Rousseau or dear
Wieland, placing in them a pair of lovers, would make so
enchanting—did I find myself by the side of my lover, my
husband ; therefore, if I thought of you, surely it was a
compliment, and I did think of you and wished you to be
present. Yesterday it rained incessantly, but I was equally
happy as the day before and the day following. When we
were together he read to me ; I went to our child, and wished
for nothing more in the wide world. How long in reason
should I flatter myself with expecting the continuance of
such happiness as that which has been mine now for near
a year ? I often check my foolish impatience for time to
pass, when wishing myself in Cheshire, least when I have
reached the summit of our wishes I should look back and
regret the sweet days past, at the time not sufficiently
valued.

Rev. Norton Nichol[1] to M. J. S.

Lee : August 3, 1797.

Right or wrong, I cannot resist an impulse I feel to
congratulate you on the birth of a daughter. . . . I own, when I
turn the eyes of my mind towards Sheffield Place (for I have
seen it with no other since the last happy days I passed
there with poor Gibbon), I feel a degree of melancholy,
which I cannot conquer. What revolutions have happened
of all kinds since we first met there ! The sincere pleasure,
however, which I derive from the establishment of you and
Louisa with every prospect of happiness casts a gleam of
sunshine even on that gloomy reflection. . . .

We have an overflowing neighbourhood and good in
quality, as well as abundant in quantity. Lord and Lady
Guilford have formed a very pleasant part of it. . . . It
is impossible, I believe, to be a ' North,' male or female,
without being agreeable. He seems to wish to live well with
his neighbours, and takes the proper means to succeed, by
the most obliging civility. My lady[2] does not appear to

[1] Rector of Blundeston, Suffolk. Friend of Gray.
[2] George Augustus, 3rd Earl of Guilford, married secondly, 1796, Susan,
daughter of Thos. Coutts, Esq.

think that her new title has added an inch to her stature, is perfectly unaffected, and is both a botanist and a musician, sympathising with us in her tastes. . . .

Nothing would give me more pleasure than to hear from you. . . . Be assured of the sincere and lasting regard of your faithful old friend   N. N.

M. J. S. to Serena.

Blyth : September 8, 1797.

When I am at Alderley I will tell you, and never again will I pretend to say I shall be there one time more than another.   Such happiness is farther off than ever at present. Orders arrived yesterday evening for the Cheshire and Shropshire regiments to march into Scotland, and they are to set off on Monday next in four divisions, by Berwick, Carlisle, Coldstream, and Kelso.   I hope it is more a case of precaution than of necessity.   I could not be tolerably easy if I did not follow the regiment, not knowing exactly what they would have to encounter, or where they may go, and fortunately my beloved, though he made a few prudent objections, is as desirous I should go with him as I am myself.   So far so good.   The painful part of the business is that we must part with our little treasure, who is daily gaining upon our affections . . . therefore as the best and safest plan we send her immediately to Alderley with Foley.   About nine miles from Carlisle we stopped to see Naworth Castle, Lord Carlisle's, which is kept up on the true antique style.   Mrs. Radcliffe's spiral staircases, secret passages behind the wainscot, and concealed doors are not exaggerated.   I could easily imagine the ghosts must run about like tame mice at midnight behind the tapestry.   We saw many pieces of armour, and I clothed my hero in as much as he could bear.   I assure you a helmet and a barred vizor is a very becoming head dress, and his visage looked terribly grim, *à travers*. . . . I am in excellent health and spirits, except when I think of Alderley and its new inhabitant travelling to it; but she would have been sadly off marching with the regiment, poor little love! Our footman is gone with Foley, to take care of 'Crab' and her and Bounce. We have one dog with us; he is a beauty: a Pomeranian that we purchased in Blyth.

[Great trouble followed next day, as the Pomeranian dog was lost.]

M. J. S. to Louisa.

Dumfries: September 25, 1797.

We met with a gentleman of the neighbourhood who is a curiosity himself, and amused us much. As he was riding on the road, we inquired if he had seen or heard of our dog. He answered, 'Are you one of these officers?' 'Yes.' 'What is your name?' 'Stanley.' 'Oh, Stanley! Well, is that your sweetheart?' 'No, she is my wife.' And after getting all this information, and not before, he told us he had not seen our dog, but would make inquiries; and in his turn he satisfied our curiosity, but unasked. 'Sir, everybody knows me. I have a singular name—my name is Cock, and that is my wife, daughter to Major Heron, and her two daughters in the carriage behind; they are taking a little jaunt towards Gretna Green, and if you are riding east, we will go together, if you please, a little way.' . . .

A very unpleasant affair happened at Newcastle when our second division passed through. The Lowlanders, and even some of the Dumfries, attacked several of our men with bayonets. They had quarrelled before we went to Blyth, and in one affray two of the Cheshire were severely wounded. The Lowlanders were brought to a court martial, and sentenced to forty lashes. To revenge this they waited at the corner of the streets till they saw any single Cheshire man coming, and then cut at him. Twenty-five were wounded. Our fine fellows behaved wonderfully well: one man snatched a bayonet out of the hand of a Lowlander, threw it away, and then gave him a hearty fisticuff licking. They likewise threatened this was only a beginning, as they had written to their friends in Scotland to give us a good reception. However, our soldiers behaved with so much propriety that I doubt not they will continue to do so. General Musgrave next day paid them a handsome compliment, and, after expressing in strong terms his concern and surprise at what had passed, offered a reward of ten guineas for the apprehension of any of the culprits. For as this attack was made at night and it was very dark, it was impossible for our men to swear to any one in particular. . . . I am very glad you have had the treat of seeing and hearing two sensible men. I have experienced the want of such society (except the dear pocket dictionary I carry about with me) for some time past; you have been better off than me. You had Fred North and some others at least in town sometimes. You have surely heard talk of Mrs. Nesbitt. She makes a conspicuous figure, you see, in the late revolution at Paris. The best beloved is at this moment writing to her; if papa still takes in the ' Morning Chronicle '[1] you will have seen a very fair account of her, except that I do not believe she married the D. of W.; she refused him once actually, however. Alas! the delusive hope of peace is then at an end. I think Lord M. will not like to go on a third fool's errand.

I have just got a letter from Foley, dated Alderley. Alderley, with a young Stanley in it! The dear thing arrived safe and well.

What do you think of grease to grease the wheels of the ammunition waggons and guns, from Dumfries to Glasgow, forty-eight shillings—forty-eight pounds at 1s. a pound! I am sure Mr. George Rex ought to settle a pension on us, for all the money we save him.

We have got our dog again. He returned after wandering for three days. He is the most beautiful Pomeranian I ever saw. We call him 'Loup,' and when my Man calls ' Poor Loup, pretty Loup,' I cannot help looking for you.

Hamilton : September 28, 1797.

We rode yesterday to the Falls of the Clyde, about nine miles from our inn. . . . As I was galloping on a flat road,

---

[1] See Appendix.

and rather stony, down came Tyger upon his nose and knees
as if he were shot, and down came I in the road. I jumped
up as soon as I could recollect myself, which was in less
than half a minute, quite safe and sound; but that half-
minute scared my poor dear companion out of his senses.
Well, we examined Tyger's knees, which were not much
hurt, and dusted his nose, my Man gave me two or three
hugs on the king's highway to convince himself I was whole,
and up I got again (he looking at me as if he expected me
to turn into a skeleton every moment, like Leonora's William).
We went on with great success. . . .

We have had a very pleasant march from Carlisle, and
seen all worth seeing within our reach. While we were at
Carlisle we rode to Corby Castle, which belongs to Mrs. H.
Howard—Neave *ci-devant*. She is campaigning in the south.
I went knowing it was a pretty place, but chiefly because it
belonged to a friend, but did not expect to find the most
beautiful spot I ever saw. Nothing can exceed the romantic
scenery of wood, waters, and distant mountain. Skiddaw
looked finest among the fine. The whole range of Keswick
Fells is beautiful.

Theresa Parker to M. J. S.

Saltram: October 25, 1797.

. . . I cannot grumble at anything, after three such
delightful months as the last. This is the first time these
eight years that I have passed above three weeks at a time
with my brother, so you may imagine how delightful I felt.
To be sure, Admiral Duncan's victory was a glorious thing;
you may imagine what a sensation it made at Plymouth.
As to peace, if it comes I shall be very glad to see it; but I
never again expect it. We went some days ago to see the
four great Spanish prizes taken by Lord S. Vincent, which
are now in the harbour to be repaired. Their size is
beyond belief; we rowed round them all. 'Tis astonishing
how much they are shattered.

Harriet Clinton to M. J. S.

Broadstairs: October 26, 1797.

. . . Our sea view has been enhanced by the number of men-of-war, frigates, &c., that have passed and re-passed close inshore to and from the Downs. Captain Fairfax landed here with the first despatches from Admiral Duncan, and great were the rejoicings. All the towns and villages illuminated; and I must tell you of our butcher at Ramsgate, who instead of sticking candles in sand or potatoes, hung round his shop all the poor muttons he had killed, and placed a fine fat tallow candle in each rear, which most famously illuminated the apartment, to the great amusement of the surrounding mob. We had a ball on the occasion, and the master of ceremonies did not limit us to twelve o'clock, so that it was kept up with spirit till two. Even the famous Mr. Erskine danced country dances and reels, and the Chancellor seemed in such high spirits that I believe, had he not had on a gouty shoe, he would have set aside his dignity and joined in the dance. Lord Hervey is determined to marry Miss Upton, notwithstanding Lord Bristol will not give his consent. And it is reported that the wedding will soon take place. Lord Stanley is to marry Miss Hornby; and Lord Sheffield, I hear from everybody, is to have Lady Anne North. There is the most comical story in circulation respecting Lady C. Luttrell I have heard for a long time. You may remember, perhaps, she has been in the Fleet some time past. Being allowed one day to take a drive, which is usual, after going ten miles from town, she stopped the chaise; asked the postboy if he had ever seen two hundred guineas, and upon his answering in the negative, she promised to put that sum into his hands if he would marry her directly, which he consented to do; and she immediately set off for Dover, and from thence to Calais, while the postboy husband found himself in the Fleet on account of the lady's debts. This pretty unlikely story I have been told by more than one person.

M. J. S. to Louisa.

Falkirk: October 22, 1797.

Mr. M., Lord Lieutenant of the county and M.P. for Glasgow, is a very delightful man, and I made believe as prettily as possible to remember his being at Sheffield Place, though I'd be hanged if I recollect a bit about it. He spoke of Mr. Gibbon and his conversation with great pleasure, and said he had never passed so pleasant a day as in his company at S. P.

We have received a very civil note from Lord Adam Gordon, saying, if we wished to pass a few days at Edinburgh he should be happy to see us there. This was a polite way of allowing us to ask leave to set off for Cheshire, for there is permission from the Duke of Y. for half his officers to go on furlough till March 10. Indeed, I do not think lieutenant-colonels or majors of militia should be married men with families!

To-day we have had our answer. . . . Lord Adam tells us we may be gone when we like. He did not answer as he did Lord Feilding when he asked leave to go to England, and how soon—' O my lord, the sooner the better.' We hope that on Thursday I shall be at the long wished-for home!

Edinburgh: October 26, 1797.

To-day we have been at Leith, and walked upon the pier, the scene of Captain Stanley's glory as commander of the ' John ' of Leith, bound to Iceland.

Sunday, as soon as we had swallowed our breakfast we went to the high church, to hear Greenfield, the next in request after Blair. He gave us an excellent discourse. The prayers I liked much, and particularly the exhortation preparatory to the Sacrament, which is here only twice a year, and is to be next Sunday s'ennight. It was less terrifying to weak minds, and yet I think more solemn and impressive than ours; there is more psalm singing than I like; otherwise, if our Litany was introduced I should approve their service more than ours, as I think the prayers better, but it should be remembered I am speaking of the

L

prayers made by a first-rate preacher. To close the day
we supped at Mr. Dalzel's, Greek professor, and met very
pleasant people. The men were Greenfield, Playfair,
Rutherford, professor of botany, Mr. Russell, a clever
medical man, and Mr. Arbuthnot, a young man who has
lived at Lausanne, and only left it three months ago. You
may imagine I catechised him. Mr. Gibbon's terrace and
garden remain much as they were; the dear dear acacia is
still there, perhaps neglected, therefore unshorn by the
barbarous gardener; but I am afraid the Goths have taken
away the summer house at the end of the *berceau*, for
Mr. A. said he did not remember any building there.
How could people read that beautiful sentence at the conclusion of his work, and not preserve every bit and atom
of the room and *berceau* with holy reverence for the
departed eloquence and science? Mr. Arbuthnot says
Sévéry is not married yet, because his 'future' is not old
enough. She is a Mlle. de Polier, daughter to Polier de
Loys, who, if you recollect, dined at Mr. Gibbon's a few
days before we left Lausanne. The Cerjats, Chanoinesse
Polier, and St. Cierges are *in statu quo*. He saw at
Lausanne Mr. G.'s miscellaneous works very well translated
into French. Necker is still living at Copet, in much better
spirits than when madame was alive. His grandchildren
are with him.

J. T. S. to his Brother-in-law, Captain W. Clinton.

Alderley: November 21, 1797.

Dear Clinton,—I have been very ungrateful in not having
before now returned you my thanks for the trouble you
gave yourself about my leave of absence. My arrival at this
place, on many accounts, has been of serious consequence to
me. I should have suffered a loss of some hundreds of pounds,
by inattention and neglect, had I stayed but a little while
longer with the regiment, and the sufferings of anxiety and
impatience from perpetual disappointment would soon have
been intolerable; but I look back no more. My present
enjoyments are great. I have found my child well. Maria

is happy and placid, and pleased with everything about her. To live at Alderley with such a being to love, has ever been the wish of my heart. I shall close this letter with my thanks for your trouble in collecting seeds of forest trees for the further decoration of Alderley. I shall want hundreds of bushels to accomplish all my projects of planting. Some I must have from Sussex, to comply with a family custom; our beech wood was planted by one of my predecessors [1] on his marriage, with seeds he got from his wife's county.

Adieu. Yours truly, my dear Clinton,

J. T. STANLEY.

M. J. S. to Louisa.

Alderley.

I was surprised to find the house as comfortable as it is from the account he had given of it, and everything of furniture &c. left in plenty and in nice order; a good stock of linen to begin with, stores of all kinds, and wine. The dear old Man is as busy as fifty bees all day long, and plenty of employment there is, for it would vex anybody to see some of the most beautiful ground possible in a state of wilderness beyond anything you can conceive.

Lord Sheffield to Serena.

Alderley Park: December 11, 1797.

I had intended to send the enclosed yesterday from the excellent and very dear Lady Pelham; but, although I expected all the kindness and sentiment expressed in the letter, it unhinged me so much that I deferred writing. I have heard from Pelham, who offered to come out of his way to see me here, if he could not depend on meeting me in London or Sussex. There is nothing but what is highly pleasant to mention from this place. The good sense the dear Pol thinks proper to display; the propriety; and

---

[1] Sir Thomas Stanley married Elizabeth, daughter of Sir James Pytts of Kyre, co. Worcester; and beechnuts from Kyre were the origin of the Alderley woods.

attention to the Man is everything that could be desired.
They seem eminently made for each other. She strokes
and pats him, and does not seem particularly to prefer her
own way. Many reports had reached her of my prospects
of happiness, and when I spoke to her, the dear Bratt
expressed all possible satisfaction and joy in her best
manner. She has also written to Lady Anne, that the connection proposed could alone restore me to happiness. . . .
If you should meet Lady Katharine Douglas, there can
be no impropriety in singing 'Hallelujah' on the event.
Lady Anne desired to have it mentioned to her near connections. . . . There is not the least affectation in anything
the dear Lady Pelham says. She feels it all, and now she
has the advantage of the real piety she possesses, which
another kind of Christianity can know nothing of. That
alone could support her under such losses,¹ such constant
severe attacks on the health of Lord P. and the very delicate
health of their now only darling, the dear little princess
[Emily Pelham].

Yours S.

Theresa Parker to M. J. S.

Saltram : December 1797.

I cannot think how 'the Man' could have been such a
ninny as to go out of Parliament, which would have obliged
him to stay in town, and moreover he could have franked
our letters! I am sure any sensible man would have
thought those considerations outweighed all nonsensical
ideas of dependence or independence and such trifles, and so
you may tell him, with or without my love as to you may
seem best! . . . We have been, and are still I believe,
surrounded with French prisoners who have made their
escape from the prison at Plymouth. Three of them were
in the stable yard here t'other night, and are probably
still lurking about the place. I do not like it at all, and
never venture my sweet person in any woods or close walks,

---

¹ The Hon. H. Pelham and his sisters, Lady Sheffield and Lady Leslie, had
died within a few months of each other.

as I should be under some apprehension, if I met them, that they would despatch me into t'other world to prevent my informing against them in this.

Yours ever, T. P.

Theresa Parker to M. J. S.

Parliament Street: December 17, 1797.

The St. Paul's business[1] on Tuesday seems to be a foolish thing, and everybody grumbles amazingly, and indeed with reason if it rains. Alas! poor Lord Mayor! he is to go bareheaded before the king from Temple Bar. I should have liked very much to have gone too to St. Paul's had it been practicable, as I suppose it will be rather a fine thing, and what one would like to say one had seen fifty years hence; but there are no places appropriated for peers' daughters, and the difficulty of going to take one's chance would be so great. 'Le jeu ne vaudroit pas la chandelle.' We are going to breakfast with our friend Dolly Stainforth, and from her windows see the royal family set out. We called on her yesterday morning and found her very properly in company with a blind dog and a tabby cat. . . . I can tell you but little about fashions, everybody is as black as coals from head to foot for the old King of Prussia. The heads are quite flat and tied up in handkerchiefs, hardly showing any hair, than which nothing can be more ugly and unbecoming. In other respects our dress remains much the same as it did. Now for news. The chief and almost only topic of conversation is the new taxes. How people are to live if the bill is passed I know not! I understand the Opposition are much elated with the hope of the bill's being passed, as they consider Mr. Pitt infallibly ruined if it does, and that he must go out. How true this may be I know not, nor do I care, for I doubt whether Mr. Fox could bring us into a worse predicament than we are in at present. We have some little consolation for ourselves, as, if my aunt's[2]

[1] Thanksgiving service held at St. Paul's after the Battle of Camperdown.
[2] Miss Robinson, sister to Lord Grantham.

assessed taxes were to be tripled, the sum would exceed the tenth of her income, and she may in consequence appeal, and pay only a tenth ; but as to tradesmen, they all say they must be ruined. I would not be Mr. Pitt on Tuesday for something, as I think he has a good chance of being knocked on the pate.

M. J. S. to Serena.

Alderley Park : December 1797.

I have intended all day sitting down to write a long letter to poor dear aunt, who has been so good and written such a nice epistle ; but how was it possible ? From break-fast to this moment, near five, I have been in the ecstasy of putting up my books, the shelves being finished yesterday. . . .

Poor, poor little me is quite alone by myself. He left me this morning. . . . Of your coming I do not admit a doubt. The militia will not affect it. Alas ! it may be the means of your company being a charity as well as a pleasure. If all this French blustering comes to nought, he will quit the militia in the spring, as really his absence from here would be of the greatest detriment to his affairs, and I could not be with him. For myself I do not trouble my head much about it, since events so frequently turn out, both in public and in private, different to what is expected, that it is very absurd to *enjoy grief* beforehand ; for grief it would be, to be divided for any length of time. . . . The little thing gains in-telligence visibly every day. Foley will spoil her sadly, I am afraid, by-and-by. Miss will have a will of her own, if ever young lady had. You must come and give lectures, and do worse yourself than those you lecture. I have seen Lady Jane Stanley twice. She is just what you described, and what I expected. She entertains me much with her strong sense and strong manner of expressing it ; but I should be sorry to live with her. Adieu, dear old aunt. Pray write again soon to me. I love to receive letters better than ever.

Yours ever,

M. J. S.

Serena to M. J. S.

Welbeck Street: December 27, 1797.

This neighbourhood suits me particularly well, the streets are so clear and quiet that folks walk about. . . . I am hitherto in brilliant health. Lewis Way last night declared himself in love with me and my new velvet bonnet, and I am told, so as not to doubt it, that I grow younger and more charming every day! . . . I cannot go on without congratulating you on the dignity of aunt [1] as well as mother, and I do not insist on your loving the little brattikin better than I do my two dear girls; but I should like to see you all together and make the little cousins shake hands. It was very pleasant to see my brother just come from you. He brought the lady to see us, and all was quite easy. I must think him a wonderful lucky man, after his cruel loss, to gain such another woman. What annoys me is his not waiting a little longer.

One morning he brought two miniatures of the dear Lady Sheffield in his pocket to take to the painter, and in the very same pocket his articles of marriage to Lady Anne!

Adieu, ever and ever yours,

S. H.

[Words of caution are added by the old friend Miss Firth.]

. . . I hope the horses will be so well broke that you will venture to be drove by a servant; but I should not wish you to trust to the major for driving, unless he will condescend to wear spectacles.

It is the *only* thing in which I should not wish you to be guided by him.

A. FIRTH.

[1] Little Lou Clinton, born December 1797.

CHAPTER II.

AT HER OWN FIRESIDE.

1798–1799.

Soliloquy—The new Lady Sheffield—'Anti-Jacobin'—Shipwreck of Lord F.
Osborne and Lord Talbot—Lady Holland at Gloster—Mr. Mellish—Theresa
Parker's marriage—The Lady of the Bedchamber—Grattan—Napper Tandy
—Serena's Salon—Daniel Holroyd—Tuft's exit—Lord Nelson's letter—An
ovation to his wife—Hannah More's early impressions of J. T. S.—Flight to
London—Royalty at Weymouth—Wilberforce—Baby cousins at Alderley—
The mysterious 'Cadabber.'

Soliloquy supposed to be spoken by Lord Sheffield.

BY THE BISHOP OF W.

> Say, lovely Hymen! am not I
> Thy true and faithful votary?
> Resolved at every age to prove
> The chaste delights of wedded love.
> In youth I followed, free and gay,
> Where Fancy led, how sweet the WAY![1]
> In Manhood told by Reason's voice
> 'Arms and the Senate be thy choice.'
> Fair PELHAM's very name had charms
> To fire the Breast Ambition warms.
> In Age when nought so well can please
> As sage Retirement, lettered Ease,
> Then Temper, Talents, Virtue, Worth
> I sought—and found them all in NORTH.

Serena to M. J. S.

London: January 20, 1798.

. . . This day, by special license, at the Honble.
Frederick North's, was married the Right Honble. Lady

[1] Lord Sheffield married, first, Abigail, daughter of Lewis Way, of Denham
Place, Bucks; secondly, Lucy, daughter of Lord Pelham.

Anne North to the Right Honble. Lord Sheffield. The
ceremony was performed by the Bishop of Winchester,[1]
and immediately after it was over, they set out for his
lordship's seat in Sussex. An event, my dearest Maria,
that, all things considered, we ought to be glad of, for he
cannot but be happy with such a woman.

They asked me to be at the wedding; but I thought
Lady Anne, having her brother to part from (probably for
ever), besides other agitations, would be much obliged to me
to spare her, and, as Louisa could not go, I gave my brother
my reasons and he acquiesced. I hear that at the wedding
every one cried bitterly; the bishop was so pointedly solemn,
and poor Lady Anne felt parting from her brother Fred.
Old Mr. Williams, her great-uncle, gave her away and *he*
cried. . . . Two days ago was our christening, and I was
informed that Mrs. Holroyd carried the babe with particular
grace to Parson Way and did not drop it; she also was the
only sponsor who spoke out boldly and answered for her.
She is called Louisa Lucy, which last is a pretty name,
and one that we all like, as it belonged to the 'dear lady.'
My brother whispered William Way not to drown it, as he
thought he threw so much cold water on it; but she was
fast asleep the whole time. I have told Louisa your kind
thought about her monkey, and she rebelled at your throwing
away money, as she says she knows the old girl loves her,
and she wants no proofs &c. However, as I thought you
would like it, I got the saucepan for brattikin, and we will
put your cipher on it.

(Anne) Lady Sheffield to M. J. S.

Sheffield Place: January 29, 1798.

My dear Mrs. Stanley,—I can no longer refrain from
making use of the privilege my near connection gives me,
and I must plague you with a letter to say how anxious
I am to improve the acquaintance which has so long sub-
sisted between us, and which the little I already know of

[1] Brownlow North, Bishop of Winchester, 1781-1820.

you gives me every possible inclination to increase, and I most sincerely hope you will not grow to like me less by knowing me better. I am extremely sorry to hear that we are likely to see so little of you for some time; but Lord Sheffield gives me hopes that perhaps next spring Mr. Stanley will be able to quit his regimental duties, and his improvements at Alderley, and pass some time with us in London. You know there is a very comfortable apartment at Whitehall which will be always at your service, and which I shall never think so well occupied by any other person.

I hope my little granddaughter is quite well. I wish very much to see her and give her my blessing. I will now torment you no longer. . . .

Most affectionately yours,
A. SHEFFIELD.

Serena to M. J. S.
February 13, 1798.

I am as much pleased as you with Lady Anne's letter. . . . I do believe her most intrinsically good and sensible, and all that is pleasant and amiable. . . .

As Mrs. Kennicott is in town and is in the habit of living not merely with divines, but with the best of them, I shall consult her before I answer you on the subject of Divinity. Have you read Paley's last work on Christianity? I think it is the best on the subject. . . . Also 'Watson's Apology' (I don't like the phrase, though it has been explained away) ' for the Bible.' Lady Jane Stanley is learned in Divinity. She wrote really pleasant things of you to her grand favourite, Lady Hesketh.

I beg you to assure Mrs. Foley that the anodyne necklace was the very best that could be got—the last patent anodyne, that they are never more ornamented, and that they are as ugly as I believe them useless, though so long used.

Yours ever,
S. H.

Theresa Parker to M. J. S.

Stanmer: January 21, 1798.

People make a monstrous fuss about the invasion now,
and poor I am reckoned a democrat by the wise people here
because I happen to be of your opinion and think the idea is
certainly much encouraged by Mr. Pitt in order to get
money. 'Tis a sad thing to find now that these quintupled
taxes will not after all produce half what was wanted or
expected; so that we shall probably have something worse
next year.

As to my long-deferred gift, the plateau, I will trouble
you to put your extreme modesty in your pocket for five
minutes, and during that time to inform me really and truly
what size you wish it to be. . . . I am happy to think I shall
be the means of rescuing your table from that old-fashioned
ornament, an épergne. It may perhaps be reckoned genteel
and elegant in your outlandish place; but from its antiquity
is now thought vulgar in the ' Païs des Vivans.'

Do you take in the 'Anti-Jacobin,'[1] a weekly paper inter-
spersed with poetry written by a set of the cleverest men in
London? I am sure you would like it amazingly; it is
universally allowed by all sensible people to be one of the
best performances of the day, and really a good and proper
thing to circulate in the country. It only comes out during
the sitting of Parliament. It began with the last session,
and if you have not already seen them I would advise you to
send for the whole set that have appeared; the expense is
but 6*d.* a week. As you know Lady Mary Osborne, you must,
of course, like her—*ça va sans dire*—and will therefore be interested in hearing what a miraculous escape her youngest
brother, Lord Francis, and Lord Talbot have had. They sailed
from Stockholm in November, intending to go to St. Petersburg, but, through the ignorance of the captain, steered a wrong

[1] Edited by W. Giffard, inspired by Canning with the object of attacking
the doctrine of the French Revolution. Among the contributors were Hookham
Frere, Lord Liverpool, Lord Mornington, and Lord Morpeth, but the boldness
of the language so alarmed Government that after eight months the *Anti-
Jacobin* was stopped.

course, and two nights after, during a violent storm, they struck upon a rock, and were for many hours in constant expectation of death, having no alternative but drowning or starving. At daylight, however, they got to another rock by the help of a sort of bridge, made by cutting down the mainmast of the ship, and from thence discovered an island, with an uninhabited hut, to which they went in open boats. After they had been five days and nights on this desert island, a boat full of Swedes providentially came to their assistance, and informed them they were near the coast of Finland, some miles from Abo, to which place, with the assistance of these Swedes, they arrived after a passage of two nights and days in open boats. 'Tis a sort of escape one would hardly credit if one read of it as having happened in days of yore.

Ever very affectionately yours,

T. PARKER.

Theresa Parker to M. J. S.

Parliament Street: February 26, 1798.

. . . As you have never seen the ' Anti-Jacobin,' I can forgive your supposing it dull (though, by-the-bye, it was no great compliment to me) ; but if you ever had, I should not have so good an opinion of your taste and judgment in those matters as I have hitherto had. It has been of very essential use in promoting the public spirit, that is now so high. Few people appeal (but shabby politicians), and my aunt is determined to pay the whole taxes ; I remonstrated furiously at first, but my brother has converted me. . . .

Now for your plateau ; it is not begun nor bespoke, but is thought of, if that will satisfy you. I am in hopes of getting a shape that pleases me in a day or two, when I shall begin my labours with alacrity, and shall be too happy to be brought to your recollection at your daily meals. I lay all my friends under contributions for pretty prints to put on it.

Lady Holland has taken it into her head that she is ill, and has persuaded two physicians to say it is a Bath case.

She has therefore made Lord Holland accompany her there, because he has a particular aversion to the place. It is a most extraordinary thing, but no less true, that she is visited by everybody, literally even the oldest, properest, and strictest people, and some who only sent their names to her formerly, now desire to become intimates! 'Tis the more wonderful, as she is more universally disliked than anybody one ever heard of.

Yours ever,

T. P.

Louisa to Serena.

1798.

Sir Gilbert [1] and Lady Afleck being at Gloster on a visit to Bishop Beadon, the Right Honble. Lady Holland, daughter to the said Lady Afleck, came with her lord to Gloster, and sent in to inform her mother of her arrival, who went to the inn and passed the day, apologising to Mrs. Beadon for leaving her, Mrs. Beadon entreating her to do what she liked.

Next day the same. No attempt from Mrs. Beadon (who had been intimate with Lady Webster) to wait on Lady Holland. In the afternoon Lady Afleck wrote from the inn to beg Mrs. Beadon to give her and her daughter places in her box at the play. Mrs. Beadon returned answer that her *whole* box was at Lady Afleck's command, who went there with her modest daughter and her new lord; while Mrs. Beadon and some friends went to a distant box, and took care to go out early, so as not to meet the Hollands or be forced in any way to know them. Next morning Lord and Lady Holland drove close to the bishop's windows, looked up, and left her little boy Webster there for her mother, and so, in her phaeton and four ponies, drove out of Gloster, and drove through this place; where next to exhibit is not known. This history I had from Lady Peyton, who dined with the bishop the day after these

[1] Sir G. Afleck married (1796) Mary, daughter of T. Clark of New York, relict of Richard Vassall of Jamaica.

brilliants had left the place. You may send this ' Morning
Chronicle' to Maria, as I know she is *fond* of *dear Lady
Holland.* . . .

Isa and Lou Stanley to M. J. S.

Grosvenor Place: March 1798.

We hear London is dull, with few carriages, parties, &c.,
the opera and St. James's church being the only public
places frequented. I should have had respect enough to
have mentioned the church first; never was it fuller than
this morning: many ladies stood in the aisles. This multi-
tude of fashion, you have probably heard, is attracted by the
eloquence of the Bishop of London,[1] who reads lectures
every Friday in Lent, I need not say how well, for his
excellence is well known, and must be powerful to rouse
the gay and dissipated from their beds and entice them to
church at so early an hour as half-past ten. . . . My father
heard at Boodle's yesterday that several persons in Ireland
were apprehended on suspicion of being concerned with
Mr. O'Connor &c., amongst whom was Lord Edward
Fitzgerald, who married Pamela. His inclinations always
appeared to be that side of the question. . . . In reading the
papers I am most thankful not to be nearly connected with
the Irish Union. What warm altercation there seems to
be at Dublin! Sure there will be many ' Tay and pistols
for two ' go forward in Dublin!

Last night we went to the opera, which, notwithstanding
the court mourning (which very few wear, since the Lord
Chamberlain told us we might let it alone), looked gay
enough. The dance of Bacchus and Ariadne is very
pretty, but they have been over-attentive to the bishop,
and besides putting dark green instead of pink garments,
have added thick petticoats to the bacchanalian gentlemen,
which look ridiculous; some say the effect was better before
it was bishopised.

[1] Beilby Porteous, 1787-1809.

M. J. S. to Serena.

Alderley: March 21, 1798.

We are as busy here as possible. He is making me seats and walks and bosquets, intermixed with more necessary operations of planting, fencing and draining, &c. In the few months we have been here much has been accomplished, and yet the very first moment it can be done, we must build a quite new mansion. The dear old rogue sends his love to you. He delights in his idle, busy, lounging, active life. He is never indoors except at meals, and does not come in to dinner till six o'clock.

Theresa Parker to M. J. S.

Parliament Street: March 28, 1798.

What I am now going to tell you is likely to be the happiest event of my life. I should be sorry you should hear it from anybody but me, as I know you will rejoice at the intelligence. From this *début* you will perhaps guess at the nature of the subject, which is, in short, that in spite of the Sieve [fortune-teller], I am actually going to emerge from the spinning state. When you have recovered your surprise (for I think I see you making *les grands yeux*!) you will next exclaim, Who can it be to? You may spare your guesses. You never, I believe, saw the person, probably never heard of him, though you may of his family, at least in days of yore, when his ancestors made a great figure. *Enfin*, it is a Mr. George Villiers, Lord Clarendon's youngest brother. You will perhaps suspect me of partiality if I attempt to describe him; but I believe, if I was to use my aunt's or my brother's words, I should say he was a man of a most unexceptionable character, good principles, an excellent heart and temper, and perhaps my thorough conviction of his being very sincerely attached to me may be no small recommendation. It has been going on, on his side, for three years. . . . To my infinite satisfaction, when my brother was informed of it, he most heartily approved, and is, if possible,

as happy as I am with the thoughts of it. Indeed, if
anything can exceed the kindness I have uniformly experienced from that dearest of brothers, it is in this instance.
Mr. Villiers is old-fashioned enough to prefer a quiet
domestic life to the gaieties one meets with. I am afraid
my taste is sufficiently corrupted to agree with him, so we
shall be but humdrum sort of people.

His house in town is in Upper Grosvenor Street; but
the place I look forward to living at with the greatest
satisfaction is in Hertfordshire, thirteen miles from London,
a distance which admits of his attending his office in town.
He is Paymaster of the Marines, which requires much
attention. He is in such a desperate hurry, he thinks everything may be done in ten days! but as no one thing is yet
begun, I very much doubt the practicability of the measure.
. . . God bless you, dearest old Polly. I must leave off.

T. P.

Alas! the poor plateau! I hardly dare mention the
word. My intentions were good, and an immense book of
Lady Lucas', with drawings of the Vatican, has been lying
in this room for the last month for the purpose of being
copied, but has, alas! never been opened. Adieu.

[So end the good intentions of superseding the old silver
épergne.]

M. J. S. to Serena (at Miss Firth's house, Doncaster.)

Alderley Park: April 26, 1798.

'Grimalkins' are not infallible; for instance, how could
the pussies think a letter going round by London would be
no longer on the road than coming perpendicularly here ? . . .
We are *in statu quo*—that is, well and busy, forgetting there
is any place beyond Alderley—almost too much ; yet I think
there is not much fear that we should ever become quite so
torpid as to prefer total solitude when the option of good
society is offered us. . . . We shall be most happy to see you
whenever you please—the sooner the better. We have two

goodish spare rooms and one indifferent one. Miss Huff[1] shall have the second best, on condition that she turns into the indifferent room (which has a ghost in it without a head) if necessary. . . . When you come I shall make a violent effort to breakfast at nine : don't try to prevail upon me not to put myself out of the way ; because I sleep more than is good for me. The poor old Man tires himself in the day standing over the labourers, and begins to make the deuce of a clatter about going to bed between nine and ten, and I believe you will allow that eleven hours is more than is absolutely necessary for sleep. . . . What a shocking accident, or rather catastrophe, was that of poor John Mellish![2] I hope the brutes will be discovered and convicted, for such wanton brutality is too bad to pass unpunished. Who is to have the care of his poor little orphans?

Is not Grimalkin Hall a very comfortable, neat, and pretty little mansion? Say everything to both the Grimalkins —its owners—and believe me

Ever affectionately yours,

M. J. S.

Mrs. Howard (née Neave) to M. J. S.

Corby Castle : April 1798.

Howard begs his compliments and sends you a copy of his translation of the ' Wild Huntsman,' which I hope you will approve. The assessed taxes, which come very high to us, have deprived me of horses this winter; it appears to me like being without legs, it makes one so dependent. . . . I am sure you will have been much shocked at Mr. Mellish's most unfortunate death. I never heard of a more rascally action, for the villains fired at him after they had robbed him

---

[1] This refers to Miss Ann Firth.

[2] J. Mellish of Blyth, cousin of Lord Sheffield, was returning to town with two friends, Mr. Bosanquet and Mr. Peter Poll, after a few days' hunting with the King's staghounds at Windsor, when they were attacked on Hounslow Heath by three footpads, who fired pistols into their carriage and robbed them. Mr. Mellish, mortally wounded, was carried into the ' Magpies' Inn,' and a surgeon sent for, who was, however, stopped and robbed on the road by the same gang. See *Annual Register*, 1798.

M

of everything. Mr. Mellish lived from the Tuesday to the Monday, and remained quite sensible till the Friday, with tolerable nights, even after he was trepanned; he made a will, with a long calculation of figures, and wrote two letters. His head was opened, but the ball not found in it, which is singular, but the skull was much fractured.

Serena to M. J. S. (after her first visit to Alderley).

Welbeck Street: August 3, 1798.

You will readily believe how much you have filled my mind since we parted. . . . I had no accident on the road, though one or two of the postillions were so drunk I expected every moment to see them under the horses' feet, and they drove furiously. . . . I am desired to ask Mr. Stanley if a gentleman, Mr. James Six (who was believed to be his tutor), translated ' Oberon ' ? . . . I have a note from Gosling to say my Irish remittances have come; *ergo,* no hope of my tenant being a rebel, as he has paid regularly. . . . Also a letter from Harriet Bowdler, who has been conversing with Mr. Grattan. He has hopes the rebellion may begin again ! . . . Adieu, my dear Maria. I knew you would like to hear my little body is safe in town. . . . If I knew a wish beyond your continuing as happy as you are, I would send it from my heart.

Yours ever,

S. H.

M. J. S. to Serena.

Alderley Park: September 1798.

We are rejoiced to hear you have survived all the misfortunes of travelling post and sleeping at inns, and that you escaped without having your neck broke by drunken postillions or your bed pulled from under you. We have missed you very much. The dinner table wants a balance sadly, and the poor old rogue has had more headache since you went, which must be attributed to the want of your reviving presence. . . . The haunch of venison would be eat on Thursday, as it had not patience to wait for yesterday in good condition; so we had Mr. Carr and family to eat it, which he liked better than meeting Mrs. Davenport, to whom he has taken a great antipathy, for telling Mrs. Carr whom she met at Bath some time ago, that Georgiana was the greatest fright of a child she ever saw. To be sure it was not a tender speech to make to a mother, but if I was the father, I should form my own opinion of the person who could make it, but should not object to meeting her in a third place. . . . Mr. Six, who travelled with the beloved, and of whom you heard him speak with regret one day, and of his being buried at Rome, *did* translate ' Oberon,' but did not publish it. I believe Lady Stanley may have the translation; we have not. I long for you to be at S. P. to talk us over with the folk there. You can give Louisa an idea of us, our walks and our children and our dogs, our plantations, &c. &c., much better in one conversation than I can in twenty letters. . . . The three weeks you passed here have been indeed pleasant to us, and I love to hear you say they have been so to you.

Yours ever and ever,
M. J. S.

Serena to M. J. S.

Shabden : August 10, 1798.

. . . I routed about on Saturday and did all my twos and threes, and dined with Mrs. Ord and Lady Lyttelton. Mr. Garrick, who had heard I was to be in town, came on purpose and brought baskets of fruit from Hampton. . . . You will be glad to hear that Mr. Cowper is almost well—I mean the poet. He has now recovered so as to write and seem happy and see his friends. . . .

I do not like to talk to people about what they know already, else I have a sort of a budget almost new to me. *Imprimo* : Yesterday Admiral Sir H. Calvert sent us notice that an order from the War Office went the day before to recall William to his post of aide-de-camp to the Duke of York. Have you been told of the new Lady of the

Bedchamber to the Princess of Wales? It is supposed the attendance may be made easy, else it seems breaking up domestic comfort.

M. J. S. to Serena.

Alderley: August 19, 1798.

Our letters crossed on the road, and well they might, as each was a week on its travels.

I do assure you, *poor* as we are, that I can afford to pay for your letters; and unless some good spirit moves you occasionally to send double or treble letters, I had much rather you would despatch single ones perpendicularly. Mine not having much in them originally, will I am sure improve by travelling, or at least they will not lose in value, which is more than can be said of all the monkeys that have seen the world; and as your correspondence is numerous and your tenants not attainted, I think you may as well be saved paying for my letters.

Lord Sheffield to M. J. S.

Whitehall: August 21, 1798.

The very dear Ria's fragment is just received, as was an excellent account of the state of things by the Huff yesterday. We were brought here by express yesterday se'ennight. Lord Guilford is seemingly better, but he cannot last many days. His dear sister sits by him from morning till night, and I am in waiting to alleviate her grief. It is a great comfort to hear you have such an excellent nurse, and that the brattery is in such good condition. Tell the Man that his friend Gilpin called on me yesterday. He is just from France, of which country he knows much; was at Marseilles when Buonaparte departed, and has been throughout Switzerland since it was overwhelmed. He entertained me extremely. Now for a secret which you are not to mention till further orders except to the Man or Huff. Lord Cholmondeley desired to have the honour of waiting on me with a message from the Prince of Wales. It was an offer to my lady to be Lady of the Bedchamber to the princess. I since find it was the suggestion of the latter, and the wish and act of the prince. At first we were not sure that we liked it. The few to whom it was mentioned approved it highly, and it is esteemed the highest honour that can happen to a woman. She has accepted. The association with her friends Lady Cholmondeley and Lady Carnarvon (Lord Egremont's sister) is agreeable. The salary 500*l.* per annum; the attendance very little. When in London four or five dinners with the princess, and an opera during her month of waiting.

Yours ever, S.

M. J. S. to Serena.

Alderley Park: September 8, 1798.

. . . The important period of hay harvest is concluded, and we have got two very fine stacks. Old Peter says, 'as foin a ruck of stuff as you shall see.' We had yesterday what is generally called a harvest home supper, but here a 'shutting;' and I really do not think the grandest Lord Mayor's feast with turtle and venison, and the finest court ball afterwards, could have given me as much pleasure. All the labourers, carpenters, bricklayers, and weeding women, to the number of about two or three and twenty had their meal on a long table placed in the coachhouse, at five o'clock. We went to see them eat, and drank their healths in a bumper of ale which they very obligingly returned. Old Peter—I hope you remember him, the old labourer who has worked on the estate for forty years and served four generations of Stanleys—danced the Cheshire Round on the table after supper with Charlotte Alcock, one of the women. They all played afterwards at prison bars in the park till it was quite dark, and then came to the house to sing and dance over a bowl of punch, till eleven—I believe as happy a party as ever assembled. . . .

I suppose you know Lady Jane Stanley is gone to Cheltenham to Lady Hesketh. She called here a few days before she went, with a doll and a looking-glass in hopes to propitiate Rianette, but it did not succeed : she cannot overcome her alarm at the *tout ensemble* of long ruffles, countenance, and manner of speaking. Moll Peg sends you a dear little soft kiss. I wish you could return it upon the little dimple in her elbow or her little rosy mouth. Adieu, with my beloved's best love.

Ever yours,
M. J. S.

I must tell you an epigram on Napoleon that may amuse you, sent me by Theresa Villiers. Somebody wrote on an inn window, ' Tutti questi Francesi sono Ladri, sono Ladri,' to which another person added underneath : ' Non tutti, non tutti, Buona-parte, Buona-parte.' Pray be amused therewith. Now adieu.

Isa Stanley to M. J. S.
Highlake: September 1798.

Dear Maria,—Your letters are always welcome. Edward will be very happy to spend a little time at Alderley, and I hope he may have rubbed off his shyness, that you may see him to advantage. The lace we send will, we hope, become the face of the little black Lucy. She will be a good companion to Rianette, whose nose would have been put out of joint, and been as misshapen as Aunt Isabella's [referring to herself] had a lord of creation arrived. Now, come when he will, she will have a good companion.

You are a very spiteful dame, and deserve to follow the Alderley fashion of having three *shes* before one *he* thing to inherit the estate. It is fortunate the moat does not surround the park house as it did the old hall, or the damsells might be tossed in ; but I trust they will escape, as your heart would relent before you get to Radnor Mere. Tell my brother his old Iceland nanny goat is trotting about in good health ; she sometimes lies by the kitchen fire and singes her sides. Adieu, with all loves.

Your affectionate
Isa and Lou.

M. J. S. to Serena.

Alderley: September 13, 1798.

Colonel Campbell [1] arrived the day you left us, and has remained unmolested ever since, and will, I hope, so continue, in consequence of the surrender of the French, which is now, I suppose, certain. . . . The gentleman is very silent; when he does speak he is sensible and pleasant, and has a great deal of humour; but he is one of those sort of men who let time pass itself, and with whom I rejoice it is not my lot to have to help them to pass it.

However, partridges will be *killable* to-morrow, and that is a great resource. . . . We dined with Mr. Carr on Tuesday, who sent for turtle from Liverpool and claret from Manchester to treat us with. He was in full epicurean glory.

Serena to M. J. S.

Sheffield Place: September 13, 1798.

I am now sitting on the identical sofa where you might suppose yourself with Lou and me, which would be delightful to realise. *Mais passe pour cela*, and let me proceed with my history. I came here the moment I heard of the landing in Ireland. I conceived Lou alone, disappointed, and perhaps alarmed, and sent for my chaise and went to her, and I scarce ever did anything I enjoyed more from seeing the effect on her, and from her confession that she wanted the comfort. . . .

This business in Ireland is very wearing. We can't comprehend Lord Cornwallis's meaning, unless to give time for the rebels to collect, and to have the pleasure of a grand battle. . . . Since I wrote, the Sheffs came to us, and brought the welcome news of the business in Ireland so happily concluded. It seems that I have been all in the wrong, and Lord Cornwallis all in the right; but thank

---

[1] Sir Harry F. Campbell, old school friend of J. T. S., shot through his mouth at Talavera.

God ! it is so well over.   It is a good thing that the French
landed, as it made so many Irish wretches discover themselves to be sad devils, who might otherwise have escaped
notice.   What will your dear Man say of his friend Grattan,
who my brother says is one of the very worst rebels, joined
with the French ? . . . Your account of the ' shutting ' was
delightful, and after my own heart.   It has often been a
grief to me that these old customs were so much laid aside.
It seems the most natural way of attaching the people and
of gaining influence. . . . Lady Sheffield is indeed so
amiable and pleasant that one must be a savage not to take
to her. . . . She is by no means so delighted with being
Lady of the Bedchamber as her lord is, but says nothing
can exceed the good-humoured pleasant manner of the
princess, and that she is so good, she will excuse attendance
whenever it is really difficult.   The day she went to kiss
hands on being appointed, the lady happened not to be there
in form to present her ; but the princess, hearing she had
arrived, called her in, stepped to her and kissed her, and
said how long she had wished to have her ; then asked her
to dine, but saying ' Now pray don't if you would rather
not,' and let her go when she confessed she wished to be
excused, with great good-humour.   All this makes it as
pleasant as such things can be.

Lord Sheffield to M. J. S.

September 1798.

It has been stated that on Wednesday evening between
six and seven hundred French arrived at Killala.   During
the night and next day they landed artillery and arms,
which they immediately delivered to the people, who
received them in numbers.   The whole number of men that
landed were between seventeen and eighteen hundred.   Few
troops in those parts ; but Lake went at the invaders
immediately, and Lord Cornwallis was to go to Carrick-on-
Shannon on Sunday evening. . . . I have letters from the
Speaker ; from the colonel who had reached Dublin ; from

J. Corry &c. Yesterday brought so many rumours of an engagement with Buonaparte, both in foreign Gazettes and public and private letters (most of them supposing victory on the side of Nelson), that it is generally believed there has been an action. Yours ever, S.

Harriet Clinton to M. J. S.

Sunday, September 25, 1798.

My brother Henry mentions the alarm there had again been of the French landing on the north-west coast. On Sunday morning a brig hoisting English colours came to an anchor off the Isle of Arran. A Custom House boat's crew went on board, on which the men were seized, and the boat soon returned to Rutland filled with Frenchmen, and Napper Tandy [1] ventured to accompany them. They landed in all about a hundred men, among whom were several Irish. They immediately posted sentries round the island, distributed inflammatory handbills, and even erected two green standards on which were written 'Liberty or Death.' On the arrival of the post, the bag was seized and carried to Napper Tandy. By the papers he learnt that the French who landed at Killala had surrendered : this, he told the people, was news very prejudicial to their cause, and such an effect had it on himself that he immediately embarked, and next morning stood to sea. There are, however, hopes of the brig falling in with some of our cruisers ; two frigates sailed from Lough Swilly in quest of her. The Custom House men, who were detained on board, report that the brig had about twenty field pieces, saddles, accoutrements, and above a thousand stand of arms, which, had the country been in the state they expected, and General Humbert [2] still at the head of a French and rebel army, would have proved a useful reinforcement ; but in addition to their disappointment at Humbert's ill-success, the people refused to accept the arms offered them by the French.

[1] Chief of the United Irishmen, 1747-1803.
[2] Joseph Amable Humbert, French general, 1755-1823. His sword is now in the possession of the Knight of Kerry, to whose ancestor the General delivered it up.

I long to see you, and never thought we should be so long separated. I am, however, still precisely the same person. You will not find me less sincere and open with you; but you are changed. ‘Voilà la différence, madame !’ And in writing to Mrs. Stanley I cannot say all I used to Maria Holroyd.

Isa Stanley to M. J. S.

Highlake: November 14, 1798.

Our note from Chester will have informed you we were safely arrived so far on our journey. . . . My brother's kind last words were bidding me keep off vexation. When I wish to drive it off, I turn my eyes to the domestic comfort you have given him by your own most amiable disposition, and the two dear little ones left in your arms, forming a picture of family happiness fit for any romantic mind. We have been much annoyed by storms, which, however—to use the ideas of the good people in this neighbourhood—have not been favourable to this coast; in other words, have sent us no wrecks. Good fish is remarkably cheap here. If you think it worth while to pay the carriage from Liverpool, we will be grand, and treat you with the prime cost. We think it might be convenient for you to have 40, 50, or 60 lbs. to salt for winter stock. It is often twopence the pound if you take a quantity, or less. So write quickly, that if ‘Dilly, dilly, come and be killed,’ he may have his eyes and ears stuffed with salt, and be hoisted on board the market cart next Saturday. At the same time as the muslin, will you send a slice of his Honour's pigtail ? We want to put it in his picture when we get it set in town. H. Carr has copied it most faithfully. My love to the brats and their papa, and a friendly pat to the quadrupeds.

M. J. S. to Serena.

Alderley Park: December 16, 1798.

Have you any evening parlour work on hand ? because, if you have not, I want to know if you would undertake to net a breadth of netting, the size of the enclosed pattern. It is stripes for a gown, mixed with muslin, and if I get several friends to assist me I do not think the undertaking will be so very desperate as it appears at first sight. . . . If the accounts of Buonaparte's death are true which we have got to-day, it is a fortunate event for England, as somehow he seemed to be getting a footing in Egypt. The extinction of that army may perhaps lower the pride of the Directory a little, and make them seriously think of peace. Heavy as the taxes are, I think if we can continue without absolute ruin it is better than to make peace with the French in their present disposition. . . . I wonder how the country in general will approve of this tenth of income being taken. To those who appealed before it will make no difference, and we were among the number.

Serena to M. J. S.

Bath: January 3, 1799.

No, indeed! The 3rd January shall not pass without sending blessings to the dear old thing; and don't you believe, my Maria, that I have no small joy and comfort in reflecting on what you are at this moment—such a happy and good, dear, amiable woman, that I can't invent scarce a wish beyond it! . . . As to any little alterations of a few boys running about you, and a few thousands for income, we will not object. . . . Catharine Fanshawe[1] reckoned only fourteen at my levée yestermorn, and afterwards came in Lady Waterford and the Lady Beresfords and Lady Inchiquin. Her husband was my brother Daniel's[2] intimate friend, and once I hated him because he led him into all his wild dissipation; but two years ago he came to me in such a friendly manner, saying that the name of Holroyd would ever be dear to him for Daniel's sake, that I forgave him his sins. Now, indeed, he has laid that life aside, being very

[1] Poetess and artist.
[2] Daniel Holroyd, distinguished at the capture of Belesse and Martinico. Killed July 24, 1760, when in command of ' Forlorn Hope ' storming Moro Fort, which led to the surrender of Havannah. He was buried on the glacis of the Moro Fort.

happy with his pleasant wife. I told him I had hated him, and he said he knew it; but that he and dear Daniel were only wild and idle, not wicked. Did I tell you I had got a puppy from Lord Pelham? My brother called it Damietta in compliment to our victories, and for the sake of the abbreviation, which the little puppy's tormenting tricks often provoked from him in the few days it was at Sheffield Place. *I* call it ' Fanny,' after its mother.

M. J. S. to Serena.

Alderley Park : January 9, 1799.

We have had our merry Christmas kept by the labourers and tenants eating much beef and plum pudding. . . . We have been quite alone, which is next best to having the company one likes. Our Scotch bullock did not turn out very profitable, but was fat enough and excellent beef. We calculated at the market price our gain was only twenty shillings, including the fifth quarter, which scarce pays for the keep of the gentleman, considering he came from Scotland and eat accordingly on his first arrival, besides all the turnips he put down afterwards.

What a true farmer's wife I am, with all these details! We are as busy as bees with bricks and mortar, adding a dairy; *now I make cheese.* I wish we had a salt work or two to pay for it.

Serena to M. J. S.

Bath : January 15, 1799.

. . . You are a dear child for your kind thought of me on January 6. Catharine Fanshawe, who has always some pretty thought, found out my birthday, and when I went to breakfast, there was an elegant little silver leaf to take up tea with, and a few words in pencil on the occasion. It happened odd that the very day I received your letter, poor old Tuft was released from his painful state. I certainly was glad, though having nursed it so many years, I felt a twitch. . . . I have taken your netting with me to little parties, but I can seldom work at it, as I cannot insist on a candle near me, and cannot net without it, as my eyes, though beautiful, are older than they were! Many loves to your beloved; tell him that I am reading over your letters to lay by for him, and if they did not really give me great pleasure, and make me covetous of them, I should like to send them now. I suppose you have heard how gay my brother begins his London campaign by dining with the princess, and a gala at Gloster House, and so on.

M. J. S. to Serena.

January 1799.

. . . I do not think this is one of the very *spirituelle* epistles worthy to be preserved to after-times, but I thought you would be in a quandary about my contradictory orders relative to the netting. I do not by any means approve of the rogue's laying his *pattes* even upon my *ci-devant* communications to you. Howsomever, I do not disturb myself much about what is, I hope, at a great distance— unless we pay you a visit and he reads them. If we were ever par hazard to wander your way, would you take us in? Good-bye. My Man's best love.

Ever and ever yours,

M. J. S.

Serena to M. J. S.

Bath: February 2, 1799.

. . . What an unlucky business this is of the Union! It seems strange that Mr. Pitt was not better informed, than to undertake such a measure without being sure of success. It has taken away some staunch friends of the Government. It was all in Foster's [Lord Oriel's] power, I dare say; but nothing could gain him to promote the Union. . . .

Did you ever hear of Lord Nelson's letter to his wife before his victory, and just after the tremendous storm that for a time dispersed his fleet and almost shattered his ship to pieces? I would give anything for a copy of it; but I will try to give you the substance, though it will lose greatly by not being in his own words. He begins by saying he cannot call it by the cold name of Chance what had happened to

him, for he was fully convinced it was the immediate
hand of God to humble his pride, and as such he bowed with
submission to the salutary chastisement. Behold him (he
adds) but yesterday a really proud ambitious man (recollect
this is a private letter to his wife) at the head of a proud
fleet, and almost secure of a glorious victory. In one night
it pleased Heaven by a tremendous storm to scatter and disperse all his ships, and to dismast and tear his own almost to
pieces, so that the smallest French frigate would seriously
distress him. He concludes with begging Lady N. to let the
Lord of the Admiralty know (lest his letter there should be
lost) that he has got safe to land, though in this condition,
and gives an account of the masts &c. of his ship washed overboard, but that they must refit as well as they can—and it can
be done quicker there than it would be in England—but by
no means to be restored to its original state. Recollect now
that with this very ship he soon after gained that glorious
victory, as if indeed Heaven meant first to humble and then
to reward his power of submission. Recollect, too, the modest
pious letter he wrote to give an account of his victory, and
you will allow the whole to be very fine. Lady Nelson has
been here a long time with his father, and she keeps
modestly quiet. Once she went to the play and was received
as a queen. Sir Harry Englefield gave me a print of Lord
Nelson, taken from a portrait in his possession.

All the world is trying to get places to see Mrs. Siddons,
who is come here to act six times, and had two overflowing
houses already.

M. J. S. to Serena.

Alderley Park: February 1799.

. . . What I meant by asking if you would take us in if we
wandered your way, is founded upon the chance of the Love's
being obliged to take a journey into Somersetshire, as Sir
John is about selling an estate in that county. . . .

As for the Man, he is grown such a terrible fixture that
I do not think any of the beech trees are more firmly rooted
in the Alderley soil; but for myself I always find going from

home a little change that makes the return more sweet, and endears home more.

We have just succeeded in getting a school-mistress established at the village, by giving house, rent, and 6*l.* a year for teaching fourteen children, and I have no doubt she will have a very large school. There has been a boys' school since the middle of January.

The volume of 'Sunday Readings' contains a short tract I particularly wanted, and the clearest arguments I ever met with on the duty of receiving the Sacrament; likewise the explanation of the Ten Commandments. I should really like to be acquainted with Hannah More, in the hope that in the next world she would recognise me as an old acquaintance, and that I might thereby chance to approach the very exalted station in which she must some day be placed. My Man says she ought to have a statue of gold erected to her in every parish in England. She must feel the good resulting from her endeavours as the most grateful statue she could receive. . . . I am trying the success of subscribing to Hookham for one year. . . . A new novel of Madame de Genlis, 'Les Vœux Téméraires,' interested me very much, though I did not think it the only novel fit to be put into the hands of young people, as the authoress does, *mais au contraire.* I have been much entertained with Lord Oxford's correspondence.

[An allusion then follows to the servant recommended by Serena.]

I did not mean to make a serious complaint of poor Mr. George James, as he is not wanting in readiness towards us by any means; but what I meant was a ridiculous sort of *grandeur* he has about him—towards the other servants. The man is very civil, which is the great point – he is only no *Solomon.* Lord Nelson's letter is highly interesting. Lady Jane has interrupted my epistle by a morning visit, and I read her your account, which she was much pleased with.

. . . Both the animals are quite well; but Rianette will never talk, I am afraid. Adieu.

Serena to M. J. S.

Bath: March 1, 1799.

I have been inundated with new-comers, and with the necessity of asking them to parties. I more and more only feel fit for little snug societies, such as Bath affords for us dowagers; but we that have houses and are so very agreeable must sometimes do what we don't like, and I believe it is best not to subside as soon as inclination would prompt me. . . . Pray, when next you see Lady Jane Stanley, desire her to let you see Catharine Fanshawe's ' Elegy in a Wash-house,' for I think you will be much pleased with it. You would be surprised to see what an immense large folio Lady Jane writes, all sides close and small, to her favourite Lady Hesketh here. Old women nowadays are very miraculous ; but if poor little I should spin out so long, I believe I should not be of the number.

How dare any storm blow down one of your noble beeches or any of their descendants? I delight in your simile, and say Amen to your wish. What, indeed, can be compared to taking deep root in every virtue, as in him to whom your happy lot has joined you ! I scarce ever knew characters of great excellence that had not strong biases. With much energy one can do nothing by halves. While one can rest on the head or heart of a friend, all the rest is nothing. I admire Rianette's prudence in not talking till she gains sense to speak what is more to the purpose. She follows the example of her great-grandfather; my father [1] [Mr. Isaac Holroyd] spoke not till two years old, and was often told he made amends afterwards. If she is as sensible and amiable as him, without partiality I may assure you of her being a blessing to you. . . . Did I tell you how charmed I was with Mr. Stanley's translation of the ' Generous Lye ' ? It really seemed the original, and with all its absurdity, is quite beautiful. I read it to Lady Hesketh and two or three more, but it was never out of my hands.

[1] Gibbon alludes to the mutual devotion of Serena and her father, and speaks of them in his letters as Pater and Sorella.

Louisa Shipley desired me to ask if Mr. Stanley had translated the 'Legation of Moses.' I think you would have told me.
Hannah More will be delighted with what you say, because
it will prove your religious principles; not because it is praise
to her. She takes to me and lets me into her bedchamber
tête-à-tête, because she thinks me good, and I don't un-
deceive her, in hope she may make me better. She once saw
Mr. Stanley when he was very young, for a short time, and
in that moment he gave a little trait of his character that
did not escape her, for he happened to say to somebody he
should go in the stage, and by saving the money he should
spend in chaise-posting, he could buy the more books·
When I talked over his life she said he had double merit, for
that his talents, vivacity, &c. had thrown him in the most
dangerous intimacies—viz. the modern philosophies—in his
early life. Now I felt this the greater security, knowing
your dear Man as I do. . . . I won't go on talking to you
all day, no more I will. I am rather ashamed of being so
idle about your netting, but of all mysteries it appears to me
the most obscure, because you sometimes say it is to be but
twenty-five stitches in breadth, and sometimes fifty or forty-
six. . . .

   Adieu, dearest Maria.

Ever most affectionately,
S. H.

Lord Sheffield to M. J. S.

Whitehall: February 11, 1799.

   I have been in a constant course of grunting and growling
and threatening on the subject of not hearing much about
you. . . . It is too soon for the Man to be laid up with gout,
but his activity will long delay essential malady. . . . I
should like to see the stupendous brows of Lucy; are they
much larger and blacker than Lord Thurlow's? My lady
and I shall rejoice when we can make an expedition to
Alderley Park; . . . but although I have a sincere admiration for yours and the Man's deliberation and decision in
respect to a journey hither, I do not like the relinquishment

N

of it, and my lady and I have deliberated on sundry
arrangements at several times . . . the expense need not
exceed 40*l.* You would require a male servant on horseback, but 15*l.* would pay for him, and other additional
expenses; and you now seem to be grown so wise and
matronly, that I must not suspect you will want to buy
everything you see in every shop. I think the Man has
been subject to control himself in such respects; but you
could both make a vow not to purchase anything during
your peregrinations, except what you want positively for
Alderley. . . .

I wish to write a long letter to the Man, although there
is nothing pleasant to communicate, for Europe seems to be
au comble; and no one seems to flatter himself otherwise
than that the wretch the emperor will yield to the peremptory
French requisition that the Russians should quit the empire,
and you will see that only fourteen days from the first of
this month are allowed for an answer, and it is thought
there was still less chance of the King of Prussia's stirring
I am sorry you had not better weather for your trip to the
neighbourhood of Liverpool. I should like to have been of
your party. I suppose you are now a bit of a commercial
character. I can give you some comfort by stating the
prodigious increase of our imports and exports.

In 1785 the imports were	15,948,167
In 1797 „ „	21,013,956
In 1798 not exactly known, supposed 24 millions.	
The exports 1785	16,986,711
„ 1797	28,655,396
„ 1798	33,564,385

This may be curious to some of your Liverpool friends, for
it is only just known.

Irish Union is entirely suspended for the present, and
the utmost that can be attempted will be at the end of the
session to lay the proposition before Parliament, that constituents may be consulted. Mr. Pitt will want for the
country and Ireland about twenty millions. Buonaparte
was well on November 14. Egypt is likely to remain a

substantive possession to France, and I must go and attend
the wet docks. I have been but once at the House of
Commons since I came to town.

I am ever the dear Poll's and the dear Man's,

S.

M. J. S. to Serena.

Alderley Park: May 1799.

. . . The Man has translated the 'Legation of Moses,'
but never published, or indeed written it out fair. I am
very glad you liked the 'Generous Lye.' There are very
beautiful natural passages in it, though the plan is so German.
I see two translations of the 'Noble Lye' published. It is
very odd that the German translators will always present
themselves to the public in pairs.[1] If he was within reach
Mr. Sotheby should be made an absolute Jack in the green,
with wreaths of myrtle and bay leaves, for having given us
such good possession of the sweetest poem ever written in
any language. In general, I am disappointed with any
translation of any play, poem or fragment which has not
first been translated to me by the Man; and not only because
Adam the relator is to be preferred before an angel, for
reasons too tedious to insert, but because the literal version
of the original which he gives, though it would not do to
set down, often preserves more of the spirit and peculiar
beauty of the German sentiments than a polished and
Englishified translation can do. Now, Mr. Sotheby's
translation of 'Oberon' has at once the merit of being a literal
translation, and of its being in elegant and flowing verse:
many of the images which delighted me at first, delight me
ten times more in this translation, and from the exactness
with which they resemble what has reached my memory.
. . . We are rejoicing in mild weather. Grass and leaves
springing *à vue d'œil*, and birds singing as if they were
making up their leeway. I do wish you would make up
your minds at once to come and sit in my arbour. Neither

---

[1] The translation of Bürger's 'Leonore' by J. T. S. had been soon followed
by another.

you nor Lou could do better, I think—till **William's** return. If we found a little more gaiety than **Alderley** furnish might be desirable for us all, we *have talked* of passing two or three weeks at Buxton this summer, and which we might do or not as we liked when all together. I mention it in case you should think that though Louisa might like woods and groves, hamadryads and fauns, yet the total retirement would not be good for her nerves.

My Man has been uncommon busy in the most arduous task of comprehending the Income Act, and the various instructions &c. sent by the Tax Office. He is a Commissioner of Appeal for this hundred, but as there have been three named for each hundred in the county, the trouble will not be near so great as I apprehended it might be. Most of the farmers have come to him to have their incomes made out, and that has been a long tiresome business; but no one could understand how to set about it themselves.

M. J. S. to Serena.

London : June 1, 1799.

I am not surprised that you should be a little astonied at our sudden start for this part of the world; and yet, somehow, it happened so naturally, that if I did not find everybody in a general fit of amazement, I should not suspect we had performed any extraordinary feat. You know I have had all the winter a wish to migrate, and had only been quiescent in the country because I found it would have been unpleasant to the Man had I persevered in expressing that wish, since it would have given me no gratification to prevail with him *à contre-cœur.* But about ten days ago a happy moment offered in which country business of all kinds seemed at a stop for some time. Commissioners of Appeal would not meet till August, and hay season had no chance of beginning till the middle of July. I made the little observation how easy it would be to go to London, as things stood with us, for a very short time, before the Sheffs went into the country, and pass what time we could then

spare at S. P. When I made the above observation, with very
little idea of success, I found it made a little impression, so
there I left it to pursue its progress in his mind till the next
day and tried again how it had acted. To my great surprise
(if I can be surprised at kindness from him, when he knows
how to oblige me) and pleasure, he said: ' Well, we will go
to London,' but bid me take all the arrangements on myself;
and I instantly wrote to milord, having but just time to save
the post, and this is our history:

    We left the babes in perfect health . . . and I have
begged Mr. Holland [1] to visit them as often as he can. Now
I hope you will not think us so crazy and wild as perhaps
you did at first. I am quite happy to see all my old friends,
and very glad to make more intimate acquaintance with the
excellent lady of the family, with whom I can find no other
fault than that she appears to me faultless, and therefore I
cannot find any excuse for disliking to see her in the place
of that other angel. . . . As to Louisa, I never was so surprised as at the alteration in her looks. She struck me with
having a strong likeness to mama, which formerly was the
last resemblance I should have thought of finding for her.
I am delighted with little Lou, the most good-tempered,
good little animal I ever saw. . . . We dined with Louisa yesterday—i.e. the Man and I—as milord and lady dined at Lord
Palmerston's. . . . I have not time to mention half the
people I have seen, and seen with pleasure. Yesterday I
and J. went to the exhibition by water; after seeing which,
we walked to the Lyceum, to the Orleans Gallery, then to
the Panorama in Leicester Fields, and then to Berkeley
Square, where Lady Stanley lodges. In the evening we were
at a party at Lady Glynn's, and music at Mrs. Palmer's,
where the heat made me ready to wish myself in the country.
This morning I am quite quiet, to rest for the new play of
' Pizarro ' this evening, which I am to see in Mr. Coutts's box.
Milord and lady dine with the princess at Blackheath. It
appears to me very odd to be writing to you upon my own
old table, in my own old room, about London enjoyments. . . .

[1] Mr. P. Holland, physician at Knutsford, father of Sir H. Holland.

M. J. S. to Serena.

Sheffield Place: July 19, 1799.

. . . Poor *u* is certainly in danger of remaining in
profound ignorance, but I will be good and write constantly.
. . . Milord and the Man have gone to the assizes to-day.
The judges are expected to-morrow. . . . I do long to be at
home again, and am almost sorry I have promised to stay so
much longer here than we intended, though indeed I am
very happy and comfortable; but it is odd how I want to see
all the things at Alderley. May all your dear visions of
blue sky be realised and continue bright to the end of your
days! You deserve blessings because you are thankful for
them and think of the Hand whence they flow. . . .

Serena to M. J. S.

Weymouth: July 1799.

I hope I am in time to catch you at S. P., my dear Maria.
You have no idea how many things I have to do; every
moment is taken up with these boatings and strollings and
arranging for Lady Hesketh and the girls. Our life is so
pleasant I do not complain. You can't think what a pretty
scene it is! The very long line of soldiers two and two
marching by on the esplanade, with their bands of music,
under our window. Beyond, on the sands, a variety of pretty
open carriages, sociables, phaetons, &c., and beyond that the
beautiful sea covered with little sails and pretty boats. . . .
We go on doing ourselves good. Lady Hesketh is as lively
as ever in conversation, though totally helpless in body.
We enjoy ourselves greatly when, after the day's business is
over, we call for candles and get our books and work. Were
you sometimes to step in and see us laughing *à gorge
déployée*, you would hardly believe there were two old ladies
of the company.

Hannah More is rambling on the seashore to recover
her health, and forbidden to undertake her usual labours.
We are preparing for royalty next Saturday. The arrival
is to be very pretty; but I shall not like our illuminations or

firing. We are to have a fine transp...
Royal Library, which will be *magnifiq...*
Christopher Sykes's family? She is the d...
Park in your neighbourhood. We talked over...
of Alderley Edge most delightfully. Lady Jane ...
seventy-six writes the most lively letters and generall...
lines of playful poetry which she calls ' prose run mad.'

Harriet Clinton (engaged to Colonel Chester) to M. J. S.

Grove, Chiswick : August 6, 1799.

. . . It would have given me real pleasure to have seen
and talked to my dear old Poll once more as H. Clinton. I
expect you to drink my health next Tuesday, and think of
me as often as you please. Sir Francis and Lady Willes are
to be of the party, and my particular friend, Mrs. Anstruther,
stays in town on purpose to go with me. I am not quite
sure whether Susan Charteris [1] will be able to come up. . . .
The beautiful gown you gave me has been more admired
that anything ever was. The Duchess of Newcastle has
given me two more muslin dresses and a veil. Did I tell
you Lady Grey likewise gave me a muslin-worked dress.
Write to me now and then, my dear Maria.

God only knows how long Colonel Chester will remain
in England. Poor Charles Dawkins is shot through the
legs; his being a prisoner is such an additional misery.

M. J. S. to Serena.

Alderley Park : September 4, 1799.

. . . Louisa has had this morning a charming long letter
from William, dated Schaffhausen, August 16. He has been
on ground as familiar to him almost, by his father's narratives,
as the nursery where his infant days were spent, and he has
seen some of the principal towns of Europe not commonly
visited by young gentlemen making the 'Grand Tower,'
Dresden, Prague, Vienna, Augsburg, Munich, and now
Schaffhausen and Zürich. From Zürich he could see almost

[1] Daughter of Lord Elcho, engaged to Henry Clinton, the prisoner abroad
afterwards General Sir H. Clinton.

the whole of the French line settled peaceably among the mountains in huts, where they had been about two months without a movement, and both armies, French and Austrian, grown so polite, that though the sentries of the advanced guards were within fifty paces they never fired at each other. William, however, had a narrow escape of seeing more active service. By the Paris papers it appears that the French army made their attack upon the Austrians under Hötze [1] the very next day after William left Zürich for Schaffhausen. . . . And what do you at Weymouth say to the opening of our expedition to Holland? Glorious and honourable has certainly been the conduct of our troops, and I am glad they have in part succeeded, but I hoped there would be less opposition. I am afraid things will not go on as smoothly as we expected. . . . Louisa seems very easy, however, as she has reason to be, since next to the Duke of York himself, no person is likely to be so little exposed to danger.

Is it possible that she wrote to you and did not mention that we spent a day at Woburn on our return home—where the Man went over the farm with the principal steward, to whom Mr. Pelham gave him a letter—and saw the extensive and princely works carrying on by the duke in great perfection. The dairy, it is said, cost 5,000*l*., and is the most magnificent of the kind I ever saw, fitted up in the Chinese style, with painted glass and a profusion of fine old china.

M. J. S. to William Clinton.

Alderley Park: September 30, 1799.

My dear William,— . . . I hope no evil reports of actions will reach us before we get letters from you; that is the worst of your vicinity to the seat of war, otherwise it is very agreeable to get news as speedily as we do. I quite grieve that you did not reach Suwarrow's army. Besides the pleasure of seeing Henry Clinton, the whole scene would have been highly interesting to you. I am afraid the Russians in Holland are not equal to their countrymen in Italy and

[1] Austrian general, 1740–1799.

Switzerland. Pray send us good news very soon after your arrival on the other side of the water, and finish the campaign gloriously that you may come to us at Christmas to escort Louisa and her babes to town. Little Lou very often talks of papa in the Swiss print of the 'Soldier's Return,'[1] which she discovered of herself. Mrs. Firth is a great favourite with her, and the comfort of our lives, with her cheerfulness and good sense. I think we should like to make a shuttle-cock of her between us if we could.

M. J. S. to Serena.

Alderley Park; October 19, 1799.

. . . There were a few lines from his lordship to-day, in which he mentions letters had been received from Henry Clinton just before the surrender of Tortona, by which it appeared he was going to Switzerland with Suwarrow, while Lord W. Bentinck remained with the army in Italy. How very providentially William's motions have been directed! Sent abroad and avoiding a dangerous service; sent for back when the danger of that service is over, and that in which he was engaged beginning to become critical. Then again being detained in London to carry despatches, by which he was out of the way of the last action. May the same Providence guard him to the end![2] . . . Louisa desires me to thank you for the letter she received yesterday, which found her exactly as you thought possible, with a new baby at her side. Now I do desire, you greatest of all geese, you will not go for to be at all fanciful about me. I am as well as possible.

Adieu, dear old great-aunt of four great nieces.

Ever yours affectionately,

M. J. S.

Serena to M. J. S.

Bath: October 28, 1799.

'If it is not a boy, what can one do?' So ends your letter. To be sure it must be a boy or you will be divorced;

[1] By Freidenreich; coloured prints brought home after visit to Gibbon, 1791.
[2] During Colonel Clinton's absence his wife remained at Alderley, where their second daughter was born.

but don't drown the girl, for I would rather breed it up myself to save you the sin. You are a dear Maria for all the
comfort you bestow in various ways and your good accounts
of the nursery. I must tell you of my amusements. Yester
morn I had taken out one great double tooth, the dentist
admiring my courage because I was quiet; but in fact I
trembled with fear and pain. If I was to be hanged
I should do exactly the same, equally unresisting, as
thinking it the best way. . . . Lady Loughborough herself
is not here, but did I tell you I beat the chancellor at
cards?

. . . I am just come from breakfasting with Mr. Wilberforce, who is really as lively as possible, though called a
Methodist. He showed me two nice children. His wife
spoke of his eyes and the business he was worried with &c.
By-the-bye you are the greatest of all favourites with Lady
Jane, who is not apt to like the world in general. I never
heard her say so much in favour of anybody, and when I
spoke of Mr. Stanley and what a jewel of a man I thought
him, she said, 'Why, yes, I like my cousin very well, but
really Mrs. Stanley is' &c. . . . It is a pity that she has
sometimes a roughness of manner that conceals from those
who are unacquainted with her the valuable qualities of her
heart. Her vivacity, memory, strength of body and mind
are wonderful. She is very poetical too, and such a con-
noisseur in painting, statues, &c., as quite surprised me.

November 29, 1799.

To be sure I ought to have thanked your dear Man
for his kind letter long ago, and it is an age since I have
talked to my poor old Maria and her three girls. . . . Mr.
Bolsius inquired about you. 'If a son he would have
thought it worth while writing to congratulate, but indeed
not for a girl.' But you, poor dear child, never mind;
your girls will be blessings, and the boys will come in time.
I am so content with girls that I ordered all my family to
drink their healths in the best brandy, and so they did. I
had a sweet letter from Lady Sheffield—she is going to give

me an Edridge drawing of herself. She and my brother seem determined to go next summer to Alderley. . . .

I believe I told you Mrs. Kennicott comes to Bath in February. She lately puzzled me greatly by the word 'cadabber,' which I begged Lady Harcourt to explain after I saw twenty or thirty lines all ending in rhyme to 'dab.' Probably you know that in one of Fred North's embassies, where the language required an interpreter, Fred observed the word 'cadab' made use of by the sovereign very often, and each time it was used Fred bowed more and more profoundly, taking for granted it was some gracious expression, and he took his leave highly flattered with his reception. He afterwards begged one of the attendants to tell him the meaning of the word 'cadab,' and was told it was 'you lie!' . . . . Three days ago I was surprised at the entrance of Lord and Lady Guilford and their two children. Little Lady Maria[1] presented me with a note of introduction from Aunt Sheffield.

M. J. S. to Serena.

Alderley Park : December 3, 1799.

Dearest old Aunt,—I have really borne my misfortune with much greater magnanimity than you might suppose possible, and the little intruder[2] is so good and quiet that one cannot find it in one's heart to drown her or even to give her a pinch. . . . Both the little babs sleep with Foley. In the daytime Mrs. Huff is the greatest comfort in assisting to take care of the five little pussy cats, who would, every one almost, take up the whole attention of one person apiece. . . . Adieu, dear Mrs. Aunt. Pray don't be so frisky and fancy you can outwalk me.

Yours ever and ever affectionately,

M. J. S.

[1] Afterwards Lady Bute.
[2] Louisa Dorothea, born November 1799.

CHAPTER III.

'SO WISE AND MATRONLY.'

1800.

Royal Institution—'Entertain me, Gran!'—Fashions in shirt collars and cropped tails—Cruel inoculation—'The sauciest of Cheshire cats'—Buonaparte striding on—Sir J. Banks amphibious—The Ladies Colyear, in death not divided—Visit of Lord and Lady Sheffield—The salt mine—Death of Madam Owen—The prison tutor—Poor Jeremy—The pussery—Lou Dolly.

Louisa to M. J. S.

January 3, 1800.

Though in the midst of all the important avocations of settling myself, which is more retarded than usual by the presence of two children and the absence of one maid, I must write to dearest Ria many happy returns of this day in the next century, and that this time three years you may have three screaming boys outbawling their three sisters. William desires me to say for him all sorts of fine things to you, but lest they should make you vain I shall leave them unsaid. I wish we could both drink your health round the comfortable fire at Alderley. . . . I must give great credit to all our travellers for their good conduct. Heckla [Iceland dog] was somewhat of a nuisance to be sure, but the little fellow took so kindly to me that I was quite sorry to part with him; but Sir H. Calvert, who called last night, unfortunately admired him so much that we could not withdraw our promise. F. says she has lost all appetite for supper, though she has neither cold nor malady of any kind, except Alderley mania; so don't be surprised if you should see us all driving back again in the course of a week. Even the old shoes Simson made me, that William used to abuse so much, I now wear with the greatest pleasure, being quite fond of them for the sake of dear Alderley.

March 1800.

. . . Monday, dined at Privy Gardens, met Mrs. Pelham there. The jewel of a Man lent me one of his tickets for the Royal Institution,[1] and I went with Lady S. the next morning, when the first lecture was read. They are to be six times in the week, and would entertain me much, but Albemarle Street is sadly out of reach.

I would have been tempted to have subscribed the two guineas could I have attended regularly. The lectures only last an hour, which is too short except for fools, who had better stay away. It is as unpleasant to me as when you sit down to play, knowing you will leave off before I have had half enough music.[2] I stayed the day I went, near an hour after the lecture, with Lady Sheffield, as we had to walk all over the house with Count Rumford; and there was Mr. Pelham, Mr. Bernard, Sir H. Englefield, and all sorts of pretty kind of people there. In the evening I was so very good as to go to a blue-stocking party at Miss Leighton's. . . .

I have been to concerts at Lady Congreve's and Mrs. Palmer's this week, and to-day I should have gone again but for want of a carriage. One thing, I have quite determined never again to submit to live in London without a carriage. It would be better to vegetate among my own cabbages or

[1] Founded 1799 by Count Rumford, Sir Joseph Banks, Earls Spencer and Morton, and others. First lecture March 4, 1800, by Dr. Garnet.

[2] 'Impromptu' by Hayley, 1795:

> Maria of melodious skill,
>   Thy magic aid impart,
> When misery's plantive Sonnets chill
>   The Horror-troubled Heart ;
>
> Thy Fingers rapidly command
>   The Antidotes of Care,
> And thou canst chase with potent Hand
>   The sadness of despair.

potatoes at The Lodge than be continually annoyed and
tantalised as I am here. I have vowed never to be prudent
again in that way. I had rather wear horsehair shirts,
sleep in sacking and cattle rugs, eat sheep's heads and
barley bread; nay, give up my writing-box and armchair
before I would again depend on my own feet and my neighbours' charity.

M. J. S. to Serena.

Alderley Park: January 21, 1800.

. . . We are buried in snow, and the trees are looking
beautiful with their powdered wigs. I am affronted, however, that I cannot go out and look at them but I should be
over shoes and boots, and, I believe, knees into the bargain. . . . Alderley may bless its stars at having its present
master this winter. The necessaries of life are so dear, I do
not know what would have become of the poor without
assistance. There has been a subscription raised in the two
Alderleys, which amounts to above seventy guineas. This is
allotted to selling meal or other food at a reduced price to the
families who are thought proper objects by a committee:
but this reduced price is so much higher than what it is in
general, that I think even his lordship cannot accuse us of
encouraging the consumption and thereby increasing the
scarcity of corn in the country. I have tried, but found a
soup shop would not answer here, where the population is
scattered. Enough could not be disposed of to pay for
trouble, fuel, and material to any one doing it for their liveli-
hood; but I find a demand and thankfulness for forty
gallons a week which we make here, where trouble, fuel, and
vegetables are so many plums in the house.

Miss Huff is quite a grandmother to the little ones, and
spoils them accordingly. With her they never can contrive
to amuse themselves. It is always 'Entertain me, Gran!'
like their worthy mama.

Adieu, dear old aunt.

M. J. S.

M. J. S. to Louisa.

1800.

. . . I dote upon the German authors, whether they are in the tender, passionate, or horrible style. In all, I think, they excel. There is a play by Goethe—'Stella'—some scenes of which the Man has translated, and I never read anything equal to it for passion mixed with the greatest delicacy of sentiment. The 'Robbers' and 'Fiesco' you have read. The 'Sorcerer' and the 'Ghost Seer' are two of the terribles not dramatic, which perhaps you have seen. Do inquire if there is a good translation of Gessner's[1] 'Idylls' either in French or English. They are such sweet things, I want to make them my own. Now and then I catch the Man to translate a little, and am as pleased as Punch. Last night I had an idyll and a half read to me.

Theresa Villiers to M. J. S.

Upper Grosvenor Street: February 5, 1800.

. . . Our babe[2] is not to be christened this fortnight yet, for, as Mr. Villiers has set his heart on making it a grand gala, I want to be quite stout. He is named after the King, 'George William Frederick,' as he is to be his god-father, and my brother and Lady Essex, junior, the other two responsible people.

Two kisses to each of your babes. When am I ever likely to see them? How I should enjoy showing you my boy!

Very affectionately yours,
THERESA VILLIERS.

M. J. S. to Miss Ann Firth.

Alderley Park: February 19, 1800.

We miss you sadly. . . . I can in all verity thank you a thousand times for having given us so much of your company

[1] German idyllic poet, 1730–1788.
[2] 4th Earl of Clarendon, Lord Lieutenant of Ireland 1847-52; Secretary of State for Foreign Affairs; died 1870.

and for your great kindness to the babes.   Rianette watched
you round the corner of the plantation, and when quite out
of sight turned to me very reproachfully, with tears rolling
down her cheeks. I believe she thought I had sent you away.
She always says at breakfast, ' Miss Huff went in a coachey.'
I assure you I have not scared her much since you
went. . . .

Milord is in a great rage with the reports of the committee
on corn. It is very odd, with his knowledge of the consumption that takes place in England, he should not recollect
that probably one-half of the kingdom do not subsist entirely
upon wheat at any time; therefore his calculations must be
erroneous, and the saving in general would not be what
he supposes by ordering his standard wheat only to be
sold. The saving would only be in London and the southern
counties. I do think they give themselves much more
trouble than necessary about limiting the consumption ; the
high prices will do that effectually with all but the very
rich.

Serena to M. J. S.

Bath : February 20, 1800.

. . . I felt very affectionately all that you feel in regard
to our good Mrs. Firth, and loved you for that well-drawn
character your heart so justly prompts. Indeed, I believe
my dear girls have not in the world a more sincere friend than
she is. . . . There are so few left now who know all about
us and are like one of our family, that I can't reconcile myself to her leaving us, as long as she can enjoy life
tolerably.[1]

I had indeed intended she should come and close my
eyes if I had notice long enough to invoke her aid, for she is
exactly what I should like to have about me. I should not
like to have my children near me, either on their account or
my own, for it is assuredly the tie that would most keep my
thoughts on earth when they should be elsewhere.

[1] ' Mrs. Firth ' lived to complete her hundredth year.

M. J. S. to Louisa.

March 9, 1800.

What in the world is this deep plan of milord's about corn which he has been so long in announcing to the House ? I suppose he is like our great Cæsar, saying *Ero, ero, ero*, at the Corn Committee reporters, and that his pacific friends are pulling him back by the tail. We have got some barley out of Nottinghamshire, which we hope is sufficient to last our labourers till next harvest. Flour is lately fallen a little in consequence of a considerable importation at Liverpool from America, and more expected. Have you seen Moleville's ' Annals of the Revolution '? He lets out a few cats, I think, in regard to Louis' sincerity in accepting and promising to preserve the constitution ; and the Jesuitical distinction without a difference of declaring but not making war, alluded to in the letter to Fox, is curiously absurd. . . .

Pray, is it the fashion for the shirt collar to stand as high as the corners of the eyes? for it is of consequence I should be informed before the new set I am making is finished. The old shirts must be greatly tugged up before they will equal Ned Davenport's !

Your cropped tail must be very comfortable. But I cannot cease admiring the extreme pitch of folly to which the world is arrived, and that for fashion, i.e. for something new, people with good hair cover it with a wig, or spoil it till it looks like one. It is really too ridiculous.

Louisa to M. J. S.

March 1800.

. . . I inquired of William respecting shirt collars, upon which he only made a violent philippic on the folly of man's dress at present, and did not seem to know anything about the matter. . . . Oh ! *à propos* I do not think the state of womanhood is quite so pitiable, now that it is the fashion to walk the streets in black cloth gaiters ; they are the comfort of my life. . . .

I will not begin to talk politics and all the evils of our administration, as I have many things to say, and it is a bad

o

plan to encourage the malevolence of disposition I feel when thinking about the matter. I doubt whether Plato would give me any hopes of his heaven, when I so fervently long to see the day when they may be thrown from their arrogant height and be judged as they deserved (I do not mean *hanged*, but generally abused by the public), and obliged to hear the truth which now reaches their ears as seldom as it does an Eastern prince in his seraglio.

M. J. S. to Louisa.

1800.

Pray inform me if there is anything like a shirt annexed to the hideous ears you have described, because I think that part would be very comfortable to keep one snug from flies and sun. As to the ears, I hope I may get my health for some time without accommodating myself to the fashion, for there is nothing I have felt a stronger aversion to in men than that same fashion which I have seen in a few puppies. By-the-bye, I am very sorry; but you have not done with that business yet—I mean of dress. Miss Huff has really a more fearful bonnet than ever I saw her in possession of yet. It is made, I believe, of a bit of old shift with a small portion of green riband annexed to it, and by its being mounted on the occasion of paying a morning visit with me, I conclude it is her best. I shall wish to make her a present, and I find she has a handsome worked muslin gown to make up for the christening; therefore, if you could meet with a decent smart bonnet that you think would suit her, I shall be much obliged to you, as my nerves cannot bear the sight of this unfortunate piece of apparel all the time of her visit. Get a bonnet or hat for me either of muslin or straw, giving more shade than the brown, but not a slouch, and a spencer cloak of cambric muslin at the same time. . . . There never was anything more provoking! After I had taken the trouble to write all this, I find she has got a chip hat to trim for best, which I think I can bear the sight of; therefore, if you can think of anything nice for Miss Huff, about a guinea or so, I wish you would get it. The hat which you got for me has been my constant companion all last winter and this, habit or no habit. Do you see anything of a *she* beaver hat which you think I should like as well as a man's hat? If you see nothing very delectable I will have only the *he* hat, and wait for winter to get another.

M. J. S. to Serena.

Alderley Park: April 6, 1800.

I am afraid you have given me up as supposing that we have emigrated at least, if not dead and buried. Since I wrote my mind has been a good deal engaged and a good deal anxious about my poor little baby. She has been inoculated a fortnight ago, and the place seemed to die away, so Mr. Holland thought it advisable to inoculate the other arm. On the eleventh day after the first inoculation, fever and inflammation had increased so considerably that Mr. Holland applied five leeches to the poor little arm, which in a very few hours gave great relief. Last night she had fever, and the other arm is very much inflamed in the usual way, so that I am puzzled to know whether she had the disorder last week or is going to have it in this. I hope in a few days the dear thing will be quite herself again, and all her arms restored to a convalescent state. My Lucy is always in motion and wanting to be where she is not, and as complete a little Stanley as you can imagine in eyes, eyebrows, and complexion.

Dear old aunt, pray send me your forgiveness for all past offences. I want to hear from you and all about you. Levade's letter is very interesting. Many thanks to the Legards for the reading of it.

Yours ever,

M. J. S.

Louisa to M. J. S.

April 1800.

I am very glad to find that upon a more complete investigation your opinion of ' St. Léon ' tallied so perfectly with mine. Your resolution of never praising a work till you

o 2

have finished it, is wise and similar to those of two very sage personages : Solon, who advanced that no man could be pronounced happy till removed by death from the possibility of misfortune, and Mrs. Louisa Clinton, that none can be pronounced virtuous till equally safe from temptation.

. . . Would you believe that my impudent fellow dared to make an April fool of me, by writing a note in long-legged De Luc's name, saying he proposed coming to break-fast with Mr. Traytorens ; and the vile dog vowing he would not let him in, I began wasting my precious breath to per-suade him to be civil for once, before I found his face was not so savage as it would have been had he not raised the difficulty himself. . . .

I haven't subscribed to the Royal Institution, as I have had Mr. Pelham's ticket from the beginning, nor shall I now, as it is raised to three guineas. . . . Sir John, Lady, and three Miss Stanleys are subscribers. To the latter I have several times acted as chaperon. . . . The Royal Insti-tution is an excellent centre for meeting one's friends, which it is a vain attempt to do at home ; and were the lectures all in the evening it would be very pleasant, but a morning assembly I dislike. Lady Stanley and Emma very in-genuously confessed that the certainty of having six more parties every week was the sole cause of their subscription ; and would two-thirds of the party be as honest, I am of opinion they would be found actuated by the same motive. . . . I am sometimes made very indignant by Dr. Garnett wasting much of his time in playing tricks to amuse the pretty creatures who surround him. The last lecture was on electricity, the latter half-hour of which was employed in playing the fool, without explaining a single circumstance more than in the first. It may be excusable this year when the object is to get money and render it fashionable, to court the attention of fine ladies ; but when fully established, I shall have a poor opinion of the managers if they suffer such child's play. The information one picks up from time to time is very superficial, and without reading also, would not overburthen one with knowledge. . . . I enter into it much

more than I should have done, from the ideas I received from
your Man and his books. . . .

Though the sauciest of Cheshire cats, I must take the
opportunity of thanking you for your letter, now my husband
is dining at Sir John Sebright's, and my child composed to
sleep. We have continued *tête-à-tête* every evening, Monday
excepted, when I drank tea with a blue party at Mrs. Good-
enough's. . . . The usual Clinton bad luck will probably
prevent an event of the last fortnight being beneficial to the
family, or present appearances wear a most favourable aspect.
Lady Chapman died, and left Lady Willes [1] full possession of
her town and country houses, estate, and everything she possessed except 12,000*l.* in legacies, so that she will probably
have between 2,000*l.* and 3,000*l.* per annum to dispose of. . . .
I have been entertained with you and Miss Firth sending me
scoldings about Lady Willes. You guessed very right, for
it is certain that William and I have lately been less attentive than we should have been had her favour been less
worth cultivating. I do so hate being supposed to be kind
to people on such motives.

Lady Chapman has been left everything by her husband.
She has been acquainted with Lady Willes thirty-six years,
many of which they were most intimate friends; she appointed William one of Lady Willes's trustees; the house,
Cokenhatch, is in Hertfordshire, forty miles from London.

M. J. S. to Serena.
Alderley: June 22, 1800.

I am extremely affronted that you care so little about
me as never to have made any inquiries if my remains have
been decently interred, and if Mr. S. and the children are as
well as can be expected. . . . I wish I could convince people
of the propriety of writing me two letters for one. I heard
from Lady Jane that you was leaving Bath for Clifton with
Lady Hesketh, and I wish you may be so invigorated that
you may feel equal to undertake the expedition into Cheshire.
My little Louisa is a great love, and has always a smile ready

[1] Sister of the late General Sir Henry Clinton.

for any one. I meant to have written a longer letter; but
how do you think I have been interrupted? By the old
fellow insisting upon my dressing up a flower-pot, and as he
gathered the flowers, I could not help myself. Adieu, then,
and pray write soon, and do not take for granted that I
know anything of your history further than that you exist;
for you know Louisa never tells me anything of details.
How do you like their scheme of a villa at Fletching?[1] I
think it a good plan as things are.

Serena to M. J. S.

Clifton: June 27, 1800.

It is certain that the less you write the more you will
dislike it, and you must remember your poor old aunt can't
give it up, and when she is gone to heaven you will say, 'I wish
I had gone on writing a little longer, not to deprive her of
her little affectionate enjoyments;' and so pray, dear Maria,
spider-like, draw out of yourself your inexhaustible fund of
playful pleasantness, and be assured I shall delight in
it. When I read a thought or so to Lady Hesketh, she
says 'There is nothing like you.' She has herself the
liveliest imagination, and so perfectly comprehends all
things of taste, humour, &c., that half an idea is for her
a chain perfectly complete to know a person by. She really
is, in spite of no voice, a charming companion, and her
beautiful countenance does one good to look at. . . .

O mirabile dictu! A mother loving her children and
yet not blind! I am glad of it, because you will take more
pains with their minds and manners. Teach your girls to
wish to please and oblige, and I'll answer for it they will
do so. . . . The Jamaica fleet has just come in. Every
ship passes under our windows. Alas! I must not talk of
politics at this unhappy moment, when Buonaparte (who was
christened Abdiel) seems striding on to desolate the world;
and yet must we not particularly feel the blessing of
our navy, which preserves our trade so wonderfully when all
seems to go against us?

[1] The village near Sheffield Place where a house was being fitted up for the
Clintons.

. . . Sir J. Legard showed me a very interesting letter from Levade, in which he speaks of the state of Lausanne; that though the French are masters who *cut off the legs* under pretence of giving liberty, yet they have not been much molested. He speaks of the good order and discipline of their soldiers as being a great comfort. He describes a place he is building upon quite beautifully, almost *à la* Rousseau.

The Legards[1] and Grimstons were much gratified by your remembrance, and seem to forget nothing of those days And now, dear Soul, Adieu.

Blessings to your Man, your little ones and self.

Yours ever,

S. H.

M. J. S. to Serena.

July 16, 1800.

I am all alone to-day and to-morrow, as the Man is attending quarter sessions, from whence he will return a justice of the peace. . . . I have never been able to grieve for the defeat of the Austrians in Italy, because I live in hopes that peace may be something nearer in consequence. . . . I cannot help admiring Buonaparte. He may be acting a part (I mean independent of his victories), but at least he is acting a noble part; and if he keeps up to his present conduct, whether it is acting or natural, I insist upon it, he must be called a 'great man.'

We had a famous merry-making here on Wednesday last. I don't know whether it is a North Country, or only Cheshire and Lancashire custom, on Easter Monday, for the men to lift the women; and on Tuesday the latter returned the compliment. The men dressed a chair very fine with ribands and flowers, and when I came down to breakfast offered me a ride, which I of course declined; but, as was expected, bought myself off with half a guinea. On Tuesday the maids actually did lift the Man in the chair, but he thought he would give them a handsome treat, or I had not properly provided him with half-guineas, so he gave a guinea. The servants got fines from others, and subscribed

---

[1] Sir John Legard, guardian to Lucy and Maria Grimston (Lady Wilmot and Mrs. Fawkes).

among themselves in all 2*l.* 13*s.* wherewith they got a
fiddler from Macclesfield, bought tea, sugar, cake, and rum,
and, I assure you, made out a capital dance in the laundry.
We went to see them, and a very good ballroom it made,
taking down the pipe of the stove and the handle of the
mangle. The fiddler sat on the fine chair on the dresser,
and performed capitally. So you see we have galas as well
as Mrs. Walker, and other gay people in London!

Serena to M. J. S.

Weymouth : July 16.

I must say I am glad there are not such Newhaven
parties[1] every day. I perfectly remember the whole scene—
the farmhouse &c.—as if it were yesterday, and how much
we enjoyed it with Lady Cath. Douglas, Sir Joseph Banks,
&c.; the latter proving his amphibious nature whenever
you wished for an aquatic plant by stepping out of the boat
into the water and back again as readily as a Newfoundland
dog would have done. . . . I intend that this should be an
uncommonly happy year to me, and that I should have
nothing to vex me. Only think of my having four children
and five grandchildren, who so lately had but two dear girls
for my whole stock! having my brother also as happy as man
can be, and having in his wife, one that I can really consider
as an old friend. I even intend that this next year should
make a great change in public affairs, and that the demons
of discord should be crushed.

Thus rapidly am I dispersing all clouds, to make room
for a clear blue sky, my natural climate. Amen to all my
bright visions. Amen. So be it!

Lady Sheffield to M. J. S.

July 9, 1800.

. . . I have just heard his lordship order a horse for
his cousin, Mr. John Godley,[2] to accompany Mrs. Clinton

---

[1] Referring to a boat accident and narrow escape of the Sheffield Place party.
[2] Born 1731. Member for Baltinglass in the Irish Parliament 1778-1783;
great-grandson of Susanna Holroyd (*m.* John Godley, Sheriff of Dublin), and
grandson of Ann Ellwood : both great-aunts to Lord Sheffield.

and Miss Cooper in their ride. My lord is very busy
brushing up Mrs. Page's house for the Clintons; it is
now called Clinton Lodge. He is going to build them a
room, and you shall have a plan of the proposed alterations
very soon. I flatter myself you will think his lordship in
great beauty when you see him. I am sure you will not
think the same of his lady, for nothing can be truer than
what Mrs. Coutts told me the other day, that I looked at
least ten years older than my lord. I dare say all your good
cream and Cheshire cheese will make me grow fat, and I
may, perhaps, return nearly as young as my husband. . . .
I still hope we shall be with you about the middle of August.
The princess means to honour us with another visit this
summer; but we have given her notice that we mean to
leave this place on the 10th of next month. God bless you,
my dear Mrs. Stanley. Yours sincerely, A. S.

Louisa to M. J. S.

August 1800.

What do you dear loyal souls say to these immense
expeditions when the country is threatened with invasions?
and what think you of persisting, contrary to all advice
and common-sense, in having 8,000 French prisoners at
Plymouth, when such an enterprising enemy as Buonaparte
is likely to take every advantage? But my wrath is so
beyond bounds I cannot bear to think of it, so I will look
over your dear long letter, which I am sure contains more
sense than can be found in all the proceedings of ministers
for years.

. . . The two poor Colyears were sitting on the same
sofa, Dr. Jenkins reading prayers to them. Lady Mary
fell back without a groan, seeing which her sister fainted,
and, before many minutes, expired also. How little did
Lady Portmore and her daughters [1] think a year and a half

---

[1] Lady Mary and Lady Julia Colyear were the daughters of 3rd Earl of
Portmore, and died at Bath the same day, August 11, 1800. M. J. S. and her
sister remembered them as beauties dancing minuets at the court ball,
1791.

ago that in so short a time they would be carried off by that horrid disorder!

Serena to M. J. S.
Clifton: September 12, 1800.

I saw in the papers the death of Madam Owen. I am sorry it happened just now, but otherwise she has lived to a good old age.

['Madam Owen,' grandmother to J. T. S., was Margaret Bold of Bodwina, in Anglesey, a woman of remarkable character and ability. She was left a widow at nineteen by the early death of her husband, Hugh Owen of Penrhos, 1742; he had gone to take the waters at Bristol, and did not live to return to Wales and see his child, who was born during his absence. Madam Owen managed the property for the little heiress, and in order to give her educational advantages took her to London on a pillion behind her, crossing the Welsh mountains on horseback. Margaret Owen married Sir J. Stanley 1763.]

M. J. S. to Serena.
September 1800.

Poor dear old Aunt,—How ill people do use you! I know I am very good for nothing, and yet when your last letter arrived I really was so pierced, I did not think I could ever be idle again.

. . . Lady Sheffield has told you of my disappointment in regard to the little Welsh tour. I did not think poor Madam Owen's exit could have occasioned me so much grief. The only recompense I can think of, is that you should promise to pass next summer with us, and accompany us to see the Llangollen ladies, who feel intimately acquainted with you beforehand. After the retired life I had led, the scenes of visiting and gaiety I have lately been engaged in seem quite dissipation to me. Alderley never was so full of company; Judge Downes spent two days here a fortnight ago, while the Sheffs and Miss Stanley were here. We have been twice down a salt pit within a month—once with the Sheffs, and once with two gentlemen who came here in the course of a mineralogical tour: one was an acquaintance of S.'s at Edinburgh, Mr. Playfair; the other, Lord Webb Seymour, brother of the Duke of Somerset. I never met with a more pleasing young man, in regard to the universal knowledge he had acquired, and the total absence of conceit notwithstanding. I thought it a great undertaking for Lady Sheffield to descend the pit, 330 feet in a low bucket, but I was very glad she did, as the sight underground amply repaid the trouble and risk. . . . I am afraid the good folks will depart long before we are tired of them. I believe we shall usher them as far as Manchester and see the lions there, but no farther. . . . Rianette is a great favourite with grandpapa, and he is disposed to spoil her prodigiously, which the little villain has discovered, and whenever I am out of the room coaxes him to do all the possible things which I don't allow. . . . And now adieu. If you will write very soon and ask all sorts of questions about all sorts of things, I will incontinently send you a categorical answer. Poor me has quite lost the talent of writing, from shameful disuse. Once more, adieu.

M. J. S. to Louisa (after her visit to Manchester with her father and Lady Sheffield).

Alderley Park: September 1800.

I never saw anything that gave me such satisfaction as the jail at Manchester. The attention to the management of the interior of the prison is so well directed that I imagine very few equal it. There was a melancholy number of young boys there; but in one of the parts of the prison we went into unexpected, there was a man, one of the prisoners, teaching them to read. The governor told us it was regularly done every day, and that many young people who came in totally ignorant went out able to read, and instructed in the Catechism by the minister, who reads prayers and lectures twice a week, besides Sundays. Besides this instruction, they are kept so constantly employed that they cannot be discharged from prison worse members of society than they came in. They are likewise, if they behave well, allowed a third of their earnings on leaving prison, therefore are not tempted to return to their old practices from pressure of want.

Lady Sheffield to M. J. S.

Halifax: September 28, 1800, 5 o'clock.
'In the worst inn's worst room, with mat half-hung,' &c.[1]

We found the roads so hopelessly bad that we did not arrive at Huddersfield till half-past five o'clock. I really thought our crazy equipage and my crazy back must have broken to pieces; the jolts were beyond all imagination, and when we got to our destination, our host came out to receive us and informed us that he had waited till his dinner was spoilt, and then, despairing of our arrival, he and his friends had sat down and devoured it! I confess this news appalled me, for I was almost famished; however, I had to submit to fate and Mr. Atkinson, who handed me into his drawing-room, which was filled with ladies who were filled with the dinner of which I ought to have had my share. I was presented to them all in turn, but the only names I could distinguish were Mrs. Tinkler, my sister; Miss Tinkler, my niece; Mrs. Atkinson, my daughter-in-law; Mrs. Edwards, her mother-in-law; Miss Firth, my niece, &c. I believe there were a dozen of them, dressed out in long drop-earrings and covered with necklaces. I took the first opportunity of sitting down in a corner by ' my sister Tinkler,' who, if I had not been informed of her relationship, I should have taken for 'my good old nurse Tinkler.' In this manner we sat conversing about the jolting roads and the bad harvest, till it was quite dark. At last I heard a clattering of plates, and there arrived the remains of a half-cold boiled chicken and some hot mutton chops. I think I never was so happy in my life as at their entrance, and I eat and drank till I

---

[1] Pope's *Moral Essays*, iii. 299.

was equal to listening to the account of all the Norwich balls, related by Miss Firth, a young lady of that town, who danced at the last ball with a Mr. Stoven, who did not speak a word to her though she had been told he was very clever, and she happened to say to a friend of hers that Mr. Stoven might be very facetious, but she could not find it out; and, do you know, she told this to him again, which was so provoking, was not it? Mrs. Edwards had married a man who had a cousin married to a man who knew Mr. Groves, so we had a great deal to say upon that subject; and Mrs. Tinkler thought a little warm *punch* and wrapping yourself up warm in your night *gownd*, going to bed, was the best thing for a cold. . . .

The next morning we went over Mr. A.'s manufactory, and then dined with a Mr. Whitacre, a very gentlemanlike man. They asked us to stay all night, and so we did, and I am sure it was lucky for us, for we should otherwise have slept here. We set out from Mr. Whitacre's very early this morning, and arrived here in time for me to go to church, and his lordship to visit Mr. Lees, a friend he met with at Mr. A.'s. When I came home I found there were no horses to be got in the town, and we are condemned to wait here till midnight. His lordship is returned from Mr. Lees', and, in a fit of despair at being kept in this horrid inn, has sent for the landlord and asked him if he knew of anybody of the name of Holroyd in the town, and he has discovered to his great joy that there is a Jeremiah Holroyd, a woolstapler, and we are actually in the middle of a dispute whether Jeremiah shall be sent for to comfort us. I confess my opinion is that his company is by no means necessary; but his lordship finds he cannot do without him; so poor Jeremy is sent for.

I can assure you I was very sorry to leave you, and shall always think with the greatest pleasure of my visit and with the greatest gratitude of the kindness I received both from you and Mr. Stanley. It is now eight o'clock. No tidings of any horses—not one to be got in the town—and poor Jeremy has sent word that he is too ill to come out; so we must make up our minds to sleeping in this wretched place, and not seeing poor Jeremy. I wish I could reconcile myself to the one misfortune as easily as I can make up my mind to the other! His lordship's best love.

Yours most affectionately,

A. S.

[The inquiries after ' poor Jeremy,' however, appear not to have been without results.]

Benjamin Holroyd to Lord Sheffield.

Honoured Sir,—I hope you will excuse me for making an address to your lordship. By the advice of some gentleman with whom I was acquainted, I sent you a letter about six months ago and desired your answer, but perhaps might not come to your lordship's hand. My reason for troubling you is this. I was informed that you was down in Yorkshire some time since, but understands your stay was very short. I was told your honour called upon one Jeremiah Holroyd ; he is my own uncle. I was also told that your lordship was then making inquiry for an heir to enjoy the honour of your lordship's title. Some time after, I was advised to send you a few lines to give you a true account of the same, which was thought might give your lordship some satisfaction ; so now I'll inform you as follows : viz. my grandfather's name was Benjamin Holroyd, having three sons, Michael, Elkanah, and Jeremiah. Michael was the oldest brother, and I'm his oldest son ; my name is Benjamin Holroyd, and lives in Halifax, Yorkshire. The above is a true account, hoping it may satisfy your lordship. I understand your lordship is related to the Holroyds, and believe myself to be the nearest heir. And if you should consider any time to dispose of whatever you think proper either to me or mine, I shall esteem it as one of the greatest favours, and always acknowledge myself humbly thankful.

Please to answer this the first favourable opportunity,

and direct ' For Benjamin Holroyd, Innkeeper at Boars Head, Corn Market, Halifax, Yorkshire.'

Sir, I'm your most obedient and humble servant,

BENJAMIN HOLROYD.

M. J. S. to Serena.

Alderley Park : October 6, 1800.

I suppose you now comfortably settled at S. P., and must write to congratulate you thereon ; likewise to mention we are all alive and well, which is about the sum total of events that I have to relate. What a fool of a thing human nature is ! I did not like to be always going out, and in a bustle, and thought I should be mighty glad when we were quite quiet again ; and now we are so, I think it is rather dull, and am considering what a long dreary winter there is between the present time and the chance of seeing any beings but our neighbours. . . . I depend, however, on seeing you here, I hope, in the spring. . . . I heard this morning from Lady Sheffield at Doncaster. . . . I do hope my lord will soon get a secretary, for he does employ all the poor lady's time terribly, and has gained so many new correspondents at Liverpool, and so much information to disperse, that there is no end of his epistles. I have taken to her, more in this visit than ever ; she is, indeed, a most amiable woman, but has such an extremely humble opinion of herself that it is necessary to be very thoroughly acquainted with her to discover her high merits. . . . I suppose you have been told the old rogue has commenced his career as justice of peace, which finds him plenty of employment. You will have a vast deal to see next year, and such a walk as will be quite after your own heart, with seats near the house. . . . I long to hear from you all about S. P., the little kittens, the old cat, and the pussery preparing at Clinton Lodge. I hear you are soon to have the delectable company of Lady E. Foster and the little Caroline. I don't think Lady S. is much fonder of her or more bewitched by her charms than I am.

Yours ever affectionately, M. J. S.

M. J. S. to Serena.

November 2, 1800.

It is terrible gloomy weather, for it has been raining and snowing without ceasing; and if there were ropes enough in the kingdom, all placed in tempting situations with convenient nooses, up and down the country, I should be surprised any English man or woman in the Campagne abstained from hanging themselves. Long evenings are not pleasant. When I am read to by the Man I want nothing, not even the opera; but headache often interferes. Oh! that Sir John was in Abraham's bosom, for he gives him nine out of ten headaches!

The price of every article has gone up very high indeed, and I do not wonder the patience of the poor should be exhausted. They are, however, quiet and uncomplaining in this parish. At Macclesfield they have been very troublesome on market days. In consequence, the farmers do not take their corn and potatoes where they are likely to be insulted and their property taken by force, which is, of course, a great inconvenience to the inhabitants.

As your letters are, like mine, worth four or five of any other person's, I wish to procure myself one of these valuables; though Louisa is, for her, very good, and really sent me several marriages and some divorces, and, wonderful to relate, said a good deal about her own little child. My sweet little Lou Dolly is the liveliest-looking animal you ever saw; she will almost talk by the time you come. . . . I wrote to Miss Huff to bespeak her as soon as ever she can find it convenient to leave home. . . . I long for her among the children, now that they are growing more intelligent. What would I give in another year for such a person to be about Rianette and Lucy! I am not equal to having them all day with me, nor have I patience to teach. I speak very feelingly just now, for Lucy has been plaguing me with questions without end, and now I have exchanged her for Rianette, and have not mended myself one bit.

CHAPTER IV.

ON THE THRESHOLD OF A NEW CENTURY.

1801.

Bread and beer limitations—' Growlery '—The Queen of the Feast—Three little fairies—Medusa wigs—A miniature Serena—Mr. Pelham's marriage—' Yet another girl '—The host alone survives—Good news by the coach—*Patte de velours*—Princess Charlotte's cleverness—Bishop of Killala—The Duchess of York and Hannah More.

M. J. S. to Louisa.

1801.

I will be obliged to you to recollect if there are not a good many more events which you dare say I have heard, but which nevertheless I am as ignorant of as if I lived in the moon, and, to be sure, Cheshire is very near as much out of the way. . . . I like to be *au courant* of how the world of which I know anything goes on or off, and yet it is something like servants or common people in general who always are in such haste to communicate melancholy or bad news, saying ' I thought you would be glad to hear it, ma'am, for it is a very melancholy thing,' &c. . . . . Now as to bread. I cannot find it in my heart to spoil good flour with putting such a quantity of rice into it as you mentioned. Mrs. Crooky Johnson sent me some made with one pound of rice to four of flour. Nothing could be better mixed, not a particle of rice was visible ; but it gave the bread a sweet taste and a dampness. I have put the family on their allowance of a quartern loaf, which I am glad to find is quite sufficient. It is not till Christmastide is over that I can confine our consumption to as many quartern loaves as persons in the family, because of the several dinners we have at this time of year. We had yesterday our labourers' dinner—thirty-three personages. We have made some additional regulations about ale

P

and beer which caused a little growlery at first, but the insurrection was very trifling and soon appeased. It is not allowed for ale to appear on any occasion of gentlemen's servants or others having refreshment, which was the principal cause of lamentation among the male part of the family.

Our own people have a pint each on Sundays, the housekeeper's room have half a pint every evening to supper ; and the washing days the maids are allowed a pint each. Small beer, which was very good and went very fast, has undergone a limitation. A load of malt used to be brewed every fortnight. It is now only to be brewed every three weeks, and it makes rather more than a hundred gallons. We have been mighty comfortable lately, i.e. not stirred from home. The Man execrates all dinners at this time of year. I try to combat a too great love of the fireside, not merely to support a wife's privilege of contradiction, but that folks may not think us savagely despising them and their society. Lord, have mercy upon us ! When will this letter come to a conclusion ?

You may well suppose the seedcorn has cost a mint of money. Oats are 10s. a bushel, and it takes ten bushels to sow a Cheshire acre; yet I hope our capital buried in the ground will be returned with interest.

M. J. S. to Louisa.

. . . It is not what my ' lazy servants ' tell me, but what others have tried, and I have tasted : and we have at home mixed ground rice with the best success. I do therefore assert as positively as your ladyship the contrary, that there is no doubt ground rice is better than whole, all but the additional expense, viz. $\frac{1}{2}d$. per lb., which I am very glad to hear may be saved by the use of a coffee-mill. I must exculpate my poor female servants, to whose lot breadmaking falls, from the charge of being lazy or of having little to do. The men have certainly as little to employ their time about, except fiddling, fluting, cobbling, and car-

pentering for their own amusement, as any men in the kingdom; and if you can mention any precedent or give me any
hopes of success if I request either the groom, the coachman,
the footman, George Blackbeard or old Mr. Radcliffe, to knead
dough, I shall be quite happy to make the attempt, and the
rice shall be insinuated grain by grain. But cast not your
evil reflections in the meantime on my damsels! I have no
dairymaid, and Hassall and the kitchenmaid are not a little
employed in cooking for the poor, the labourers, and eighteen
school children that frequently come twice a week to eat
their dinner here. . . . I could enumerate several other em-
ployments they have, but I dare say you have got enough for
the present, and so adieu.

Serena to M. J. S.

Wednesday, January 21, 1801.

. . . Our Christmas at Sheffield Place was after my own
heart, and your ball [1] was really the happiest thing of the sort
I ever saw. How we did wish you to pop in! I must inform you it gave me spirits to dance one dance down twenty
couples, as gaily as ever I did in my life. It was quite a
pretty scene, the hall pillars all festooned with wreaths of
variegated holly &c. If you had seen us at supper and heard
120 of us all joining in loud chorus of ' God save the King,'
after drinking you as Queen of the Feast, it would have done
you good. . . .

M. J. S. to Serena.

Alderley Park : January 25, 1801.

Dearest Mrs. Aunt,—A great many thanks for your
letter. I thought you were to spend rather more time in
London, and I would not bother Lady Sheffield about my
cotton in the midst of her princess, her birthday, and her
Cape of Good Hope sister [Lady Glenbervie], and yet I
believe you were as fully employed during your week.
Though I need no fresh proof of your holding me in

---

[1] Given January 3 in honour of the birthday of M. J. S.

remembrance, yet I do take so kindly to receiving marks of affection that had you only sent me a wooden tray I should have felt gratified ; but in sending me a Wedgwood supper tray, you have chanced to hit upon one of the few things I wished for and had not. One of these little dears will be particularly convenient to us, as I always have the supper brought as much as possible all together on a little round table to avoid bustle and fuss. . . . I quite long for you to enjoy our nice home, walks, arbours, and seats. I shall be very cross if it does not prove a fine summer, for it will be so funny to see the three little fairies running about on the hill among the flowers. Rianette and I get on tolerably well, considering my want of patience and her want of application in b–a ba, and a–b ab. I have got a delightful new-invented spelling book, and expect a new-invented spelling box, which makes these studies much easier than before. You can easily know if Louisa has them ; if not, I wish you would get for me, for her, the 'Doll's Library' and Mrs. Teachwell's 'Spelling Books.'

Louisa to M. J. S.

February 1801.

A great many thanks for the 'Doll's Library' and the spelling book, which will be very useful, as Lou has nothing of the kind in town, and I must soon begin to 'larn' her a little. . . .

What do you think I did Sunday? Augusta seduced me by giving me two tickets and persuading me to use one myself for Lady Dashwood's masquerade; and so— never having been at one, and thinking I might never have a better opportunity—I gave my other ticket to Caroline Lyttelton, and I was in for it among all the fools till half-past four.

Lest I should forget fashions, I hope you country folks are not so vulgar as to fancy white arms pretty ; the beauties all have something round the middle of their arms,

where the sleeve ends, so extremely tight that the arm looks
like raw beef. You have probably read in the papers of the
' Medusa wigs ' which are worn.   Some of the women
seem to fasten their hair with a dagger. By the time you
return to the civilised world, I think you may hope for
much amusement in the fashion.

Mrs. John Villiers was lately walking about in Brighton
in a muslin gown over a pair of grey pantaloons tied at the
ankle with black twist, like those you may have seen William
have !

O that I had a few people about me with but an atom of
soul ! I shall begin to think it a bad thing to give a girl an
idea beyond following the Ten Commandments and dressing
in the fashion, as one a little more improved must be so
continually disgusted in after-life.

I suppose you have heard from Privy Gardens of
Mr. Pelham and Lord Glenbervie being engaged in the
new administration. I rejoice at the first for the sake
of the nation, and the last for Lady Sheffield, who is over-
joyed.

M. J. S. to Louisa.

Alderley Park : March 8, 1801.

How very much I should like to be in town this extraordinary spring, and hear what folks say of the singular
events of the present crisis. The accounts of the king's
health seem very favourable, and I wish a regency may be
dispensed with; but how or which way shall we get
out of this *embrouillement* of ministers and no ministers,
Papists and Protestants ? I forget if you share William's
horror in regard to the danger of Catholic encroachments.
I do not think they are now much to be feared ; the Man
leans very much towards the side of Mr. Pitt in this question,
and upon the whole is more inclined to think well of him
now than heretofore. I am of opinion that the matter
should have been well considered before the Union, and

before any promises were made—and that it is now not
subject to be debated.   Is Horne Tooke[1] to remain
Parliament or not? The circumstances of his getting th
are curious enough; and I hope he will be reputed eligib
that we in the country may have the amusement of !
speeches.

I was very glad to hear from you this morning.   Lit
Dolly has always walked just like Aunt Serena, to Fole
and my great amusement.   Instead of putting out her ha
like most children, she tucks her elbows into her sides, a
trots away in a most famous waddle; she has scarce e
fallen but with the assistance of her sisters, who are apt
overlook and run over her, and she is always disposed to
one of the party.   I, or I should say we, have been extrem
pleased with Wraxall's ' Memoirs of Continental Courts.'
is a book which some day or other must be added to
collection.   One would think the time of which he tre
must be at a much greater distance than thirty years.   H
like an impossibility would have appeared to Maria Ther
a prophecy of Marie Antoinette's end, at the mom
when she had gratified her utmost wishes for her worl
welfare by an alliance with France!

Louisa to M. J. S.

March 18, 1801

I shall hope for no good, either public or private, if N
Pitt comes in again, which I much fear he will.   On t
particular subject of Catholic Emancipation I am sorry
be obliged to doubt whether he may not be right.   For thou,
I hope I am a *good* wife, I never can bring myself to th
necessary perfection of an excellent one, thinking it i
possible for my husband to be mistaken like any other fr
human creature, and consequently defending to the dea
every opinion he chances to hold, were it to change eve
fortnight. . . .

[1] Political writer, 1736–1812. The trial of Tooke, Hardy, Joyce, Thelwr
and others on a charge of constructive high treason caused a great sensatic
They were taken into custody May 1794.

Emancipation may be necessary, but till the question is better understood I must doubt whether politically it may not be as dangerous as religiously it would be indifferent ; for it is little to be expected that the R.C.s would be satisfied without still more essential advantages.

Your Man, who likes truth and justice, and has no estates in Ireland, may say the avarice of individuals should be sacrificed for the good of the whole. . . . I agree with you in thinking Mr. Pitt by no means so blameable in this instance as the general cry would make him, as I have no doubt he meant rightly, and it seems doubtful whether he did not *judge* equally so ; but still I rejoice that anything should pull him from that gigantic and arrogant height of popularity to which he had ascended on the ruin of Europe and the incapacity of his countrymen.

Serena to M. J. S.

Lincoln : March 18, 1801.

I feel nearer to you here than when in London, and yet I have so little dependence on cross posts that I may just as well save your pennies and send this to town to be posted, particularly as I dare say you have heard my adventures. To say truth, I have felt a kind of remorse and twitch at my heart that I hardly ever felt before, from the very affectionate alarm that all seem to have had at this exploit of mine. Lady Sheffield tells me that on receiving my take-leave note and finding me *gone*, my brother, contrary to his usual custom of concealing his feelings, burst into tears and was wretched till he heard I had got as far as Peterborough and not the worse for the journey.   Poor Lou dined with them the day I went, and cried instead of eating.   The good-natured Lady S. kept her company.   In short, I was very wrong, but I really was so long ill, that in despair I determined to try change of air ; and having once taken leave, when my illness stopped me, I did not like to do all that over again, and was sure they would not consent to my going, as I seemed indeed very unfit to travel.   I therefore did steal away, and though it has ended happily in my being restored to health, I certainly never will serve them so again. Most assuredly I should leave them with sincere regret at any time, and never was I more happy in my life, nor could anything exceed their kindness. I have been fortunate in being safe at Lincoln before all this snow fell, and worse roads, except in Sussex, I never beheld. Of the wildness of the country it may give you some idea when I tell you that within four or five miles of Lincoln there is a *lighthouse* to direct the travellers that they may not be absolutely lost. . . . Here we are situated at the top of a high hill, quite out of the town of Lincoln, overlooking the country; and with good prebendal houses and gardens, we enjoy a fine, pure air and the most exquisitely beautiful cathedral possible to imagine. It is called the wife of York Minster, as more elegant and even more beautifully ornamented, but not so vast. It was very near being burnt down just before I came, by the carelessness of a plumber, who left a candle in the steeple, and it was in flames. Had they reached the great bell so as to make it drop, the mischief done would have been irreparable, but the fire was discovered in time. The Coxes are most happily settled here. . . . Dr. Paley and family are now our next-door neighbours, and he is uncommonly lively and pleasant. Dr. and Mrs. Pretyman [1] are also very agreeable, and I meet the Dean, Sir R. Page, the members of the county, and a Dr. Herbert, who gives me a power over his fine library. I have promised not to leave till May; then I belong to you for the rest of my rambles from home, and much delight am I sure of, with all my dear Stanleys, great and small. I went a few days ago to Castle Howard, which reminded me of Blenheim on first entering the house, and would alarm me to live in, though I should greatly like a lodge in the beautiful woods and grounds. What, however, was to me the greatest treat was a new acquisition of pictures from the Orleans Gallery, added to the fine collection before.

[1] Bishop of Lincoln, 1787–1820.

M. J. S. to Serena.

Alderley Park: March 29, 1801.

Indeed, I was very happy to receive your letter from Lincoln, and to hear that your extraordinary *échappée* from Privy Gardens had not produced any bad effect on your body; neither did it appear that your poor mind and brain were so much deranged as I at first agreed with his lordship in supposing they must be. Seriously however, I am glad you went as you did, all but the occult mode of it, which I do not like at all; for now suppose you had become, as Lucy calls it, dead and killed and put into a big hole— don't you think it would have been very disagreeable to recollect they did not even shake hands and say ' God bless you!' at departure? However, if you were determined to go— and I believe you judged right in leaving the smoke of the metropolis as soon as possible—perhaps you took the only means of carrying your purpose into execution; as, with milord's opinion of the insanity of the measure, he might possibly have had recourse to a strait waistcoat. I shall be impatient to show you all the creations at Alderley. If we might have a tolerable summer I think it might be good economy to let all but the bedrooms, as I expect to be so little in the house during the day that it will be quite extravagant keeping parlours in use. . . . Little Lou Dolly is a sweet love, a countenance and gestures of extreme intelligence. She has been thought very like you by others who have seen her, as well as Foley and myself. She has certainly a Holroyd countenance : grey eyes, which the others have not, with dark Stanley accompaniments of brows and lids, and the shape of the face is like. She has, moreover, the Holroyd space between her upper front teeth in full perfection; but, notwithstanding my regard for the family, if you please, I should wish that to be rectified in her new edition of pegs. Now I think I have given you a full account of the little animals; I need only add, the great animals, their papa and mama, are likewise very well, and much the same in every respect as when you left them in

August 1798, and except a desirable perfectibility in goodness and knowledge which they may annually wish to acquire, that they may for many years continue in the same *statu quo* of calm enjoyment of life, without experiencing great calamities, is the prayer in which you are requested to join with your most affectionate   M. J. S.

M. J. S. to Louisa.

Alderley Park: March 30, 1801.

I have never seen the 'Pleasures of Hope.' I have tried to get it two or three times from Hookham, without success. He is a tiresome old dog about these little things; he should send for new copies of what he has not by him. Five of your books, 'Robinson Crusoe,' two Hannah More's, and two volumes of 'Parent's Assistant' were given yesterday at the boys' school as prizes. If you had seen, as I did, a poor girl, daughter to a very small farmer who works as day labourer here, reading 'Calisthenes' Reproof to Alexander,' I am sure you would feel great pleasure in having assisted to procure them more suitable studies. . . .

I am quite delighted with Mr. Pelham's [1] match. I always fixed upon Lady Mary Osborne for him, and I wonder what the foolish man has been so long about in finding out that she might suit him.

Isa and Lou Stanley to M. J. S. (after the birth of her fourth daughter).

Grosvenor Place: June 15, 1801.

Dear Maria,—It was so long since we had heard from you that merely seeing your handwriting would have been a treat had the letter only conveyed the intelligence of your welfare; but though I wish it had been more satisfactory as to the kind of article, you begin by finding merits in this

[1] Hon. T. Pelham, their agreeable fellow-traveller when the Sheffield Place party were in Paris, 1791, on their way to Lausanne. He succeeded his father as 2nd Lord Chichester; he married Mary, daughter of 5th Duke of Leeds.

nice babe to make up for the disappointment she has caused.
I hope she will make a strong body with her sisters to guard
the four noses from being distorted by dislocation, which
must take place when the long-expected brother does arrive.
Edward came off honourably at St. John's, and intends
studying to come off creditably in the Senate House and
obtain a good degree. . . . We are sitting in a room filled
with flowers, and balconies almost vying with your shady
arbours, having high shrubs for a background and shade
from passers-by; sweet mignonette with other gay flowers
in front, and our opposite trees afford us choristers of the
wood, though not at this moment the most harmonious, being
rooks and jackdaws chattering and cawing most vociferously;
so we have the mock rural.

I had almost forgot the cloak for which you wish
instructions. We have a good pattern of one, which is a short
pelisse trimmed with lace. A bedgowny appearance in
morning dress is now the *ton*, and were I a fine-figured
beauty I should adopt it. Headdresses are very little
different to last year; I think, instead of bags, the turbans
have long tails for full dress; the feathers are inclined,
instead of perpendicularly erect. Adieu for the present.

Yours affectionately,
Isa and Lou.

M. J. S. to Louisa.

Alderley Park: June 16, 1801.

I never saw Mrs. Aunt look better than she does, and
I was surprised that she seemed so little fatigued by having
come from York to Manchester in one day. The day after
she arrived here she sallied forth and invaded every part of the
beech-wood, which, though it tired her enough to give one a
good right to swear at her for youthful folly and impetuosity,
did not knock her up as I fully expected.

. . . Mr. Brick came to read the churching; but I have
not had the babe named, as she seems so healthy. I hope
there is no danger of her poor little soul not reaching
heaven by any short delay in baptising her, and Miss

Stanley said Sir John talked of the beginning of July fo
quitting Grosvenor Place. As I think I told you, this lad
will only have a single name, Isabella; and Oswal
Leycester is to be godfather. The three elder misses, hor
shocking a number! are all well.

Isa Stanley to M. J. S.

Grosvenor Place: July 13, 1801.

Dear Maria,—We begin to feel our consciences a littl
galled with the idea of our nameless niece continuing s
long a pagan; and I wish the half-ceremony had beer
performed, lest, contrary to appearances and probabilities
she should slip out of the world in an unbaptised state—not
I think, to the danger of her future welfare, but to the
scandal of the commonalty, who will look on you and us a
demi-pagans to suffer such a shocking thing to be possible.

M. J. S. to Louisa.

August 1801.

I will not believe anything—no, not the testimony
either of my memory or my pocketbook—that says it is three
weeks since I wrote to you. However, more time has
elasped than I intended since I talked to you last; but
sundry things have prevented me, among others the races,
though, thanks to my pagan babe, they have not had the
honour of my attendance to do penance there. But we sent
all the family, which for two days caused me to be nurse in
chief; and who can think of anybody or anything beyond
the extent of one's own farm when the weather is so
heavenly and so propitious? Every appearance promises
plenty: I wish I could see some to promise peace; but Lord
Nelson's expeditions do not meet my approbation, and
hitherto appear calculated to raise the spirits of our enemies
and depress those of our own people.

I begin to be much in fear that on William's return
old England will be still under the direction of Mr. Addington and not of Buonaparte, which must vex him much, for
nobody likes their prognostics to fail entirely. And now

having enraged you completely with my extreme ignorance and consequent impudence of security, I will proceed to something else.

This is a very anxious moment for every one, whether they only love themselves and their near connections, or whether they love their country also; for I feel much inclined to think the next six months may be a very important era in British history. In regard to Aunt, however, if our apprehensions were ever so strong we should conceal them from her; and I dread the words 'Egypt' and 'invasion' beyond anything, lest she should be unpleasantly affected.

Serena to M. J. S.

Bath : September 18, 1801.

. . . Mrs. G. Coxe has a letter from her son, Major Lyon, from Egypt. I will copy an extraordinary paragraph out of his letter :

'On March 20, the day before the desperate attack of the French upon our lines, five officers dined in my tent. We were all in remarkably good spirits. The conversation turned, however, on the uncertainty of our existence, and the little probability of the same party meeting again that day week, for we knew it was intended to advance on the enemy the 23rd. When we parted we agreed to meet again the next day, the 24th. After the action, on entering my tent, I inquired for my friends, and found only *I* had escaped. They were all killed ! Should not such a circumstance inspire a military man with religious awe, and me in particular with gratitude?' This excellent young man is not twenty-five years old.

Yours ever, S. H.

M. J. S. to Louisa.

Alderley : October 4, 1801.

What is anything to the delightful news brought to us by this morning's mail? I suppose you will throw cold water on my transports on account of our promised peace, and say

either that it is not finally settled, or else that the peace
will be a short one; or else, who knows whether the general's
wife may not think, in spite of risk, there is better pickings
in time of war? However, I will rejoice, and I will hope.
The rumour reached us last night. The drivers and guards
of all the coaches were adorned with ribbons; they blew
their horns and dispersed their good news wherever they
passed; the bells were everywhere rung, and even Alderley,
to our great surprise, set up a peal between nine and ten at
night.

Louisa to M. J. S.

October 11, 1801.

What says the Man to our peace? It is surely a fortunate thing that France is governed by a man like Buonaparte, who has moderation to relieve us from such a war,
with a couple of islands in our pockets to put John Bull in
good humour. Dismal as necessity has rendered the peace,
it is absurd in the ministerial papers insisting upon its
being glorious; . . . if it had not been for the fortunate
success of our Egyptian army, how miserably must have
stood the military character of England at the beginning of
the nineteenth century! But I will have done. I wanted to
splutter a little at the folly of the newspapers, and probably of two-thirds of the nation.

M. J. S. to Louisa.

Alderley Park: October 30, 1801.

You are much more outwardly rational than I expected
about peace, and your own fate in consequence. I congratulate you on being delivered of an expression of approbation
relative to the conduct of the Egyptian business; that has
indeed been a theatre of glory for the British army. They
did not meet with an army inferior in number, courage, or
discipline, and the French were certainly more experienced
in fighting, having all served many campaigns. Many of
our soldiers probably saw an enemy for the first time. If

peace is to be received as a blessing, and the terms such as we ought to approve, I suppose we may thank our army in Egypt; for if that enterprise had not been successful, may-hap Buonaparte would not have dealt so leniently by us.

I desire you will always date your letters, that I may know whether you are writing at S. P. or on your own sofa. I am quite happy you have got that same piece of furniture for the sake of past times. When the old man and I are Darby and Joan, we will come to visit you, and you will allow us to sit upon your sofa, and we may talk over many a scene of 'recollected love' before our 'gentle spirits fly to scenes where love and bliss immortal reign.' My virgin tables and chairs, too, I shall like to see in your possession; pray never be too grand to keep them in use, or if you should perchance, sell them to me at a fair price.

Looking over an ancient letter of yours from London, I see you mentioned that you was to hear and see Lady Hamilton at Lady Bath's. You never told me anything more—what did you think of her?

Isa and Lou to M. J. S.

Highlake : October 19, 1801.

Oh happy, happy peace!' Now this is rejoicing without drawback. Our neighbours at Liverpool prefer war to peace, to their shame and sorrow be it spoken. Having no opposite neighbours here on the land-side, and fearing to mislead the pilot in his course should we attempt to rival the lighthouse, we have not shown our joy by illumination, but contented ourselves by ringing the church bells and waving our colours. General Clinton has got his commission just in time, and may sail back again and commence 'farmering'; his Lou will be better pleased that he should handle a ploughshare than a sword. So good-night, and may every happiness follow those two great blessings of peace and plenty, pray your ever affectionate

Isa and Lou.

M. J. S. to Serena.

Alderley Park: October 20, 180

. . . But what are all these people's doings about pe
and plenty to ours? You have seen the Feast of Plenty, a
if you had been here last Saturday you would have witnes
the Feast of Peace. May we never again, however, have
rejoice over peace or plenty in the same way—that is, af
such long suffering of war and scarcity. I must tell y
our opinion exactly coincides with yours on the subj
of the said welcome unexpected peace. Everybody m
rejoice, everybody almost will think the terms as good as
could reasonably expect from such a powerful adversar
but I fancy very few pretend to call it a glorious pea
Buonaparte is a great man, and a hero in my opinic
but anything but a good or principled man. Therefore
think it depends very much upon whether peace or w
suits him best for his private ends whether it is lasting
otherwise. Just now I suppose it flatters his vanity to
called the Pacificator of Europe, and certainly he saw 1
immediate prospect of conquering us. Except, howeve
that I don't like taxes or thousands of men killed, I a
half inclined sometimes to think that war *à toute outran*
might have been safer for us than peace with devils, for
do not imagine them much better yet, and the *patte e
velours* may do more mischief to Old England than tl
griffes découvertes of their double 'Chats d'Enfer.' . . . Bi
really the story of our bonfire and fireworks and our eatin
and drinking may entertain you as well as my politici
reveries. . . . All the labourers, nearly as many as at th
harvest home, sat down to dinner at half-past four o
Saturday last. At six the great bell rung to summon ther
to attend the lighting of the bonfire, and as a signal for th
commencement of the fireworks. The former was a mos
famous stack of faggots and trees, with a tar barrel in th
centre, suspended at the top of a large beam, so you ma
imagine the fine blaze. A barrel of ale was placed by the sid
containing thirty-six gallons, and all comers were welcomec

Three guineas' worth of sky rockets, catherine wheels, and roman candles were let off at intervals. Volleys of musketry were discharged, drums beat, and men shouted. ... At nine there was a supper and punch for the farmers, their wives and daughters, and a dance which lasted till twelve, when as many as were capable of getting home did retire peaceably, but I believe many spent the night under our straw shed. There were fifty gallons of ale drunk in all, and great plenty of beef and plum pudding consumed. . . . All's well that ends well; and I rejoice in the hope that William will soon be at home, and that he brings with him the rank of general.

Lady Sheffield to M. J. S.

Sheffield Place: November 14, 1801.

My dear Mrs. Stanley,—It will be impossible for me to express how very sensibly I feel your kindness and Mr. Stanley's. You were very right in supposing your letter would make me cry, for it certainly made me shed many tears, but they were tears of pleasure, and could therefore be of no bad consequence. It is certain no woman can be a wife without wishing to be a mother, at least according to my way of thinking. . . . I am sure you will believe that my joy on this occasion is much diminished by the idea that a blessing bestowed upon me should in any degree interfere with the future prospects of people I so sincerely love as I do you and Mr. Stanley; and though you despise females, yet if it should please God to bless *me* with a little girl, I certainly shall not mind. . . .

Most sincerely and affectionately yours,

A. SHEFFIELD.

Serena to M. J. S.

Bath: November 13, 1801.

I have had the Princess Charlotte's Miss Hunt in my house: her health made it absolutely necessary for her to stay longer at Bath, and so I took her in for a fortnight.

Q

She is a sweet young woman, full of information, ta
and genius. Miss Hunt has left me, but I know the
thing she had printed for the use of children was an i
duction to Astronomy. It is quite a pity, by-the-bye,
the royal child is not always in such good hands, for s
very clever. One day, after admiring the beauty of (
trees &c. Miss Hunt said, ' *You* know, Princess Charl
that God made them ; but what would you say to any one
took it into their heads that they made themselves ? '
should desire them to go and think,' says the little girl.
who could answer better ? Miss Hunt had a most hands
letter from her royal master, directed with his own l
and sealed by him, giving her leave to stay with her fri
till her health and spirits were restored. What a very pi
hand he writes, and what a pity he *won't* be what he *m*
be ! I suppose you know that the 'Arethusa' sailed
Saturday for Brigadier-General Clinton. He speaki
particular winds being necessary which do not blow
next month, and he has 1,100 men to bring home ; bt
hope the winds will be propitious, and that he maybe at h
before Louisa is confined. It must be a great affron
produce a child and not have a husband to say 'Thank
my love.' . . . Dr. Maclaine comes to me to-morrow
meet the Bishop of Killala [1] whose letter is published v
an account of his spirited behaviour when the French w
at his house in Ireland. The Bishop is a very anime
character. My good Dr. Maclaine, alas ! looks declini
and reminds me but too much of his being eighty yt
old. Yet at times his fire and spirit are still alive. (
evening he and the Wilberforces drank tea with me, i
the conversation was so lively and pleasant, I never thou
of age in the good old man.

Serena to M. J. S.

The last day of the year 180
No, you poor old thing ; though you are married i
live a few hundred miles distant, I will not forget after

[1] Joseph Stock, Bishop of Killala, 1798–1810.

that you were born, and lest you should forget that little circumstance, I intend this remembrance should arrive on the 3rd of January. I shall not indeed celebrate it as we did your last at Sheffield Place, which only wanted you and your dear Man to complete the pleasure of it, but in my heart you will be as warm as you were when numbers joined to do honour to your birth. I have not now, as formerly, wishes to offer up for the improvement, the establishment of Maria Holroyd, but I have for her continued happiness as a wife and mother, and they will never end but with my life. You can't imagine the delight I have in a little trunk full of your letters, some of a long date, and one I was reading directed to me on my own birthday, when you tell me you can't well return the compliment I generally paid you in wishing for your improvement, but that, as I had often said my happiness more or less depended on your conduct, you could not choose a better wish for my birthday than that you should prove all I wished you to be. You dear child : how true is that thought, so well turned and yet so natural as is all you write, which makes the great charm of your letters, though they are besides incomparably expressed. I hope you will some time hence enjoy the pride and pleasure a mother feels when her children are promising to turn out happily. At present they are but playthings; . . . when they become companions and friends, it is then they excite all the interest and anxiety. I can so well conceive that. I can hardly at times believe Louisa and you are not really my own. . . .

I am going to-night to Hannah More, who is ill with the ague and alone. I must tell you a pretty thought of the Duchess of York. She has sent Hannah More a most elegant gold aromatic vinegar-box with her pretty hair in large plaits at the top, and a sweet letter saying she loved to associate the idea of sending what she remembered used to relieve her headaches, with an affectionate token of her highest regard. It was peculiarly well timed, when she knew how cruelly Hannah is attacked. . . .

Q 2

CHAPTER V.

'CAN'T BELIEVE IT.'

1802.

Epitome of education—Storms and wrecks—Ed. Stanley declared Wrangler —Master Holroyd—The royal sponsors—Conway and Menai bridges—(defenders—Joy at Sheffield Place—The guillotine at work—Baron Sheffi of Sheffield—Colonel Clinton's appointment—' Such a piece of news ! ' Heaven bless them ! '—Ann Firth the comforter—Mr. Pitt and Duchess of York attend Dr. Randolph's church.

M. J. S. to Louisa.

Alderley Park : January 3, 1802

I wish either that William was come, or that you wei certain he would not come till the destined hour, and th you knew that hour ; for I think nothing so uncomfortat as the daily, hourly, momentary expectation you must in. . . . I do not give up the idea of a possible visit fro you all next summer. Now I hope no feelings except a fe little tender scruples of trouble, expense, and suchlike, c act either on you or William in the way of keeping y away from Alderley ; but that the attraction is so stron it will be impossible for you to resist its influence. T separation of my animals into two pair will much condu to the quiet and peace of the seven ; besides that, both yo and my eldest will be more manageable and less troublesor than they were two years ago. I long to see the whole ga upon the hill. I must mention that the Man is as desiro of your coming as I am, and does not dread numbers. Y and Lady S. are two ninnies to insist on Baby Lou's beii twice cowpocked. I have had thirty-six children of all ages i oculated in Alderley within the last month, and all doing we

Poor old me! I wish myself, however, a great many more happy birthdays, and hope I shall grow a great deal older, though not happier, for in this world I should be frightened at being much happier!

January 21, 1802.

A very good child you was to mention books to me; mind you always pick up knowledge in that way when you can. I have not got Miss Hamilton's two volumes yet. The first is, I think, by far the most sensible work upon Education I have seen, and by no means difficult of comprehension to middling capacities. Such, however, have so little business to study any system of education, or, if they do, are so little likely to make any hand of it, that it is rather a good thing when a work of the kind is in language above their comprehension, that the few ideas they have may not be bothered. It would be a happy thing for the community at large if nine-tenths of the young gentlemen and ladies who are turned out into the world, thoroughly well educated, had never been taught more than to write a good hand, read their Bible, be taught what some would call a 'religion of prejudice'—by which I mean, not led to make inquiries, which has mischievous effects on ordinary minds—the Hes to be instructed in regard to the profession they are about to enter, and the Shes made perfect in plain work.

I am writing in the midst of such tempests and storms that the barn only can stand unmoved in the commotion.

Alderley: January 28, 1802.

I am sure you and Miss Huff have bewailed our misfortunes in Thursday's storm. You can sympathise with the groans of the forest, and are ready to shed tears with our unhappy hamadryads. I went with great anxiety to see if your tree with the sunny seat was safe, and was right glad to see it unhurt. The trees on the Edge are tossed about in a most curious manner, and scarce a fir has

escaped without some wound. We rode a tour of the
estate the next day, and saw nothing but mischiefs, which,
however, all hide their diminished heads before the thirty
trees in the park. . . .

Lou Stanley to M. J. S.

January 28, 1802.

Oh dear ! Oh dear ! What a pitiless storm to have no
mercy on the fine, dear beeches, the king of birches, and
the stacks that had been built with so much rejoicing ;
however, you are doing all you can to supply the loss by
planting. We heard of this calamity from Edward,[1] who
showed the letter to my father. He read it more than once,
and seemed very sorry. Edward is not a little pleased at
his labours being crowned with success beyond his hopes,
in being declared a Wrangler, of which there are only
sixteen ; so he is one of the sixteen wisest students of the
university. We have just had a letter from Penrhos ; the
storm was earlier there than with you. My mother[2]
mentions the wreck in the harbour, which first struck on a
rock under Llanfawr, and another wreck at Towyn y Capel,
where St. Winifred landed before her head was cut off.
You know she ran after it as it rolled down the hill at
Holywell, where I believe it was put on again by a pious
man, and a spring rose where the head stopped, which cures
lameness. A Dutch vessel was wrecked under Penrhos ;
some of the crew were dead, some brought on shore and
revived at the kitchen fire.

M. J. S. to Louisa.

Alderley Park: March 7, 1802.

I am very glad to hear Lady Willes is to be godmother :[3]
I rejoice to hear of everything that connects your family
and her more together. . . . I saw about William's fine

[1] Afterwards Bishop of Norwich.
[2] Margaret Owen, Lady Stanley, was accustomed to fly to the help of crews
on noticing signals of distress. She eventually met with a serious accident
while helping the sufferers when a vessel was wrecked on her rocks.
[3] Henry Clinton, born February 1802.

sword in the newspapers, and was gratified by the complimentary expressions addressed to him. I wonder Mrs. Dawkins should wish a French governess. I had much rather my four daughters—or my fourteen, if I should have so many—should speak French with an accent somewhat less correct, and be more secure that their principles were perfectly so.

I have a commission or two for you. I enclose a bit of my hair for you to hand over to Marshall as a pattern for a fillet of hair for the front; I have cut off my tail for comfort, and as my front hair is always coming out of curl in the damp summer evenings, and as I find everybody sports a false *toupée*, I don't see why I should not have the comfort of one too. I wish it to be fashionable and as deceiving as possible.

Send me a cap for Rianette, whom I mean to shave when the warm weather comes.

M. J. S. to Serena.

Alderley Park : March 1802.

And so Master Holroyd is arrived ![1] I hope like me you are well content now suspense and anxiety and doubt are at an end, and I am sure, like me, your first idea was pleasure that the dear lady had got over her business so well. . . . Prince and princess sponsors he is to have, and most assuredly it is decided we do not visit London this year. If we can persuade William and Louisa to move towards us in a patriarchal way, I shall be very well content to remain fixed here. My lord's letters have been very natural and unaffected, just as he ought to write upon the subject. I think myself lucky to be out of the way of congratulations and condolences. What delightful accounts we have of Louisa and her boy! Well, I hope my turn will come next, if I am not hoping for a curse instead of a blessing; and, to be sure, it is a great matter of uncertainty, which a son and heir may prove.

[1] George Augustus, 2nd Earl of Sheffield, born March 16, 1802.

Isa Stanley to M. J. S.

Grosvenor Place: March 23, 1802.

. . . But here have I talked of all these minor concerns, without one consolatory word on the little lord in Privy Gardens. Why would he not be a girl, instead of what Ralph Leycester calls ' an unnecessary little boy ' ? But here he is, and all one can now say is, May you be happy with what cannot be intercepted ! Nobody can suppose him very welcome to you, but all give you just credit for the manner in which you have expressed yourself on this trying occasion.

Lady Sheffield to M. J. S.

April 10, 1802.

My dear Mrs. Stanley,—I received your very kind letter when my eyes were weak, and I was not allowed to write or read, or I should certainly have told you before how very sincerely obliged to you I felt for writing it. I can hardly believe it possible that I have got a child and that I am alive and well. I thank God he is very healthy and now begins to look more like a Christian. He will not deserve that name till Thursday, when we are to have a grand fuss. The Prince and Princess of Wales are to be godfather and godmother, and if they both stand in person, I wonder what will become of me ? I fear I shall not be equal to having a ' scene ' in my drawing-room, though I suppose it is what I ought to wish for; for as the prince knows the princess is to be here, he certainly will not come unless he wishes to meet her.

Ever most affectionately yours,

A. SHEFFIELD.

Miss Ann Firth to M. J. S.

April 1802.

Mrs. Clinton is writing, and she will inform you of the disappointment when every eye was turned to the door in expectation of the princess—behold ! her bedchamber woman

Mrs. Lisle entered, to the great dismay of the company, with excuses that her Royal Highness was prevented by indisposition ; she was bled at four o'clock, and was too unwell to come.   His lordship and Lady Glenbervie had been waiting some time in his lordship's room to be ready, and Colonel Clinton to carry the lights.   Lady Sheffield stood for her Royal Highness and his lordship for the Prince, and Mr. F. North for his brother.

There were only relations present, except Miss Vernons. The prince it was not expected would go ; for he has never wished to meet the princess anywhere, therefore he certainly would not in a small circle and on such an occasion.   The child is called George Augustus Frederick Charles.   The Bishop of Winchester performed the ceremony.   Mrs. Holroyd looked very well, and had on a new muslin gown, made for the occasion by Madame Friand.   This is what I have heard of the day.

A. FIRTH.

Isa Stanley to M. J. S.

Grosvenor Place : April 11, 1802.

I think I told you the petitions for the bridges—one over Conway and one over the Menai—were signed by my father.   The Carnarvon people are very strongly opposed to this bridge on account of the navigation, which the Bridgeites say will not suffer, as the arch will be sufficiently high to admit vessels at full sail that can pass the heights. Rennie is now surveying the coast.   Mr. Assheton Smith strongly opposes the bridge and proposes to remove the packets to Porth yn Lleyn, in Carnarvonshire.   If that harbour is a good one, and if the road is made good, and if I preferred three additional leagues of sea to thirty miles on land, and if I was often going to Ireland, I should vote for it. But, as I am not, I hope Porth yn Lleyn is a bad harbour, that the road cannot be made to it, and that the bridge will be built over the Menai, and the packets remain at Holyhead ; for certainly your future property must suffer if the mail

coaches, the travellers, and the road are lost. . . . Edward
will be here next week. He has now no dry study, but must
attend a certain number of divinity lectures *pro formâ*. His
tour is in agitation.

M. J. S. to Louisa.

Alderley Park : June 6, 1802.

I positively have not written since last Sunday, which
furnished me with more of an event than our usual course
of sleeping, eating, and walking usually does. The 42nd
Regiment were on their march through the town on
Saturday, and the sudden thought arose it was right and
proper to pay some attention to our brave defenders.
S. called on the commanding officer, made his speech and
invitation for next day, which was graciously accepted.
Accordingly six officers, four of whom had been in Egypt,
came to dine. We got as many people to meet them as we
could in so short a time, and as good a dinner as Hassall
and I could compose for an impromptu, and had really a very
pleasant party. The Colonel was a crosspatch of a stupid
old fellow as ever was, contradicted every word the others
spoke, and I wished him in Egypt again ; but the others
were sensible men, tolerably communicative in regard to the
country and natives, but not fond of talking about their
battles. I thought of the famous day when the Invincible
Standard was taken by them.

. . . I think I like the shape of the three-guinea mug
much better than the other, which looks as like a porter pot
as it can stare. Pray have engraved upon it ' L. A. S., June
30, 1802,' in a little oval, and take care to have it done before
that date. You know this is the grandmama Sheffield's
present. . . .

My box is arrived. The wig is the comfort of my life.

Lord Sheffield to M. J. S.

Whitehall : June 25, 1802.

I was glad to see the dear Ria's manuscript. The Man
does well to amuse himself not only with the ideal but with

the actual providing for the defence of the nation. The original conscript measure—which I stated to be as inadequate in respect of the object as the means were oppressive—was greatly softened from the first intention ; and although that circumstance was not answered in the House of Lords, it was stated by the Secretary at War to the Commons. The original project was not to have any exemptions. You now observe all are to be exempted who have a child under ten years old. Tell the Man I am somewhat appeased by finding there is some other great project behind, not yet matured, that will be something like a real militia, not liable to be called from home until the enemy actually lands, and in this he may be useful. I have been occupied by a great degree of fever ever since the surrender of the Hanoverian army. The immense team of artillery, horses, &c. were captured by the French without the least effort of any kind on the part of this country. The most obvious of all things would have been to have sent immediately on determining on war, transports to Stadt to bring away the army. It was publicly known at Paris and here that Hanover would be attacked immediately on the commencement of the war. Just at the time the army surrendered we were beginning to think of sending transports to bring them away. The same tardiness, the same inertness may bring our militia into the same situation. I have much to say to the Man : but I never was so worried with business in my life.

Yours ever, S.

Sheffield Place : June 26, 1802.

I write incessantly, because privilege of franking will cease most probably on Tuesday next. We arrived safe—six maids in the new coach (which is as smart as possible), three more in an hack chaise, and my lord, my lady, the young nobleman and nurse in my chaise ; but Muff, the favourite dog, was fortunately forgot. As soon as we entered Sussex we were accosted in every village by personages with congratulatory handbills. When we arrived here, instead of assisting the family, we were infested with a triple discharge of artillery, and the parish bells seemed to ring all night and this day. . . . Very dear Ria, your S.

Lou Stanley to M. J. S.

Grosvenor Place: July 9, 1802.

In spite of all Edward's exertions he has not been able to get a sight of the chief consul. He has taken his station opposite his box at the opera, has attended the relieving guard early and late, and has taken various measures within Paris, all in vain. He has been told by Englishmen that the people have gained by the revolution; but the few natives he dare speak to on the subject vehemently deny the fact. Chantilly is converted into a public tea-garden; the Duc de Montmorenci's château and garden likewise, and he has been told the duke often frequents the spot. The Baron of Montpelier told us that most of the nobles' hôtels in Paris, *ci-devant* private property, are now made *hôtels garnis.* The term 'citoyen' is only used by the soldiers to those not of their own cloth. 'Monsieur' is the universal appellation of other ranks of people towards each other, and of late they have resumed the old-fashioned custom of pulling off their hats when they accost each other. 'Place de Louis' is now 'Place de la Concorde.' . . . Gaming is the ruling passion from the highest to the lowest. There is a public gaming table at the Frascati every Sunday evening. . . . I do not know whether we told you that Edward's phiz has been taken, and very like too, by Green, a painter of no great eminence at present, but in a fair way of becoming so. He drew Edward as a gentle shepherd, and Crab and Stanley too. He drew us two with a harp. . . . My father goes to Boodle's as usual, where, as everywhere else, the common topic is the elections. . . . We went through Covent Garden yesterday, which was quiet though the good people are polling away. No marrowbones or cleavers have molested our ears as yet, and cockades are not very common.

From Edward Stanley.

Lyons: July 20, 1802.

At Dijon, beautiful Dijon, we arrived on the evening of the 10th. The army of rescue was encamped for some time in its neighbourhood, and the many respectable families who lived in or near it rendered it a sad prey to the hand of Robespierre. Its churches and convents are in a deplorable state. The best houses are shut up, and its finest buildings are occupied by the military.

We arrived at Lyons on the day of the Grande Fête. We saw the town illuminated, and a review on the melancholy plains of Buttereaux, the crimson tomb of so many Lyonese. Of all the towns I have seen, this has suffered the most. All the châteaux and villas in its beautiful environs are shut up. The square of St. Louis le Grand—then Belle Cour, now Place Buonaparte—is knocked to pieces; the statue is broken and removed.

Every mule and jackass I meet with panniers reminds me of Louisa.[1] I wish I knew where she had received her foreign education and learnt the rudiments of the French tongue. I should certainly have visited the cottage. I have been witness to a scene which my curiosity would not let me pass over, but which I hope not to see again—an execution on the guillotine. On looking out of my window the morning after our arrival here, I saw the dreadful instrument in the Place de Ferrant. Five men were to be beheaded in the morning, and two in the evening. They were brought to the scaffold tied, each with his arms behind him, and again to each other, attended by a priest and a party of soldiers. The time of execution of the whole five did not exceed five minutes. Of all situations, I can conceive none half so terrible as that of the last prisoner. He saw his companions ascend one after another, heard each fatal blow, and saw each body thrown aside. I

[1] Louisa Stanley, Lady Leighton, born at Lyons, had been put to nurse as a baby with peasants in the country.

shall never forget his countenance when he stretched out his neck on the fatal board. He shut his eyes on looking down where the heads of his companions had fallen, and instantly his face turned from ghastly paleness to a deep red. The wire was touched and he was no more. Of all deaths it is far the most easy—not a struggle could be perceived after the blow. The sight is horrid in the extreme.

The next morning I saw a punishment a degree less shocking. The prisoner was seated on a scaffold for public view, there to remain for six hours, and then to be imprisoned in irons for eighteen years—a term (as he is forty-one) I think he will not survive.

Lady Sheffield to M. J. S.

Sheffield Place: July 22, 1802.

The Gazette has this moment announced his lordship's being a peer of the United Kingdom. . . . He has just received a letter from William which announces the safe arrival of Lou and her babes at Alderley. I hope all my grand-children enjoyed their fête on Rianette's birthday. I heartily wish their little uncle was old enough to romp with them! I have not heard from Sir Joseph Banks when they mean to come to us, but next Monday is the wool fair; so I imagine they will arrive to-morrow or Saturday.

Serena to M. J. S.

Barley Wood: July 22, 1802.

From the house of Hannah More. With *her pen*, taken from the inkstand which Dr. Kennicott used to write his Hebrew, and on the other hand a most curious stand made of Shakespearian wood with his arms carved upon it, and engraved on a silver label as follows:

> I kissed the Shrine where Shakespeare's ashes lay
> And bore the relick of this Bard away

—seeing from my windows one of the most heavenly

prospects of a rich country, including the British Channel at a distance, what ought not all these circumstances give of brilliancy to this letter? The first, too, that will be franked by Baron Sheffield of Sheffield in Yorkshire. . . . I had made an agreement with H. More to pass a week with her, and I came yesterday, when I parted with my dear Sir Thomas Rivers, who was a fortnight at Bath. It is credibly reported that more than once we were seven hours *tête-à-tête* and greatly surprised when, forgetting supper, we heard the clock strike eleven! The worst of this indiscretion is that my poor Dr. Maclaine is terribly jealous and very unhappy about it; luckily the rival is removed! . . . It is time to tell dearest of Marias that I did very much delight in her letter; there was so much good sense and discrimination in it as particularly pleased and struck me, and at such times I ask myself, ' Est-il bien possible que cette tête-là peut jamais être folle?' You see, therefore, the responsibility of good sense. In order to pursue that reflection properly, I looked off my paper, and saw just before me the monument given by Mrs. Montague to Hannah More in memory of the great Locke, who was born at Wrington, the village just by. . . .

I saw a letter with an account of a day passed with Epictetus Carter [1] last week: she is wonderfully well at Deal; she is in her 86th year, with faculties perfect.

M. J. S. to Louisa.

Alderley Park: October 9, 1802.

And now for such a piece of news! Louisa Margaret Anne Stanley is about to be married! To a colonel in the army, named Baldwin Leighton,[2] of the 46th. The Baronetage mentions the great antiquity of the Leightons, and they are connected with William Clinton by the marriage of the head of the family in Queen Elizabeth's time with the daughter of Edward Baldwin of Diddlebury, in the

[1] Elizabeth, daughter of Dr. Nicholas Carter, considered the most learned woman of her day. Translator of Epictetus.
[2] General Sir Baldwin Leighton of Loton, 6th Bart., born 1747, died 1828.

county of Salop, who was descended from the Baldwins,
Kings of Jerusalem. There's blood for you ! and an honour
to you personally to possess estates that belonged to such
grandees ! We hear Sir John has given his consent and
behaved kindly.

Lou Stanley to M. J. S.

Highlake : October 15, 1802.

. . . As you may be somewhat anxious to know more
particulars of the fate of Louisa M. A. Stanley, be it known
to you that she is in future to reside at Shrewsbury (by the
way, the Wrekin and the Beacon may again be responsive),
where Colonel Leighton's relations and early connections
live. This place is no unpleasing speck in the prospect, as I
shall be within view of all my friends in Cheshire. As for
those in London, I must not hope to pay them frequent
visits, though I hope I shall never be lukewarm towards
those who have been kind to me. Our income will probably
not exceed 800*l.* per annum. An equipage like my father's
is therefore out of the question. A gig and a travelling
chaise form the extent of the stable establishment. . . .
Instead of the spacious rooms in Grosvenor Place, a small
house on the banks of the Severn will be my abode, and not
one sigh do I heave on the exchange. There is philosophy
for you ! In lieu of parties and operas, I hope to receive
the affection and kindness of a most amiable and estimable
man, and that is no bad equivalent for the follies of London.
. . . Colonel Leighton's first appearance, to take a retrospect in my memory, is not so favourable to him as his
intrinsic worth deserves. He is not young, turned of
fifty ; he is not handsome, though far from the contrary ; and
not altogether *unbeauish*—his black coat used to raise our
admiration at its nice well-brushed appearance. He is
rather bald, but his coiffure has a particular spruceness in
it. From having been so long a soldier, his first manners
have not the smiling suavity of a court, which, however,
on further acquaintance, is amply compensated for by the

truth and honesty of his principles; and the latter rested more on my ears than the former on my eyes. My father is very kind and pleased with the whole business. The colonel behaves like a prince, leaving all to my father's arrangement about business.

Mrs. Howard to M. J. S.

Corby Castle : 1802.

Dearest Maria Stanley,—I should be rejoiced to introduce my stout boy and my pretty, gentle girl to you. My darling Philip is almost as broad as he is long, and has got a little Brutus head, for his hair curls beautifully; but we do not give way to our feelings, for my nursery hours are like clock-work. . . . We have internal peace in the county of Cumberland from Lord Lonsdale's death.[1] He perhaps was the most singular character of this age; his great power gave him many opportunities for exercising his propensity for contradiction and tormenting, not only neighbours and even friends, but all those who were obliged to apply to him as Lord Lieutenant of the county. His successor, Lord Lowther, is much approved. He is come to an estate of 40,000l. a year. There was 40,000 guineas found in bags of 5,000l. each, at Lowther—some had never been in circulation—10,000 guineas were found in his house in town, and still he owed his bankers 25,000l. . . .

I am surprised how similar Mr. Stanley and Howard's pursuits are. Howard is overseer of the poor these seven months, and I believe is the first gentleman who ever over-looked, *himself*, in this country. It is generally left to butlers and stewards. . . . I think these times of hardship call for such interference. Added to this he is overseer of the high roads, or I mean the roads in Corby quarter, which work he also attends himself, and he is one of the Commissioners of Appeal and of the Income Tax.

[1] 1st Earl of Lonsdale, son of Robert Lowther, Governor of Barbadoes. Succeeded his great uncle, 1750.

R

Louisa to M. J. S.

. . . *A propos* of children you are really like Aunt, who suspects me of thinking religion an unnecessary prejudice, because I do not agree with H. More respecting the danger of taking a governess who has not the most clear ideas about original sin; when you persist in supposing I wish to educate Lou to be masculine in manner, I can only repeat, nothing was ever further from my thoughts. . . . Time must convince you that I am not quite such a Quixote on the subject as you suppose. . . . William found on his arrival in town a very flattering letter appointing him to Brownrigg's office of secretary to the Duke of York. William has written a very pretty letter in answer, declaring he is by no means fit for the situation; but I trust the duke will keep to his own opinion, and so prettily force him to accept it, as I do not think so high and advantageous an offer is to be refused, though it is a difficult situation and will confine him much to London. What think you, good folks? You will crow and say, ' Did I not tell you he would not be forgot, Mrs. Lou? ' Remember this is a great secret, as it is not by any means settled. How I should like to squeeze a few of the intervening counties a little on one side, so as to approach Cheshire within a day's journey of London !

Were it not that I cannot find a single objection to the man you have got, and that I never saw another to whom I would ever for a moment wish you married, I should be much inclined to grumble that the only conversible relation (of my own standing) belonging to me should have planted herself at 170 miles off. . . .

Serena to M. J. S. (*on receiving the news of the birth of twin sons*).

Bath : Monday, November 1802.

I can't believe it ! It is all a dream ! I am shaking away and reading the letter over and over, and I did not come in till near four ; but write I will, to bless the dear

precious mother of boys. Heaven bless them! There is no
danger. They will live and do well, as many other twins
have done; and it was but right, for it would have been
nothing to follow Lady Sheff and Louisa in the common,
vulgar way of one at a time. Maria shows her superior
spirit. I will rejoice that there are two. A thousand congratulations to dear Mr. Stanley! May these dear boys be
worthy of him and never give him anything but pleasure
and honour! I should delight were I to live to see how he
will educate sons—but I must not talk more of that before the
poor dears know how to see or breathe. . . . A thousand
thanks to the dear Firth for all her intelligence! My heart
beats to think how near she was to not being with you, and
somehow I should not think them well born without her. . . .
The Legards will all rejoice. Lady Rivers and her son
Sir Thomas are here, William Coxe also, so that I live in a
whirlwind. Lady Hesketh met my party at dinner yesterday, looking all beauty. Mr. Pitt is still here; he looks ill, but
is better. . . . Only think how lately no boy in the family,
and now four! How very grand it sounds! I am no
longer forced to say, ' O, Maria has girls enough!' My
servants shall positively get tipsy this good day. As for
Alderley, I expect to hear there was not a sober person in
the county, and at least a dozen houses made into bonfires.
Best wishes to all who care for me, and a thousand blessings
of my own.

Ever and ever yours, S. H.

Serena to Miss Ann Firth.

Bath: November 22, 1802.

There are few in the world better entitled to the name
of Comforter than you are, my dear Miss Firth, for you are
a messenger of glad tidings with all the interesting circumstances one so much wants to know. . . Maria was
piquée d'honneur to outstrip her competitors, though she
started last; therefore she could not help having twins.
That she is so well and has two boys, is sufficient to be glad

R 2

of, and all my great family above and below got tipsy to celebrate the event. What a pity poor old Peter did not live to enjoy an heir to Alderley! Sheff enjoys having four young males in the family within the last ten months. I saw Mr Pitt yesterday at church in the seat with the Duchess of York, amongst all the brilliants who attend Dr. Randolph's oratory. I was surprised Mr. Pitt was not gone to town on this horrid business of a plot. It makes me tremble and feel how tottering our state, though thankful to Providence for the discovery. Lady Sheffield has got over her presentation at the drawing room and returned home to her blue-eyed boy.

[During the year 1802 Lord Sheffield's own son and three grandsons had been born.]

M. J. S. to Louisa.

Alderley Park: December 5, 1802.

I wish you could see these boys. I think it impossible they can ever grow alike; they are so totally different. . . . I believe it is owing to your conversing so much about Celts and Scandinavians! William is a perfect Celt, though not quite so black as Lucy when first born, and Edward seems as if he would be as fair as Bella. . . . We measured them at ten days old, and the elder was two inches longer than his brother; and though you affront me with the notion that your giant boy is to vanquish by force of arms not only his uncle, but both his cousins, I would have you to know that I expect Edward will be a very tolerable match for Henry in single combat. I wrote to old Bill yesterday and told him so, for fear he should encourage in himself such contemptuous ideas of my progeny and insolent ones of his own.

Lady Stanley has written in a very kind manner upon the event, and seems much pleased at being asked to answer for William Owen, and at Lord Bulkeley being requested to be one of the godfathers. She may flatter herself with the hopes of her grandson being a Welsh squire some day. Lord B. is almost the only relation she has.

M. J. S. to Serena.

Alderley Park: December 19, 1802.

Thou poor dear old aunt that ought to have been written to by my own paw long ago. I have intended it every day for some time past; but indeed the succession of children that annoy me all day long in some shape or other, with the addition of eating, drinking, and airing, have made the days vanish like smoke. All continues as prosperous as heart can wish. Edward is large and stout, little William continues to keep his proportion, but has grown and is always in perfect health. He is extremely dark, and Edward is almost as fair as Bella, who is quite a fair beauty and does not seem to belong to us. . . . I wish you could hire a balloon to take a peep at our festivities on January 4. The christening is to be on the 3rd, and we shall have as many neighbours to dinner as our room will hold. Next day will be the feast for the tenants and labourers, attended with fireworks, bonfires, &c. . . . I am very glad my youngest is a boy, and I like two strings to my bow; and as to hardships, there is a great deal in their father's power, if he thinks proper, to make amends to the youngest for the misfortune of not being able to bustle into the world first.

CHAPTER VI.

KEEPS OPEN HOUSE.

1808.

Old English hospitality—Rejoicing nearly turned to mourning—
ground—Galvanism and Calvinism—Liberal presents of heirs—to
Cowper—General D'Oyley—'Delphine'—Retrospect of twelve h
A ruffian—Volunteering discouraged but established—Prison b
Mameluke.

M. J. S. to Louisa.

Midnight, New Year's Eve.

A many happy new years to you, say I, in the first mo
I can send you the good wish. What miracle, will you
or dreadful insomnia, has caused such an un
occurrence in the annals of Alderley? Anxiety that
raise very little sympathy in your breast, I doubt. Geo
is gone to Monksheath to bring back, if I am fortunate
cook and pots of turtle from Liverpool, and a box fi
London, containing a christening robe for Edward and
for both. . . . Mrs. Firth and I have been playing at ch
till the clock struck twelve. . . . You may imagine the M
is not a companion of our revels. He has been as busy a
whole hive of bees for some days past in fitting up
theatre.

The box is heard of; the cook is come. So good nigh

We are within two days of the great day, and I be
to breathe more freely than I did six weeks ago. . . . If o
of the boys had failed, or if either had been weak and sick
I could not have received any pleasure from rejoicings, a
every preparation would have been a big thorn; but th
are so well and promising, I try to cast away all fear. . .

M. J. S. to Louisa.

Alderley Park : January 5, 1808.

All is happily over, and we are alive and the barn is
standing. Had you seen the crowd on Tuesday, you would
hear with no little surprise that no damage whatever has
been done to our premises. Monday and Tuesday were
days of great fatigue to us both; but we are not much the
worse for them, though the evening I despatched my last
letter to you had as nearly as possible turned our merriment
into mourning. The poor old fellow met with an accident
which makes one tremble at the thoughts of. He carried us
into his theatre to witness a rehearsal, and we were indeed
surprised at the good effect of his contrivances, and in full
glee at seeing him perform harlequin to show the step to a
very stupid clown, when in one minute he fell through a
hole left in the floor, and for some time I could not tell
whether he was able to pick himself up or not. The
distance was not so great; but, when I tell you that he fell
backwards with his head against a brick wall, and that a
large axe was just below, you will think I have reason to be
thankful that he only got the blackest eye I ever saw, a
broken shin, and a bruise on his hip. A most severe headache followed next day, though he saved himself at dinner
as much as possible. All his guests, however, were as
drunk as ever I had the pleasure of seeing anybody. We
sat down to dinner twenty-six. Lord and Lady Bulkeley;
Mr. Davenport; four from the Carrs; the Thorneycrofts;
Oswald Leycesters; Croxton Johnson; Mr. and Mrs. Glegg;
Mrs. and Miss Leigh of Twemlow; Mr. and Mrs. Atherton;
Mr. Bell, the curate; and Mr. Brown, of the Addington
family. Cannot you imagine how happy I was when dinner
was over? More so when the last carriage left us, not till
near twelve o'clock. . . . And now for Tuesday's entertainment. A floor was thrown over the thrashing floor, so as
to make a room seventy-two feet long: at one end the
stage was raised seven feet from the floor. The rest of the
apartment was filled with tables, and held, I suppose, about

160 people at a time. The roof was covered with evergreens. A bench was placed for our reception at the upper end, flags forming a drapery. Two very handsome flags were sent as a present from Liverpool, made for the occasion. 'Edward and William Stanley, 4th January 1803,' were on each flag in large gold letters. No description can give you any idea of the general effect, which was beautiful; and at night, when the lanthorns were lighted, which were disposed with great taste among the beams and green boughs, it was the prettiest sight imaginable. People began to assemble about eleven. At two the first set sat down to dinner. At the upper end, three tables abreast, each holding twenty or thirty people, were set out with roast turkeys, hot rounds of beef, cold roast beef, and joints of mutton, succeeded by plum puddings and mince pies. These tables held the principal tenants, their wives, and the Macclesfield tradesmen. The other tables had not turkeys, but were in other respects the same. The labourers and their wives dined in the new stable. There was a hundredweight of plum pudding, ten pounds worth of mincemeat for the pies, the greater part of a bullock, and two sheep: nothing but bones left. The toasts were each announced by a discharge of artillery placed on the Hoblington, the green knoll near the gate. The Knutsford and Macclesfield bands played during dinner; and afterwards on the stage were exhibited performances of various kinds, mummers, snapdragon, a pantomime, including harlequin and columbine and the clown in proper dresses. The scene would have been thoroughly pleasing and have continued an hour or so longer had not the mob outside, comprised of all the cotton devils in the neighbourhood, begun to be clamorous to get in and wanting ale. The Man—who only wants some evil inspiration from Satan to aim at popularity with a mob, and acquire it—talked to them and received three cheers; and when the monster was once patted down and quieted, he thought the best way was to divert its attention, and shut up the barn. He told them first, in a very big tone, that he would have order; and having made them stare, he said two barrels of ale were sent to the

bonfire for their own property, and that he was sure Cheshire men could assemble on such an occasion and conduct themselves with propriety and no tumult, and turned their hearts, or at least their feet, another way, at a very critical moment. The bonfire was lighted, the ale carried down, the fireworks began flying about, the music marched out of the barn to play at the bonfire, good humour prevailed through the evening, and you may guess at the number assembled when I tell you 320 gallons of ale were drunk, and no drunkenness ensued; at least, not that extreme of intoxication which causes men to be swine. By ten the whole of the premises were cleared. Our servants and a select party of labourers had great merit, for they were constantly attentive, and kept sober that they might watch others. As a reward they are to have a dance in the barn to-night, and this will be the last time of representation. The boys are well and growing every hour.

Isa Stanley to M. J. S.

Grosvenor Place : January 13, 1803.

I thank you for your very interesting account of Alderley fête, which describes, as the most perfect of all possible things of the kind, how many people were made happy who will talk of that day to their latest day. May little E. J. and W. O. answer the good prayer of their toast, and dispense happiness throughout their lives, as they did unconsciously at this festivity on their account. I am rather surprised W. O. did not win the race; as he is smaller and more healthy, he ought to be the most active. Let him learn by this very early lesson the value of five minutes. . . . War is not talked of, and some say Lord Pelham will go out. I begged the Chancellor to hang Mr. Hatfield,[1] and he promised he would if he could.

M. J. S. to Louisa.

January 1803.

Do not make yourself unhappy lest any of our offspring should be too white. What a villainous way of describing

[1] English swindler, executed 1803.

my sweet Bella! Little Owen will be even more like the Man than Lucy, and really, when the little fellow puts on a frown of indignation, his countenance has a resemblance to his father's when fighting for the invincible standard against the 42nd, or assisting in bringing any other truth (as he calls it) to light in spite of the devil, politicians, or Scotchmen.

Lady Sheffield to M. J. S.

Privy Gardens: January 16, 1803.

My dear Mrs. Stanley,—I congratulate you most sincerely on having got over all your fêtes with so much success. I would have given a great deal to have been present. There is nothing I love so much as such sort of festivities, where one has the satisfaction of knowing one really makes one's company happy, as well as drunk; whereas in giving a ball and entertaining fine folks, you affront many people, please a very few, make many drunk and yourself miserable. At least I know, at the ball I was fool enough to give in this house three years ago, I thought none of my company was pleased, and I was tired to death. I hope the two young gentlemen are not the worse for the quantity of ale drunk to their healths.

M. J. S. to Serena.

Alderley Park: January 20, 1803.

If I had not been frozen to death as soon as I had recovered being tired to death, after having been previously frightened to death, I should not have allowed Mrs. Firth to be the first narrator of our festivities and their successful performance. Thursday's entertainment gave us an opportunity of seeing the theatricals much better than on Tuesday, and I assure you that Thomas in Harlequin, and Jenny as Columbine entertained us in high style; a Wild Man, *i.e.* a man in bear's clothing, afforded great amusement to the world in general, and one of the Mummers from Winston sung extremely well. Indeed, it is quite foolish to say so often how I wish you had been here, but I cannot help it.

Mrs. Firth told you of a silly speech which the Man, in the delirium of his headache, made to the assembly in the barn when my health was drunk. It was not fair to take one by surprise, when I was standing most conspicuously at the top of a bench, luckily with my little Lou in my arms very conveniently to hide my blushes—and he had just before been giving a little twitch to one's feelings in a speech about the boys. Whatever he says of this kind one knows to be so to a tittle the real inspiration of his heart, and not the production of his head only, and it adds very much to the effect of such a scene. I should have liked seeing how others took it, if I could possibly have seen or thought of anything but myself and him.

Only think what reason I have to be thankful that we can laugh at the Man's Harlequin trick. There could scarcely have been a more frightful narrow escape; in what an instant every preparation for rejoicing, every twig of evergreen, and every additional plank about the barn might have been turned into a dagger as looked upon the next day. Indeed, I had never been cordially happy in seeing the preparations going on, but my fears were not of Stanley's breaking his neck or knocking out his brains as he was so near doing, but I had always in my thoughts the many chances there were against these dear little twins living out their six weeks. . . .

I should like you to kiss Edward John's fat cheek and elbow with two holes in it, and admire little William for his resemblance to his papa, and his *spirituel* look. You ask why my Man's name was not given to one. I thought you had been told it was added to the prettier name of Edward to the eldest. Besides our dislike to the sound of John or Jack, it would be objectionable to have three baronets—*de suite*, as we hope—of the same name.

I have seen Gisborne's 'Sermons,' and am very much pleased with them. The 'Infidel Father' I have read likewise. I am sorry to say, as I fear it may shock you, that I expect more entertainment from 'Delphine,'[1] which I have not as yet seen. I have much more to say, but must have done.

[1] By Mme. de Stael.

Mrs. Howard to M. J. S.

Corby Castle: January 1803.

Without being capricious, my dear Mrs. Stanley, we have certainly double cause to be angry with you for not announcing to us the birth of your two sons. You promised to let us know when you should be possessed of *one*, and the claim was greater when you had outshone your relations and friends and presented Mr. Stanley with two. I did intend to go to London next spring, but really cannot find it in my heart to leave my children. After so many years' absence, I find the comfort of being some use at home, where every one interests themselves for you, and you for them. I sometimes think of you and your little basket going to visit the old woman. Nothing would give me more pleasure than to take a peep at your improvements. . . . William Lyttelton stayed here on his way from the Hebrides; he is so clever and entertaining, and the handsomest young man I have seen for some time.

M. J. S. to Louisa.

Alderley Park: January 30, 1803.

I enclose a little brooch made of a bit of my wig—I mean that which grows upon my head. Long's brother made it.

There is an excellent tiny book of catechism and prayers for the use of children under eight years old, by Dr. Watts, printed for Longmans, Paternoster Row. I want a couple of dozen for the use of the schools, inasmuch as it is more easily comprehended than the Church Catechism. I forgot to make answer about Madame Roland's works. I am sorry that ' the Man ' should have lost the very copy he was reading in his tent at Brighton which furnished the conversation at the ball which made him first appear so interesting and unlike other men. The book is classical ground in our history.

[This book had been the ' subject of discourse ' between M. J. H. and J. T. S. when they met at the Brighton ball, 1795.]

. . . Cobbett will really lose all power and effect by the vulgar and bulldog abuse which he bestows on all who do not please him. He has now and then been happy in laying naked an abuse, and he has humour, and frequently writes a sentence of sound good sense; but his eternal badgering of the Addingtons in such violent forms, and his insolent attacks on Wilberforce, *passe permission*. . . . I should have liked being of William's party to Aldini.[1] I wish I knew how to make a battery and try some experiments on the ox's and sheep's heads, and I wish I could hear what the wise folk say about it. Mr. Holland does not seem disposed to think it different from the electric fluid, and he is the only person I have seen who knows the difference between Galvanism and Calvinism. And so good-bye.

February 24, 1803.

The set of Donovan's 'Birds and Insects' is ready, and I would wish you to see if it is a good copy. I must mention that on my birthday next ensuing, owing to the handsome and most liberal present of heirs which I made to my husband, he thought it but right to make me a handsome present.

Now for a gown. You and Madame Friand are very much in the right in lifting up your eyes with astonishment at the idea of a ringed, striped muslin being worn in the morning by an Alderley exile. It is not intended for that purpose, but for afternoon wear at that same gay place. Long sleeves, by all means; either of the same or white. Now do you understand?

Serena to M. J. S.

Clifton: March 1803.

. . . To be sure, I long to see your Gemini and all your children not a little. If you have not got 'Cowper's

---

[1] Giovanni Aldini, nephew of Galvani, came to London and performed experiments in Galvanism.

Life,' by Hayley, and have not another guinea in the
world, you must get it, unless Lady Jane Stanley can
lend it to you, for in my life I never read anything so interesting. . . . I am sorry to tell you that when it is the
fashion to suppose your aunt so correct and good, that all the
careful mothers are happy if she will but talk &c. &c. to
their daughters, yet she feels that, without taking pains to
deceive any mortal, she has much more of the d—— in her
than is generally imagined, and it is possible she might be
more entertained reading ' Delphine.' It is true she only
read the first volume, where the cloven foot does not appear
openly, and she really believes you will be shocked if you
read the whole, such as she has heard it described.

Have you heard that Buonaparte, who now finds religion
and morality useful, has forbid it, and says that Necker
having ruined France as a financier, his daughter, to complete the work, tries to ruin its principles and all bonds of
society.

Louisa to M. J. S.

March 1803.

Care is very necessary, as the influenza is laying down
two-thirds of every family it gets into. I never before knew
apothecaries complain of their fellow-creatures' sufferings,
but they are so completely harassed with attending on them
that they say, like the Esquimaux, ' Too much coughs, too
much fever, too many draughts wanted.' They say there
has been nothing equal to it these two-and-twenty years.
It seems of the same kind as that you suffered from in '95—
total loss of strength, after pains in bones &c.

. . . General D'Oyley[1] was at the concert at half-past
eleven on Thursday night, and by one was dead. He was just
settled so as to think himself most comfortable for life, with
a wife of a very desirable sort, and a regiment for which he

[1] Francis, son of Dr. T. D'Oyley, Archdeacon of Lewes. He entered
1st Regiment of Foot Guards, 1769. Served in Flanders under the Duke of
York ; was wounded in the action of Lincelles. He commanded a brigade in
Holland, 1799. Appointed Col. of the 67th Regiment, February 1803. He
married Anne, dau. of Dr. Hugh Thomas, Dean of Ely ; and died March, 1803.

had only kissed hands. Really all these deaths, and an east
wind, while reading Hayley's 'Life of Cowper' (which is
most melancholy perusal), is enough to give one the blue
devils.

M. J. S. to Louisa.

April 13, 1803.

A word for 'Delphine' and Cowper, lest I should again
finish a letter without having mentioned them. From fifteen
to twenty, perhaps longer, I should have been enchanted with
the 'All for Love' of 'Delphine' and have overlooked its real
beauties and real defects. In my present state of sobriety,
and past thirty, I am exceedingly offended at finding that
I must be past all possibility of happiness in this life; and
besides that, as I have not been a first-rate beauty, it is a
physical and moral impossibility I ever can have known
anything like felicity, and—before I read 'Delphine'—I
thought I had been, and now was, tolerably happy. Yet I
could not help being often pleased with observations which
mark knowledge of human nature and genius in the author.
. . . The Man is indignant beyond measure. He read about
three volumes with patience and some interest, but was so
disgusted by the time that he came to the last, that I could
hardly prevail on him to finish it. He has all along been
comparing the simplicity and many beauties of the ' Tableaux
de Famille ' with 'Delphine,' a comparison which the latter
could not possibly bear. . . . Neither the Man nor I agree
to the truth of the motto that men should brave, women
submit to opinion. I acceded at first, till we examined the
matter and produced examples, and the result is that man is
as much bound as woman, woman as much as man, to brave
public opinion, if their principles of religion or morality call
for one line of conduct, and public opinion for another. At
all events (an elegant proverb will suit me very well), ' what
is sauce for the goose is sauce for the gander.'

I can only now speak of Hayley's 'Cowper' shortly.
I have been deeply interested throughout, and I am rather
angry with you for blaming the publication of the letters,

and calling Hayley methodistical for so doing. There is not one I would wish omitted, or that I do not think contributes to throw light on Cowper's character and turn of mind. His religious opinions, as contained in the letters published, are rational and in no way extravagant. . . .

And now a truce to literature for the present. You ought to thank me, for I have sat at home to write in the most lovely weather possible; but I am more inclined to agree with the proverb 'Delays are dangerous,' than with 'Ce qui est déféré, n'est pas perdu.' . . . If you could help being absurd and ridiculous, I should like to ask how Sévéry looks? what difference twelve years have made in him? and what stay he makes in England? Anglétine is, I suppose, in Switzerland.

[These were members of the happy party at Lausanne at 'Château Gibbon,' 1791.]

Oh! what a silly figure administration makes in the debate of this morning's papers. I long for Cobbett next Monday to attack Captain Markham and Addington's fifty ships ready without men in them!

May 1803.

There is some truth in what you say of the consequence of writing long letters, that you are less likely to have them circumstantially answered, on account of the undertaking of reading them over. You will be under a great mistake, however, if you suppose they can be too long for my gratification; but sometimes I set to write in such a hurry that I have not time to look over a volume and see what is to be answered. Upon my word, six children under six years would have tired Job's patience sufficiently, without Devil or wife to help, if he had only been condemned to have one or other with him all day long, but without some peculiar dispensation of providence to condemn thereto he would have probably shared the happier fate of the Man, who sees but as much or as little of his children as he sees agreeable.

I am glad you have read Lady M. W. Montagu's

Letters. She seems to have led a very pleasant life at Louvere, and to be as well contented there as a person can be anywhere totally void of religion, and having been very careless of reputation—which latter cause I imagine to have been the reason of her living abroad, her conduct having been very light, I believe, in England in the early part of her life. You must perceive in the whole course of her correspondence that she had shaken off prejudices till she was quite on a level with the modern philosopher, and it must be impossible for the unbelieving old woman to face death with satisfaction. . . .

I return you Cat. Fanshawe's verses, and I wish you would coax her out of some more. . . . The last Paper you sent us is indeed alarming, because the plan is well imagined and likely to succeed. If Otto[1] planned and proposed such a scheme, I shall hardly have patience to wait for seeing him fry in the next world; and while this diabolical system of revolutionising continues to prevail in the French government, the most expensive war must be better than peace which obliges us to harbour devils and serpents.

. . . War is a bad thing, and our present ministry a bad thing, and bankers' failures are bad things, and altogether we may suspect ourselves in a bad way; but anything is better than the continuance of the peace which followed the Treaty of Amiens. So far Cobbett has made a partisan of me; but I am not of his opinion that it is bad the peace was made anyhow. War begins again on new grounds and much more popular ones than the just, necessary and religious war we were engaged in. . . .

I do want badly to write to aunt; but the days slip and slide away like—soaped pigs, I believe, would be a pretty simile. Do remember me to Sévéry. I should like to see him. Be sure you see Edward's Swiss sketch-book. It was an odd feel to see Gibbon's acacia; the steps; the basin of the fountain; and even the very pots of flowers on the terrace. Twelve years seemed annihilated in a moment.

---

[1] Ludwig, Count of Moslay, German diplomatist in the French service; 1754-1817.

How gladly would I go back to be secure of passing twelve
such again! Few people would say so much. May the
next twelve pass with one half the happiness and content, I
shall have reason to be thankful.

M. J. S. to Ann Firth.

Gayton, near Parkgate : July 25, 1803.

We are in a very pleasant, but the smallest of all cottages,
belonging to Mr. Glegg, close to the water, where though
the name of sea is almost too grand for its proper description, yet the water is perfectly salt, the bathing good,
and at high tide it is seven miles across to the coast of
Flint, which, with the Welsh hills peeping out from behind,
gives the water the appearance of a large lake. . . .

Last Friday we went to Liverpool, and the party would
have been pleasant but for a disagreeable affray with which
we concluded our day. We took a large boat from the ferry
this side, had a very delightful sail across the Mersey, saw
all the docks and shipping, and I was much entertained.

We took Foley, Edward, and Lucy. After an agreeable
day we took boat at sunset to cross again to the Cheshire
shore, but instead of pursuing our course some evil genius
prompted us to go out of our way to see a French prize just
come into the port. Our boatmen hailed the vessel, inquired
if there was an English captain or mate, and if they would
allow Mr. Stanley to go on board.

We were answered insolently by several voices in broken
English, but at last a well-dressed man in good English said
we were welcome to come. . . . Prudence would have led
us to sheer off, but unfortunately she was asleep at that
moment in my Man's breast. He went on board and
wanted me to follow up the ship's side.

I tried to excuse myself, but while he was speaking to the
French prisoners, one of the roughest of the *broken English*
men, who said he commanded, came into the boat, said a
great deal about our going up, took Edward out of Foley's
arms, and he seemed so drunk and odd one did not know
whether to refuse him or not.

I thought the best way to end it was to go up myself, leaving the children, Foley, and James in the boat. When I got into the ship all but the prisoners seemed very tipsy. They were very urgent that we should go into the cabin, but that I would not do, and at last I went back to our boat. . . . A few minutes after S. came down, and the rough man I spoke of earnestly asked him to take two young girls, French passengers, and, upon his answering he could not, d——d England and the English. You can imagine this was rather too much for the Man's philosophy to put up with. As we pushed off, he called them to account for such treasonable words, and appealed to the people standing on the pier-head, and to the well-dressed man who appeared a prize-owner, if such expressions should be allowed on board a French prize from the captors. In an instant the man gets into a boat alongside, comes to ours, jumps upon the gunnel where S. stood (we thought he was going to make an apology), asks what right he has to say what he did, and gives him a blow on the face, which being as instantly returned, and followed by the brute seizing hold of S. by the shirt, which he tore almost from the collar, I threw myself between them. James then came forward and collared the man; he turned upon James, struck him violently, and a great scuffle followed—poor Edward, Lucy, and Foley all squalled in concert. We were in a minute surrounded with boats. Ours was filled with people, yet none interfered so far as to take the brute of a fellow in custody. The language he used was such as I had never had the honour of hearing before. . . .

Two Liverpool gentlemen, seeing women and children in such an unpleasant situation, came to us and wished much to take me and the babes away, but when they found I would not stir, thinking my presence might keep my Man cooler and be some restraint on the others, they good-naturedly came into the boat and promised they would not leave till all was settled. Someone from the pier-head hailed the revenue cutter. One of the mates coming with his hanger under his arm was of some use, as the good folks were afraid of being pressed. When the boat stopped our man made a violent push at James, but the two gentlemen and the boatmen all laid hold of him while we got out. When we came on shore the idea of a constable and quarter sessions at last quieted him, and he was forgiven; but you can have no idea of the unpleasant voyage we had. . . . It was twelve o'clock before we got home.

Miss Ann Firth to M. J. S.

Doncaster: Aug. 20, 1803.

My dear Mrs. Stanley,—I have to thank you for a very interesting letter, which made my blood run cold to think of the situation yourself and family were in. I think it a great mercy that the boat was not overset, when one reflects that such brutes half drunk do not care what they do. James will feel himself very proud to have been of such service to his master, and I have no doubt would have ventured his life to serve him. I do not see why you should blame yourselves for going on board. . . . I have heard from Mrs. Clinton, and Lord Sheffield seems very happy in preparing against the French, should they come; he had had a gratifying letter from the Duke of Richmond on his conduct and plans. . . . Since we have heard from each other what a dreadful explosion has taken place in Ireland. I recollect Lord Kilwarden was a friend of Mr. Stanley, and an amiable man. I suppose any person at that moment going in a carriage would have met with the same fate.[1] What a situation for the lady! one thinks it was quite enough to kill her. The uncertainty as to the fate of her friends was enough to make her mad. . . . I wish Mr. Stanley had been in a higher station as to the defence of this country,

[1] Arthur Wolfe, Viscount Kilwarden, Chief Justice of Ireland, was murdered (1803) in the streets of Dublin. He was accompanied by his nephew and daughter. The latter, when the attack took place, was permitted to escape, but Lord Kilwarden and the nephew were killed. Lord K.'s last words were: 'Murder must be punished, but let no man suffer for my death but on fair trial, and by the laws of his country.' This outbreak was the last important event of the Irish rebellion. Lord Kilwarden had shortly before this attack been pall-bearer at Lord Clare's funeral.

because he has more head, I think, than those who are.
But if he should be called on by circumstances, I think he
will not let any little punctilio prevent his exertions for the
benefit of the country. It is much to be wished that men
of energy of character were in high situations. . . . There
have been meetings at York and Leeds, and large sums
subscribed—Lord Harewood 2,000*l.*, and many 500*l.*, some
confining it to the volunteers of their own place, others to
the county at large. I heard the Archbishop of York had
subscribed 2,000*l*. Nothing but drumming and fifing is
going on here. We hear nothing but ' Right ! Left ! ' from the
children in the street, as there is so much learning to march
going forward. . . . Mrs. Clinton mentioned Lady Jane
Stanley's release. My love and best wishes to Mr. Stanley
and all the family of young ones.

I am, my dear Mrs. Stanley's
Much obliged and affectionate
ANN FIRTH.

Lord Sheffield to M. J. S.

Sheffield Place : September 1, 1803.

Last post brought me the very dear Ria's letter of the
29th, and I think I may now give an opinion that none of
your volunteer corps will be established. I shall be sorry
if the Alderley company should be rejected, as it appears
that you and Stanley wish its existence ; but independent
companies are particularly discouraged, and I hardly think
there is any chance of your getting arms. I have not
leisure for detail ; but a letter from Mr. Yorke to the Speaker
on the subject of the North Pevensey legion is very satisfactory, and establishes the corps exactly on the principles
and terms proposed, but it has the following remarkable
paragraph : ' There is not a chance of getting to Kidbrooke,
till we have fairly broke the neck of this volunteer business ;
if it is not soon done, it will break our backs.' It may be
better not at present to mention this. You will have already
discovered that a complete check has taken place in respect

to all volunteering. I shall be able to send you more particulars about this business soon. . . . If anything can be done about the Alderley company I shall write forthwith. The Bishop of Bristol[1] and his lady are now here.

Yours ever,

S.

M. J. S. to Louisa.

September 10, 1808.

I received your scolding this morning, and the 'Alderley Independent Company' received his Majesty's gracious approbation and acceptance yesterday. Edward has been to Lord Stamford this morning about arms &c. The last order says only half the number are to be provided with muskets, the remainder with pikes; that is very well, if no lessening afterthought should come down. He says that as soon as he receives an order and begins to act upon it, a counter-order arrives. If Addington stands the general displeasure against him which his weak conduct has excited all over England, I shall think we are in a very fit state to be conquered by Buonaparte, and that it matters not how soon it happens. . . .

To-day, till this present eight in the evening, I have been so fully employed in coursing six hares, and assisting in the harvest home dinner given to our usual number of about seventy persons, that I have not sat down quietly since breakfast. We had a famous game of prison bars this afternoon, and the soldiering spirit that has seized the greatest part of Alderley has added great liveliness. At this present moment I am sure Buonaparte would have a bad time of it if he were to visit Alderley, for its inhabitants are wonderfully valiant. I do not know if they will continue so till the next drill day. Some of our heroes are rather afeared, and some few determined cowards; but upon the whole our folks have come forward surprisingly, and continue drilling with the utmost patience; the awkward

[1] The Hon. George Pelham, afterwards Bishop of Exeter and finally Bishop of Lincoln.

figures of some would furnish excellent subjects for the pencil of a Bunbury. I am impatient for their muskets, that they may begin to look like soldiers. . . . Have you seen Gilray's excellent caricature? George III. as the King of Brobdignag holding Buonaparte in his hand as Gulliver, and a quotation from Swift. The print is worth anything as a portrait, for I never saw a stronger likeness than the king's. Are you not almost tired of expecting Buonaparte? Edward has made a very good sketch of John Bull, yawning dreadfully on Dover cliffs, wearied out with watching for gunboats. I suppose you wise folks smile at our security, but really the day has been so often fixed for invasion that I must be allowed to think it possible it may be put off *sine die*. I wish, as the old woman said of the thieves, Buonaparte were come and gone.

Sunday evening, September 25, 1803.

I have not missed a single drill, and I am much interested with the progress the Alderley company makes in various manœuvres, beyond the most difficult of all, that of distinguishing the right hand from the left. There are a few who have not quite mastered that science yet. This morning, having no service till evening, on account of the curate's being gone to ordination at Chester, we had a famous field day, which concluded with a swearing-in of volunteers. Some few had already sworn to their wives and mothers not to take this dreadful oath of allegiance, and begged to consider of it; but seventy-four out of ninety present cheerfully took it, and as cheerfully took a shilling each to drink the health of Captain Stanley[1] and success to the volunteers. I think the uniforms will be good and reasonable. The jacket made of very good cloth, with a comfortable shirt, duck trousers, black gaiters, and a round hat, came to 2*l*. 0*s*. 9*d*.; but the unanimous desire of the whole corps was to have blue cloth pantaloons, which will make the dress five or six shillings more. On Monday the report was very strong in

[1] Rev. Edward Stanley.

Macclesfield that the French had landed in Wales and
Devonshire. It proves premature. If we had wiser
ministers and generals, I should wish it true; for it would be
as well for the people to hear the attempt has been made,
and I trust they would hear nearly at the same time that it
had failed. One feels a little tender of wishing the enemy
too strongly to come, as you lie rather in their way, and there
may be no joke in the business. William sends most alarming threatenings of sudden invasion; but I am more disposed to believe Emmet, that Buony's policy will be to
attack only our finances and exercise our fears for this
autumn at least.

Not having anything else particular to fill my paper, I
must flatter you by mentioning what comfort I have found
in following your fashions. I bought a man's hat as I came
through Chester; my hair is cut snug, and it now seems un-
natural to me to put any clothing on my pate, with a riding
habit which I have worn constantly, almost since I got the
habit by the seaside of doing so.

M. J. S. to Serena.

Alderley Park: November 6, 1803.

Occasionally Louisa has mentioned your existence and
wellbeing, which has contented me, though it ought not, as
you are so good as to love my letters a bit. To be sure, I
should have made a few violent exertions in your favour; but
till my governess came, my days were quite employed, and
I was not disposed to write in the short happy period after
the children retired to rest. Since she came I have given a
good deal of attention to my dear little Lou-Dolly, who is
really the cleverest, most engaging child I ever saw, and of
whose company I had less than I wished, because her sisters
required attention still more. Have you given up all
thought of a journey hitherward before you settle at home?
We have much to show you. Our Alderley volunteers are a
very fine body of men as far as they go, viz. 120. There
was a fear of the oath, which caused a delay; but all diffi-

culties are now got over. . . . Good-bye, my poor little dear old aunt. I punish myself for my remissness; for I love one of your volumes of all things, and it is a long time indeed since I had one.

Serena to M. J. S.

Whitehall : November 9, 1803.

I left them at Sheffield Place on September 11. Possibly Louisa told you that I eloped with the little judge [1] you put down into the salt pit. . . . I do not actually wish the enemy to land, for fear of some confusion; but I wish such destruction of every ship as to prove the invasion is a wild undertaking, and if afterwards Buonaparte is torn to pieces by his own people it would finish matters more completely. I cannot think he has any serious expectation of hurting this country but through Ireland, and a slow ruin by the expenses of such a war; and in that way he may succeed in time, if it pleases Providence to permit such a scourge to live much longer. A mameluke, whose life he spared on some occasion, has devoted himself to the guard of his master, and every night lays his bed across the door of his bedroom for security. An English maidservant who lived with Mr. Harcourt is married to the mameluke, and sent this account, which Mr. Owen told me from her. What sensations the French princes and other foreigners must have felt on seeing our fine old king heading his thousands of volunteers! What a contrast! I was told the king was never so affected in his life. H. More has sent me some loyal songs.

[1] Downes.

CHAPTER VII.

AN ALDERLEY EXILE.

1804-1805.

Volunteer corps—Prince William—The flag—The ' Edinburgh Review '—Duc
d'Enghien—Serena's dream—Hannah More's miners—J. T. S. visits
Serena—Lord Webb Seymour—Queen of the Fairies—A feast—Alethea—
' My better angel '—My millionth Man—The brattery.

M. J. S. to Louisa.

Alderley Park : **February 9, 1804.**

We had a grand day yesterday. The Alderley volunteers
were reviewed by Prince William. Edward found that
every other volunteer corps in the neighbourhood had been inspected, and therefore asked if H.R.H. would like to see the
Alderley company, which he most graciously condescended
to agree to. The men looked very well, and appeared to
great advantage after the cotton-spinners of Macclesfield who
had been inspected the day before. Our six feet high men,
as you used to call them, looked like giants, and I was glad
they were seen by the prince, and I think they did themselves and their commander credit. The prince and his
party from Capesthorne, after our journey to the Beacon,
returned to a cold collation here, and we had the agreeable
sensation of seeing the back of his carriage about five o'clock.

Serena to M. J. S.

Clifton : **February 20, 1804.**

For some days past the horrors of our public situation
spread such a gloom as I never witnessed before, so profound
and general. And though the account of the king yesterday
was more favourable, I cannot suppose any durable amend-

ment. I went yesterday to the cathedral, where I heard a sermon that struck me particularly, as I had heard our poor king was dead, and it was almost to be believed. The clergyman, without adulation, spoke of his character with so much feeling as went to the heart of many. Even the rugged soldiers, of whom there were many, looked affected and sad.

M. J. S. to Louisa.

March 1, 1804.

I really think, on the strength of the 500*l.* saved to Government in stationery, you might save me the trouble of hunting out the concatenation of fragments last sent. I ought, however, to feel gratitude that you take the trouble of numbering these sibyl's leaves. . . . In the first place, Cat. Fanshawe's Botany is herewith returned. I beg you will make the best excuse you can for me. It was buried under a heap of the Man's rubbish in his writing-table, and when brought to light I always forgot it; pray say I have been translating it into Latin verse, or anything you can think of as an excuse; only I am too modest to show my copy, therefore I hope she will not ask to see it. . . . There was one little soft parcel sent to William, which he forwarded. I hope he has forgiven me, for that was really in the service of the Crown. The Alderlian flag could not be completed without some crimson silk to shade the folds of the crown. It is now finished, and will look very handsome in the great hall of the castle, which is at present in the air; but which we hope may some day prove a flat reality, in the piping times of peace; probably when we are a province of France, the only chance, I perceive, of prospective peace and plenty.

Can you inform me whether the 'Conversation' bonnets, as they were called last year, deeper on one side than the other, are now worn? I bought a very pretty one at Chester, which is now my sheet anchor—muslin lined with yellow.

M. J. S. to Serena.

Alderley Park : 1804.

I have just read Hayley's third volume of 'Cowper.' I am afraid my opinion will sound treason in your ears, who have been reading it with Lady Hesketh; but surely Hayley has been much too prodigal of his communications to the public. The first two volumes interested me very much; but I do not think Hayley shines in this part of the work. Most of Cowper's letters are delightful; but as to Mrs. Unwin, I can never forgive her cattish jealousy of Lady Austen, a woman who seemed sent by Providence to enliven the drooping spirits of Cowper. Probably if he had enjoyed more of such society as Lady Austen and Lady Hesketh he might not have ended his days so miserably.

Have you seen the 'Edinburgh Review'? and tell me if you hear who are the principal people concerned in writing for it. It is extremely clever, and conducted in a very superior style; and since no work is without faults, and that publications swarm, perhaps they are right in the severity with which they expose and lay open the defects of every author. But I think they are sometimes too severe and illiberal in the style of their wit. They are likewise sworn enemies to sentiment, therefore not qualified to discover the beauties of some modern works which have no other merit to recommend them.

M. J. S. to Louisa.

Alderley Park: April 18, 1804.

What effect will the murder of the Duc d'Enghien produce in the continental Powers, or in France sufficient to be of any use? It is some satisfaction to think how wretched Buony must be from his apprehensions in the midst of his ill-acquired greatness. The manner in which he executed the duke shows his fears, and his folly likewise, if it is true there was an assassination plot against him; since the only way to have opinion on his side was to make the particulars of the trial public and give proof that such a plot did exist, and that the duke was engaged in it.

[The following account of the murder of Louis Antoine Henri de Bourbon, Duc d'Enghien, was received through Serena :]

Colonel Laborde, in whose custody the Duc d'Enghien was put on being brought a prisoner to Paris, gave Mrs. Henry Hamilton, daughter of Lady Longford, the following account.

'He was put into a common jail. He had fasted a long time and was very hungry, and, finding the prisoners eating something, he desired to have a little. They gave him part of their food, and a wooden plate and wooden spoon. After he had eaten, he complained of being extremely tired and desired to lie down, which he did, and fell fast asleep. Colonel Laborde, knowing that the grave was actually dug in which the duke was to be put, after a short time awakened him and told him, if he had a lock of his hair or a letter to send to any of his family, that he (Colonel Laborde) would take care to forward it, and would only part with it with his life. The duke replied, "I understand you." He cut off a lock of his hair, wrote a short letter, and desired that a confessor might be sent to him. He was soon afterwards led out. Five of the soldiers refused to fire at him. They were immediately shot before his face, and their bodies thrown into a ditch. They desired to put a bandage before his eyes. He answered he had looked death in the face before, and could face it again. Seventeen soldiers fired at him.

'Madame Buonaparte did everything possible to save the duke. She implored Buonaparte on her knees, holding the skirt of his coat, which was torn off by his violent manner of going from her. She seized the other skirt, which was likewise torn off; and Buonaparte declared he would never go to bed till the duke was dead.

'Lucien Buonaparte also exerted himself to the utmost, and, finding he had no success, in a rage took out a watch Buonaparte had given him, dashed it on the ground, break-

ing it in pieces, and said to his brother, " You will be treated
in the same manner." The two brothers have never been
friends since.'

Serena to M. J. S.

As I have seen a letter from an intimate friend of mine
to Lady Hesketh, lamenting, with only too much affection
and kindness, my death—which she knew to be true from
undoubted authority—you may perhaps like some news
from the next world, and be glad to find my spirit still
hovering about you with affection. As I passed through
the Inferno I met crowds hurraing Buonaparte and his
myrmidons, and particularly rejoicing in the murder of Duc
d'Enghien and Pichegru.[1] Some among them, however,
muttered how *poor* his inventions were to cover his deceit
and wickedness, for that none but idiots could possibly
believe his fabrications; and, as Pride and Barbarity were
pushing him on so fast, they feared he might be destroyed
before he had done all the mischief the great prince wished
him to do. As I went a little farther they showed me a
high seat of honour intended for him, but I saw through a
mist the horrid tortures he was to suffer, with the never-
dying worm of remorse, in which he had many associates,
such as Robespierre &c. I was right glad to leave that
scene of horror and go to the next place, where I saw the
victims of those monsters waiting for judgment, hoping they
had atoned for their sins, and by repentance might be fitted
for Heaven. I wanted to join them, but I was told I must
not yet be admitted; and this is all I am allowed to tell you.
In some of the passages I met people about whom I have
often been puzzled. In Heaven they would meet nothing to
suit them. Too insignificant and selfish to feel the benevolent
joy of the happiness around them, incapable of looking up
to sublime objects, their idea of the Supreme Being is only
fear which they try to forget, but death obliges them to recollect. No employment on earth but cards, dress, scandal,

[1] French general, 1761–1804.

and folly, what enjoyment can their poor souls find even in Heaven, if, through mercy, they should be admitted there? These people I met chattering and disputing for place, and I was not allowed to see the end of their destination, as I wished to do. I feel in a great fright lest I should be reckoned in that class; for though I may never have been exactly like them, yet, if I had been taught better and have had more advantages without making the use I ought to have made of them, I may be glad to get even into those passages with the hope of no worse punishment than such associates would be. . . . If I can now recollect anything that happened before my death I will tell it you. I felt a hope that, had you been at liberty (as much, at least, as the mother of seven or eight children so young can be), I might have had a chance of seeing you. All my hope now is, that I may be permitted to become the guardian angel of the dear children I so loved on earth. Were I worthy, I should like the employment of guarding them through their earthly pilgrimage. I remember I was very pleasantly settled at Clifton, and was greatly delighted with the third volume of ' Cowper's Letters,' which I read to Lady Hesketh before it was published.

I was so well at Clifton that my death [1] must have been very unexpected!

[1] On the occasion of a similar report about Gibbon reaching him in 1785, Lord Sheffield wrote to the Rev. Norton Nicholls:

The Gibbon is pleasant on the subject of his Death, with which all the English newspapers amused themselves last September. He says as a celebrated Historian has not written to any of his Friends in England, and as that respectable personage had always a reputation of a most exact and regular correspondent, it may be fairly concluded that he is or ought to be dead. The only objection he can foresee is the assurance that Mr. G. himself read the article as he was eating his breakfast, and laughed very heartily at the mistake of his brother Historian. He affirms, however, not only that he is alive, but that his head, his heart, his stomach, are in the most perfect state, and that the Climate of Lauzanne has been congenial both to his mind and Body. He confesses, indeed, that after the last severe winter, the Gout, his old Enemy from whom he hoped to have escaped, pursued him to his retreat among the mountains, and that the siege was long though more languid than in his precedent attacks. After some exercise of patience he began to creep and gradually to walk, and, though he can neither run nor fly nor dance, he supports himself with grace and firmness on his two

I wish I had the privilege from these regions to see you and your children and your dear husband; for, even were I admitted among the blessed, I should still take pleasure and interest in you all. In the last year of my life my greatest regret was not having visited you.

Heaven bless you ever,
S. HOLROYD.

Serena to M. J. S.

Barley Wood: July 6, 1804.

I wish you were sitting by me just now, looking on, I really think, the most beautiful country I ever beheld. . . . The parish is very wild and poor, kept only by the working in the Mendip mines, and for that reason particularly sought out by these benevolent women. The ignorance of the miners was beyond all conception : they really knew not the name of God. Hannah More tamed them first by good offices, and then by taking their children and getting matrons to teach them to work and to be good. The parents came to listen and were gradually civilised. The first seven years was sad labour and would have made any one else despair. The men who were such savages are now perfectly honest and good. There is a company of volunteers entirely com-

legs, and would willingly kick the gazetteer, though more easily to be forgiven than the impudent courier du Bas Rhin, who about three years ago amused himself and his readers with a fictitious epistle from Mr. Gibbon and Dr. Robertson. He gives a great detail of Persons and things. He says he begins to view with complete indifference the combat of Achilles Pitt and Hector Fox, for such, as it should now seem, must be the comparison of the two warriors. He inquires whether I am patient in my exclusion from the House, whether I am satisfied with legislating with my pen, whether I had resumed the pursuits of farming, &c., what new connections, public or private, I have formed, and adds a tour to the Continent would be the best medicine for the shattered nerves of a soldier and politician. I wish I was near Blundeston.

. Yours ever,
S.

This etter with others, written from Sheffield Place to the Rev. N. Nicholls, are now in the possession of the Rev. Canon Moor, St. Clement, Truro.—ED.

posed of these *ci-devant* savage miners, but the officers and all
the neighbours say they know no regiment that can boast of
better-disciplined soldiers or of more industrious men. They
exercised before us yesterday. Hannah ordered every man
a little loaf of plum bread, and as much strong beer as they
could properly drink with it. They drank the king's health
with cheers and rural joy. They drank their colonel's health
with singing, and played ' God save the King.' They have
a little band of music, and every one joined in the chorus.
They then lined a way for our carriage and saluted. . . Miss
Hamilton's ' Agrippina ' is, I believe, ready, and you will see
it advertised. She begged my pardon for reproving Mr.
Gibbon amongst other dangerous writers, and I told her
my only objection was that it would not be new. I shall
like to know that you and yours are all the better for the
sea air, for somehow I am really and truly

Yours ever affectionately,
S. HOLROYD.

[In the summer of 1804 business connected with the sale of
the Somersetshire property caused J. T. S. to journey south.]

J. T. S. to M. J. S.

Compton Bishop : July 27, 1804.

We arrived last night, having left Bath at twelve. Our
amiable aunt took me, as she promised, to Lady Hesketh's,
though there was some balance of thought in favour of a
party where Mr. Mulso was to read certain manuscript
letters of Mrs. Chapone. Lord Webb Seymour accompanied
us. We left the ladies soon after tea. Mrs. Holroyd gave
me the opportunity of escape by saying I must see the
gardens, and Lord Webb Seymour having never seen them
had the same duty imposed upon him. Lady Hesketh's
conversation was very agreeable, but I was nevertheless well
satisfied to have my lord and the gardens for an hour to
myself. The three days spent at Alderley, and three or four
meetings we have had at Bath, gave us the feelings of old
acquaintance, and many of our opinions and thoughts had

T

to be exchanged. The more I have sounded his mind, the richer I have found it, and strong on almost every subject we have touched upon. Every branch of philosophy, science, *belles-lettres*, or taste has dropped some of its fruit for him. He kept up the conversation with as much ease as I heard him converse on Mineralogy at Alderley. If his principles of conduct, moral sense, and temper correspond with what I have seen, and we should meet again, from acquaintance we must become friends.[1]

M. J. S. to Serena.

Blackpool: August 5, 1804.

I have three letters to thank you for, dear good little aunt, and very pleasant they were to receive. To be sure, it was rather improper, throwing out your lures to detain a poor man from his duty; but as you did not succeed, I will not be very angry with you this time. I wish he could have stayed a day or two longer in the delightful circle you could have drawn about him. We shall leave on Wednesday. I shall be very glad, for nothing can be more disagreeable than this Blackpool—all the disadvantages of a public place and none of the advantages such as a good library, good shops, pleasant walks, or interesting places to see at a distance.

M. J. S. to Louisa.

Alderley: September 16, 1804.

I am well pleased that you think it possible you may migrate to the Land of Potatoes. It ensures me a sight of you

[1] 'It would be doing injustice to the memory of Lord Webb Seymour were I only to dwell on his intellectual character, or even on his love of truth and desire of improvement. Not only was he a man of the most untainted honour and scrupulous integrity, but of the greatest benevolence and the warmest attachment to his friends. . . . He scarcely knew anger or any of the violent passions, and perhaps in considering the mild stoicism of his character—the self-command which never degenerated into selfishness—we are not mistaken in fancying some resemblance between him and Marcus Aurelius!'—From sketch of Lord Webb Seymour's character by Hallam. Died April 1819, aged 42.

and your tribe. Have you read Miss Edgeworth's 'Popular Tales'? If not, get them as fast as possible; they are equal to anything yet published by her. There is one story that is my delight—'The Limerick Gloves.' . . . The Life of Richardson is written in a clever manner by Mrs. Barbauld, and many of the letters are very interesting. . . .

I know of nothing I want from London unless it is a loup dog. Seriously, if you knew where to get me one I should be very glad; though I should not insist on William's bringing it, for it could come by the waggon. I should prefer a French dog like my old Bounce, but I am disposed to indulge the Man in his rage for the loup species, and have desired long to try if you could find a beauty. I know you pity me for liking to add the torment of dogs to the torment of children; but I really think they are necessary to make the group complete. . . .

I have just given dear old Bill a hug. It is a great pleasure to see his face again. He is gone to the drill. . . . So! you are to have a royal sponsor! I wish you joy, as I know it gives you satisfaction. I like the name very much, and I am glad the little fellow [1] is not to be loaded with names like his little uncle.

M. J. S. to Serena.

Alderley Park : November 1, 1804.

Little miss was indeed the Queen of the Fairies at first, but she has increased so much in size and plumpness since her first *entrée* into this vale of tears, that she is now a very decent sort of a baby. . . . I believe I told you our volunteers have been on permanent duty, and that nearly all our household were of the number. They returned home on Monday, and to-day are partaking of a grand feast at this house. The officers are at dinner with the captain and squire in the parlour; and the non-commissioned officers and privates, between ninety and a hundred, are devouring geese, hares, beef, mutton, pies and puddings in the hall &c.

---

[1] Frederick, Colonel Grenadier Guards, of Ashley Clinton, Lymington, m. Mary, dau. and co-heir of Lord Montagu, d. 1870.

Of course, all this must be washed down with a due proportion of ale.

All the children are well. The boys are the greatest
darlings possible, and indeed it is not because they are boys,
I do assure you; for had they had the misfortune to be girls,
they must be thought nice clever babes. I wish Mrs. Firth
was here to sing their praises, or rather speak to the truth
of mine.

M. J. S. to Louisa.

Alderley Park : December 27, 1804.

Nobody tells us nothing. To be sure, in some respects it
is a comfortable thing not to have a certain brigadier-general
as a correspondent from the seat of knowledge, as in the
absence of his explanations and hints we may flatter ourselves with existence as a nation, at least a few months
longer; still I like to hear something, especially of this said
personage, and your epistles are equally scarcy in number as
in matter.

A little work of Madame de Genlis has pleased us well—
' La Duchesse de la Vallière ; ' and I will be in one rage if you
do not tell me whether you have read the ' Popular Tales ' of
Miss Edgeworth.

If you have any hopes that your letters will ever appear
in print, I think you should have some regard to the trouble
of the compiler and affix dates.

M. J. S. to Serena (her birthday).

January 6, 1805.

My best thanks for your letter shall be returned on *this*
day, and all your good wishes sent back again, not the less
warmly and sincerely, because, if I enumerated all the good
things of this world—of which I pray you may continue in
the enjoyment many years—I am so conceited as to think
I must include our health and happiness as one of your
sources of content. Little babe was christened the beginning
of last month by Mr. Oswald Leycester and named Harriet
Alethea. The second name was a fancy of her papa's. The

word in Greek signifies truth, which is such a favourite virtue of his, that the name happening to have a very pleasing sound, he wished to bestow it on a daughter. I wish it may be ominous, and that a love of truth may be innate in Miss Alethea.

Do you plan a tour this summer or autumn? The temptation you had to visit the Lakes is, I am afraid, gone with Sir J. Legard; but is there not temptation here to come halfway? I am very glad to hear of Lady Sheffield doing so well. I was not sorry it turned out to be a *Miss* Holroyd, more especially as I do believe Lady S. is as well pleased, and this little thing may turn out a great comfort. I hope you are mistaken in what you say of my lord's health; I may join you in the wish you express of his retiring to calm enjoyments, but I think neither you nor I can expect it will ever be the case. I most ardently wish and hope that his powers of activity in mind and body may never fail him;[1] for if they did desert him, I am sure he would be miserable. From the temperate life he has always led, and the excellence of his constitution, I think we may hope to keep him as he is for many years more. He seems to have been much shocked with hearing of Lord Rosslyn's sudden death, in a very sudden manner.

M. J. S. to Louisa.

January 23, 1805.

I was much grieved to hear of poor Mr. Rose's incurable malady a short time before I saw his death in the papers. He was a friendly, warm-hearted, well-informed man. S. took to him when we met him at Sheffield Place in 1799. It is rather melancholy to observe from the distance at which we are placed, how many are dropping off, of those who were in middle life when we were young. It is the first warning. I was thinking of Lord Chichester, Lord Rosslyn, and Sir Richard Heron, as well as many more

[1] 'Lord S. is and will ever continue the same active being, always employed for himself, his friends, and the public, and always persuading himself that he wishes for leisure and repose.'—August 1, 1792.—E. Gibbon to his stepmother.

whom we shall not so much miss, but they serve for very
good *memento mori*. . . .

I am expecting a box from Hookham, and shall be much
disappointed if I do not get the ' Life of Sir W. Jones.'   It
is a pleasure to contemplate such characters ; but I declare
I think they rather put me out of humour with human
nature by their great rarity, and one is inclined to growl at
not having some of these folks thrown in one's way sometimes instead of the stupid blockheads and soulless people
by whom one is surrounded.   However, I confess myself
favoured by the lot I have fallen in with, as my days are not
spent with a common character.   Good Lord ! what fools I
might have yoked myself to, if my better angel had not
taken care of me !

January 31, 1805.

So you have the impudence to insinuate, though you do
not say it, that I am rather improved than deteriorated by
my residence in the country with my *millionth* Man.
Perhaps there may be something of foundation in the idea.
He is one that would make anything with the least spark of
the mind I have mentioned, think ; and whoever thinks,
improves.   Let me see now for your unanswered letters, and
I will talk to them regularly.   In the day I can scarce ever
write, and in the evening could I quit Sir W. Jones do you
think ?   Never surely was there a more interesting noble
character.   I regret there are not more private letters, with
less of Hafiz and more of his sentiments on political, moral,
and religious subjects.   I want to write a great deal about
this work—perhaps I may be so good as to resume the
subject. . . . I have just read the ' Bravo of Venice ' and
thought it very grand.   I began it in the evening, could not
leave it unfinished ; so when the Man began his usual clatter
for bed about half-past ten, I very quietly carried the
' Bravo ' upstairs with me, and placed myself too firmly by
the fireside for any arguments to remove me till the clock
had struck five !

Lord, have mercy upon me now !   Your next letter is

that vile criss-cross composition. Well! the first part is only about giving poor innocent babes physic, not because, but for fear they should be ill. I am glad it pleased heaven to make me your sister instead of your child. And such a nasty mess too—salts, of all things for poor babes!

March 31, 1805.

William has not mentioned the tenth report. Probably scenes of the kind are so extremely familiar to his knowledge that he is not surprised or shocked as we county people are. Oh! if a few Lord Melvilles were to swing on Tyburn Tree we might escape a revolution; but surely we cannot long do so, if he comes off with flying colours.[1] I almost wish to see a Crash, that things may be put in better Train. Mind, I only say 'almost,' for I fear no Crash could take place that would not more or less injure every individual now existing. Were I viewing the affairs of Britain from the moon I should be impatient for a thorough Revolution, a new Dynasty, New Men, and new Measures; but it may be a too serious matter to wish for, since I am on this planet with a large family, and more to lose than to gain by any change whatever.

And now, having vented some of my public spirit, I must descend to the discussion of meaner subjects. The management of the Anglesey estate is seemingly given up to S. In consequence, he is to visit Wales in May. . . .

My master has been graciously pleased to consent to be troubled with my company to Wales. It is a favourable opportunity not to be missed.

Alderley: May 5, 1805.

We left Holyhead on Tuesday, and returned through the new Capel Curig road, now making through the finest

[1] 'In April a vote was carried which led to an impeachment on charge of peculation of Pitt's old friend, Henry Dundas, Lord Melville, First Lord of the Admiralty. Ultimately Melville was acquitted, and there is no reason to think that he was guilty of more than neglect of the forms needed for guarding against embezzlement; but Melville's necessary resignation was a sad blow to Pitt.'—S. R. Gardiner, *Student's History of England.*

scenery imaginable, under the auspices of Lord Penrhyn.
The Conway ferry is avoided. The new road carries you
winding through valleys by the side of a torrent-like river
close to Lord Penrhyn's slate quarries. We slept at
Corwen, and next morning passed through Llangollen,
where we introduced ourselves to the ladies,[1] who were
delighted to see us. Their abode is quite a little paradise,
though I was rather disappointed in the situation; but the
ladies did not disappoint me, though they did not answer
my ideas. I found them more unaffected and less clever
than I expected. . . . Lady Eleanor hoped Mr. Stanley did
not join in the 'cry against poor Lord Melville.' But in their
Garden, and amongst their new Books just arrived, they were
delightful, and seem to lead a most enviable and happy life.
I am glad to have seen them, and hope to see them again.
If I had any hope that you had a right idea of politics, I
should like to say a great deal; but I know you would not
agree with us. I think we are more annoyed by such as
my lord [Sheffield] and William wanting to join the Ministry
in the Cry that the Opposition wish to establish a 'Poissarde
Government,' than we are at the Depredations discovered,
or the shameful endeavours to screen the Delinquents, or
by the total omission of any public expression from a high
quarter of his displeasure at the discoveries made. I look
upon him as perfectly incompetent to form an opinion on
any subject except a tie, a wig, or a waistcoat. I am glad
we are not in town, for fear we should not hear Sense from
any we associate with. The 'Morning Chronicle' and
Cobbett are our Delight. . . .

I feel impatient for the 'Logographic Spelling Book.' Is
it too big to be franked from the Agricultural Board as a
Treatise on Breaking-up Grassland, or some other such
matters? Or by William as Instructions to the Country
Magistrates, relative to the best method of receiving and

[1] Lady Eleanor Butler and Miss Ponsonby when quite young determined to
live together. Their cottage in the Valley of Llangollen became celebrated,
and all travellers between England and Ireland sought their acquaintance.
Lady Eleanor died 1829, aged 90; Miss Ponsonby died 1831, aged 72, and they
were buried in the same grave.

lodging the French in their march through the manufacturing counties. For my part, I think, in such a case we might find it as necessary to beg assistance from their troops against the natives, as the Bishop of Killala did in Ireland —but this is an episode.

I never knew anything so perplexing as the infinity of patterns submitted to my inspection. I think the blue gingham from Christian's pleases me best of all, so I will decide on it, and seven yards is sufficient. I abhor long tails— which cause the poor children and dogs many more scoldings than they would have with short appendages to my apparel. As Christian in his list holds forth that he or she makes ladies' dresses, order it to be made up there instead of sending it to that tedious Mrs. Friand.

What fits you, will me, I dare say. If I am wrong, I beg you, fashionable London lady, will set me right.

Lord Sheffield to Serena.

Whitehall: July 14, 1805.

Fox's health is said not to be materially better. It is supposed he can only be patched up for a few months. . . . My lady dined with the princess and a large party at Blackheath yesterday. There is reason to believe that some of her servants have been spies upon her conduct; and notwithstanding all the pains I take in admonishing the sex, I can conceive it very possible that many of them are highly indiscreet in their communications. My lady and brattery are quite well.

CHAPTER VIII.

ON POLITICS AND LITERATURE.

1806-1807.

Dismal forebodings—Death of Pitt—Young Holland—Cheshire all alive—
sixth daughter—First-rate folks—Long's parentage—Dick Turpin's sis-
Dieu merci !—'A Paddy nurse'—'Corinne'—Scylla and Charybd
Journey to Wales—Cattle swimming Menai Straits—Death of Sir John

M. J. S. to Serena.

Alderley Park : January 20, 180

I had really a better opinion of your poor dear und
standing before I discovered you could have a doubt th
visit from you would be at any time a great pleasure to
both.   The resignation of Carr was the greatest bless
almost that could happen to Alderley.   Edward Stanle
likely to make a very different clergyman.   He has st
principles, religious and moral, and a very proper idea of
duties incumbent on his profession. . . . Politics at home
abroad are too melancholy a subject to touch upon.   N
Buonaparte is more formidable than ever, and he will s
have leisure to turn all his attention towards us, and I
nothing and nobody in our Government that gives me
encouragement to hope he will not easily conquer us as s
as he seriously attempts it.   With which agreeable pros
I must conclude.

Serena to M. J. S.

February 18

If I live, and am able, it is not undecided that I go to
in May—I am meditating tremendous things for my old bo

. . . I have had a packet from Louisa with a full account of the state of Dublin. She concludes saying she can scarce press my coming merely to make her happy, when she thinks of the trouble to me, and of my leaving Paradise to go to Purgatory. She feels no fear of invasion ; for she says, as soon as the enemy appear at Cork, she and I could go off directly in a packet with the children. I imagine it would not be so easy as Louisa thinks to get away ; but for myself I cease to fear. I like to share the fate of those I love, and if you told me they were going to put you to death, I would go to you directly to have a scratch at the people to try to save you or go along with you. . . . I want to see the dear Sheffs, Lady Cremorne and Lady Charlotte Finch, and poor Epictetus. I have promised to call at Windsor to see the Kennicotts, and a visit to the Legards. I shall do more or less of these things as it will bring me to May ; and thus, dear Maria, I lay before you my plans. . . . I have had a little party—Lord and Lady Leven and four sons, all the race of Elchos, Lady Frances Traill, Lady Elizabeth Magennis, and Lady Florence Balfour, Lady Willes, Sir C. Talbot, Admiral Sotheby, and a few smart men ; the Bishop of Salisbury and his daughter, and Lord Bernard and his brother. Lady Hesketh writes still, though too blind to read her own writing or distinguish anyone's face ; but she is quite cheerful, and receives company as brilliantly as ever—few of seventy-five so handsome. I say nothing, dear Maria, of public affairs. It makes me sick, and I never felt so little of my blue sky. . . . I pity the poor K., who has behaved with temper and good sense. The loss of Mr. Pitt seems to me a great national loss. I confess, however, some of his schemes might be mistaken, but I really know not any man left that possesses the same ability and integrity. His loss and that of Nelson, and now Lord Cornwallis, seem to me as if our strength in their different stations were removed from us to prepare us for sharing the fate of other nations. My brother writes with moderation, but allows what I have said of the loss Mr. Pitt is. It is time for that same brother of mine to give up *ambition*, and I trust he has done so, and will end his days in tranquillity, if the time will permit any of us to do so. Adieu, my dearest Maria.

I am ever most affectionately yours,
                                    S. HOLROYD.

Sheridan was literally not to be trusted as treasurer to the playhouse avowedly, and he is supposed a fit person to be Treasurer of the Navy. Grattan, a curious person to be Chancellor of the Exchequer in Ireland. Several equally fit for their offices. Well might Mr. Pitt, dying, cry out, ' O my poor country ! '

M. J. S. to Louisa.

February 7, 1806.

If I did not appear joyful enough at the disappearance of Mr. Pitt from the stage of existence, it proceeded from my writing the very day of hearing the news, and one cannot help feeling some repugnance at first to rejoice in death when it attacks those in the prime of life, as one may call Mr. Pitt. But if some natural feelings of human nature withheld us from saying an immediate Te Deum, I beg you will believe that subsequent reflection has confirmed us in the opinion that nothing more fortunate in the way of casualties could have happened to Great Britain, unless, indeed, the death of Buonaparte, and I cannot find in my heart to wish heartily for that, from a curiosity to see what pitch of greatness a man may arrive at in this world. I think he is on the high road to outstrip all the heroes of antiquity.

I am very glad, upon the whole, at the total change of administration, for I look upon the prince as sovereign now, and I hope he will act so prudently as never to lose the power he has acquired. It is impossible to approve all the appointments. Surely Sheridan must be very unfit for Treasurer of the Navy. It is a sad misfortune that when a party comes into power, of whose members in general one approves, one is forced also to have all the tagrag and bobtail of that party as bad as the same fag-end of the opposite party. . . . I suppose poor aunt is blessing her stars that she will possibly not live long enough to see the miseries which must inevitably befall the country with prince, Fox, &c. at the head of affairs, but I have not now time for politics. You will see a great many J. T. S.'s in the Cheshire report, which will direct you to his share of the work. The Salt is entirely Holland's, which is most interesting to readers in general, not being found in any other work in so complete a form. Young Holland is come into the country to practise with his father for two years. He aims at being a London physician, and, if information and good sense could ensure success, he would have a fair chance of rising in that line to great eminence ; but I think ignorance and plenty of small talk and flattery are more likely to succeed.

I have read 'St. Clair,' and I so dearly love the senti-mental that many passages please me much ; but my sober old fellow has so lost his taste for these kind of things that he would not finish it. He is a very different kind of animal to that which used to read poetry, pick off thorns from sweetbrier, and sing French songs. Do not mistake, however, that I mean he ought still to be gallant to his old matron wife ; but I quarrel with him every now and then for having forgotten his old feelings in the romantic and sentimental.

Serena to M. J. S.

48 Gloucester Place : April 18, 1806.

. . . I bring you a gauze rag for a gown that looks pretty and takes up no room. I take not an atom to the Clintons, but I am obliged to take gowns to my Irish cousins, and shall be in jail unless Buonaparte disposes of me otherwise. I am afraid he could not contrive to make me of any use but to teach children English, and he would not care for that, so into the ditch or fire I should be con-veyed. I hope to find the Firth as young as ever. In proportion as I myself see my beauty decay, and wrinkles and age wither my face, they think it the more necessary to tell me I am not altered. But I beg you to prepare yourself for seeing more than the year since we have met, for it is a period when the ravages of that sad old fellow, Time, come rapidly on.

M. J. S. to Louisa.

Alderley Park : May 4, 1806.

All Cheshire has been alive this week past. On Mr. Egerton's death, a fortnight ago, General Broughton, Parker, and Mr. Davenport declared themselves candidates for the honour of representing the county. From last Monday the Man has been in a state of permanent bustle— out by eight in the morning, and sometimes not home till midnight. Mr. Davenport had the support of almost all the principal landholders in the county, and S. was of great service at Macclesfield, Northwich, and Stockport. I believe Mr. Davenport had doubts whether he should have S.'s support ; but, setting personal considerations on both sides out of the question, S. considered him as the most proper person, and as the one who had most claim on him for support.

I do hope you will not take pleasure in annoying poor old aunt on the subject of Ireland and Irish folk. I am sure you often say more than you think, and as she really takes what is said so literally, it would save you both a great deal of trouble if you would for a while say *less* than you think.

Many a wise observation do you lose by my not writing oftener. As I have told you before, I compose many letters to you which never appear in black and white. Would that a wish—a thought—could put them on paper ! Many an occurrence, a book read, or a paragraph in a newspaper, suggest observations which, for want of being speedily committed to paper, escape my memory when the pen is in my hand. . . . I have been delighted with Cobbett of late on many subjects, except on that of the princess, and I cannot imagine why he takes that side so violently. The 'Morning Post' is too violent on the other.   Cobbett is to me unintelligible.   I do not know what he aims at.   Surely not working to have her thought guilty!   The 'Morning Chronicle' is grown quite stupid since it became ministerial.   The 'Courier' is now the best paper we see.

[A sixth daughter, Maud, was born June 10, 1806.]

Alderley Park : July 10, 1806.

We had our christening on Tuesday.   Edward was so absurd as to have such violent scruples about baptising any-where but in church, that they could not be made to give way in consequence of my being unable to go.   Oswald Leycester was so good as to perform the ceremony.

My uncle said something about Abigail in his answer to our request; so we have tacked it on as a second name to please him, and called little miss, Matilda (Maud) Abigail. Maud is not a family name, but a fancy of his worship's.

Benjamin Way of Denham Place to J. T. S.

My dear Sir,—From the 'Morning Post' of last Monday I read to my wife, the birth of your daughter, at the same time exhorting her to offer her service for godmother.   She told me she had so done on a precedent opportunity and was ready to do so now.   Your very kind letter since received settles this point.   We are both at your service now and in future.   For Christian names I have no ridiculous partiality. Abigail was my dear sister's name, and Mrs. Stanley can inform you that it is recorded she was the tenth in suc-cession of that name in our family.   Whatever may be the customary fee in Cheshire I shall be happy to place to your account at Gosling's. . . .

Yours most sincerely,
BENJAMIN WAY.

[After the christening, Serena joined Lady Longford at Chester, and proceeded to Ireland, from whence she wrote to M.J.S.]

Never was a journey more delightful through Wales ! But I have only time to say that at Llangollen you and dear

Stanley are held as first-rate folks, and many wishes for your
return.   Lady Longford had never seen the ladies before, and
went as my party, but they soon took to her. I hailed the Eagle
and Child at the inn at Holyhead, and in the distance I saw
Lady Stanley.   That jewel of a man, Captain Skinner, took
as much care of me as if I had been a princess, and certainly
I never was in such a ship so neat.

M. J. S. to Serena.

Parkgate : September 14, 1806.

I was very glad to persuade S. to come here. I do not
think it is necessary to deny ourselves the expenditure where
health is the question.   Thank you very much for your
generous kind offer of forwarding my wishes if I could not
have attained them without.   I assure you the Man felt it as
strongly as myself, though I could never have borne to accept
such a sum from you, who have too many generous wants for
money.   Though from never running into debt, you would
not be poor were your income less, yet were it much larger
you could not be rich, as you would then only indulge yourself
with giving away hundreds, where now perhaps you give
tens or twenties. . . . We came here on Friday se'ennight,
bag and baggage, eight children and seven females !

M. J. S. to Louisa.

Alderley Park : October 10, 1806.

When I got to Chester, I was met by the intelligence
that Kitty Leycester was dangerously ill of a fever. She has
been in great danger ; but the last accounts are so favourable,
I trust she will get over it.   The extreme anxiety shown by
our rector has convinced me still farther of what I told you
I thought likely to be in his contemplation in regard to
future establishment.

I have pressed Mrs. Long to get her mother into an
hospital, but have desired she will not think of returning to
me while she lives, unless she could make herself quite easy.
She is a most worthy good creature as ever lived.   Her

father[1] absolutely refused her coming to live with him, under the idea that she ought not to leave me, or she would have shared his misfortunes long ago.

Lord Sheffield to Benjamin Way [President of Guy's Hospital], Denham Place, Uxbridge.

Sheffield Place : November 19, 1806.

My dear Uncle,—Maria Josepha is in great distress. The father of her lady of the bedchamber is dead. The mother is somewhat crazy ; moreover there is nothing to maintain her. The daughter (Mrs. Long) came from Alderley, where she is much wanted, some time ago to attend her parentage in London. Can you, as an extra favour, introduce the mother into that nice place called Guy's ? It will be a great charity. It is believed that she can last but a very short time. Alderley is greatly inconvenienced

---

[1] Long's father, Mr. Tilney Long, was a person of education and superior position. He had had reverses of fortune, as is shown by a letter to him from Lady Anne Lindsay, authoress of *Auld Robin Gray*. She writes : ' If any assistance respecting the establishment of your pretty, genteel daughter is still necessary, I think you would do well to mention it to my sister, Lady Margaret Fordyce, who is at present in Cavendish Street, at Lord Hardwicke's; but I hope she is comfortably settled long ago.' The ' pretty daughter ' entered the service of M. J. Holroyd in 1794 and remained the devoted friend of the family for fifty-three years. She was in turn attendant, nurse, and housekeeper, beloved and trusted by all, though her particular charge was the younger twin son, William Owen.

The Tilney Longs' old home was near Chingford. Mr. Long writes to his daughter : ' In my last I described to you that I had sometime since repaired our family vault in the old cathedral church at Chinkford, and I do intend to erect a proper tombstone thereon, inscribed at the entrance of the vault " Long," and on one side thereof, " This vault was built by direction of George Long, the Elder, of this Parish, Gentleman, in the year 1738." The race for the next presentation, I think, lies between myself, your mother, and Squire Moses. There is still room for from fifteen to eighteen coffins. I am informed that there is now living, in a very advanced age, in the house my father formerly inhabited at Chinkford, a woman who had been for many years servant to my father and married his gardener. She is now a widow, having buried three husbands, and it is my intention to see and have a little gossip with her, whose maiden name was Turpin, sister to the noted highwayman, Dick Turpin, whose history is more remarkable for benevolence than violence. His haunts were the then almost impenetrable thickets of Epping Forest.' Dick Turpin, born 1711, died 1739.

U

through the want of Mrs Long, more especially as the ... ... is so little delectable that she must depart and with ... I am just going to Stanmer to attend the christening ... Emily Lyssa Pelham ... I am very busy all day while ... with a famous Mr Pusey, author of the 'Forest ... The same impetus which set me in motion forty years ... keeps me going on, although I do not think the present ... with the help of our ministers and Buonaparte ... ... longer.

> Yours and dearest Aunt's ever.

Series to M. J. S.

Fakenham Hall: December ...

On the ... of November Lady Longford, Mr ... Caroline Fakenham, and I set out from ... Lodge together, and went to Summer Hill to Lady ... sister to Lady Longford ... Lord Longford dies ... ... but no one man can do enough against ... numbers. You will be told that the insurrection has ... ... but I happen to be on the spot where a week ... within seven miles of this house, it was necessary to call ... a considerable military force to disperse the numbers ... had collected and were hourly increasing. Several ... killed and many taken prisoners who are to be tried for their ... lives. Lord Longford and his yeomanry are out ... every night for some hours. He conceals his time of ... to be the more sure of all being right and they may ... ... as they might be if they expected him; and ... ... many other precautions are taken.

M. J. S. to L. ...

Alderley Park: April 1st

The 'Letters from the Mountains' I like better ... letter every time I open the volume. I shall not ... till I am well acquainted with the authoress, and I shall be ... wretched if I can discern she has any unpleasant quality

I think I can discover that though she submitted to rear children, and even thought she took pleasure in them, that she looked upon it as a subordinate employment, and almost envied her childless friend in America. Well ! *Dieu merci !* I do not make a virtue of necessity ; but feel thoroughly convinced that no possible torment the eight I have can give me could be so irksome to me as having led a childless married life. Nothing could have carried me through my long exile but a family of children. I know, in the bottom of your heart you think this is a mark of want of high sentiment and of a strong philosophic turn of mind. Maybe so ; but I do not wish to be otherwise, any more than I do to be a man, another proof of my grovelling disposition.

I cannot write a long letter to-day because I enclose one to aunt. I have made an attack on the new ministers in particular, and the present principles of government in general, that will frighten her out of her seven senses and make her think me as bad as you yourself. On the Catholic question I was certain William could not side with the late ministers because of the Rat Hole. What I want to know is, what danger there can be in rendering Catholics eligible to high offices, unless we put a Catholic king at the head of affairs. A good Protestant will not be obliged to prefer a Catholic, and yet the ideal advantage might conciliate the Irish. . . . The Man is half tempted to build castles in the air and wish himself (though without hope) in some snug place with something to do, to enable him to emerge from obscurity. . . . If Cheshire should ever have a free representation and a more general power of electing members to speak for its rights, I shall hope to see S. the popular member, and I think more unlikely things have happened. I should be very sorry to live with a servile set of placemen who would never dare to speak their sentiments, if they did by accident feel ashamed of growing fat at the expense of the people ; and in whose company one must never call a fool a fool, or a knave a knave, if in high situations. What do you think of the outset ? Perceval and the Chancellorship

of Lancaster, to induce him to condescend to become
Chancellor of the Exchequer! It beat the first job of the
Foxites out and out. . . . So much for last night; and, as all
the family of subalterns have been at church this morning
and I am going now, I can add no more except my sincere
hope that all placemen in Ireland may not be murdered
before you leave it! Tell me how you take to a Paddy
nurse. Does she hold the child the right end up?

Yours ever,
M. J. S.

[On hearing of Louisa's sorrow in exile, an old friend—Hon.
Caroline Lyttelton—writes playfully:]

Stourbridge: 1806.

Dear Sister Cabbage,—You talk of vegetating in Potato
Land; I have root in a much heavier soil. Oh! unhappy I!
I shall transmit to you several articles of impeachment
which have reached me against the Hon. L. D. C. They
come from Ireland, but are not directly or indirectly the
work of Lady L. Barry.

First and highest Misdemeanour.—That General Clinton
is a very handsome and agreeable man, and disposed to be
sociable; but that his wife will not let him go anywhere,
and when he did dine at my Lady Vandeleur's she cruelly
and despitefully carried him away before all the rest of the
company.

Second Misdemeanour.—That the said Louisa Dorothea,
on her first arrival, was visited by all the best company
in Dublin, who were very desirous of making it agreeable
to the Louisa or Maria of Gibbon (they could not tell
which it was), and that the said criminal gave them to
understand that she did not choose to have anything to do
with them.

Thirdly.—That she, L. D. C., being obliged of necessity to make her appearance once at the castle, looked
much distressed with her hoop; the latter article was
particularly marked as an offence against the Irish
drawing-room, because the Louisa of Gibbon must have

been used to a court hoop so frequently that it could only be from affectation that she did not carry it well at the castle.

These articles were heard before council on the side of the defendant, whose answers were as follows:

That though it might be granted that General Clinton was a handsome and agreeable man, he was far from loving dissipation any better than his wife, and that perhaps he was not unwillingly borne away; that the defendant was fond of selecting her own friends, was given to study, and had usually remarkable good manners; that she might carry her hoop ungracefully at the castle without any intentional contempt, for that, after ten years' persevering instruction from Mons. Olivier, she had never been able to accomplish a walk across the room with her toes turned out, or her head held up. As for dancing a minuet, General Clinton could just as easily perform the pyrrhic dance.

.   .   .   .

Pity me for having a half brother-in-law who has taken it into his head to turn author, and to single me out as the fittest person to be presented with two very thick quartos about Roman and British roads by an old Welsh monk, by name Giraldus Cambrensis; half a dozen pedigrees of Welsh princes; long dissertations upon the tombstones of the Cathedral St. Davids; and, in short, all that kind of information which in the case of Mr. Hearne the antiquarian produced that elegant couplet:

> Says Father Time to Thomas Hearne,
> ' Whatever I forget, you learn.'

But if you wish for any little agreeable anecdotes about Gruffyd ap Rhys, Prince of Wales, I am well qualified for that purpose, as I now take regular dozes over them every day, out of my great civility to Sir Richard Hoare.[1]

Serena to M. J. S.

Gloster Place: June 2, 1807.

I dined at my brother's on Monday to take leave of Lady Sheffield, who goes to pass a month with her princess. On

[1] Married (1783) Hester, daughter of 2nd Lord Lyttelton.

the birthday the princess dressed in the parlour at
Gardens. Lady S. then attended her to court, and
wards had her to dine, and she stayed with them till t
at night. I was kindly pressed to share all this, but dec
On Sunday they dined with her at Blackheath—twent
at dinner, all the foreign princes &c.

I rejoice for your sakes that the harbours between I
head and Dublin will be made really safe. It seems
lutely necessary, now that Parliament obliges cont
crossing the seas.

Lord Redesdale told Catherine Fanshawe that conv
tion existed not in Ireland at the dinner parties, for th
avoid the splitting on the Scylla rock of political differe
they rushed into the Charybdis whirlpool of the most d
mined and deliberate trifling.

God bless you all,

S. H

M. J. S. to Louisa.

Alderley Park : August 9,

Have you read ' Corinne,' Madame de Stael's new n
for which it is said she was banished to Copet, in
sequence of Buonaparte's displeasure at the prefe
given to the English character in the work. We have
greatly pleased with it in many respects, though by no m
recommending it as a work which may defy criticism.
character of the Frenchman is admirably drawn, a
think the English national character is much better dep
than by any other foreigner ; but I think she need not
been banished for having represented it faultless, as th
much excellent and well-deserved satire upon our man
There is a tea-table conversation which delighted me be
measure, for it is really not exaggerated, as you woul
if you had dined out much in Cheshire. The pruder
emptiness of Lucille, as a model of the English fe
character, is certainly *outré*, but there is much truth i
and an unprejudiced reader would undoubtedly long to l

the character of Corinne and Lucille; and, however one may be sensible, such women as the former would not be calculated to people the world to the best advantage, any more than a world full of Miss Berrys or Cat. Fanshawes, yet no one could hesitate a moment in choosing which character they would desire to pass their lives with. Corinne's character made us both think of the ladies above named.

Where do you think I am going? To Penrhos, with Rianette and Louisa. S. went there last week, and his mother has given us a direct invitation, which I did not think it proper to decline. I am much pleased and gratified by the invitation and kindly expressed wish of seeing as many as I can bring.

M. J. S. to Louisa.

Penrhos : September 8, 1807.

Having two M.P.s at my command, I must send you a few lines to let you know how we are going on. William and Henry Clive are both here, on their way to Ireland.

From my experience of the lady of the mansion, I should ascribe to her every good quality the human character can possess—good temper, benevolence, ease, liveliness, and everything that is charming.

We arrived here on Thursday evening. She has received and treated me and the children with all the attention and affection you can possibly imagine. She seems much pleased with Rianette and Lucy, and, without over-fondness, extremely indulgent and kind to them. Most fortunately the dogs and they are on the best terms possible—the dogs are delighted to be caressed, and the children are delighted that they will let themselves be pulled about like their own dogs. Lady S. seems to think S. the first of human beings. The pleasure she receives from her grandchildren is a perfectly new sensation, and I think she must wonder she has denied herself that pleasure so long. There is not an appearance of the least jealousy whatever of S.'s interference in the management of the property, all he does is right, and she is equally desirous of improving that part of the estate which will be his at Sir J.'s death, as that which will be hers for her life. She takes every opportunity of showing him she wishes him to consider the house and everything about it as much his own as hers, and is delighted that he should give his orders for any little alteration or improvement he wishes to make.

Sunday and yesterday have been two of the grandest and most interesting days that could have been bespoke for my special entertainment. At seven o'clock on Sunday morning it was a dead calm, and in half an hour the most tremendous storm of wind and rain arose which has been known for twenty-five years. From one of the windows we could watch any vessel that entered the harbour; and after seeing Captain Skinner's packet pass safely through a very dangerous entrance which is never attempted but in case of necessity, we saw a large three-masted ship at the very mouth of the harbour miss the entrance and go upon the rocks, where, after rolling dreadfully for about an hour, one mast after another fell overboard, and she became a perfect wreck. Two brigs ran ashore and were much damaged, and several others got safe with great difficulty.

I went out to look at the sea nearer, but it was scarce possible to stand. I saw, however, the most magnificent waves rolling after each other and breaking on the fine black rocks which bound the park, throwing up spray like a cloud as high as the top of a house.

M. J. S. to Serena.

Penrhos : September 19, 1807.

. . . I hope the capture of Copenhagen and the Danish fleet has revived your spirits a little. . . . Is Ireland in any particular bad way, that you speak with such alarm about Louisa ? I should think Dublin as safe as London almost, as probably Buonaparte will not begin with taking it, and it would always be easy to cross over to Holyhead. . . .

The worst thing I look forward to is the croaking and alarm we shall hear of, for some months to come. At least I insisted upon it to William that disastrous events must give him pleasure, since they prove his prognostics to be right, and his 'Mind my words!' always to be strictly wise and correct. I am afraid the success of Copenhagen has disconcerted his expectations.

The business here is nearly concluded. . . . All has gone on perfectly smoothly in all respects. The lady's confidence in S. is unbounded and her kindness to me and the children uniform. She does not fondle them as much as many a granmam might do, but quite as much as I wish and desire. She lets them sit in her chair, likes to have them in the room, and always proposes first their having any little indulgences of fruit, cake, &c. that come in the way, without pressing it on me if I am desirous of declining it for them. She is not at all tenacious of keeping me always with her, but proposes my walking out with S., Emma, or by myself, whenever she thinks I should like to go. I have bathed several times, and the children are delighted here : they are quite unwilling to go home.

M. J. S. to Louisa.

Alderley Park : October 1, 1807.

At Bangor we fell in with a cattle fair, and saw the ceremony of swimming the poor beasts over—a more unpleasant sight can hardly be imagined. The people tie ropes to the horns of five or six bullocks at once, get into a boat, and drag as hard as they can, while others on shore beat them cruelly to force them into the water; and when they have plunged in, it seems impossible they should not be drowned, as their heads often get under the boat's bottom. The people keep beating them all the way to *encourage* them to keep above water and to swim, which they do most awkwardly.

. . . The Edge has become a very busy scene. The steam-engine is finished and set to work. An offer has been made of 1,000*l.* per annum for the cobalt, and a tonnage payment for all beyond a certain quantity. I hope this year the concern will begin to be profitable, though I do not expect my diamond necklace quite yet; when the Man has made 5,000*l.* by the mine, I am to have a very handsome one.

M. J. S. to Miss Ann Firth.

Alderley Park: October 29, 1807.

Maud is a very nice little thing ; Alethea quite a beauty. I never saw such a spirit as the little Maud's ; but she is a very sensible babe. My lord was much pleased with Teddy's manliness and spirit, though he was rather disturbed by the little urchin's telling him that he knew his little uncle was not so strong as him, and that he should pin him down as Boaty does Pompey, unless he said ' Pray, pray ! ' What a strange idea for the child to take into his head !

M. J. S. to Louisa.

Alderley Park: November 30, 1807.

Though I have but a few minutes before the post goes, I wish not to lose a day in telling you we have this morning been informed by express of Sir John's death yesterday morning.... To feel sorrow is impossible; but death is always very awful. S. set off to-night by the mail. Edward could not have reached London in time ; and Hugh Leycester, who wrote at Isabella's request, said he supposed S. would come up immediately.

December 8.

The funeral was on Saturday, at South Audley Street Chapel. S. and Edward attended. S. is going to Sheffield Place for a few days. Though I miss him sadly, yet I would not wish him to hurry back without doing all in his power and seeing his friends, now that he is in the land of the living again. I shall not be able to reconcile myself to the name of ' Sir John ' for a long time. I wish it was Sir ' Nicholas ' or Sir anything else rather.

CHAPTER IX.

AT HER OLD LONDON HOME.

1808-9-10.

Lord Sheffield visits his sister—Dr. Kennicott and Moses—Purchase of Privy
Gardens — Mrs. Nisbett — Joséphine Beauharnais — Serena meets Duc
d'Orléans—Alfred's christening—' Mother Goose '—Ode to a Bonnet—
Humphry Davy—Sir John's discernment—To-morrow's earthquake—Mrs.
Siddons—Rogers—Pleasant dinners—' The Devil's town '—Miss Holroyd
found—The new plaything—Cobalt and Portugal—The Jubilee—Sir John's
enforced studies—Regent v. Buonaparte—King of Sweden.

M. J. S. to Louisa.

February 1808.

I hope I may enjoy myself a little before I am forced to
turn chaperone and take those parts of the world's amusements which would now give me the least pleasure. It will
be a curious transition of taste and sentiments from ' Miss
Holroyd of 1796 to Lady Stanley of 1809,' if that year
should see me in the same scenes again. I am more than
ever desirous now that William should determine on a house
in London and not in Dublin. Do go and ask the duke for
something in England, or else convince William, Buony will
be in Dublin this next spring, and that you will be safer in
London. . . . These east winds are abominable, and I have
not yet exposed myself to them on foot. I have been out in
the carriage a few times, but the coachman having the same
suspicion of the skill of regular-bred physicians as Mrs.
Clinton—and, moreover, what I believe she has not, a great
faith in quack doctors—determined to go to a famous one,
under the idea that his arm was not properly in its place,
though Mr. Holland had examined it thoroughly and

pronounced it all right. The blacksmith was his authority
for doubting. The quack of course said the arm was not in
its place, and three men pulled and pulled till they said it
was ; and the coachman is returned for the present less able
to drive than before, but convinced that he has received great
benefit from the operation. So now we have a coachman
and postillion, four horses and a landau ; but I have not the
means of going out, for the postillion, being the coachman's
son, was to learn to drive when he came, and now his
father cannot instruct him.

Alderley Park : April 5, 1808.

I have got the house we were in at Parkgate the year
before last, for two months. It is close to the sea, and with a
walled garden, where the children can be as safe as possible
from everything but one another. I should be very glad if
my breed had not so much game in it ! But the chicks
fight, kick and cuff as soon as they can move, as naturally
as the fighting-cock race peck each other before they are full-
fledged. The future hero, Edward, is a troublesome boy as
needs be. Maud is a great favourite and prime scholar of
his. For sure there never centred in so many little human
beings so much quicksilver.

M. J. S. to Serena.

Parkgate : May 15, 1808.

I came here with part of the family on the 5th ; Mrs.
Firth and the remainder followed. Our number, though
twenty-one, is well accommodated. Alfred improves very
much. My Man has been absent near a month. From the
assizes at Chester he went to Penrhos, where he is very fully
employed with agents, tenants, &c. He went by Llangollen,
and spent a charming evening with the ladies. He found
they had not seen ' Marmion,' and wished me to order a
copy to be sent in my name. I have read it and been much
pleased, though the ' Lay ' is far superior as a whole. . . .

Mrs. Chapone's [1] 'Life and Letters' interested me much, and when one thinks of the time when her letters to Richardson were written, it is surprising what learning and cleverness is displayed, both in respect to her age, and that in those days it was much less usual than at present for women to know anything but needlework and pudding-making. To be sure, an improvement has taken place in education; but it is a pity that in making an alteration the world did not stop short of going into the very opposite extreme, as nowadays one may almost venture to say young people are taught nothing that is useful. . . .

Serena to M. J. S.

Bath : Saturday, July 9, 1808.

I have no malady but extreme weakness, which indeed is the least of all infirmities while spirit and mind keeps so well as, thank God, mine does, and I will give you a curious instance how that same spirit can wind me up like an alarum clock for many hours and then drop dead. My brother was so good as to come to see me. Never was any one more kind, pleasant, and with that sort of good humour that a tranquil happy state gives, and which I delighted to see in him. One of the first things he said was that Lady Sheffield had charged him not to let me walk much, for she had observed my great weakness when she was with me. The only answer I made, ' Oho! I'll take a chair when tired, and only just show you a few of our new streets.' We dined at six, went out at eight; I walked him down Great Pulteney Street to Sidney Gardens, and when there I said 'We'll go in; we may meet friends.' Accordingly in we went, never sat down, stopped to talk to people (nothing more tiresome), walked the whole way back. Called and drank tea between nine and ten at Lady Isabella Douglas's. Went home, ate supper. Went to bed, but not a bit of sleep. However, nobody knew that but myself. He was to go away before two o'clock, and he called for breakfast

[1] Hester Chapone, English authoress, 1727–1801.

between eight and nine. We then walked to St. James's Square, where we visited a few folks. Had a sort of early dinner, and he went away, leaving me as happy as possible; but the stimulus was gone, and I literally dropped on the sofa almost lifeless. I desired Watts not to let a soul speak another word to me, but to leave a book by me, and thus I lay, stretched and motionless, till ten at night, when I went to bed. . . . I fell asleep for *seven hours,* and waked well. I don't wish my brother to know quite how it affected me, though I told him how like the clock I was. I am glad they are now at Sheffield Place. Since you wish it, I hope you will get their house [Privy Gardens]. All your plans, dearest Maria, are wise, prudent, and good; it seems to me as if you could not manage better about your children. What you say as to your enjoyment in town is natural enough, yet I think you will find it better than you imagine; for though you may not be entirely the dancing Maria Holroyd, you are certainly not less agreeable than you then were, and are in a situation of fashion and affluence to be on a level with the first people in London. You have the added consequence of your fine train of children, and though your amusements may not be of the exact same sort, yet surely there are abundance to fill the place of them. And had you begun your married life in London, you would not be half so happy as you are at present. You are now the tried friend of a most sensible, affectionate husband; your character established in really the highest way, you yourself attached to domestic life. Therefore, my own dear Maria, be sure of happiness, and you will find it wherever you go. May God grant you every best blessing, but above all, that of feeling every blessing. . . . You are naturally sprightly and lively, those happy elastic spirits will never quite forsake you. Thus I have settled, and am ready to take Uncle Toby's oath, that you *shall* be happy even in that vile metropolis.

If I live I shall see you, and if I do not I shall not perhaps think of it; and yet I rather doubt it. I am ready to cry out with Dr. Kennicott, when he heard people doubt

of knowing their friends in the next world, 'What! do
you think I should not know Moses?' My cry would be,
' Shall I not know my children?' and yet—but I will talk
no more nonsense. . . . The G. Coxes will make me go to
them this summer, at the hazard of being in gaol for want
of money. So, after two nights with the William Coxes at
Bemerton, two nights at Winchester with Lady Rivers, I go
for two months to Blackbrook Cottage. I must return to
Bath in October. I expect the Chief Justice Downes to
come there on purpose to see me. All the Fanshawes quite
brilliant this year, but now gone to Sunbury to meet Mrs.
Grant of Laggan, at Sir John Legard's. . . . Mrs. Dring
felt, without my saying it, that I should go no more north-
ward. What I most love in Yorkshire is that dear, good
Firth; but I trust she will many years be able to travel
about, and will come and pass some time with me.

Adieu, now, my dearest Maria. Heaven bless you all.

Yours most affectionately,

S. HOLROYD.

[The wish of M. J. S. that her father's house in Privy Gardens
might become their London home was gratified, and Sir John
went in August to arrange the purchase.]

J. T. S. to M. J. S.

Privy Gardens: August 1808.

I rode down to Norwood and found Mrs. Nisbett very
glad to see me. She was in the midst of bricklayers,
plasterers, &c. The whole house was undergoing thorough
repair. She contrived, however, to give me an excellent
dinner. Venison to eat, and burgundy to drink. She is
very little altered in person from what she was twelve
years ago. The accounts of my purchase and my getting
this house were fine subjects for conversation. . . . She
related many of her adventures when she was in Germany
and Switzerland, and brought to my mind one circumstance
which I had forgotten. When I was at Paris with her she

was visited by many great ladies, and I remember two being in the room when I came to her with the news of the Hôtel de Castres being stripped of its furniture by the mob. One was Madame de Châteauvieux, the wife of the general and colonel of the Swiss regiment of that name. Who, think you, was the other? I had not adverted to her at the time. She was Madame de Beauharnais, *alias* the Empress Joséphine. Mrs. Nesbitt has the most curious kind of connection with the world that ever any woman had.

M. J. S. to Louisa.

1808.

Oh for a good swing of generals! Shooting is much too honourable. If this sequel to the battle of Vimiera[1] had been performed by Prussian, Austrian, or Russian generals William would have cried out upon bribery. What will he say of our folks? What will Buonaparte say? What will Europe say? and if they are not mere machines, what will our brave soldiers say who have bled in vain? . . . If our admirals fought like our generals England would have long ago been at the feet of Buonaparte. These last never follow up an advantage. . . . Could Buonaparte have desired anything better than that we should set at liberty his troops in Portugal, who could do him no good there, and civilly transport them over to him where they might be of infinite use in Spain? . . .

Serena to M. J. S.

Blackbrook Cottage, Fareham: August 23, 1808.

Do you remember 'Orontes,' my dear Maria? I am now with George Coxe and his pleasant wife. It is five years since we met, and never was reception more cordial.

The strange conclusion to the glorious victories of our generals in Portugal has made us all wild. A letter from Gregory Way—a prisoner—shows him to be a noble fellow.

[1] Sir A. Wellesley's victory in Portugal, August 21, 1808.

I shuddered at his escape, yet was happy in his conduct towards his gallant and lamented colonel. Let us praise a Frenchman for saving his life when he was taken prisoner.

The next point interesting to me was Colonel Lyon, the son of Mrs. G. Coxe, who distinguished himself in both battles. He wrote on the field the very hour the battle was over—just three lines to his mother, thankful to Providence and full of affection to her and G. Coxe. He has since then written again, just before this terrible convention was made, in high spirits, saying that all was now in our power, and of course the surrender must be unconditional. I have had two letters from Lady Longford, who is indignant, but cautious of remarks where her son-in-law, Sir Arthur Wellesley, is concerned. She has four sons besides engaged in different ways in Spain. . . . Louisa has sent me a sketch she drew of Winnington; it gives me a good idea of being a very fine place, but I want to know if it is to take the place of Alderley, or if both will be kept. I am afraid it is many long miles further from Bath; but if we can meet elsewhere I must give up my wish to see your homes of all sorts. On Monday last I was conveyed thirteen miles in a chaise to St. Boniface, where the scene was a sudden surprise. The foreground consists of rocks and copse. Behind this the bold promontory or mountain called Bonchurch—midway—is literally the region of choughs and caws. (One of the choughs, with its scarlet bill and scarlet claws and legs, lives tame at Mr. Bowdler's.) You cannot see sheep on this hill above halfway, yet, O *mirabile dictu!* up to the top of that mountain did I ride single on a fine tall horse, attended by Mr. Bowdler on his little white horse, and passed an hour riding all about the top of it. I believe it is twenty years since I rode single at Sheffield Place, and yet I felt no fear, for I was all delight, and for three days rode the same horse over rocks and all sorts of places.

I met my good George Coxe and was conveyed in the Lindegrew barge through Spithead, delighted with the whole tour. We dined with the Lindegrews and met General Whittiam, Deputy-Governor of Portsmouth, who invited us

x

to Government House, where he had kindly intended a
friendly dinner by ourselves; but lo! that very morn the
Duke of Orleans landed from Gibraltar, and he had to be the
guest of the general. After presenting us to the duke, we
sat down ten to dinner, and I had the honour of being
handed down to dinner by his Highness, who placed me
between himself and the general, at the head of the table.
Luckily he speaks English so well, I had no embarrassment
with my bad French. I thought of all Madame de Genlis'
history of his father &c. He is more like a German than a
Frenchman, fat, fair, and heavy countenance, though they
say he is sensible and well informed; but he thinks he shall
die of consumption, as two of his brothers have done. One
he had just left dead at Malta. The physicians do not think
him ill, but he is fanciful and low-spirited. It happened to
be the day after we had the news of the victories in Portugal,
and we had no other conversation. We finished that
interesting day going home at eleven by bright moonlight.
I am tired and seventy. May heaven bless you all!

Ever and ever yours,

S. HOLROYD.

In the meantime, do pray talk to me. A letter directed
here will safely reach me. Mrs. Grant, of the mountains, was
at St. John Legard's when he died. Cat. Fanshawe had
only left him thirty-six hours, and no idea of his dying
though in bed, as supposed, with gout.

M. J. S. to Serena.

Alderley: October 2, 1808.

Your very entertaining vision, dear little aunt, gave me
much pleasure and amusement in reading, and I think you
most fortunate in being able to form as clear ideas of places
and prospects in a dream as others do in their waking hours.
For that all you have told me is only a dream I am quite
convinced. That you should have ridden on a real live
horse up a real high mountain, and that with your own

real corporeal head you should have looked down without tumbling down the said real high mountain, I cannot, by any stretch of faith, believe. After thanking you a thousand times for this pleasant letter, I must thank you ten thousand times more for not introducing into any part of it one of the reproaches my long silence so well deserves.

I have certainly not had the excuse of nothing to say this summer, for it has been a most eventful one. We have acquired two houses—one the most complete in all respects. Everything in and about Winnington is well arranged and convenient. The grounds are beautiful, and the smoke of Northwich does not reach them. The opinion of the best informed pronounce that the bargain is an excellent one; that 20,000l. may be made of the purchase; and if the salt trade continues to improve as it has done till the present stoppage from shutting up the Baltic ports and the quarrel with America, there is no saying how valuable the property may become. *En attendant* the covering of the land with steam engines, salt pans, and smoke will drive us back to Alderley with plenty of money to build a palace with, if desired. . . . If the smoke does show itself occasionally in our walks, it is smoke that fills our pockets; it is mostly our own smoke, and therefore not so offensive. . . . The house in Privy Gardens is undergoing complete repair. As to the situation being unhealthy, I can conceive no idea being more ridiculous. I sincerely wish Lady Sheffield and her children may have better health in Portland Place; but even if they do have it, I shall not attribute it to change of place. . . . I think a river, especially where the tide flows, must purify the air and render the situation more healthy than a street. . . . We propose going in December. . . . Kitty Leycester goes with me to town. As it is all settled that she is to be our rector's lady, but not immediately (she is but just turned sixteen), I thought it would be a great advantage to her seeing a little of the London world first. She is a pleasing, sensible, amiable girl. In considering my letter, I think I have not clearly satisfied you in answer as to whether Winnington and Alderley are both to be kept up. For some years the former will be our chief residence. Farming will be given up here—a saving of some hundreds per annum—and the land will be let. Winnington is remarkably dry and warm, well adapted to an autumn or winter residence, and during the summer we shall frequently come *home* for a few days. Alfred's christening was last week. He had been named long ago ; but Edward insisted on our taking him to church for the full ceremony. We waited the arrival of his godfather, Hugh Leycester ; the other sponsors are Lord Chichester and Bell Way. I have written such a long letter, I cannot speak of the children in detail, but I will say Alfred is the finest baby I ever had. He is very like his papa, with the most beautiful dark eyes and animated countenance (aye, countenance !) at seven months as ever was seen.

Remember me to Orontes—but the Me he can remember was a very different person. How people will stare at me in London who have got Miss Holroyd in their recollection !

Mr. Fry has given 63,000*l.* for the Berrow estate in Somersetshire, so there is the money for Winnington. We are told our house in Privy Gardens is nearly completed and that it looks well. When my Lord Sheffield sees how different whitewash, paint, and paper make it appear, I think he will be very sorry he parted with it, for the situation must suit him better than Portland Place. The yearly rent is 210*l.*, and the taxes moderate, from the place being extra-parochial on account of its being part of the old palace grounds.

M. J. S. to Serena,

Privy Gardens : January 3, 1809.

Your dear letter welcomed me to my house in town on my birthday, a short time after our arrival this morning. I feel very happy here because I feel at home, which I should not have done in any other London house ; and the recollections attached to my residence here are all pleasurable, except that the dear lady who took such unceasing pains to promote my happiness should not be alive to witness

the success of her kind offices. Her successor is as amiable as
herself, but in this house Lady Lucy returns most forcibly
to my mind's eye, and I can hardly help regretting her.
The four children have borne their journey well. We came
into London through shabby streets which led us into the
Strand by St. Martin's Lane, and Lucy was much disappointed with London. She said it was not so different
from Macclesfield as she expected, and she is not so well
pleased as I am at the perfect quiet of the situation. A
street full of cries and coaches would be more to her
taste. . . .

M. J. S. to Louisa.

January 1809.

It is what I look forward to with the most pleasure, that
Sir John will pick up some old acquaintance and some new,
and without form or ceremony bring them in to dinner that
I may again hear conversation. For many years I have
only heard discourses. As far as one man's mind may go,
I have had within my hearing, knowledge, the fruit of reflection, and a very rare turn of thought, enough to satisfy any
one; but I long to hear him converse with others who may
in some degree be able to meet him in conversation. . . .

Pray write to Cat. Fanshawe and order her to take me as
a substitute, and to feel acquainted with me at once without
any ceremony.

I forget whether I told you that I have got a brother
and sister, children of an English merchant at Rouen, who
lost his property during the revolution in Robespierre's
time; and after the breaking out of the present war, escaped
with his family, glad to rescue their persons without their
property from the grip of Buonaparte. The young people
have been well educated; Miss Wild is a very good
musician. Her brother is capable of instructing the boys
in all we wish them to learn. It was an unexpected advantage to find a person able to teach French who would in
any degree associate with the servants. He is to breakfast

and drink tea in the housekeeper's room, and dine with the children. He has 50*l.*; his sister sixty guineas, but I must give her more if I find her answer the expectations her appearance has raised.

Kitty Leycester is a delightful girl; so unaffected, so cheerful and even-tempered a being I never saw, happy to go out, but perfectly satisfied to stay at home. Indeed Edward will have a treasure.

Louisa to M. J. S.

January 1809.

I congratulate you on leaving a due proportion of children behind you while in London; I can conceive no possibility of enjoyment with nine little Stanleys in the house. I rejoice you have the prospect of a fit person for your boys, and should consider it far from objectionable having his sister for governess. Tell me how your affairs go on in this respect, as I am very anxious you should have your first season of amusement undisturbed by such perplexities. I told Cat. Fanshawe that you intended she should make a great deal of you, and she informed me that she was much edified you were disposed to do so by her, as the intention showed. Pray do not let the brilliancy of a London *début* eclipse your rational country ideas, for I assure you she is worth any half-dozen streets full of people.

M. J. S. to Louisa.

January 22, 1809.

I have had the great treat of seeing Cat. Fanshawe's beautiful drawings in a morning visit, and I am in hopes she is willing to be well acquainted with me; but the weather has been one enemy, and old Daddy Fanshawe another, by insisting on hearing himself tell long stories about the bottoms of rivers freezing before the top, &c., to my great annoyance while I was with her. Cat. desired me to tell you she had had a letter from Caroline Lyttelton (that was), who wished you to be informed she found herself every day thinking less of poetry and sentiment and more of ducks and chickens.

I have seen Mrs. Villiers.[1] I had a very warm and friendly reception; yet I must say, in half an hour's conversation with her, I thought I perceived that she had all the ways of a true London lady, judging as all the rest of London (that is, a certain set) judges. 'Mother Goose,' with which I was most completely disgusted, she could not bear me for objecting to, which I did both on the score of personal dissatisfaction in regard to the amusement I derived from it, and also as a very improper spectacle to exhibit to children. I supposed you witnessed Grimaldi's abominable grimaces, the only merit of the performance.

[After falling out with her oldest friend on the subject of Mother Goose, M. J. S. seems to have yielded to its fascinations and took her family to see it.]

M. J. S. to Miss Ann Firth.

Privy Gardens, February 10, 1809.

I forget when I wrote to you, and whether at that time the children had begun to torment me. They have all been ill, and for six years there has not been a serious illness in the family. It has been a sad beginning of our London amusements. Foley is very unhappy about it, and thinks we shall never go to London again; and indeed I almost think so too, for plagues of all kinds have been annoying us—servants in all ways. I hired a laundrymaid and housemaid with excellent characters whom I could not keep a week; they were so ignorant, so idle and saucy. We have been changing our coachman, and I hope got a very good one and a postillion likewise, Jim Burgess, who was in the East Indiaman lost on the Goodwin Sands; he was going with an officer to India. Not being born to be drowned, but most likely to be hanged, he escaped. Kirby is going; I made some remonstrances which did not please him, and he intimated we had better part, at which I did

[1] Theresa Parker.

not grieve. He has a view to a situation with an invalid, Percy Wyndham, for which service he is best qualified. Martha's temper could not stand the inconvenience attending our first arrival : not having a comfortable nursery fire to run her nose into &c., and could not possibly brook a couple of scoldings, therefore wishes to leave. I am not sorry, though I do not like parting with anybody I have been used to.

Tell me more about your young woman. Is she very plain ? for I do not like very ugly people, especially if they look cross. What does your Mrs. Robson think of her temper ? for I cannot bear a young person who fires at being spoken to, and it will not do for me to have anybody about the younger girls who will not be on good terms with Foley. I am afraid of the daughter of an officer being proud ; but perhaps she may have got a situation.

We have not been very gay, for I have been unwilling to seek society while the children have been so ill. The Sheffs came last week. Lady S.'s waiting began only yesterday ; but the princess insisted on having her with her every day this week, so I have seen very little of her ladyship or the children. Anne is quite a little beauty, and George does not look to me a delicate boy. . . . We dined yesterday with the Duchess of Brunswick, and met the princess and Princess Charlotte. The former was delighted to see Sir John, and talked a great deal to him. The princess was gracious, but I think she appeared out of spirits. The young one is a fine girl, but I think she will be short and square. She is very pale. Her mother and she appear very fond of each other. To-day we are going to dine with the Chichesters ; on Monday we dined with Lord Ferrard.

M. J. S. to Louisa.

March 9, 1809.

. . . Envy me for the party at the Sothebys I was at on Wednesday. Cat., Miss Berry, Davy, and many more ; but Miss B. did herself sore injury with the baronet by taking it into her head to quiz the Institution and to sport a rigmarole about writing an ode and inventing a bonnet,[1] having been the only amusement she derived from attendance there. . . .

Of all the lively entertaining men I ever saw, the Saint Wilberforce for me! I never was in company with him before, and was surprised to find him possessed of such incessant powers of chatter. He sat on one side of Lord Dufferin, Morritt,[2] who wrote about Troy (was it for or against its existence?), on the other. On Sunday we had a comical collection : the two generals Clinton, and Humphry Davy, Isabella and Dr. Ash and Murdock. I like him very much, but Davy is delightful, even out of science. I cannot say your friends the generals joined much in his style of conversation ; but you know Sir John has always the way of finding out and recollecting what is every man's shining point, and setting them upon it, so I hope neither of the

---

[1] The ode was one written by Cath. Fanshawe in Miss Berry's name as a *jeu d'esprit*, describing the supposed feelings of Miss Berry and Louisa Clinton at the Royal Institution.

> Where'er a broader browner shade
> A shaggy beaver shows,
> And with the ample feathers' aid
> O'ercanopies the nose—
> Where'er both smooth and silken pile—
> Lingering in solemn pause the while
> The crimson velvet glows
> From some high benches' giddy brink,
> Clinton with me begins to think,
>
> .   .   .   .   .
>
> As both upright we sit,
> That dress, like dogs,
> Should have its day,
> That beavers are too hot for May,
> And velvet quite unfit.
> Then taste in maxims sweet I draw
> From her unerring lip,
> How light, how simple are the straw,
> How delicate the chip !
>
> .   .   .   .   .
>
> With undissembled grief I tell—
> For sorrow never comes too late—
> The simplest bonnet in Pall Mall
> Is sold for .   .   .   .   1*l*. 8*s*. 0*d*.

[2] Mr. Morritt of Rokeby, friend of Sir W. Scott, who dedicated 'Rokeby' to him.

brothers thought it a stupid dinner. . . . I was at one of
Davy's lectures, but must acknowledge I was not much the
wiser, there were so many words I did not understand: it
was as bad as the poor lady who read Locke without knowing the meaning of Idea.

Serena to M. J. S.

Bath: March 30, 1809.

. . . What a sweet girl your favourite, Miss Leycester,
must be! Indeed, I hope she will prove a pleasant friend
and companion to you through life. Among the most
polished and pleasantest and best informed in Ireland are
Lady Longford's family, and there is a sweet little woman
that I love in my heart—I mean Sir Arthur Wellesley's
dear little wife; it would delight me if you were to visit
her and tell her I desired you to like her for my sake.
Indeed, you will like her for her own. People are afraid of
Cat. Fanshawe. Her eyes pierce one. As for me, I made
a pet of her in the first fortnight, and she is now like one of
my own family. Will you believe that many families are
actually leaving Bath to escape the earthquake we are to
have to-morrow? Many servants have left their places. A
man who hires out musical instruments told me that *ten*
had been sent to him in one day on account of families going
in a hurry. One lady told me she did not believe the prophecy, but she sent her will and jewels to Clifton, as it was
of consequence to her children! I mind no prophecy; but
I wish, if the prophet or prophetess is discovered, they may
be put in the pillory. I think the mob would cure them of
divination. If you hear we are swallowed up to-morrow, I
shall have done well to have sent you and your dear Man the
warm blessings of my heart, which you certainly will have to
the end of my days, be that when it may.

M. J. S. to Louisa.

April 1809.

I thought you would know Sir James Hall, and yet I
cannot tell why you should. He is a great mineralogist

and an inventor of how the world was made, one of the
chiefs of the Plutonians. He married Lord Selkirk's sister,
and is a very clever man in his way, and one of the first
Edinburgh men of science.

Kitty and I had a delightful morning with Cat.
Fanshawe, who let me rummage her portfolio. I am sure I
should like her better and better the more I saw of her, and
only wish I were within a walk. I had a short peep of
Caroline Lyttelton (*alias* Mrs. Pole-Carew). She asked me
to a party at her house. I have been surprised to find so
little alteration in the folks I have been so long absent
from.

All the children went with us to the play last Monday,
to 'Richard III.' and ' Peyrouse,' the prettiest entertainment
for children I ever saw. The girls went to ' Mother Goose '
and ' Henry VIII.' This play is very well got up. Pope
is a capital Harry, and Kemble pleases me much in
Wolsey. In Mrs. Siddons I was rather disappointed; she
now acts too like acting, and drawls so much that I could
not form any illusion to myself, but saw the actress repeating speeches in every word she said. To-morrow I am to
hear Catalani in an act of ' Semiramide,' with the Drury
Lane company, at the Opera House.

Privy Gardens : April 21, 1809.

The bells are ringing merrily for the destruction of the
Rochefort fleet by Lord Cochrane, which I understand has
been performed completely. Austria has also declared war.
I have just seen the two Generals Clinton in high spirits
on the occasion. I consented to the rector's coming to
town a fortnight ago. He is at his friend Craufurd's, and
behaves very well, content to come when he gets leave.
Last week I was at a large assembly at Mrs. Pole-Carew's,
and met many old acquaintances—the Fanshawes, Ways,
the Abbé Nicholl, and many other friends. Afterwards, Kitty
and I went to Lady Blackett's to a masquerade, and I was
heartily tired. We dine to-day at Portland Place to meet

Davy, Matthias, Jekyll, Mr. Butler, and some others.   We
have a party in the evening, and a great assembly at Lady
Somers' afterwards.

May 3, 1809.

To-night we are going to a ball at Lady Nelson's. . . . I
expect it will be a fine squeeze. London is very agreeable
in this month of May, and we have been gay. Sir John
bears it better than I expected. He went with us to Lady
Stafford on Friday, and was so much amused that at two
o'clock he was not at all impatient to be gone. It is a noble
house for an assembly. We have made great use of the river
during the delightful warm weather. One day we went to
see the West India Docks, and dined at Woolwich, where
we saw the arsenal and dockyard ; another day we went up
to Fulham, and walked about the Bishop of London's
neighbourhood the day before he died. To-night we have
two assemblies and a concert. Yesterday we were at the
water-colour exhibitions, which were novelties to me; the
amazing improvement in the art since I had been in London
is surprising. I could not have believed that such effect
could be produced by anything but oils. . . . Rogers, the
poet, has dined with us twice; but I had not much of his
conversation, as he is a desperate admirer of pretty young
ladies, and took so much notice of Kitty, poor I had no
chance.

Louisa to M. J. S.

Dublin, May 1809.

I did not conceive it possible for anything to give me so
much satisfaction as coming up here to the cleanly coolness
and perfume of the country from the dirt and dust of the
town. You will understand this house is quite insulated
among gardens and trees in the same manner as Mr. Gibbon's
house at Lausanne. I think his ghost will haunt me to-
night for the comparison ! Getting away from the world
and meeting nothing but old soldiers in my walks is a
blessing the magnitude of which you cannot conceive.

To be sure, I have seen and heard the Irish melodies; there is seldom any singing without one being introduced. I have even been so wicked as to hear Moore himself sing them and to admire the performance extremely, though I have not heard any which pleased me equally with the old tune, 'When Time.' I suppose you know that the 'Leave-taking from a Lover to his Mistress' is by way of Emmet's adieu to his country before execution.

M. J. S. to Louisa.

London : May 22, 1809.

How would you have liked being a mouse in the corner last week, when Davy, Sir James Hall,[1] Playfair, and Lord Webb Seymour dined here? I will tell you who, unfortunately, popped in among them, and did not like playing the mouse in a corner one bit, and at last, in despair of getting in a word, walked off precipitately—my lord! The others were invited with the intention of a good set-to at the metallic world, and my alarm was great in thinking of the probable disarrangement of all philosophic ideas which would take place when this most unphilosophical of all peers made his appearance. Sir John kept the conversation general for some time after we left the table, but as Sir J. Hall came on purpose to question Davy, at last they did begin, and continued the subject until eleven.

June 6, 1809.

I do believe, as the horses are ordered, that we shall go to-morrow—that is, Kitty, myself, and the children. I do long to be off. Our last dinner was the pleasantest imaginable. All the company were pleased and pleasing, and Sir James Hall joined the party. They all talked like men of sense and knowledge, yet not too scientific.

What a charming woman Mrs. Cholmeley is! Cat. does not take so large a share in conversation, but was very agreeable. I committed one terrible error, however, which

[1] M.P. for Dunglass; died 1832.

I grieve at very sincerely; but how could I suppose that a
professor of mathematics would condescend to review a
novel? However, it so happened that I attacked the
criticism in the 'Edinburgh Review' on 'Corinne,' and on
my right hand sat the author, poor Playfair!

We have seen a great deal of pleasant society since
we came to town. Now London is going mad, and we
might be over head and ears in dissipation if we stayed and
chose it.

M. J. S. to Serena.

Alderley Park: June 22, 1809.

As a proof that I have left the Devil's town and am re-
covering my senses, I take up the pen to write to dear little
aunt, who must have thought herself quite forgotten.

At last we are here, but in a fortnight we expect to
remove ourselves to Winnington. . . . We have let our
house in P. G. to Sir J. Nicholl for three years for 800
guineas a year; but we, or at least I, hope not to remain
in the country so long. . . . Kitty Leycester came down
with me, and a few days after left this neighbourhood with
her parents to settle at his living in Shropshire. I am very
sorry on my own account that she is gone. She and Edward
are to be married next summer. She behaved in all respects
most charmingly in London. I cannot imagine a more
right-minded, cool-judging, yet warm-feeling creature. She
will indeed be a treasure to all of us; . . . perhaps you
will not think it is passing any very high encomium on her
to say she was infinitely more rational than myself in her
love of pleasure, though perhaps you hoped I was thoroughly
sobered. . . . I expected a much greater change in everybody
than I found, and I received great compliments on my
beauty! . . . I did not think my lord had recovered his
looks or his spirits after the illness he had in the spring. I
was rejoiced to find he appeared determined that the dear
lady should give up her situation about royalty. I hope he

will persevere in his determination, or I think he must give her up, for her health is not equal to such fatigues.

Adieu, dearest of little aunts, and believe me ever, whether silent or loquacious,

Most affectionately yours,
M. J. S.

M. J. S. to Louisa.

Alderley Park: July 4, 1809.

Do you know I found an old friend towards the month of May? A Miss Holroyd, from whom I had been so long separated that I had almost lost sight and remembrance of her [1]; but somehow, as the season advanced, we almost confounded our identity, and, if you remember, she was a very giddy person, and her head was apt to be turned a little in London, and I, when I was her, might easily forget what you wrote. I am happy to inform you that Alderley air has restored Lady Stanley to herself, and she feels very much at home again amongst all the vulgar cares of the country, and will be extremely happy to hear from you as often as ever you please, and will try and recollect what you say better than she did in London.

M. J. S. to Serena.

Alderley Park: July 5, 1809.

I rather flatter myself you have Cheshire in your mind's eye as you ask where we shall pass our Christmas. Certainly in Cheshire, and I should suppose at Winnington. I need not say how happy we shall be to show our new purchase to you. Here we have absolutely not a spare room, so you see it was very desirable to get a better one. I do wish we had bought one rather nearer the dear metropolis, though Sir

---

[1] 'Maria, to whom every object is new and pleasant, begins to undraw the curtain of the great theatre. . . . Your observation will soon discern whether it will be easy to brush the powder out of her hair, and the world out of her heart, or to shut her eyes after they have been once opened to the light of pleasure.'—Gibbon to Lady Sheffield, 1788, on the 17th birthday of M.J.H.

John calls it the Devil's Town. When you go to Shabden, pray remember me most particularly to the Cat., and tell her she owes me many thanks for not giving way to the violent temptation I felt to hook her into a correspondence with me; but add that the next time I go to London I hope to be nearer Cavendish Square, and then I intend to see so much of her that she shall be forced to fancy me a very old friend.

M. J. S. to Serena.

High Lake: August 28, 1809.

It is possible you may not have the geography or history of this place at your fingers' ends. The late Sir John had a small estate at the extreme end of Cheshire, on the little slip which you will find in the map between the Dee and the Mersey. He took into his head that it would be an excellent speculation to build an hotel for the reception of bathers, and consequently expended many thousand pounds in erecting a large building here, which was his country residence ever since we married. It is a dreary spot, at the world's end, but the bathing is good; there are nice safe sand-hills and fine turf for the children to play about; all the ships which go out of Liverpool pass in review, and upon the whole I accommodate myself very well to the situation. Sir John is in Wales; he is Sheriff for Anglesea, and last week were his Assizes, when he gave a ball and danced at it too, till his legs ached. Lady Stanley and he were at Lord Bulkeley's near Beaumaris, where the assizes are held. The Winnington conveyance is signed by Lady Penrhyn, and Sir John and I are every day expecting to hear the place is given up to us. I shall be very busy when I go home, moving our goods from Alderley to W——, and I shall enjoy being ' bien logée ' after having so long lived with only the necessaries of life in the shape of a house. Edward and Miss Stanley have been paying a visit to his love and her parents in Shropshire. The wedding is to take place next summer; she is a sweet girl, and thoroughly a companion for me, notwithstanding her youth. It is impossible to believe she is but just turned seventeen when conversing with her.[1]

Yours ever affectionately,

M. J. S.

M. J. S. to Louisa.

September 21, 1809.

A good memory is a very convenient quality. Now I know no more than the cat whether I have written to you since I left Highlake. Oh, yes, I do recollect that I did be so good as to scribble a short letter just to tell you how happy I was in my palace. I went to Alderley on Saturday to meet Sir John, who seems particularly well and happy; he always is, when he returns home after a ramble. But palaces and prosperity, hot-houses and poultry-houses make bad wives I am afraid, for I have let him go to Alderley all alone to see the children and his dear own trees, while I stay here to prosecute my arrangements and admire my new acquisition, and get acquainted with the Alentours. . . .

Of all the mad expeditions ever planned and executed, surely the Walcheren expedition has been the most silly— the worst planned and the worst executed.

The above has been asleep in my writing-case, and I must now write a little more to tell you how very happy and pleased I am with my new plaything. Yesterday and to-day I have been incessantly in motion, and I like everything around me better and better. . . . The warmth and comfort of this place will, I hope, reconcile Sir John to leaving his poor dear old Alderley—a south aspect will be indeed a treat —and the climate here is generally much warmer than Alderley. The peaches and nectarines on the common walls are now as fine and juicy, though there has been so little sun to ripen them, as in the hot-house elsewhere.

[1] It was of her that Sydney Smith said: 'Hers is a porcelain understanding.'

Y

M. J. S. to Serena.

Winnington: September 22, 1809.

Here I am at last. I came for a few days to look about,
and then returned to Alderley to inspect the infantry, and to
meet Sir John from Wales. Your love would be supplied
with fresh fuel if you could but see how handsome and young
and well he is looking, and though this is not quite home, yet
he was disposed to look upon me as his home, his ' household
stuff, his horse, his ass' &c., though not quite in the same
way as Petruchio.

This place is really more delightful than I expected.
Lady Penrhyn has left it in the very best of order and
little remains to be done. The mahogany is beautiful and
all the feather beds sweet and well seasoned.

I find the hours pass like lightning, though I have been
all alone while I have trotted about the house, garden,
pleasure-grounds, fields, and roads.

M. J. S. to Louisa.

October 27, 1809.

. . . Sir John is at Liverpool, where he went on Thursday
to be present at an experiment upon the cobalt ore, which is
again as firmly believed to be invaluable as that the best
proof of a victory being gained by Lord Talavera is a subsequent precipitate retreat.

. . . Nothing can be more agreeable than the prospect of
riches held out to us, and I build upon it with the same
confidence as on the expectation of hearing Masséna, Junot,
and Ney are arrived prisoners in London after the complete
overthrow of their armies. In both cases, should these
expectations be realised, we shall be well comforted for having
formed an erroneous judgment, but alas! I fear the
Portuguese business will not be a joking matter, whatever
the cobalt [1] may.

---

[1] Cobalt had been unnoticed or employed in mending the roads, until
Ashton, a Derbyshire miner who had seen cobalt mines in Saxony, searched
Alderley Edge and discovered it there.

Alderley Park : November 21, 1809.

Emmeline was christened on the eighth at Winnington and a very pretty christening it was. The gallery sets off a large party to great advantage, and the lamps lighted it perfectly well.

The boys and papa would not celebrate the thirteenth anywhere but at Alderley, and we came over for the purpose. We had a delightful bonfire, fireworks, and dance as usual, and the children were as happy as could be. The Jubilee was celebrated rather less from loyalty than from the fear of being thought disloyal, but it was a pleasure to see a great many of his Majesty's subjects eating a better dinner than they could treat themselves with under his gracious government. 208 regaled here, and I had the pleasure of seeing them stuff. The schoolchildren and old people dined on the green before the rector's door. The day was delightful and it was very well managed by Edward and Isa, who took all the trouble. The labourers had a shilling each and we went to the Edge to see the miners eat and drink. Sir John sang ' Hearts of Oak ' for them after they had treated us to ' God save the King,' ' Rule Britannia,' &c. The day went off very well, as it seems to have done all over the kingdom.

A subscription was handed about at Northwich and the principal inhabitants gave five guineas each towards roasting oxen for the populace.

Sir John does not reconcile himself very well to the change of abode notwithstanding his spacious apartment to the south. The gardens and poultry court and furnishing of Winnington have been a constant amusement and occupation to me; and it must be confessed, association apart of past happiness here for so many years, I do like the change prodigiously. Adieu, Sir John wants to go to bed.

Winnington : December 10, 1809.

. . . Sir John has begun his studies most seriously by way of passing his time at Winnington, and I really hope it

Y 2

will answer the purpose of amusement as well, and of health
better, than when at Alderley he used to spend the whole of
the winter days watching the turning of one clod by another,
or the clearing out of a ditch. Bryant's six volumes of
'Mythology,' his last study, must, I think, be no small trial
of the attention and patience of a country gentleman. He
has taken some pains to show me how Noah, Osiris, and
Theseus and Jupiter &c., are all one and the same person;
but happily without reading the whole to me. . .

Serena to M. J. S.

Sheffield Place: December 12, 1809.

My brother thinks he must attend the first levée after
Christmas Day, viz. December 27th. I mean to go at the
same time to pass a week in town to consult about the black
cobwebs and increased blindness of my poor eyes. I sit
hours idle to spare them, which to me is much the same
punishment as a solitary cell is to criminals. After my
consultation dear Lady Sheffield most affectionately presses
me to return to her again, as she intends not to go to town
till April. You rejoice, I dare say, that she has resigned
her post after ten years' attendance. Nothing can exceed
the kindness of the princess; she never ceases to regret Lady
Sheffield. Had you been here during our distress over
Louisa's illness, you would have been touched at Lady
S.'s sweet behaviour. It was piercing to see poor Sheff
so bent down, as he seemed, with affectionate grief. . . . We
coaxed my brother to play cribbage with Mrs. Robinson and
Lady Sheffield. Mrs. Firth, in a letter just received, affectionately asks if she could do any good by going to Dublin.
Thank God there is now no occasion, but often have I
wished her there.

CHAPTER X.

THE SHADOW ON THE HEARTH.

1811.

Death of Alfred—Moomie.

M. J. S. to Serena.

I am sorry to hear my Lord has required so much bleeding, and I should fear that, whatever benefit the nation may derive from his journeys to town, *he* can find none at this severe season of the year. He is very violent in favour of restricting the Regent. . . . I daresay I must shock you very much, as no doubt the loyal people, of whom you see the most, are almost as much alarmed at the thoughts of seeing the Prince on the throne as if it was Buonaparte himself. I trust, however, that when he is in power the good souls will alter their opinion and discover a world of virtues in the actual sovereign of the day. I hope I shall hear of increasing strength in your poor hind leg, and as the year advances I hope you will be able to go out in a wheeled chair. . . .

Serena to M. J. S.

. . . I love our poor, good King so much, that being convinced he can be of no use and that he must be wretched here, and blessed in the next world, I have for him but one idea, which will probably be realised. As to my opinion on the Prince, it is utterly impossible to me to look forward with any confidence to him; at the same time, I think the heir will so soon reign that shackles are absurd. I certainly prefer him to Buonaparte, and I am provoked at the rout

made with Lucien and his grand train, while the modest
spirit of the King of Sweden would accept of nothing ; he is
living in a poor little smoky house, as he got nothing from
Sweden as he expected. He walks about, has no carriage ;
in short, is absolutely poor. . . . A gentleman who was at
our house lately gave this account of him.

I am told that Lord Powis has had a hint to be less
profuse of honour to Lucien, and since then he has not been
much invited. Only think of all these politics from me,
who never like to utter them, as it is one of those subjects
on which so few are moderate ; yet it would be strange to
be indifferent to what passes. I somehow think of a line in
Racine which suits my state of mind as to the times. Someone says : ' Cher Abner, je crains Dieu et je crains rien de
plus.' [1] Were it not for that, I should see nothing but dark
clouds from every part of the horizon ready to crush us.

[The next letter of M. J. S. to Serena ends with these words]

I think much of the impossibility of a career so smooth
as mine has been for forty years continuing much longer in
the same course. I am only anxious as to what remaining
period of prosperity and what absence of real sorrow may
yet continue to me, to prepare my mind either for a reverse
or for leaving so many blessings without regret. I think the
former would be more easy than the latter.

[The first real sorrow was close at hand. In the absence of
the parents at Sheffield Place, Alfred, the youngest boy, died after a
few hours' illness, and Nurse Foley (Moomie) writes :]

Alderley Park: March 28, 1811.

My dear Lady Stanley,—I do most sincerely sympathise
with you for the loss of this fair flower, and can only console
myself by knowing he is taken to everlasting happiness.
We must feel so sudden and unexpected a blow, but for the
sake of your other children you and Sir John must try and
bear up. He was the dearest of all your children, and in

[1] ' Je crains Dieu, cher Abner, et n'ai point d'autre crainte.'
Athalie, Act i. t. 64.

affection as much my child as yours; to his last moments
he knew me, and clasped his dear arms round my neck just
before he died. I think I could write a volume about the
dear boy. But it only makes your heart bleed again. I do
think nothing could have saved him had he had all the
advice in the world. . . . I was glad in having so good a
creature with me as Miss Davenport. I wish our leaving
this world may be like this dear boy's; then we shall meet
him to part no more. On Monday I have fixed to part with
his dear remains, and I beg you will not send any orders to
prevent me following him, for I must do it and everything
that is proper shall be done. . . . I have preserved a bit of
hair; tell me if you would wish it sent you.

I conclude and remain your faithful servant,

E. FOLEY.

I find it is not customary to give mourning for so young
a child; of course I have not ordered any unless I had
your orders, but all who attend will be in black with white
hat-bands and gloves.

M. J. S. to Moomie.

Sheffield Place: April 2, 1811.

. . . I depended on your cutting off some of poor Alfred's
hair. I wish you would send it. . . . Was he able to speak
during his illness and did he complain much? I hope the
boys will spend part of a day with you this week. Tell both
of them, especially Edward, that it should be their endeavour
to prevent our ever looking upon the loss of a child as a
lesser evil than the existence of one, and that the pain we
now feel is light and trifling in comparison to what we
should suffer, if either he or his brother should behave in
such a manner as to disgrace themselves in this world, and
leave us no ground of hope that we should meet where we
should never part again. Put them in mind also of the
suddenness of this illness, and make them consider how
either would feel if such a separation took place between

them. . . . There are many ways in which this evil may be turned to good, in the effect on all our minds, if we use it aright.

Mrs. Edward Stanley to M. J. S.

Alderley Rectory: April 1811.

I have seen both the boys. Holland went up to tell them when it was over, and they stood for a minute perfectly motionless, as if they could not understand or believe it, before they burst into tears. When they came to me at dinner they had got over their crying, and were only more grave than usual. They were anxious to know what the croup was, and I explained as well as I could to them and read them an account of the windpipe out of Paley's 'Natural Theology.' Both expressed great concern for what you would feel. Billy said, 'Poor mamma, how happy she is now, and what will she be this time to-morrow?' Few people in such a situation would have had Foley's presence of mind and good sense, having done everything that could have been done. The dear child seems to have been even more affectionate than usual to her. When you were gone and the carriage out of sight, he turned to her and said, 'Taff got Mam;' and the first thing that alarmed her in the night was his calling out to her, 'Taff come to old Mam to-night.' He seemed uneasy if she left him for a moment, and when she came back smiled upon her and held out his hand to her. In the last struggle he clasped his little arms about her neck, and a little time before, when he saw her crying, said, 'Taff can't speak.'

M. J. S. to Mrs. Edward Stanley
(at Alderley Rectory).

1811.

In pursuance of my intentions we went to St. George's and heard Gardiner preach on the Resurrection. . . . I liked him much better than formerly, but perhaps the subject attracted more of my attention. I was in dread lest it should be brought too home to our feelings by a direct appeal; but he only dwelt on the evidences of the truth of a Resurrection and a general recommendation to apply the conviction to our benefit and comfort. We did not stay the Sacrament. I do not like the crowds of a London church and should have had my thoughts too much occupied by Alderley chancel to receive with the composure I should always wish to preserve if possible and especially in a strange place. . . .

Louisa D. Stanley to Foley.

1811.

Dearest Moomie,—Pray write to me again, I am so happy to receive any of your letters. Lucy's and my picture is quite finished with regard to the figures; but Alderley church is to be put in the picture for Lucy and I begged papa to let something of Alderley be put in. . . . In your next letter remember not to call me 'Dear Miss Louisa,' but to leave out that horrid word Miss. I shall now conclude, dearest Foley,

Your most affectionate dutiful child,

LOUISA DOROTHEA STANLEY.

[In 1811, it was feared that 'Moomie' might marry again and M. J. S. writes:

'Thomas Grange, thank God, is not yet come back from Guernsey, so Foley is pretty quiet. She is full of aches and pains and rheumatisms, and I should no more think of falling in love with her in any way than as a Nurse, than I should think of falling in love with old Molly if I was a gay young man—but there is no accounting for tastes.'

Shortly after Foley writes: 'I feel I am more happy than if I were Thomas Grange's wife. I am determined never to change my situation.'

In spite of this determination Moomie became Mrs. Ryder a year after, and eventually made a third marriage, though these were only episodes and she invariably returned to her Lady.

M. J. S. to Louisa.

December, 1811.

Edridge has finished the drawings of the four girls, which he began in London, and also done the boys and Kitty—he has made a very pretty picture of her, and taken her most pleasing and animated expression; her background is taken from the woods on the Edge, where I daresay you remember scrambling when we had our dinner in a field. The boys are very like, especially Billy. Edward is taken standing, with a stick just going to strike a ball, Billy kneeling with one leg on a fallen beech tree, playing with Pompey—the mere and deer house in the background. Ally and Maud are to be grouped with me in another drawing, which is not yet begun. Edridge is charmed with Alderley, but not much less so with Winnington. You have no idea what beautiful walks there are along the banks of the river and canal, within four miles; the river also, and vessels upon it, are great temptations to a painter, not to mention the Salt works, which figure upon paper much better than you would expect. . . .

They are going on prosperously, and the smoke and the profit increase annually. Marshall is proceeding famously on the top of the hill opposite us. He is likely to double the number of pans he engaged to erect.

To be sure, I do like Alderley a thousand times better as a residence. There is nothing in favour of Winnington but a better house.

it. I talk nonsense and laugh most of the time. Bath began the season thin, but now there is not a room to be got. The style of the place is sadly altered, for the hours are changed to London hours. . . . I have been much interested in McKenzie's 'Iceland' which Lord Leven lent me. I quite love and venerate the Icelanders and their taste for literature with such disadvantages as might have damped any such tendency. . . . I liked Sir John being mentioned, and Sir Joseph Banks and Mr. Holland—I felt among acquaintances. I am now reading two manuscript tours, most entertaining and interesting, written by a Miss Wilmot, whose sister was idolised by the Princess D'Ashkoff,[1] and was several years in Russia, introduced to the emperor and all the first people there. The lady, who lived several years with the princess, is here, one of the most engaging, elegant, little women I ever met ; and happily has taken so kindly to me that she has indulged me with these tours on condition of keeping the secret, and I have only made the good Firth share them with me. She sings Russ very sweetly and knows a hundred languages, and is as gentle and humble as if she knew nothing. She landed with most valuable presents, curious as well as rich, and was left 18,000*l.*

M. J. S. to Serena.

Winnington: February 26, 1812.

I rejoice to hear such a good account, and hope you did not die in the service of Master Betty. Do send him to us in London, for I never saw him in his glory. . . . I rather long to be there, for the party of philosophers you say hover about the Catherine will be our society and not a very disagreeable one. Mrs. Apreece has proposed to go shares in an opera box with me. Mrs. Sotheby has planned a dining club of four families to meet by turns at each others' houses—she, Mrs. A., the Morritts, and ourselves to be the four. There cannot be a pleasanter house than the

[1] Princess D'Ashkoff, 1744-1810, friend of Empress Catherine, took an active part in the conspiracy in which the Czar Peter III. lost his life.

Sothebys; every man of genius, especially in the poetic line, is sure to be there. Sir John laughs and says we shall be very *blue*, but indeed there should be no colours chosen by the wise ones of the present day, for they are of a very different nature to the ancient Blues. We shall probably see much of Davy and of all the Edinburgh Reviewers with Mrs. Apreece. . . . I think I told Miss Huff that the E. Stanleys were to be with us during the month of May. Kitty is delighted at the thought of visiting London, and I am no less so to have her again as a companion.

M. J. S. to Mrs. E. Stanley.

Portland Place, 1812.

Oh that I could write only a hundredth part as quick as my thoughts gallop to you whenever I see and hear anything which I should like to see and hear together! . . . I have been obliged to turn General Clinton and Sir John out of the room that I might have half an hour for you. I must draw a hasty sketch of the outline of my engagements. Saturday I was much pleased with Kemble's performance of Hamlet; he does not look the character well, for he is too old, but he speaks and acts it almost as well as I can imagine, though not quite. It is said Monk Lewis has composed a new heroic melodrama, in which Kemble is to make his first appearance on horseback, and that he gets up every morning at six o'clock to practise. Yesterday we dined at General Campbell's, and a party at the Churchills' was very pleasant. Davy came late, he looks guilty of being in love, and has been very desirous of fixing some morning to take Sir John to see Mrs. Apreece, which is settled for Monday. I have not yet seen this conqueror of professors. The lectures at the institution began this week. Davy's first lecture on geology is to take place to-morrow. Yesterday was Catalani's benefit, and Sir John dined with the Royal Society and begged to be excused attending us, and I was very near in despair; however, by good fortune, in came your cousin George Norbury, on whom we laid an embargo.

A journal in the month of May! Clarissa (being a very early riser) might have contrived to keep her promise, had she made it. Cecilia Beverley did really perform the wonder, and God knows how she managed it, but as my pen will not follow the lightning of my thoughts, and an hour in London certainly consists of no more than thirty minutes according to country reckoning, you have been sadly neglected for almost a fortnight. I have a great mind to place myself 'au courant,' by leaving out the whole fourteen days and turning over a new leaf dated from yesterday, when a dinner of Aucklands, Sheffields, Bishop of Exeter, and Henry Clintons would give me little trouble in describing; neither would the party at the Churchills', or a grand assembly at Lady Coventry's, furnish much interesting matter for you and I. However, you are making believe to admire green trees, black beetles, sweet briars, air and solitude, and hardly are worthy to hear of dissipation and hurly-burly. You have not succeeded in making me long for grass or trees; that triumph was reserved for the lilac tree and garden upon the Thames where we dined on Sunday with the Clancartys. . . .

I wrote last on the 10th when we dined at Lady Penrhyn's, and the Wiltons, High-Leghs, Derbys, and Leycesters were there. On Saturday the 11th we went with Mrs. Clinton, Cat. Fanshawe, and Peggy Craufurd, to hear Davy, who is lecturing on geology. The dinner at Kensington on the 12th was better than the Brunswick dinner, though there was not a great deal of lively conversation. Canning and Frere [1] were there.

We spent a delightful day with Sir Joseph Banks at Spring Grove; their place is small, but their garden and plants beautiful. . . . Only think what a singular dinner we shall have on Friday next! Four Iceland travellers—Sir Joseph, Hooker, Bright, and Sir John Stanley. Possibly the four may never meet again at the same table,

---

[1] Hookham Frere, a contributor to the *Anti-Jacobin.*

there are so many chances of their dispersion. Hooker is a very pleasing man indeed, and his book interesting and amusing. He has brought over a magnificent Iceland dress for us to look at. There are no great expectations in regard to Sir G. Mackenzie's book. It is much in his favour that Hooker's book is not published. The questions asked even in London are curiously ignorant. A gentleman asked Sir John on Sunday if the island had been lately colonised!

June 1812.

Only think of poor me! Staying at home one, two, three, four days with a pulse galloping away at something between 80 and 100. . . . Sir John had to dine at Sir P. Warburton's and the Abercrombies' without me, and I had to give up Lady Stafford's last night and refuse a box at the Opera to-day. . . . Must not I be very ill to relinquish so much pleasure, and must not Sir John be a great barbarian to take so much without me? . . . I was obliged to give up Davy's concluding lecture, but it had little to recommend it except a handsome compliment to Sir John Stanley upon his excellent description of the geysers. Davy has not made the lectures so interesting as he might have done, but if love has been galvanising his brains it is no wonder. He dines here to-morrow without Mrs. Apreece. The time he dined here *with* her they filled two chairs for each other's amusement only.

Wednesday.

I went through my dinner very well, but only think how ill off I was, Sir Harry Englefield on one side, who, having Cat. Fan. on his other side, never thought of dividing his attention, and she speaks so provokingly low that I could not share in their talk. In the morning Sir John had picked up the Dean of Chester, and his unfortunate most Reverendship placed him on my left hand, and I leave you to guess how amusing he was and how I wished him back in his cathedral. . . .

M. J. S. to Louisa.

We have got Sir George Mackenzie's book, and cannot absolutely say we are disappointed, because we had not raised our expectations high. The introductory chapter by H. Holland on the 'History of the Island' is well done, and Sir George's chapter on 'Mineralogy,' Sir John says, is very good. . . . . It is possible that the book may contain more that is novel to the world in general, than to us who are so well acquainted with Iceland. While there exist Justices of the Peace who inquire if the island is inhabited, and the daughter of an earl who supposes it is peopled with negroes, much information may be acquired from what is no news to the connections of the few who have visited that country.

Edridge told us he had seen you, and you were very angry with him for finding anything to admire at Winnington. . . . He has some thought of putting Kitty's and my portraits into the exhibition. I think mine is the prettiest of all, I do not mean only because of my prettiness; but the group has such a good effect, and Maud kneeling on my lap is such a sweet little figure. . . .

Serena to M. J. S.

Llangollen: Friday, July 9.

Though I cannot sleep well in a carriage, I always find it a good place for reflection, and as I drove through the treeless forest in my way to Chester, I thought most affectionately of all my dearest Maria's kindness, not indeed forgetting Sir John's, and all I enjoyed while under your protection. I had a longing desire to see your children of all sizes as well as yourself and your abode, and this wish could not be more delightfully gratified. Your horses and servants still seemed a tie, and when they went away it was like the last trace of all the dear beings I so lately lived with. The day you know proved fine, and really the two stages that brought me to Llangollen were beautiful. The postillion had taste and took me out of the high road for two miles, through the sweetest wood imaginable. I went directly to the cottage and was welcomed as usual. We drank tea in the midst of haymaking under a large tent.

Every new book, poem, &c. is here and in such bindings ! They greatly admire the 'Lady of the Lake.'

Serena to M. J. S.

Sheffield Place : August 5, 1812.

Not an hour can I defer telling our dearest Maria the delight I have had in her letter. I often say that Cat. Fanshawe in her pictures tells her story better than anyone, so you in your letters have the same happy art. From no one else have I had any but a general account lumped together. I am quite delighted with your poetess Lucy, not only with the easy natural style, but the affectionate thought throughout. I could not help showing it at breakfast to the Sheffs. Tell your Louisa that George was in an ecstasy on hearing hers and Lucy's poetry, and Lady Sheff begged a copy. . . . I wish Matty Wilmot's marriage may lead to her publishing the Princess D'Ashkoff's 'Life,' written by the princess and dedicated to Matty. I also wish she may publish two tours she took herself. One was with Lord and Lady Mount Cashel to Paris, where Buonaparte and all his people were the characters she lived with. The second tour was into Russia with the princess, the most lively and interesting possible.

M. J. S. to Serena.

Park Gate : August 5, 1812.

Lady Sheff sent me a most welcome letter from dear little aunt, informing me of your pleasant journey and safe arrival. I am very glad you liked your visit to Stoke so much and saw Hawkstone. You were much stouter and more enterprising than I expected possible in reaching the castle, for the ascent, though as easy as it can be made, is long and steep. . . . We have been at Liverpool and seen the cobalt works going on very prosperously. It

z

is discovered that pale smalts are in great demand among
the linen-bleachers of Ireland. The Seacombe Company
can provide this article equal in goodness and can afford to
sell it at a lower price than the foreign market, even if the
trade with Holland becomes free again. . . . Our partners
have another concern in hand, in respect to fishing on the
coast and in the rivers of Iceland, and they have just bought,
fitted up, and sent out the 'Sir John Thomas Stanley' to
that island, with an intention of making two if not three
trips each year. Sir Joseph Banks has been of great service
to them in various ways by the interest he takes in whatever
relates to Iceland, and the advantages he has procured for
our adventurers from Government.

Immediately after you left us, Mr. Glegg was so kind as
to offer me their snug cottage here, and as soon as Sir John
was off to Penrhos, Mrs. Firth and I came with seven of the
children. . . . Sir John is busy at Penrhos with his lands,
and there have been two meetings about the harbour, but no
prospects of anything being done about it immediately.
General and Mrs. Leighton and the little boy [1] are there. . . .
'The Lady of the Lake' arrived just in time for Sir John to
read it aloud to us, which always increases the pleasure of a
new poem.

M. J. S. to Margaret Owen, Lady Stanley.

Winnington: December 25, 1812.

In the first place, my dear madam, let me wish you a
great many Christmases and happy New Years, according
to the old phrase, although I fear it must have something
the appearance of mockery to you, who generally find this
soi-disant jovial season one of trouble and care. Hoping,
however, you have nearly despatched your business, as you

---

[1] Sir Baldwin Leighton, seventh Baronet. In 1841 B. Disraeli writes to
his sister from Loton Park: 'Sir B. Leighton's, one of the most charming
old English halls, and filled with a family in their way as perfect. A complete
old English gentleman, whom I first met at Stamboul. A most agreeable wife,
the finest amateur artist I know, and children lovelier than the dawn.'

expressed a wish to know more of our fête and which play of
Madame Genlis was performed, I take up the pen to answer
your enquiries. The play was 'L'Ile Heureuse' . . . they all
performed much better than I expected, but Louisa was the
most at her ease. One third of the dining room was
partitioned off with a large arch in the middle hung with
festoons of flowers very prettily manufactured by Miss
Lander,[1] and mixed with evergreens for leaves. The stage
was raised a foot with lamps in front, green curtains to
let down, bell to ring, all 'comme il faut,' the recess filled
with greenhouse plants and others in front of the stage on
each side. I think I have seldom seen a happier party, and
there could not be a prettier scene. It was Sir John's
planning, and you know he has a great deal of taste in these
kind of things. There was a dance afterwards till twelve
o'clock.

Believe me, yours very affectionately,

M. J. STANLEY.

Serena to her great-niece, Louisa D. Stanley.

Bath: 1813.

Christmas day arrived a most nice turkey and hare from
Winnington. The Bishop of Winchester had sent me
one, but I shall like this better than any other because
it has been born in Cheshire. The first use I make of
the pretty little memorandum book will be to record your
name as the giver, also to put down the day of Octavia's
birth. By the by, I thought that was too witty to occur to
anyone but me, and after I had sent it off to Winnington I
was greatly affronted to find that Mrs. Leighton had done it
also. Your description I like in regard to dark blue eyes
and I must insist upon long eyelashes and have them clipped
for that purpose as soon as they are grown enough. Shall
I tell you what I took your vignettes to be? I supposed that
it was the great Napoleon that was hanging, and that the devil
was in triumph over his own work. That after leading him

---

[1] Governess for many years, and a devoted friend until her death, 1848.

to all wickedness, he was going to claw him and got him
hanged. It is but poetical justice. . . . I admired the owl
as being a strong resemblance, but thought you were quizzing
yourself, and meant it as an emblem of wisdom. They are
put up among my treasures. . . . I suppose you hear of the
Christmas gambols at Sheffield Place—to-morrow a masquerade. . . . And now, dear Louisa, with all sorts of bene-
dictions in and out of Christmas salutations, I am

Your very affectionate
S. HOLROYD.

[Louisa Stanley, aged thirteen, received the following reports
of the festivities of Sheffield Place from her little uncle, aged ten.]

Sweet Madam,—Last night we had a masquerade. I was
first a Turk and then a country girl with Maria's brown
frock on. Anne [1] was first a gipsey, with her doll tied behind
her and then a sailor boy in my clothes. There was a pedlar,
a watchman, another gypsey, a madman, a lawyer, Mrs.
Clarke, a flower girl and a French nun. Abbé was first an old
French gentleman, then a great giant, then a drunken old man,
then an old woman selling matches. I think his last was
the best. Maria was a Swiss girl in a high crowned hat and
a green silk embroidered apron. Freddy [2] was drest in our
Anny's clothes, Anna Maria was drest in Freddy's. I could
not write to thee because I have been to school and am just
come home. I hope you are going to town and will be
there next holydays if Mama stays there. Give my love to
Rionnet and I am, my dear Madam &c.,

G. HOLROYD.

Dear Miss Lou,—I forgot to tell you my second character
was a quack doctor, and I made some black doses with liquorish
water, and others of Rhew tea, and I rammed them down the
people's throats. I did not learn to skate but there were
some beautiful slides. I thought Billy and Teddy were
coming to Eton soon. It is ten times better than a private

---

[1] Afterwards Lady Anne Legge.   [2] Colonel Fred. Clinton.

school with only 150 boys instead of 500 and something. How is your puss? Our old thing is as well as ever. I have got 2 frowsy dogs besides, and I had a Syrian ram that used to follow me about like a dog : but he is sent off with a flea in his ear for knocking down some maids, dames, and so forth. As mama says you are coming to town then, I shall see you I suppose, so I remain, your affectionate husband,

G. HOLROYD.

M. J. S. to Serena.

Alderley Park : December 1813.

Dear little Aunt,—Mrs. Firth fancies that woodcocks are worth their carriage to Bath or at least that you will like to have them ; I therefore send a brace with a hare by to-night's coach. Elfrida[1] continues to be everything that is good and amiable. Her eyes are at present dark grey, but I think hazel eyes are so at first sometimes. However, they are bright and large and I am sure she will be very sensible. Our girls and Billy enjoyed their visit to Sheffield Place very much, and Billy suited George. Our rectory prospers amazingly, nothing can be happier or more agreeable in every way. Kitty is, what she ever was, faultless in temper and excellent in understanding and sound judgment, and has one of the most sensible manly boys I ever knew. He is as forward at two and a half as many children at four or five, and indeed more sensible than many grown up acquaintance at any time of their life.

Yours ever affectionately,

M. J. S.

Serena to M. J. S.

Bath : December 31, 1813

Yesterday I walked to Sidney Place and back again with my good Mary Watts and a stick to support me and I really only was tired enough to like staying at home. After all the evening having no news of Lord Wellington, the bells rang furiously and what they call ' fired,' which they never do but

[1] Eighth and youngest daughter.

on great occasions, and which electrifies me greatly, for
merely victory without particulars makes me quake. The
news came by Plymouth. To hear that no General was killed
gave me comfort, and I sent my man to the Libraries, where
bulletins were instantly put up and he returned much
pleased that the French had run away and would not be
caught; but I thought it would have been better if we had
got them! Would to Heaven all this would give us a good
durable peace, but I confess while the present ruler of
France continues to govern I have only fear on the subject.
Mrs. Nugent, a niece of Lady Longford's, is at Bath, and
had two days ago a letter from Lady Wellington written
with such spirit and hope as quite surprised me, for no glory
can prevent her anxiety at such a critical period; so much
at stake! Her darling brother too, Sir Edward Pakenham,
with Lord Wellington in all the engagements and several
times wounded. She lives quite retired at Tunbridge with
her two fine boys. Mrs. G. Coxe's son, General Lyon, is
attending Davout.[1] If he returns safe his mother will be all
happiness, as he has gained honour enough to content any
mother.

M. J. S. to Louisa.

I have not made up my mind to blame the conduct of
the allies as much as you do. Would you have them tell
the people of France their object is to restore the Bourbons?
Would you not have them leave this to the choice and
decision of the people hereafter. The quarrel is at present
with Buonaparte. The war is to punish him for his
aggressions. The French people must suffer along with him
as long as they are willing to fight his battles. You should
give the allies credit for hitherto acting so well in concert,
and agreeing on one great point, the downfall of Buonaparte's
extensive power. If the King of Rome is not a foundling,
can you reasonably expect the Emperor of Austria to desire
the complete annihilation of his prospects of dominion?

[1] Prince of Eckmuhl, Marshal of France, 1770-1823.

I think on the whole Sir J. wishes for the restoration of the Bourbons, and, amongst other bad reasons, because a weak Prince on the throne of France is better for the interest of Great Britain. . . . It is not to be supposed Louis XVIII. can be placed on the throne without opposition, and all the property which has passed into other hands quickly pass back again to the old possessors. Is it not more for the interest of France as at present existing to continue under Buonaparte and his family? I hear the Davys [1] are gone to Nice. He has not been idle at Paris; but has been making experiments on a new gas discovered by one of the French chemists, and transmitted an account of it to the Royal Society. . . .

Alderley Park: April 12, 1814.

What wonderful events have occurred since I wrote last! Even the most sanguine must have found their expectations surpassed. I rejoice exceedingly at Paris being secure from the Cossacks, and admire of all things Alexander *the Great*— but Buonaparte Emperor of the Island of Elba! Is it possible? However, let me wish you joy of the termination of the war, as what is personally interesting is always most interesting, I believe, to everybody, and if we do not first meet the General at Paris, I hope we shall at least before the end of the year see him at Alderley. If the road is safe and open, Edward and Kitty will certainly set off for Paris in Whitsun week. . . . Sir John listens to the plan of joining the party not as to an entirely impossible event. . . .

Was there ever a novel more interesting than the daily papers, or containing events and dénouements more improbable? If anyone had betted six months ago even that the allies would be in Paris this month, received with joyful acclamation, and Buonaparte dethroned, should any of us have had a doubt the person was risking his money very wantonly? Sir J.'s chief satisfaction is to see the Senate are not willing to give up themselves and their country unconditionally, and I almost wish the Bourbon

[1] Sir H. Davy married Mrs. Apreece 1813.

fools would refuse being limited sovereigns, that some other dynasty might be called to the throne. I am not satisfied with the restoration of this family; there is no poetical justice in it.

Though it is difficult to think of anything but Paris, dignified conquerors, and degraded tyrants, yet I must answer you about Madame D'Arblay and Lady Morgan, for fear I should forget. . . . Did you read ' O'Donnel ' after the ' Wanderer '? I should think not, from your manner of mentioning it. I had that advantage, or rather ' O'Donnel ' had, and whether in consequence of that or of you and Kitty having abused it I cannot say, but sure it is, I like the work extremely. . . . But the " Wanderer ! " I give you up entirely. There, if you please, is absurdity in plenty. . . .

Winnington : April 24, 1814.

. . . Sir John enjoyed very much all you say about Buonaparte and the Bourbons, as it is entirely in unison with his sentiments. He, as well as you, kept himself in a happy state of doubt just before the late events. If I had not the least belief in the general sentiment in favour of the Bourbons, and a great deal of faith in Buonaparte's talents and genius, so as certainly not to foresee such a dénouement, I fancy a great many wise folk thought with me. For the Duchess d'Angoulême I feel with you most completely. It is Monsieur, it is all the adherents who will think only of the 'ancien régime' not being fully restored, that I think poetical or any justice you please required should not be restored to their country; but I would have given anything, almost a whole season in London another year, to have seen Madame d'Angoulême enter London, to have had a full view of her countenance, and to hear from those who have access to her what her feelings and conduct are on this occasion. You would be amused to hear Sir John rejoicing ever and anon at being out of the way of nonsense. We got a letter from my lord a few days ago just saying all we expected, and that his exultation at the restoration of the

Bourbons was much checked by the conduct of the Senate, and the King's being dictated to by five Jacobinical rascals.

Sir J. approves of all that has been done except that he thinks there may be some alteration as to the formation and number of the Senate. . . . The baronet will not hear me say one word for poor Bony, and, if I only do his abilities justice, says, like you, I have a sneaking kindness for him, but does not approve of Lord Byron's calling him ' mean and abject ; ' yet I suppose anyone would be torn to pieces who ventured to criticise this little poem and not give unqualified admiration. I have not seen the whole yet, only some extracts, and some passages Sophia Churchill sent me in a letter. The latter were all very fine; the former, which was comparing him to Sylla, had very fine lines, but I want to know what Lord B. means by upbraiding him with ' hoarding his own blood.' Does he blame him for not committing suicide ?

The account you give of Madame de Staël confirms what I have heard. Miss Tunno wrote that Madame de Staël first heard of the entrance of the allies into Paris from her brother-in-law, a Swiss, and that she appeared by no means pleased with the intelligence. In a subsequent letter she says Madame de Staël sent to the Duchess of Orleans to desire she might be informed that Madame de Staël ' approved and admired the conduct of the Emperor of Russia.' The Parisian expedition is at an end for us, even in conversation. Madame Moreau's brother is just arrived from Paris, and represents travelling as at present impossible, such are the numbers of English flocking the same way. He says there are hundreds of English at Calais, unable to get forward for want of conveyances. It would be somewhat unwise to join this party, and I should be sorry to lose the right of laughing at the folly of John Bull by being as silly myself. The frequent letters you have sent me are so interesting, pray make no apology for them, and pray do not think it selfish to stay in London. I wish you to stay a long time for my gratification. . . . If bad health was not an evil in itself not to be thought of as a trifle, I should think your way of living in London very near the pleasantest. You see a few friends, hear all the news, and your children have the advantage of seeing some of their own species and equals, and not running wild among rabbits and flowers alone.

M. J. S. to Serena.

Winnington : January 1, 1815.

We have the house full of company and expect it will be much more than full in the middle of the week, when we are to have a dance and a masquerade. The pleasure of thinking of characters &c. and preparing for the latter has been very great, and besides a number of young people in the house we expect some coachfuls from the neighbourhood. I expect to find much amusement from this masquerade, and I wish you could have an armchair in one corner of our gallery, though indeed it is more likely you would disdain such old lady accommodation and be the gayest of the gay characters.

Your remembrance of the harvest home and the pleasure you took in such fêtes makes me still more wish for you at a dinner Sir John is going to give on Tuesday to twenty-five soldiers who are pensioned by Government, all having lost leg, arm, or eye in the service, mostly in Spain under Lord Wellington. A few coming to swear to their certificates in order to claim the pension and telling various histories of perils and dangers they had suffered or escaped, put it into his head to assemble all those in the neighbourhood of Winnington, and we hear they are much pleased at the thought of their dinner. . . .

I enclose a letter from Mr. Silvertop written at the same time as Davenport's from Elba.

[The accounts referred to were written by two members of a party which included Lord Ebrington, Mr. Davenport of Capesthorn, Mr. Fazakerley, Mr. Silvertop, and Mr. Douglas, who landed from their yacht at Elba in hopes of an interview with Napoleon.]

From Mr. Davenport.

December 17, 1814.

My apprehensions of not getting an audience were at length relieved by an intimation that the Emperor would see me at 5 P.M. and the audience took place accordingly as follows :

After asking about my country, where I lived, my profession, where I had served, whence I came, whither going, and a number of other such questions, which rather proved his desire to get to his dinner than to make the agreeable, I endeavoured to give the conversation a more interesting turn by asking some political questions which succeeded in animating and making him converse with more eagerness, and thus the conversation ran, as far as my recollection serves me :

D. Votre Majesté croit-elle que la paix sera durable?

B. Mais oui, pourquoi non? Les Bourbons ne feront pas la guerre ; ce ne seroit ni leur intérêt, ni leur inclination.

D. Mais la facilité de franchir les frontières de la Belgique ne donne-t-elle rien à craindre là-dessus?

B. Mais non, ils ne peuvent pas faire la guerre à present.

D. Sa Majesté croit-elle que le Piémont soit en sûreté pendant que la Montagne de l'Echelle appartiendra à la France?

B. Oui, n'y a-t'il pas encore le Mont Cenis? Vous auroit sans doute passé le Mont Cenis? Avez-vous vu mes Moines? Vous savez que j'ai fait des moines, moi (laughing) ; vous ont-ils traité bien? Vous avez trouvé que la Montagne était une barrière, n'est-ce-pas?

D. Oui, Sire, mais il n'y sera jamais assez de troupes.

B. Qu'est-ce donc que fait ce Roi de Sardaigne? On dit qu'il chasse tout le monde. Est-ce vrai?

D. Non, Sire, mais on dit que Sa Majesté ne paye personne (laugh).

B. J'ai cependant ouï dire qu'il chassoit tout le monde qui s'offroit à son service.

D. Aurons-nous le succès contre les Américains, Sire?

B. Oh! il faut faire la paix avec elle et je conçois que cela se fera. D'ailleurs vous avez commencé——.

D. Votre Majesté me pardonnera, nous avions déjà écarté la cause de la guerre, telle que les Américains l'avouèrent, avant que nous sûmes que cette guerre étoit déclaré.

B. Oui, mais il existoit encore le Blocus; oh, croyez-moi, il faut faire la paix.

D. Sire, je conçois que si la vengeance était légitime ou politique, elle le seroit contre eux.

B. Pourquoi donc?

D. Parce qu'ils croyèrent qu'en nous déclarant la guerre au moment qu'ils la firent ils allèrent nous donner le coup de grâce (a laugh).

B. Avez-vous passé par Gênes? Que fait-on là? Elle appartiendra à la Sardaigne, n'est-ce pas?

D. Oui, Sire, à ce qu'on dit.

B. Ha! vous auriez dû la rendre indépendante, mais alors il faut qu'elle aie le Pavillon. Lord Bentinck lui avoit promis son indépendance. Il faut qu'elle appartienne ou à l'Angleterre ou à la France, car elle ne souffrira jamais la Sardaigne. Le meilleur seroit la rendre libre, si non la prendre sous votre protection. Où avez-vous servi? Sous le Général Moore?

D. Non, Sire, je n'ai vu que la campagne de Castanos et la dernière dite de Paris.

Here his Imperial and Royal Majesty turned away his head as though he should say, Don't spoil my appetite by talking about that. However, when he asked me about Paris, I again endeavoured to bring him back to it in order to put some questions touching his mad attempt upon Laon by telling him I had arrived at Paris with the right wing of the allied army, but he instantly turned the subject to the comparative price of living in London with that of Paris, and 'Que dit-on des Bourbons?'

D. Sa Majesté veut-elle que je parle franchement?

B. Oui, oui (very eagerly), dites-moi franchement.

D. Sire, il m'a paru que tous les gens tranquilles étoient pour les Bourbons, et tous les militaires pour V. M.

I did not think he seemed satisfied with this share of his

old subjects. As he seemed still upon the listen, I added that there existed a very strong feeling against England and the English individually—quatre fois plus fort qu'il n'a jamais existé de notre côté contre la France.

B. Ha! vous-avez mal fait de mettre vos prisonniers à bord des vaisseaux; j'ai fait plusieurs remontrances là-dessus, même j'ai ménacé de mettre vos gens sur mes vaisseaux, ce que vous savez auroit été bien pire. Mais enfin. . . .

I then said the ships were airy and not unwholesome prisons.

Oh! mais de mettre un soldat à bord d'un vaisseau, c'est une cruauté, c'est de le tuer.

Of the truth of the former part of the proposition, I could vouch feelingly.

B. Quand vous étiez en Espagne que pensiez-vous de leurs troupes?

D. Très mal, Sire.

B. Cependant ils ont beaucoup de caractère, mais ils ne restent jamais ferme, pas même sur une montagne, pourquoi donc cela? mauvais cadre, mauvais officiers—j'étois toujours fort mécontent d'eux. Que pensiez-vous de Castanos?

D. Il me sembloit paresseux et pas grand' chose.

B. Quelle étoit la force du Général Reding?

D. 15,000 hommes.

B. Dupont auroit bien dû le battre et le renverser avec cela.

D. On disoit, Sire, que son armée étoit en mauvais état quant aux malades et à la manque de provisions,

B. Oh, non—impossible. Cette affaire de Baylen a décidé celle de l'Espagne.

I pretended not to understand him, and he repeated it, and after saying he thought Dupont never could have seized upon Cadiz in the first instance, the conversation ended by his making me a low bow.

He told Silvertop he entertained a good opinion of the Bourbons, and of the King's understanding. Upon being asked what was his ultimate object in the Russian war, he answered emphatically, 'Pour vous rendre justes.'

I think Buonaparte in person wholly undeserving the

ridiculous account of his awkwardness and fat.   He has a
very agreeable countenance when he is pleased, and I don't
think it the reverse when he is serious.   His tone of voice
is neither one thing nor the other, a common, rather bass,
tone, and neither affected nor imposing, a particularly good-
humoured and obliging manner.   But what has struck us
all is the total absence of everything like humbug or
affectation in his speech, manner, or matter.   You would
say it was complete naïveté.

He is about my height, very strongly built, his chest very
fine, and, though he is fat, it looks like wholesome fat, and
his complexion is much healthier than has been described.
He is constantly at his snuff-box, which I suppose he finishes
pretty early in the day, for he seems always trying to scrape
up a pinch, which he never fairly gets.   His smile is in a
straight line, and whenever that appears a pleasanter
countenance cannot be.   His habits are those of his former
life, going to bed at ten, getting up again about one.   'Alors
l'Empereur travaille jusqu'à 3 ou 4 heures.'   Then he goes
to bed again and rises at six or seven, goes out after a very
good breakfast and dines at half past six.   What his
travaille is, the deponent saith not, but I conceive it to be
of a multifarious description.   For he decamped a short
time ago, and retired for two days to a hermitage on the
top of a lonely hill all alone with a Polish countess, Lord
knows who.   He afterwards brought her down, and embarked
her by torchlight for the place from whence she came.   The
inhabitants who took Musty Fusty for Marie Louise
assembled on the beach to pay her all due honours.   But the
Emperor dismissed them with reproaches, and away they
went, deploring their unsuccessful and probably their first
demonstration of servility.   Bertrand is a good creature, I
believe, but a whining, unsatisfied, and unsatisfactory character; his wife is a pleasant, very tall, and rather good-looking
woman, and will, I fear, soon be a dead one.   Drouet is a
man much to be liked, as far as our acquaintance with him
enabled us to judge; all the rest are, I believe, little better
than blackguards.   Mother Buonaparte is there giving

herself considerable airs, and her profligate but beautiful daughter Pauline, Princess Borghese.

We set off for Rome on the 20th, and proceed to Naples.

From Mr. Silvertop.

Porto Ferrario: December 7, 1814.

Lord Ebrington (who, together with Sir Neil Campbell, is living with us here) had an audience of three hours last night, of the most interesting description. Like most others he is struck with the candour, naïveté, and wonderful knowledge of the world, of this extraordinary man. But what is most curious in this interview is the avowal and justification of two most important historical points, concerning which England has been puzzling her head in vain up to last night, namely, the massacre of Jaffa and the poisoning the sick of the army. He says: 'I took a large body of Turks whom I could not feed, and whom I released upon a promise of not serving again under pain of being put to death if retaken; a short time after I found these same Turks in possession of Jaffa, which I attacked and took by storm, a circumstance which would alone have authorised their destruction, but as it was I did not hesitate a moment in ordering their death, to the number of about 2,000, having no alternative with persons who had not respected their previous capitulation.' As to the poison, it is equally true, though not to the extent described. 'Three persons belonging to the army were taken ill of the plague; to remove them would have infested or destroyed my army. To leave them became, therefore, absolutely necessary. The question then arose whether it was most merciful to these people to give them an easy death by opium or abandon them to be tortured by the Turks. I preferred the former, viewing the case as if it had been my own. I therefore ordered Desgenettes[1] to give them each a quantity of opium, to which he answered that as his business was to cure and not to kill he must decline the job, which I directed somebody else to execute. At the same time I admit it is a

[1] Baron Desgenettes (1762-1837), a distinguished French military doctor.

questionable point, and one I have often debated with
myself. In the recent case of an application from Marshal
Duroc to have his tortures shortened, I refused, telling my
friend I thought it more fitting that he should fulfil his
destinies.' Buonaparte treated the imputations against
him of having murdered Captain Wright, Pichegru, &c., as
mere idle tales, supporting the denial by appeals as to any
possible advantage to be gained by disgusting acts of unnecessary barbarity upon persons who, being entirely in his
power, could give him no anxiety. 'No,' said he, 'perhaps
my mistake has been putting too few of these people to
death. Had I acted otherwise, I might not have been where
I now am.' He then asked Lord Ebrington whether he
would be received in England? to which he was answered
with hesitation, implying doubt, 'You would not have been
well received at first, but now it might be otherwise.'
'Comment! m'aurait-on donc lapidé?' (laughing). He said
we had done wrong in insulting the French by sending the
Duke of Wellington, that the French must be dissatisfied
because they felt dishonoured by Belgium being withdrawn
from them, that their being licked would make no difference
as to their eagerness to renew the war, as they despised the
armies of the Continent, 'quoiqu'ils rendent justice à vos
troupes.' He spoke slightingly of the Emperor of Austria and
King of Prussia, but said of the Emperor Alexander that he
was a sensible, lively, agreeable man; 'mais il est léger, il est
Grec,' he said. If the aristocracy of England was double its
present number I should think England in a bad way, but,
as it is, I consider your *grands seigneurs* as your bulwark.
'C'est tout autre chose en France; le Roi est regardé comme
source de tout, il doit demeurer dans un Palais de Cristal.
One cannot help recollecting the analogy of this with the
lantern-like Tuileries. Bony also acknowledges having put
to death about 200 rebellious Muftis at Cairo; 'c'étaient
des abbés de ce pays-là.' He has imprisoned two abbés
here for complaining of the weight of taxes, and, as his party
says, for exciting a village to refuse payment of them.
Altogether he is not popular, and although his troops adore

him, and all, to the number of 800, the finest fellows I ever
saw, yet it is Colonel Campbell's opinion that they will not
remain with him beyond the spring, and that next summer
will see him deserted almost to a man. . . . I hope not, for
humanity's sake. . . . His friend and *élève* Bertrand is
suspected of an intention of making his wife's sickness an
excuse for quitting that master for whom he has already
sacrificed everything. I have great fears that the circumstance of my bringing letters to the latter may thus be the
very means of rendering me suspected, and disappointing
me in my hopes of an audience. . . . I went to Bertrand
yesterday, and sat an hour with him and his wife. All they
said tended to strengthen me in the opinion that they
intended sooner or later to decamp. She told me they had
literally brought nothing with them; that they were unhappy
in every sense, and that their prospects were still more
dreary than their present situation ; that the non-payment
of the sums guaranteed by treaty to Napoleon made them
apprehend his speedy reduction to absolute mendicity. . . .

I hear Buonaparte talks of Fazakerley with more satisfaction than any other visitor. ' C'est un savant.'

He asked Douglas, ' Vous êtes très fiers et très pauvres
en Ecosse, n'est-ce pas ? '

[Napoleon made his escape from Elba, February 26, 1815.]

M. J. S. to Louisa.

Winnington: March 13, 1815.

 . . . And now what do you say about the probability of
the war, and the income tax being renewed ? If this were
not likely, if there were any chance of our looking on quietly
without interference, if I were the inhabitant of another
planet, I would confess I rejoiced to see Buonaparte again
on the stage. If it were not for these considerations, and
others of an interested nature, would it be quite certain that
the restoration of the Pope, and the Inquisition and
Ferdinand, and fat Louis and his priests, and all the
prejudices and bigotry of the ancient *régime*, which were so

A A

fast returning to stultify the Continent, would be better for
mankind in general than the established firm government
of Buonaparte, Murat, or even of Joseph, who at least would
not embroider petticoats for the Virgin Mary? If Buonaparte
succeeded in France, if Louis returned to vegetate with his
friend the Marquis of Buckingham, who paid a morning
visit here on Friday from Vale Royal, and is just such
another as his Majesty, and if we would be wise enough to
make peace, and keep peace with him when established, it is
as much his interest as ours to remain at peace, and I do
not think we are a jot less likely to go to war with Louis
than Napoleon; but the half-hour bell rings, and I must
quit this fertile topic for speculation.

M. J. S. to Mrs. E. Stanley.

May 11, 1815.

The panorama of Elba is one of the best executed I have
seen and we had the good fortune to find the artist Barker
there, from whom Sir John gained much information ex-
planatory of the scene before us. I had no idea there was
so much beauty in the island, nor such high mountains.
Buonaparte, Bertrand, Drouot, not *Drouet*, as commonly
supposed, Campbell, and another man, one of Buonaparte's
friends and a great savage—I forget his name—are grouped
together. Buonaparte seems a very good likeness, judging
from the pictures I have seen. Barker was on the island
about twelve days, and was all the time busily employed
with his drawings. He had Buonaparte's permission to take
the views, who, however, never expressed any desire to see
the drawings or ask any questions on the subject. He
describes Bertrand as a most amiable family man, with his
children always hanging about him, and Drouot was very
careful to inform him he was not the son of the Postmaster
of Varennes. . . . The Days, Sir Harry and Lady Campbell,
Lady Keith, Mr. Abercrombie, Mr. Egerton, &c., relieved
each other to-day by sound of the knocker as regularly as
guard can be relieved by sound of drum. . . . Lady Keith
gratified me by saying she now considered Buonaparte more

formidable than ever. I gave him more than six months, but was always certain he would return. . . . She mentioned that Buonaparte had chosen for his device at Elba an eagle with its head beneath its wing. Lord Keith asked me if I remembered when I was the age of some of the young things about me complaining of the dull, stupid, quiet times we lived in, and wishing for something extraordinary.

M. J. S. to Louisa.

Winnington: July 30, 1815.

I cannot help pitying my poor friend Napoleon, but I must confess I think it is quite right to put him in a safe place, and especially not to bring him into England. There is no saying what ideas might have been hatched in his mind upon finding himself so much the object of attention as he would have been, or indeed what ideas might have been hatched in the minds of the discontented; though I hope Englishmen, when they do rebel, will not look out of their own country for a chief conspirator. What will be the probable effect of the old Louis' energy and the disbanding of the army? Will it disband itself? I have rather a fancy to see young Napoleon (as he is not born to be drowned) seated on the throne of France for a little variety!

Serena to M. J. S.

October 10, 1815.

. . . You cannot think how you delight me with your kind recollections of Bath on your first visit to me! I can myself never forget how I enjoyed your happy spirits and our supper at Mrs. Preston's with Le Ferrier, and you seeing Mr. Vanburgh with his solemn bow, meaning the highest respect, when, alas! you could not resist after a stare of wonder, a laugh in his face, which however, passed for something else; my having your hair dressed and powdered at the hazard of my brother's rage, and yet his surprise at the improvement getting the better of it; my dressing you to dine at the Norths; your dressing Brunette in my stays,

A A 2

and another time locking her up behind my books in my bookcase. All these recollections I have as if but yesterday, and they are ever real delight to me. Mrs. Preston is now at Sheffield Place. Do you remember how you plagued her brother Edward for your amusement till he called you a little cantankerous thing?

Here I am like a true old woman going over past times, but your speaking of them with such good-humoured pleasure led me on.

Mrs. E. Stanley to M. J. S.

December 1815.

Write to you I must, and write to you without telling you what is uppermost, nay, just now sole in my thoughts I can't. So know that Lady Penrhyn's will is opened, and that Mr. Penrhyn, the residuary Legatee of 40,000*l.* at the least, breakfasted with us this morning . . . in the person of Edward Leycester! . . . Edward has not recovered his surprise. May it change nothing but his name! Yet I wish she had lived three years and let him finish his studies and learn law.

Now he will never be Lord Chancellor.

M. J. S. to Serena.

December 1815.

We usually have a week of masquerading and dancing about Christmas, which was put a stop to this year by Lady Penrhyn's death. In compliment to the Leycesters we put off anything of the kind.

. . . Edward Leycester (Mrs. Stanley's brother), you have probably heard, takes the name of Penrhyn [1] under her will and a legacy of 70,000*l.*, and he is well deserving of his good fortune.

[1] Mrs. Edward Stanley's son Arthur, afterwards Dean of Westminister, was born December 1815 and was given the name of Penrhyn after his uncle.

Mr. Ed. Penrhyn married (1823) Lady Charlotte Stanley, daughter of the Earl of Derby.

CHAPTER XII.

THE ANGLESEY HOME.

1816.

Lady Stanley's death—The funeral—Lord Sheffield's earldom—
Penrhos—'Lady Maria'—Lord Byron.

Extract from Madame Piozzi's[1] Letter to Sir James
Fellowes.

Bath : October 1815.

We have an old beauty come here to Bath—you scarce
can remember her—one of the very *very* much admired
women, Lady Stanley. Poor thing! she went to France
and Italy early in life, learned 'les manières' and 'les
tournures.' . . . .

> In youth she conquered with so wild a rage
> As left her scarce a subject in her age
> For foreign glories, foreign joys to roam,
> No thought of peace or happiness at home.

Her fortune, however, as an independent heiress she held
fast, and her wit and pleasantry seem but little impaired,
but the loss of health sent her here, and she wonders to see
mine so good. . . .

PIOZZI.

M. J. S. to Serena.

Winnington : February 4, 1816.

You have perhaps heard through the Leightons that
Lady Stanley was very ill. An express arrived on Thursday
morning to say she wished to see Sir John, and he set off
immediately with the rector; but they could not reach
Penrhos in time to see her alive, as I had a letter yesterday

[1] Dr. Johnson's friend, Mrs. Thrale.

to say she died on Thursday evening. . . . I grieve much that her sons were not with her in her last illness. She appears to have been calm, composed, gentle, and preserved her intellects to the last. . . . She was not aware of danger till Monday, and in the early stage of her illness showed her usual fear of consulting any medical practitioner or of liking her distant friends to know of her state. Only the day before the express was sent off she dictated a letter to Sir John in which she mentions she had a cold, but two pages were filled with chit-chat of the neighbourhood. It is supposed to have been a slight paralytic stroke. At times she could make and hold conversation with those about her—perfectly collected, but the interviews were short.

. . . In the bustle of the morning, when the account of Lady Stanley came, we read a long list of the new peers, with all their titles. I have not had a letter since directed by my lord.

Your ever affectionate,

M. J. S.

Sir J. T. S. to M. J. S.

Penrhos : February 1816.

I have followed both my parents to the grave; all my duties as a son are over. Conscience must determine whether I have done them ill or well, whether I have failed or succeeded in this portion of my trial here on earth. . . . I have just returned from the funeral, and give you the mere narrative of the day. The company assembled here about ten. Edward and myself breakfasted upstairs, and the gentlemen invited had the rooms below opened for them. They were allowed an hour and a half to eat up the good things which they considered a very essential part of the ceremony. A funeral without feasting would not be a funeral. The coffin was carried all the way to Holyhead on men's shoulders, we walking behind. It was bitter cold; a fierce east wind blew across the sands, and rocks, and sea; the ground was covered by snow; the sky was leaden and heavy, threatening the storm which, two hours after, burst forth with fury. For one instant only the sun appeared faintly through a few light clouds. The men at times could scarcely keep the pall upon the coffin. It fluttered in the wind, and gave a wildness to the funeral procession well according with what must have been the thoughts of many who were in it. The crowd increased as we approached the town, and by the time we reached the church must have amounted to five or six hundred people; but all were silent, and whether the bell did not toll, or the wind carried off the sound, I did not hear it till we entered the churchyard. Richard Owenson read the service impressively. The coffin was laid down near the Communion Table. When the first part of the service was over I left our pew, followed by the other mourners, passed by the coffin, and laid my offering on the altar. This custom, peculiar to Wales, is probably the remains of the Roman Catholic practice of paying for masses for the dead. The coffin was then removed to the grave which was prepared at the end of the aisle behind the pulpit, close to that of my grandmother. The coffin was lowered, the prayers said, a few large slates were then laid over the coffin, and the sexton spread gently a few spadefuls of earth over them. All was done. . . . I could not, on looking into the grave for the last time, believe that there lay the being from whom I had derived mine. . . . I cannot write to-day on any other subject. I should like to have answered your letter—a letter I shall preserve for ever as a record of honour, feeling, good sense, and everything human nature may be proud of. I feel blessed in the possession of such a wife, such a friend.

J. T. S.

M. J. S. to Sir J. T. S.

Winnington: February 1816.

The letter forwarded from Chester led me to hope you might arrive in time, and I was grieved indeed to find by the account of this evening that all was over. A kind word would have been a fund of satisfaction for you to reflect upon, and even a kind look or the pressure of your hand would not have been a trifling circumstance to your feelings. It seems a dream that she should indeed be gone.

This is a moment in which I feel the full value of dear Kate as a connection. Perhaps there could hardly be another sister-in-law with whom one could feel so thoroughly at ease and certain that, let what will happen, no thought of either of our hearts need be concealed from the other.

Sir J. T. S. to M. J. S.

Penrhos: February 5, 1816.

I can scarcely believe that I am master here without restraint. Edward behaves like an angel, and I love him. So far from the will having been a cause of difference, it has united us in stronger bonds of friendship. He showed me Kitty's letter. I showed him yours. How singular that our two wives should both write so exquisitely!

My mother certainly had a foreboding of her death when she set out for Bath. She was two days employed in burning letters.

All is, as it were, dead around me, and I ask the trees, the fields, the house, Can this be Penrhos? But, adieu! Consult the Leycesters as to what you shall do about putting your household in mourning. Adieu!

Ever yours,

J. T. STANLEY.

February 7, 1816.

Love to the children. Tell them the gardens here are white with snowdrops and that the parrot is ours, and the spaniel Clinton brought here, and the bathing house and the bay and the sea is yours.

M. J. S. to Sir J. T. S.

Winnington: February 7, 1816.

It was a very pretty sort of letter I received this evening, because it said very pretty things; but I wanted more particulars sadly, and wanted to know if the mysterious chamber

had been entered or the concealed treasures in the boxes laid
open to inspection. Edward's letters have passages which
are excellent paraphrases upon yours. I gave Kitty a hug
of delight when I read what you said of Edward. I really
think it gave me more pleasure than what I read complimentary to myself. . . . If you find there is business to keep
you any time at Penrhos, had not I better come to you and
try to connect some pleasing ideas with the enjoyment of
liberty there? And will there not be many things you will
want me to help you to decide in regard to the place? I
think if we could walk about together *en maître* it would
be so agreeable. . . . Besides, retrospective thoughts might
be banished, and by talking all our talk on the subject while
fresh in memory we might in future revisit it with feelings
of a more pleasing nature. . . .

Tell Edward there was a violent protest set up unani-
mously against the little French dog going to the rectory.
I should say with one dissentient voice, for I did not join in
the outcry.

M. J. S. to Sir J. T. S.

Winnington: February 14, 1816.

My poor dear man, I am very sorry for you, and I perfectly
comprehend all your vexation. . . . I allow all this; yet
you must indeed think of a little matter of fact, and
answer matter of fact, and settle matter of fact. I do not
want to come to Penrhos for enjoyment or amusement, or
to ramble along the shore, or to say this is mine and that is
mine, but to take care of and look after what is mine, since it
has become yours, and to look after the detail while you are
looking after the grand outline; to assist you to think what
must be done, which you will possibly never think about at
all till the matter forces itself upon your observation, and
then you will cut the Gordian knot and the things in a grand
crashing style. . . .

Adieu, dear thing, *my* support and guide in all essentials,
though in smaller concerns I think I see cooler and clearer

sometimes. I am glad I wrote to my lord before all came to my knowledge; I could then affirm that all parties were satisfied. . . . But certainly that must be a judicious will, and the persons concerned must be angelic indeed, when seeds of discord do not spring up as naturally upon the opening of a testament as white clover when the pastures are strewed with ashes. I heard from William, who makes no observation whatever on his immediate share in the present event, but fills his letters with lambs and trees and flowers. Adieu!

Yours ever,

M. J. S.

Sir J. T. S. to M. J. S.

Penrhos : February 15, 1816.

. . . . I have found fifty sketches of codicils all nearly the same. . . . Edward has now Plâs Croes, instead of the difference of income given him before. . . . Do you feel yourself disposed to join me here in the present state of things? If you do, I will wait for you, and not think as yet of going to Chester to prove the will. The household consists of a housekeeper, a young woman, Suzette,[1] a cook, plenty of dairymaids, a laundress and a housemaid, besides the men-servants. . . . I have sent the coach-horses to the plough, fearful that I should have to pay the tax if I made use of them. I cannot learn what latitude in this respect is allowed an executor. Provisions are exceedingly cheap here. . . . All goes on with its old momentum. I have been paying property tax in abundance; there are very few bills unpaid. . . . Arrears come dropping in, but there is plenty of money in the house—near 2,000l. in numbers of boxes and trunks. Indeed I have not been idle. I have been up every morning as soon as it was daylight and at work in my room till past midnight.

[1] The Montpelier girl brought to England, 1784, by Lady Stanley. She was devoted to her, and survived her mistress only a few weeks.

Sir J. T. S. to W. O. S.

My dear William,—I have been too busy since we lost your grandmother to write to you. I trusted to your mama doing it. You have been named in the will as my successor to a landed estate, and you have been left besides 500*l.* on your coming of age, and after my death all the plate, books, china, and pictures in the house. My mother was very fond of Penrhos, which I need not tell you is now mine. She enlarged the gardens, planted a great many trees, and created a little Paradise in a country almost as ugly and dreary as the eye can look over. The ground is now as white as snow with snowdrops, and in a few weeks will be as blue with violets. The house stands on a promontory a quarter of a mile from the sea. There is a little bay, where the sand is as smooth and hard as a floor, and where your mother and sisters will have much pleasanter bathing than they ever had at Parkgate or Highlake, and near it are wild rugged rocks you will all delight in. I hope you will all be here to enjoy them. . . .

> Believe me, my dear William,
> Your affectionate father,
> JOHN THOMAS STANLEY.

M. J. S. to Mrs. E. Stanley.

And here I am ! And what shall I say next when so many things press upon my pen for communication? Having slept at Gwyndu last night I got here at eleven, and it has been totally impossible to sit down for one moment before dinner for the purpose of writing. . . . Tell Edward with my affectionate love that Sir John has told me what passed between them, and that nothing can gratify me more highly than the thoughts of his being appointed guardian to William should he have the misfortune to require one, except the circumstance of Sir John's thinking proper to consult me on the subject. I sincerely hope that I shall never be placed

in the painful and responsible situation of being joined with
him in such a trust, not only on my own account, but for
the sake of the poor boys, to whom the loss of a father in
early youth can never be supplied. But should such be my
fate, it would be my greatest comfort to depend upon his
upright and well principled mind for assistance and discretion
in what concerned either of them. And now no more of this,
though it has unfitted me for any other subject.

Adieu, dearest Kate. I dearly love every new trait of
excellence in Edward's character doubly for your sake. New
perhaps I should not call it, for what comes out of him was
ever in him, but I mean every one that newly comes under
my observation.

Yours ever affectionately,

M. J. S.

M. J. S. to Mrs. E. Stanley.

Penrhos: March 1816.

Clearing the Augean stable was a trifle to clearing all
these drawers, cupboards, and shelves; Edward, indeed, might
have found an expeditious mode by tumbling everything into
the fire. You would be amused with the accounts given of
his method. We are convinced he burnt many a bank-note!
And Suzette declares he broke several keys in the locks in
trying which was the right one. When I laugh at Sir John
sometimes for his over-value of scraps, apparently of no
importance and propose burning, 'Oh,' says Emma, 'you
are like Edward; he was for putting things into the fire.'
'Why,' says I, 'he would have put me quite out of patience.'
However, to return and to prove that such conclusive
measures would be objectionable, I will just mention one of
the last features which distinguished a search. In an old
damp closet, full of Daffy's Elixir of Usquebaugh, ditto of
brandy, ditto of whisky, medicines of all sorts, but a greater
quantity of spiders and dust than anything else, came from
behind several books a quarto copy of Campbell's 'Pleasures
of Hope,' with engravings luckily wrapped in paper, and a
tin box with title-deeds. There were several other books of

some value in the same collection—part of 'Madame de
Motteville's Memoirs;' the rest I had found elsewhere. I
have been trying to look over and arrange a more legible and
descriptive catalogue of the old library, but I groaned over
the task. It is nothing like ended yet, but I have nearly
classed the books. There is a Latin Bible, which I wonder
if it got Edward's eye, and I hope he will encourage the
belief I have formed respecting its owner. The date itself
must give it value from its antiquity—1590 I think; but in
the title-page is the name of William Russell in a very good
hand, both in Latin and English, and on the opposite leaf
R. Russell in a different hand. May I not be allowed to
believe that this book belonged to the beheaded Lord Russell,
and to be very angry if anybody doubted the fact? One of
our Welsh ancestors was Chancellor Wynn, of Hereford, and
a great collector. What more likely than that he should
have purchased this curiosity? I have also got a bit of the
Pretender's hair for the girls.

M. J. S. to Louisa.

Penrhos: March 13, 1816.

I do not recollect if I have written to you since I came
here. . . . I am surprised to see how regularly and well
everything seems to have gone on. No extravagance or
waste, although the plenty is something surprising to English
understandings. The labourers and carpenters are boarded
in or about the house; and when I arrived I found a whole
bull and a whole cow salted for future provision; some of it
dried for summer use. Also five large bacon hogs and about
ten large deep crocks of butter salted; but I do not think
that this could be more expensive or so much so as our
English mode of paying farm servants.

The price of meat and everything else is quite ridiculous.
The best cuts of beef are 5d., by the quarter 3½d.; the cow
I found killed was valued at 3½d.; the bull at 2d.; butter
is 1s. per lb.; lamb, 2s. 6d. per quarter; everything else in
proportion. . . . There were many unmarked boxes which
came to Sir John, in which he found little packets of money

to the amount of about 400*l*., and little old-fashioned trinkets and knives, scissors and writing paper enough to supply a country shop. . . . We have about 60*l*. in silver, 8*l*. of it in sixpences.

M. J. S. to Serena.

Penrhos: March 1816.

That is a bold person, my dear aunt, who ventures to assert on the first promulgation of the contents of a will that it will be thought just and satisfactory, and a will that gave general satisfaction was never, I believe, yet penned. I have been very busy and very much pleased here; I have found things much better regulated than I expected—the servants accustomed to economy, though I could describe the style of house-keeping here in a way that would make you stare in respect of plenty. Keeping up the place for dear little Billy, who I hope will live here, will not be very expensive. . . . I have been acquainting myself with everybody and everything, and making arrangements for a change of Government. Luckily a general change of Ministry is not necessary. We shall return in August, when the boys come back from school. . . . I should be very glad to give up Winnington, as three country houses will prevent our ever having one home. . . . To be sure, I acknowledge myself Lady Maria, and have become tolerably well accustomed to the sound, but hope always to be your Maria *sans phrase*. Is it your Lady Longford whose death I see in the papers?

M. J. S. to Mrs. E. Stanley.

Penrhos: March 20, 1816.

I have been supposing all day how you have said or thought, ' They have enjoyed this first spring day thoroughly at Penrhos,' so don't tell me you have either not thought about us, or that you have not had a fine day to elicit the thought. . . . It has comforted me to sit down to think and write of a day of birds singing and violets smelling and sun shining at Penrhos after having written to you of, I hope, the dying speech and confession of the testamentary wars of the family, for I trust nothing more will be said, altho' every-

one will probably remain of the same opinion as before. . . .
Have you rejoiced very much at the triumph of the country
over the income tax? What new *horreur* shall we have
in its place? . . . Sir John is summoned to be on the Grand
Jury at Beaumaris on the 30th.

Ever yours,

M. J. S.

Serena to M. J. S.

Bath: April 11, 1816.

. . . At that very time I heard of my dear Lady Longford's death, from whom I had never-ceasing kindness, that
neither her woeful calamities or any other circumstance ever
interrupted. . . . Never was a mother more tenderly beloved
by her family. Her mind seemed to become clearer and
more admirable as her body weakened at the close of her
life. She had four of her children, Mrs. Hamilton and
Stuart, and two of her sons by her for some hours, and she
never once spoke of herself, but actually died while giving
them advice. I had so long loved her that I own I felt her
death more than any I could feel out of my own family. . . .

A very pleasant, animated couple, General and Mrs.
Despard, live at the Grange, near Ellesmere. She is niece to
my Lady Hesketh. I had a large parcel of Lady Hesketh's
letters, and as I should not long live to read them, I have
given them to Mrs. Despard. Reading them has sent me
back to many scenes and people that were for years happy
days to me.

I am thinking of sending Henry Clive [1] the picture of his
mother by Hickey. Edward Clive told my brother he had
two miniature pictures. He supposed them to be my father
and mother, but, as my mother's picture has never been
taken, I suppose it is *mine*. I should like to know if it is so.

M. J. S. to her son W. O. S.

Penrhos: March 30, 1816.

My dear William,—Papa is still very busy and is preparing a new plantation and planning many improvements in

[1] Of Whitfield, Hereford.

building and walks He has bought 20,000 little thorns to
nurse up into hedges, which he means to plant with stone
walls and walks between. In this country the only fences
are walls or gorse hedges. Over the bathing-house there is
a large pleasant room with three windows, which I mean
to fit up for use in the summer, and we shall often bring tea
there, or eat our fruit luncheon. We went by water to the
South Stack on Monday : we had an excellent boat, with
an experienced sailor to take care of us. There is now a
bridge of ropes to join the land instead of the cradle you
must have heard of, and, as it swings about, I did not like
crossing it much. I shall be frightened when I take you,
unless you are very good children and walk quietly. The
rocks are grand, and we went into one beautiful cave called
the ' Parliament House,' which is very lofty and deep. The
birds were numerous, and from one part of the high perpen-
dicular cliffs there flew out twenty or thirty large cranes.
The seagulls were by hundreds. . . . Grandpapa has asked
about your holydays. If he wishes you to go to Sheffield
Place, I hope you will do nothing to frighten him, or to
lead or follow George into any pranks, as you know grandpapa is easily alarmed for the safety of boys, and not without good reason, tho' I don't think you mischievous.

Your very affectionate mother,

M. J. STANLEY.

Poor Gram and Hecla are dead. Papa is very sorry.
There is not one of the Iceland race left; they have all died
of distemper.

Lord Sheffield to M. J. S.

Portland Place: April 25, 1816.

We returned to town on Monday, and, having appointed
Edward and William to meet us at dinner, we passed the
remainder of the day together. William has a most interesting and I think handsome countenance, and is a very
ingratiating little fellow. I was hardly aware of the increase of George Aug. in height as well as in bulk until I
saw him with his nephews. Edward appears to me as if he

would be a stout, square, squat little fellow, just like his grandpapa Sheffield. He asked Mr. Dodson whether any boy he could lick could require him to fag. He was highly gratified when answered in the negative. I am considerably better, but my lady is strenuous for an immediate return to the country.

Yours ever, S.

M. J. S. to Mrs. E. Stanley.

London: May 6.

I was much disappointed with Miss O'Neill in the *Grecian Daughter*. She wants expression of countenance sadly for such characters, and I remembered Mrs. Siddons too well—in—— Fiddlestick !—it was not Miss O'Neill, but Kean I have to talk about. Euphrasia's failings have been recorded : but it is ditto for him. Kemble acts and looks Penruddock in a much superior manner, and Kean's shocking voice and mean appearance are horrible defects, and the rest of the actors are so bad that altogether I was tired of the performance. Lucy was much interested in watching Lord Byron's countenance and envying the lady who sat next him every time he spoke to her, and the lady, whoever she was (not Lady B.), laughed a great deal and proved Conrad was not in a gloomy fit.

Mrs. Davenport's assembly was splendid, with all the drawing-room heads. We went to Mrs. Bold's late, when the height of her glory was passed.

B B

CHAPTER XIII.

THE UNCLE'S LETTERS TO LOUISA, LUCY, RIANETTE, AND BELLA.

1816.

[About this time M. J. S. heard of plans being made by the Rectory party for an expedition to the scene of Waterloo. Her regrets at the separation involved by an enterprise in which she could not share are vividly expressed.]

M. J. S. to Mrs. E. Stanley.

April 1816.

I wish the Battle of Waterloo had been gained by Buonaparte. I wish Brussels (and Paris too) was in the hands of the Algerines. I wish you may have the asthma in June. I wish Edward may have the gout, and Edward L. another bilious fever. I wish you had twelve children all under twelve years old, and then *perhaps* your truant dispositions might be something quieted. I have not had a moment's comfort since I got your plans, or Sir John either —I from disappointment, he from fear. I try to flatter myself you are not in earnest, for if there is any chance of going farther next year there is no reason for going part of the way this. I thought you were engaged to the South Stack. I thought we should have spent June and July so comfortably together at Alderley; and then the sea, which would do you so much more good than anything else, with all the children together, and my bathing-house fitted up for your reading or writing room. . . .

I do not see a chance or possibility of our going with you this year. It would be wrong to worry him about it, as there really is so much business to settle. . . . I think we must prepare apartments in Bedlam at the same time if we were to talk to Sir John about going abroad ; and yet I see he is wishing it were practicable to oblige me.

[No picture of the family life at this time would be complete without allusion to the uncle at Alderley Rectory who was the moving spirit in all the pursuits of the younger generation.

They acted his plays and delighted in his stories, and he was always devising some fresh amusement and surprise for his nieces.]

M. J. S. to W. O. S.

Alderley Park : June 1, 1816.

My dear little Boy,—You have been very ill-used to hear nothing of us for so long. . . . We kept Bella's birthday here, and the school-children dined in the yard upon furmity, buns, gooseberry pies, and rice puddings. They played about all the afternoon and were very happy. Uncle had fitted up one of the turrets of the deer house [1] very prettily as a surprise for us when we came first and as a present to sisters. He put in casement windows, lined the whole with white moss from Soss-Moss for the ceiling and green for the walls, put seats round and made an inscription of double marsh-marigolds over one of the windows.

THE NIECES' BOWER.

On one of the window frames lay a copy of verses called Mr. Hoo Hoo's Legacy, which I send you.

The Last Will and Testament of Mr. Hoo Hoo, Professor, of this Mansion, &c., &c.

I, Mr. Hoo Hoo, do bequeath unto all,
The elders, and juniors, the great and the small,
As tenants in common, in spinster succession,
To have and to hold as their legal possession
This mansion in lease, and do further bequeath
To our nieces the items recorded beneath.

[1] Built by Sir Edward Stanley, 1750, after Lord Vernon's deer house at Sudbury.

B B 2

To the eldest the bliss of the numberless hours
We owls have enjoyed in these fanciful towers.
Long, long in possession may Rianette be
Contented and happy and gladsome as we.
To Lucy my daily consumption of brain,
Such a budget of thought, such a marvellous train.
What would she have more for a splendid romance
Than the daily results of an owl in a trance!
Above and moreover I, Mr. Hoo Hoo,
Do give and devise to the little Lou Lou
My gravity, silence, and dignified gait:
How rich the bequest if it make her sedate ! . . .
And what for the Bella?   We give and bequeath her
Our wardrobe complete, with each delicate feather.
A legacy suited, we think, to a hair,
A complexion so sweet and so soft and so fair.
It is further my will that my beak and my claws—
But shall I devise them, no, no, let me pause:
I revoke my bequest.   Dear nieces, adieu !
They shall rest in the grave of Hoo Hoo, Hoo Hoo.

E. S.

Uncle and aunt set off on Monday; they mean to be at
Waterloo on the 18th, the anniversary of the battle. Edward
Leycester goes with them and Donald Craufurd.[1] . . . Long
sends her love. I mean to take her to Penrhos, as she will
like so much to see the place again; she must look after your
plate, your old tankard, old books, and old china, that
nobody cheats you of them; but I think I shall borrow your
silver dishes, which are so much better than our plated ones,
and Long must look sharp that they are taken care of. She
remembers your telling her she should be your housekeeper,
and if she was too old to be of use she should sit in the
parlour and read to you. Some time or other perhaps she
may have some other office of the kind, for as she is younger
than me, I should be very sorry not to hope she may see you
fixed in a home before she is blind, deaf, and lame.

Good-bye, dear William.

Your affectionate mother.

[1] Captain Donald Craufurd—wounded at the Battle of Waterloo.

[Before leaving Alderley the four elder nieces were promised letters from abroad by their uncle, and the following extracts show how faithfully the promise was kept :—]

To Louisa Stanley.

June 11, 1816.

Will my dear Lou excuse one little letter from the land of her ancestors just to say that uncle and aunt and Edward and Donald have experienced every degree of prosperity since the sad and melancholy hour of parting with the tenants of the Turret.

All in the Downs the fleet was moored! and so are we —just fifteen miles from the shore we quitted last night. . . . They say a breeze is coming. The breeze came and went away, leaving us floating immovably on a sea of chrystal, where about sunset, on peeping through a telescope, I saw a little black speck which speedily increased to the size of a boat full of men evidently making towards us. All eyes were turned to the spot : in half an hour it could be clearly seen with the naked eye—very long, very warlike, very suspicious. No vessels were nearer than twelve or fifteen miles, and we of course were the object of pursuit. Was she a smuggler? was she a pirate ? was she a Press gang ? The silence of the evening was soon broken by a shot—a hint that we were to prepare for the arrival of the mysterious wanderers on the deep. Our flag was hoisted in token of submission, Donald's sword being the only offensive weapon on board. The dusk increased, and was soon illuminated by a flash and a second shot. . . .

Now the boat drew near, pulling rapidly, and now it came alongside with the velocity of a trout and demeanour of a pike ; six gaunt figures of the Bandit breed pulled six long oars in silence ; one tall figure stood motionless in the bow, with his boat-hook presented. In the stern sat two grim chiefs ; one the Jackall to the Royal Lion, who, by a word, arrested the progress of his vassals. In a moment every oar was twirled from the water and stood erect in compliment to the order. The chief arose like the Corsair ; his head enveloped in flannel to guard him from the midnight mist; a girdle of pistols and cartouche-boxes encircled his body. On his right hand were deposited muskets, pistols, bayonets; on his left reposed a pile of cutlasses; at his feet gleamed the lighted match; behind him was a lanthorn, compass, and all the et-ceteras of dire and dusky doings. He rose, he sprang, from step to step, and every hand was raised to every hat as he seized a rope and stood before us—a lieutenant from H.M.S. 'Cadmus' in a boat thirty feet long, called a 'Death' or a 'Coffin' from its extreme danger—sent to search suspicious people. He had chased us in silent solicitude for three hours, having in that time bounded o'er the light blue waves at nine or ten miles an hour. Here the mysterious tale must close, for, contrary to the wish I am sure you must feel of his having boarded the vessel sword in hand, severed our heads from our bodies and left us a blazing monument of his incendiary powers, he proved to be a very civil, well-behaved gentleman. Excepting indeed that in as civil terms as possible—*i.e.* in certain terms with it behoveth me not to express—he hinted that he had been sent on a wild-goose chase. . . .

The morning dawned upon us in nearly the same position in which the night had received us. . . . Famine began to stare us in the face; our provisions were nearly consumed; two or more days might elapse before we reached Ostend. We breakfasted on tea, fried skate, and cheese. Breakfast at an end, it was proposed to board the nearest vessel and beg or buy a dinner. In the tide course appeared a sail about five miles distant. The boat was lowered, volunteers stepped forward—Uncle Edward, Donald, and a gentlemanlike Belgian. Away we went, rowing by turns, and when midway between the vessels again we cried as on twenty other occasions, 'What would Louisa say to this?' It was like traversing infinite space in a balloon or being tenants of a trimmer which a shark might have swallowed up in a trice. By hard rowing we came alongside the strange sail in an hour. Three leaden figures, motionless as the unwieldly bark they manned, gazed curiously upon our approaching boat. Our Belgian friend hailed, but hailed in vain. They looked, but spoke not. Again he spoke, and at length a monotonous 'yaw' proclaimed that they were not dumb. We went on board and found a perfect Dutch family on their way from Antwerp to Rouen. Again we said, 'Oh, that Louisa could see this!' Out stepped from her cabin the Captain's wife in appropriate costume, her close little cap, large gold necklace and earrings ; and behind the Captain's spouse stepped forth two genuine descendants of the nautical couple. Large round heads with large round——(what shall I say?) Hottentots to match and keep up the due balance between head and tail. They were about five and six years of age, the æra of incipient curiosity—but no curiosity was there. They stood on each side their Vrow, like marble Cupids supporting a marble statue. Having explained our wants and wishes, the Captain produced as the chief restorative an incomparable bottle of Schiedam—*i.e.* gin. To each he offered a good large glass, and then, in answer to our request for beef, four bottles of excellent claret, two square loaves. . . . For all this, he asked a guinea, upon receiving which his features relaxed with a smile, and he declared we should have two more bottles of claret. Upon hearing we had a lady in the packet, he begged her acceptance of half a neat's tongue, some butter, and a bag of rusks. Loaded with them, we took a joyful leave of these sombre sailors and returned with the orange cravat of our Belgian for a flag, in triumph to the packet.

But a truce to my pen. Ostend is in sight, and now we are all rubbing our hands and congratulating each other that wind and tide are in our favour, and that we shall be in in a couple of hours.

To Lucy Stanley.

Cambray: June 24, 1816.

Come, my dear Lucy, leave this novel market-place of Ghent; leave Louisa to purchase those long wicker chests full of live rabbits. . . . Let Bella superintend the sale of those dear little milk-white goats, harnessed and unharnessed; do not, by patting upon their heads that nest of pugs in a basket or that pack of curs of all shapes, sizes and variety, lead their owners to suppose that you want to return to England like another Diana, with a kennel of hounds under your protection. . . . And now away with me to Waterloo!

We arrived at Brussels on the evening of the 17th, and at seven o'clock started for the scene of action. From Brussels a paved road with a carriage track on each side passes for nine miles to the village of Waterloo. For the first mile the country is open and diversified with fine views of the town. Straggling trees then denote the approximation of a forest, and another mile finds the traveller immersed in a long dark avenue of trees, whose shade the sun rarely penetrates, and consequently the road is scarcely ever dry. What, then, must it have been when the accumulated baggage of 80,000 men, horses, drivers, carts and carriages, waggons, &c., were all rushing through it at the same moment after a fall of heaviest rain ! . . .

It is without exception one of the most cut-throat-looking spots I ever beheld . . . and for some days after the battle, deserters and stragglers, chiefly Prussians, took up their abode in this appropriate place, and, sallying forth, robbed, plundered, and often shot those who were unfortunate enough to travel alone or in small defenceless parties.

After traversing this gloomy avenue for about four miles the first symptoms of war met our eyes in the shape of a dead horse, whose ribs glared like a *cheval-de-frise* from a tumulus of mud. If the ghosts of the dead haunt these sepulchral groves, we must have passed through an army of spirits, as our driver who had visited the scene three days after the battle, described the last four miles as a continued pavement of men and horses dying and dead.

At length a dome appears at the termination of the avenue. It is the church of Waterloo. They were preparing for a mass and procession, and the houses were most of them adorned with festoons of flowers or branches of trees. . . . In a neat house on the right Lord Anglesey suffered amputation. We went into the room and the owner showed us the table on which he was laid and the chair on which his

leg rested, still stained with blood. The leg itself is deposited
in the garden; a weeping willow is planted on the spot.
Close to this tree is an inscription descriptive of the event,
and in the room is a coloured print of the Marquis in a
handsome frame, a present from his lordship. The Duke of
Wellington visited him half an hour after the operation was
performed. In the church are four monuments erected to
the memory of officers who fell in the action. Opposite the
church is the inn where the Duke slept, dignified with a
sign on which is inscribed : ' Quartier-Général du Duc de
Wellington.' . . .

. . . We turned to the right down the Nivelle road, for
it was there Donald's gun was placed, and some labourers
who were ploughing on the spot brought us some iron shot
and fragments of shell which they had just turned up. The
hedges were still tolerably sprinkled with bits of cartridge-
paper, and remnants of hats, caps, straps, and shoes were dis-
cernible all over the plains. Hougomont was a heap of ruins,
for it had taken fire during the action and presented a very
perfect idea of the fracas which had taken place that day year.
How different now ! A large flock of sheep, with their shepherd, were browsing at the gate, and the larks were singing over
its ruins on one of the sweetest days we could have chosen
for the visit. As I was taking a sketch in a quiet corner I
heard a vociferation so loud, so vehement, and so varied, that
I really thought two or three people were quarrelling close
to me. In a moment the vociferator (for it was but one)
appeared at my elbow with an explosion of French oaths
and gesticulations equal to any discharge of grape-shot on
the day of attack. ' Comment, Mons.,' said I, ' what is the
matter ? ' ' Oh, les coquins ! les sacrés coquins ! ' and away
he went, abusing the *coquins* in so ambiguous a style that
I doubted whether his wrath was venting against Napoléon
or against his opponents. ' Oui,' remarked I, ' ils sont
coquins; et Buonaparte, que pensez-vous de lui ? ' This
was a sort of opening which I trusted would bring him to
the point without a previous committal of myself. It certainly did bring him to the point, for he gave a bounce and

a jump and his tongue came out, and his mouth foamed, and his eyes rolled, as with a jerk he ejaculated, 'Napoléon! qu'est-ce que je pense de lui?' It was well for poor Napoleon that he was quiet and comfortable in St. Helena, for had he been at Hougomont, I am perfectly convinced that my communicant would have sent him to moulder with his brethren in arms. Having vented his rage, I asked him if the French had ever got within the walls. 'Yes,' he said, 'three times; but they were always repulsed;' he assured me he had been there during the attack and that he saw them within; but added, 'How they came in at that door' (pointing to the gate by which we were standing and which was drilled with bullets), 'or when they came in, or how or where they got out I cannot tell you, for what with the noise, and the fire, and the smoke, I scarcely knew where I was myself.' One of the farm servants begged me to observe the chapel, which he hinted had been indebted to a miracle for its safety, and certainly as a good Catholic he had a fair foundation for his belief, as the flames had merely burnt about a yard of the floor, having been checked, as he conceived, by the presence of the crucifix suspended over the door, which had received no other injury than the loss of part of its feet. He had remained there till morning, when, seeing the French advance and guessing their drift, he contrived to make good his escape, but returned the following day. What he then saw you may guess when I tell you that at the very door I stood upon a mound composed of earth and ashes upon which 800 bodies had been burnt. Every tree bore marks of death, and every ditch was one continued grave. From Hougomont we walked to La Belle Alliance, crossing the neutral ground between the armies; a few days ago a couple of gold watches had been found, and I dare say many a similar treasure yet remains. At La Belle Alliance, a squalid farm-house, we rested to take some refreshment. For a few biscuits and a bottle of common wine the woman asked us five francs; which being paid, I followed her into the house. Not perceiving me at the door, she met her husband, and, bursting into a loud laugh, with a fly-up of arms and legs (for nothing in this country is done without gesticulation), she exclaimed, 'Only think! ces gens-là m'ont donné five francs.' In this miserable pot-house did the possessor find 280 wounded wretches jammed together and weltering in blood when he returned on Monday morning. If I proceed to more particulars I foresee I should fill folios. I must carry you at once to La Haye Sainte. It was along a hedge that the severest work took place; it made me shudder to think that upon a space of fifty square yards 4,000 bodies were found dead. The ditches and the field formed one great grave. The earth told in very visible terms what occasioned its elasticity; upon forcing a stick down and turning up a clod human bodies in an offensive state of decay immediately presented themselves. I found four Belgian peasants commenting upon one figure which was scarcely interred, and on walking under the outer wall of La Haye Sainte a hole was tenanted by myriads of maggots feasting upon a corpse. Here stands the Wellington tree, peppered with shot and stripped as high as a man can jump of its twigs and leaves, for every passenger jumps up for a relic. We stood upon the road where Buonaparte (defended by the high banks) sent on, but *didn't* lead, 6,000 of his old Imperial Guard. They charged along the road up to La Haye Sainte, dwindling as they went by the incessant fire of eighty pieces of artillery, many of them within a few yards, till their number did not exceed 300! Then Napoleon turned round to Bertrand, lifted up his hand, cried out, 'C'est tout perdu, c'est tout fini!' and galloped off with La Corte and Bertrand, quitting most probably for ever a field of battle. A continued sheet of corn-fields occupy the whole plain. The crops are indifferent, and the reason assigned is curious; the whole being trampled down last year became the food of mice, which in consequence repaired thither from all quarters and increased and multiplied to such a degree that the soil is quite infested by them.

Upon the heights where the British squares received the shock of the French cavalry we found an English officer's cocked hat, much injured apparently by a cannon shot; it was covered with its oilskin, now rotting away, and showed by its texture, shape, and quality, that it had been manufactured by a fashionable hatter and probably often graced the wearer's head in Bond Street and St. James's.   Wherever we went we were surrounded by boys and beggars offering eagles from Frenchmen's helmets, cockades, buttons, pistols, swords, cuirasses, and numberless other scraps and fragments. . . . I merely carried away a few bullets and eagles for Owen, a leaf of the Wellington tree for K., a piece of cartridge for you; but Donald has a nobler present for Louisa—a rib and part of the backbone of a man who was burnt at Hougomont. 'Qu'est-ce que c'est que cela?' said an astonished Custom officer to us as he poked it out from a corner of Donald's trunk when we were searched as we passed the frontier. Well might he ask; but I doubt whether the information conveyed in the reply gave him any particular satisfaction. . . . We started from Brussels on the 20th, again crossed the field of Waterloo, and proceeded towards Genappe. . . . . The road along which we jogged merrily and peaceably had last year on this same day been one continued scene of carnage and confusion—Prussians cutting off French heads, arms, and legs by hundreds ; Englishmen in the rear going in chase, cheering the Prussians, urging them in pursuit; the French, exhausted with fatigue and vexation, making off in all directions with the utmost speed.   At Genappe we changed horses in the very courtyard where Napoleon's carriage was taken . . . and were shown the spot where the Brunswick hussar cut down the French general as a retaliation for the life of the Duke. The postmaster told us what he could, and in his narrative he never called the Highland regiments 'les Ecossais,' but 'les sans-culottes.' . . .

Our landlady gave us such a tragi-comic account of her sufferings last year during the time of the retreat, and in 1814 when the Russians were there, that while she laughed with one eye and cried with the other we were almost inclined to do the same.   She had been pillaged by a French officer in a manner that surpassed any idea we could have formed of French oppression and barbarity.   At one time the Cossacks caught her, and on some dispute about a horse four of them took her each by an arm and a leg, and, laying her upon her *ventre* as flat as a pancake, a fifth cracked his knout (whip) most fearfully over her head. By good fortune an officer rescued our poor landlady from their clutches, but she shivered like a jelly when she described her feelings in her awkward position, like a boat upon the shore bottom upwards. Then she told us how her husband died of fright, or something very near it; her account of him was capital: 'Il étoit,' said she, 'un bon papa du temps passé,' by which perhaps you may imagine she was young and handsome. She was very old, and as ugly as Hecate.

To Rianette Stanley.

July 1, 1816.

On looking over my heads of chapters, for I note down briefly, I observe—

Brussels—frogs, 100 for 3*d.*
Children kissing!

It is perhaps as well to say a word upon these two strange articles. The first occurred as I was walking through the market-place at Brussels; I observed a woman busily employed in chipping, cutting, and skinning certain little nondescript pieces of gelatinous food, which I could not at once make out as belonging to either flesh, fish, or fowl, and sure enough they were legs and thighs nicely tied up in a knot of poor dear little frogs. I asked the price, and she offered me 100 for 3*d.* I requested one, which, gently taking by its dear little toe and holding between finger and thumb for closer inspection, the woman, who had eyed me attentively jumped up, saying, 'Mais, Monsieur, il ne faut pas les manger avant qu'ils sont grillés!' thinking that I was going to gobble it down as a *bonne-bouche* before breakfast. I returned with my trophy, which was deposited in Donald's egg-cup to excite his appetite when he came down.

My kissing children were performing a game in the middle of the street on the night of the illumination at Brussels round a sort of altar (I believe the said altar to have been a tub), crowned with a wreath of candles. A circle of alternate sex hand in hand danced and sang, in a style of elegance and step which would have puzzled Mr. Daniel Massey, dancing master of Alderley, to communicate to his scholars. The song terminated with the couplet, 'Allons nous, dépêchez-vous—baisez la plus belle-a,' upon which the beau *pro tempore* cast a gentle look around, and then, handing forth the fair object of his choice, made a respectable obeisance, and *salué'd* la Dame with all the delicacy and tenderness possible. La Dame smiled, and he smiled, and, placing one arm upon the shoulder and another round the waist, kissed, bowed, and retired, and song and dance recommenced. It was agreed by our two beaux that the particulars of song and dance should be revived the first happy week at Winnington, and Louisa can act 'La Dame' for the first hour till the whole party is perfect.

We arrived at the door of our inn at Compiègne. Out comes mine host: 'Pas de place'—pleasant hearing this, for hungry, tired, and shaken travellers, so we hurried to the 'Petit Barillat.' Let it be recorded, for it is deserving of record. We were ushered into a large room, in the middle of which we observed by the glimmering of our candles two tall black figures, motionless and uniform. We advanced, and lo! the figures proved to be (you will never guess)—a new pair of full-sized genuine jack boots; if I described them you would all exclaim, 'No, no, it cannot be; this is one of uncle's stories! so ask John Harrison, for I doubt whether this, his first introduction to a full-sized pair of jack boots, will ever be erased from his memory. The rest of the furniture consisted of broken chairs, rickety tables, marble slabs, torn paper, golden borders, muslin curtains, mirrors, and a couple of beds. Could we have tea? 'Oh, oui, tout de suite.' Accordingly, a cloth was laid, and in time four things called tea-cups of doubtful shape and size were placed on the table, with large spoons in each. Then after another pause up came a soup-tureen, with a monstrous ladle, filled with hot milk. 'Do,' said I to Edward and Donald, 'go down and see what is doing below; there must be some mistake!' They found the cook boiling tea which he had taken out of a bag by handfuls; 'it was almost ready, but les Messieurs would probably like to have the eggs put in before it came up;' and the artichokes were quite ready. What would have appeared but for this interference we could not guess; but probably a few minutes more would have presented us with a dish of poached eggs boiled up with tea instead of spinach. The unfortunate tea was rescued, but wonders did not cease. We called for bread, and the maid produced a loaf thirty-four inches long, about as thick as my wrist. We continued to drink our tea, and half dead with laughing and fatigue, tumbled into our beds. The whole kitchen and passages in the house were paved with tombstones from a convent knocked down in the Revolution. For our excellent accommodation and fare we were charged twice as much as at the best hotels in the Netherlands. Upon remonstrating, the waiter deducted two francs in the hope and confidence that he should see us again when we passed through Compiègne. If he does, I will consent to live in a jack boot and dine for the remainder of my days on fried tea and eggs, and coffee and artichokes.

To Bella Stanley.

Paris: July 9, 1816.

. . . It is absolutely necessary that a word or two should be said upon the palace at Compiègne, which was fitted up about seven years ago by Napoleon for Marie-Louise. Having seen most of his Imperial abodes, I am inclined to give the preference, as far as interior decoration extends, to this of Compiègne. Gold, silver, mirrors, tapestry, all hold their court here. The bath is a perfect specimen of French luxury and magnificence. It fills a recess in a moderately-sized room almost entirely panelled with the finest sheets of plate glass, and the ball-room is so exquisitely beautiful that to see its golden walls and ceilings lighted up with splendid chandeliers and its floors graced with dancers, plumed and jewelled, I would take the trouble of attending as your chaperon from Alderley whenever the Bourbons send you an invitation. The gardens are formal, like all other French pleasure grounds, but there is one part you would all enjoy. When Buonaparte first carried Marie-Louise to Compiègne she expressed much satisfaction; but remarked that, as it was deficient in a *berceau*, it could not stand in competition with her favourite palace of Schönbrunn. Now, a *berceau* is a wide walk *covered* over with trelliswork and flowers. She left Compiègne. In *six* weeks Napoleon begged her to pay another visit; she did so, and found a *berceau* wide enough for two carriages to go abreast, and above two miles in length, extending from the gardens to the forest of Compiègne, completely finished. May you all be espoused to husbands who will execute all your whims and fancies with equal rapidity and good taste! In your *berceau* I will walk; but if you are destined to reside in golden palaces, you must expect little of uncle's company.

Where shall I begin? Let us take the theatres. We saw Talma last night, and the impression is strong, therefore he shall appear first on the list.

The play was 'Manlius,' a tragedy in many respects similar to our 'Venice Preserved.' The house was crowded to excess, especially the pit, which, as in England, is the focus of criticisms and vent for public opinion. When a tragedy is acted, no music whatever is allowed, not a fiddle prefaced the performance; but at seven o'clock the curtain slowly rose, and amidst the thunder of applause, succeeded by a breathless silence, Talma stepped forth in the Roman toga of Manlius. His figure is bad, short, and rather clumsy; his countenance deficient in dignity and natural expression; but with all these deductions, he shines like a meteor when compared with Kemble. He is body and soul, finger and thumb, head and foot involved in his character. . . . The curtain is not let down between the acts, and the interval does not exceed two or three minutes, so that your attention is never interrupted. The scene closed as it commenced, with that peculiar hurra of the French, expressive of their highest excitement. It is the same with which they make their charge in battle, and proportioned to numbers it could not have been more vehement at the victories of Austerlitz and Jena than it was on the reappearance of Talma, and not satisfied with this, they insisted on his coming forth again. At length, amidst hurras and cries of 'Talma! Talma!' the curtain was closed up, and my last impression rendered unfavourable by a vulgar, graceless figure in nankeen breeches and top-boots, hurrying in from a side scene, dropping a swing bow in the centre of the stage, and then hurrying out again. Theatres are to Frenchmen what flowers are to bees, they live *in* them and *upon* them, and the sacrifice of liberty appears to be a tribute most willingly paid for the gratification they receive; for, to be sure, never can there exist a more despotic, arbitrary government than that of a French theatre. A soldier stands by from the moment you quit your carriage till you get into it; you are allowed no will of your own; if you wish to give directions to your servant, 'Vite! Vite!' cries a whiskered sentry. In this play of 'Manlius' were many passages highly applicable to Buonaparte, and Talma, who is supposed to be (*avec raison*) a secret partisan, gave them their full effect, but the listening vassals struck no octaves to his vibration. A few nights before, we were at a play in which were allusions to the Bourbons and compliments to the D. de Berri &c. These (shame upon the trifling, vacillating, mutable crew!) were received with loud applause by the majority of the pit. . . . *A propos*, we have seen the Bourbons. The king is a round, fat man, so fat that in their pictures they dare not give him the proper *contour de ventre* lest the police should suspect them of wishing to ridicule; but his face is mild and benevolent, and I verily believe his face to be a just reflection of his heart. . . . Then comes the Duchesse d'Angoulême. There is no milk and water there. . . . She is called a Bigot and a Devotee: she has seen and felt enough, and more than enough, to make a stronger mind than hers either the one or the other. She is thin, genteel, grave, and dignified; she puts her fan to her under lip as Napoleon would put his finger to

C C

his forehead, or his hand into his bosom. . . . Then comes
the Duchesse de Berri, a young, pretty thing, a sort of royal
kitten; and then comes her husband, the Duc de Berri, a
short, vulgar-looking, anything but a kitten he is—but
arrête-toi. I am in the land of vigilance, and already my
pen trembles, for there are gendarmes in abundance in the
streets, and Messieurs Bruce and Co. in La Force, and I do
not wish to join their party. In France I dare not say Bo to
a goose! So *je vous salue, M. le Duc de Berri*. . . .

The constant song of our drunken soldiers on the
boulevards commenced with

> Louis Dixhuite, Louis Dixhuite,
> We have licked all your armies and sunk all your fleet.

Luckily the words are not intelligible to the gaping
Parisians, who generally, upon hearing the ' Louis Dixhuite,'
took for granted the song was an ode in honour of the
Bourbons, and grinned approbation. Paris cannot know
itself. Where are the French? Nowhere—all is English.
English carriages fill the streets, no other genteel equipages
are to be seen. At the play, the boxes are all English. At
the hotels, restaurants—in short, everywhere John Bull
stalks incorporate. . . . About the Tuileries, indeed, and here
and there a few *bien poudréd* little old men, *des bons Papas
du temps passé*, may be seen dry as mummies and as
shrivelled, with their ribbons and Croix St. Louis, tottering
about. They are good staunch Bourbons, ready, I dare say,
to take the field *en voiture*; for once, when taunted by the
imperial officers for being too old and decrepit to lead
troops, an honest emigrant marquis replied that he did not
see why he should not command a regiment and lead it
on *dans son Cabriolet*.

At the last of the Duke of Wellington's balls a curious
circumstance took place. Word was brought to him that
the house was in danger from fire. He went down, and in
a sort of subterranean room some cartridges were discovered
close to a lamp containing a great quantity of oil, and it was
evident they had been placed there with design. Strange asso-

ciations were whispered as to Guy Fawkes and Louis XVIII. being one and the same; but the powder was not sufficient to do any great mischief, and the general idea is that had it exploded, confusion would have ensued, the company would have been alarmed, the ladies would have screamed and fled to the street, where parties were in full readiness and expectation of diamonds &c. . . .

To Louisa Stanley.

Days in Paris are like lumps of barley sugar, sweet to the taste and melting rapidly away. . . . You extorted by a *petite ruse de guerre* two letters from me, and I comply partly because I presume you will be pleased, and partly because I did not half finish our adventures in my last to Rianette. We have now seen theatres, shows, gardens, museums, palaces, and prisons; aye, Louisa, we have been immured within the walls of La Force—aye, Louisa, and that from inclination, not necessity. We procured an order to see Bruce,[1] and after some shuttlecock sort of work, sending and being sent from office to office, and préfet to préfet, at length we received our order of admission. In this order our persons are described; the man put me down *sourcils gris.* 'Mais, Monsieur,' said I, 'they will never let me in with that account.' He looked at me again. 'Ah, ah, vos cheveux sont gris, mais pour les sourcils—non pas—vous avez raison,' and altering them 'noirs,' he sent me about my business. Bar and bolt were opened, and at length we found ourselves in the presence of these popular prisoners— popular, at least, amongst the female part of the world. I have reason to believe that a few of the Miss Stanleys had formed a romantic attachment for Michael Bruce, and there are few of our adventures which would, I think, have given you more pleasure than this visit; your heart would have been torn from its little resting-place and been imprisoned

[1] Michael Bruce, one of the Englishmen who helped in the escape of Lavalette from prison. He was known as 'Lavalette's Bruce.' He had previously tried to save Ney. (See Davenport's *Narratives*, 'Escape of Lavalette.' Bruce ended his life at Taplow Lodge.

We have hired a great green coach, with which, if exhibited in town, we might make our fortunes. We go round by Rouen, where we are assured we shall be pelted, perhaps massacred, as the Rouenites hate the English: as we are in search of adventures it would be wrong to omit any opportunity of being put in prison or losing our heads.

Farewell, dear little niece,

E. S.

CHAPTER XIV.

TOWN DOINGS AND TOWN TALK.

END OF 1816–1817.

A loaded shoe—The grandson's escapade—Welcome to Isle of Man—' Childe Harold'—A gilt cuckoo—Enterprising spirits—The drawing-room—Kemble and Liston—Opera and balls—Opening of Waterloo Bridge—Royal embarkation at Whitehall Stairs—Garden and river fête—Lady Davy's sensational entry—Cath. Fanshawe—Enigma.

M. J. S. to Louisa.

Penrhos: August 16, 1816.

. . . Our journey was tolerably prosperous . . . and it was surely being very prosperous to transport ten children, seven horses, three carriages, and a due proportion of servants to such a distance, without a single accident—not a spring or a bolt failing throughout the journey, or any other evil attending travellers. We slept the first night at Llangollen, and visited the ladies; as long as they or their cottage continue in existence, they will remain objects of interest and curiosity. They are grown great believers in ghosts and second sight. . . . The entrance to the cottage, a Gothic porch, the inner entrance, staircase, and kitchen are just fitted up with old carvings of wood, the contributions of various friends, or the plunder of churches and choirs. It has a very good effect.

Lord Sheffield to Sir John Stanley.

Sheffield Place: August 21, 1816.

My dear Sir John,— . . . I do not recollect what kind of stone you have at Alderley for building, but I respect you much for using any kind of stone rather than brick. . . . Your

Cheshire miscreants seem to be still more atrocious than ours. The loaded shoe thrown at your head is a choice specimen of the undisciplined habits of your lower ranks. I respect very much the vigour of your ordering him to be whipped immediately, and also in three other towns. I hope you added solitary confinement to his punishment, and a bread-and-water diet. We have made a great impression upon our rogues lately by such means. I have been so much entertained by an exploit of Edward John that I cannot refrain from communicating it. . . . The day on which Pevensey came home, he was going in a boat with some boys to breakfast at Surly Hall. Edward John was swimming in the middle of the river. He forthwith boarded the boat and obliged Lord Spencer Chichester to lend him his breeches and to proceed in his drawers to Surly Hall, and without any other clothing he accompanied them and breakfasted in his skin. I believe the distance is about three miles. When the boat returned to the place where he had left his clothes, he found they were gone, and he had half a mile to walk, with only a pair of breeches, without either shoes or stockings or anything else. His clothes had been found, and the most complete consternation ensued; it was universally supposed that he was drowned. Dr. Keate was so affected that he was unfit for business the remainder of the day; consternation prevailed among the other masters, and the dame fainted. There was so much joy on finding Edward was not drowned that he escaped flogging. . . . We have an agreeable party here at present, viz. Lady Louisa Stuart, the Hon. Anne Vernon, Lady Emily Pelham, and Lady Charlotte Lindsay. We expect Chief Justice Downes here on Monday. I shall be heartily glad to see him.

Ever truly yours, S.

M. J. S. to Serena.

Penrhos: November 19, 1816.

I cannot allow Miss Western to return to Bath without taking from hence some signs of existence to dear aunt.

We are all so fascinated by this wild country and rocky coast that we have been delaying our return from week to week, till our distant friends think that we have forgotten them.   Sir John has business, and so he would if he remained here all the year ; but I think inclination more than business has kept us.   The last week or ten days has furnished him with plenty of employment as a justice and in the cause of humanity.   Several wrecks have been thrown on the coast, and several Liverpool packets crowded with soldiers, their wives and children, and paupers returning to their own country, all Irish, have put into Holyhead.   Great distress at sea ; and here they were, thrown on the compassion of the inhabitants, who indeed have exerted themselves generously in the favour of these poor creatures.   Nothing could exceed the horrible beauty of our coast during the hurricane, which lasted for four days with such violence that no vessel whatever could leave the harbour.   In the early part of our stay here we had enjoyments of a different nature.   We have bathed a great deal, walked and rode, and drove in our Irish car almost all day long.   There is always something new going on in a seaport, and especially one of so much resort as this for passengers to and from Ireland. It is amazing to watch the packets out and home.   There is a sloop of war stationed here to hunt the smugglers, commanded by an agreeable man, Captain Patten . . . and the children had a cruise in the vessel when Uncle Edward was here for a visit of ten days.

Our excursion to the Isle of Man was delightful, and we were fortunate in everything relating to it.   Our voyage there and back being the most favourable we could have had, and the reception we met with so flattering to the vanity and family pride of the Stanleys, that you may believe Sir John, the boys and girls were gratified to a high degree. The name, as that of their regretted sovereigns, was well known to even the lowest peasant we met with in the island, and the sight of the crest on our servants' buttons was sufficient to excite them to offer every civility and attention in their power.   I was pleased also with the island and the

inhabitants, and only wish to have seen more of the principal
ones than we had time for. Sir John was in haste to return
lest the weather should change, or in another day all the island
would have done us homage—the homage at least of a visit and
invitations without end. The absence of all taxes, especially
of the window tax, adds so considerably to the comfort of all
ranks and the appearance of the houses, that it makes one
sigh more deeply than ever at the weight of taxation which
crushes this country. I saw hardly a poor-looking person
and certainly not one beggar.

Serena to M. J. S.

Bath: November 28, 1816.

My dearest Maria,—If I wrote out a quire of paper it
would not be too much to tell you the pleasure I had in
Miss Western's account of you all. I wish you could have
heard her mention your dear Sir John in his different
capacities, as magistrate, as a humane character, with power
and inclination to do such extensive good by your assistance.
Intermixing in both your characters there is indeed everything to make you loved and beloved. Then let me not
forget your dear girls, whose constant messages to me went
to my heart; she says they were anxious that not one of
them should be forgot as desiring love to aunt, and I believe
I talked an hour to her of your dear fine boys. Lady Ely
was here a few days, and Sir Humphry and Lady Davy.
I have had many amusements. Lady Ely dined with us
and Mrs. Charter Moore (*ci-devant* Peggy McLean). I have
had both the Bowdlers to dine with me, and I have showed
them Mrs. Piozzi as an odd lion. Last night I had Mme.
d'Arblay, her general and son, and we really were very
pleasant, as it was a small number, all conversing together
and liking each other. Cat. Fanshawe was brilliant and
read parts of Lord Byron, and Mme. d'Arblay was agreeable and delighted. I set Miss Fanshawe at the head of
my table and Lady Ely at the foot, and dear Cat. and I sit
anywhere and take no trouble of any sort. . . . I am more

than ever wishing my friends to have wings, as I cannot move to them, else how glad I should be to go to you, but indeed I can be nowhere but at home. . . . I will conclude with many blessings and wishes that you may all continue long to be happy in making others so.

Your ever affectionate

S. H.

M. J. S. to her daughter Louisa.

Penrhos: December 6, 1816.

I think you will not have left Win. before this reaches you, and that you will like to hear the horses are ordered for to-morrow. . . . Captain Plumer Davies has lent 'Childe Harold' to me, and talked of it as I shall probably not hear it talked of out of Alderley, and your papa and I sat over the fire in the dining-room and fancied ourselves young people, with a baby, or two perhaps, in the cradle upstairs, and read together more beautiful poetry than any other pen I am acquainted with has yet produced; and he was not cross when I interrupted him in reading his newspaper with cries of 'Never was anything so fine!' and very soon he laid down his newspaper and said, 'Read more.' But to comfort you, if you think I mean that this *tête-à-tête* and poetry was better than a well-filled round table of young ladies with their heads full of Mermen, I will tell you that upon the whole it seemed very dull since you went, and that if I had not been very busy I should have been very wishful to have you back again. . . . Love to all, and I am

All's very affectionate mother,

M. J. STANLEY.

Serena to M. J. S.

Bath: January 2, 1817.

. . . I hope you received a letter I wrote in answer to the noble basket of game and turkey. It fed my Fanshawes and came most seasonably. It will probably be our last Christmas Day together, and I shall never forget it. Catherine drew for me a sweet picture of gleaners while sitting in the

evening together, and Elizabeth gave me many very pretty
cuttings-out, and among them the little Stanley driving his
cabriole with the goats, which makes quite a pretty and
interesting picture. I only wish Catherine had drawn pictures for me of all your family. I hear you have a very nice
group done by Edridge. Those dear ,Fanshawes did one
wicked thing : they brought me one of the fine seal shawls,
so soft and beautiful, and came stealing into the room, all
three, and each took a corner and wrapped me up in it. . . .
The good rector of Alderley did bring me himself, and my dear
Maria's letter giving such a pleasant account of your happy
home. The first of blessings you will, I hope, never cease
to possess—natural, cheerful spirits, free from all gloom.
In that alone can consist any resemblance to your ever
homely aunt, but something of manner may have given the
flattering idea of resemblance; if such an old woman can
talk of *being lively*, everybody is sure I must like to be so
flattered, as, exclusive of being handsome or hideous, there is
something pleasant in having a family likeness where there
is affection. . . .

M. J. S. to Serena.

Alderley Park : January 5, 1817.

. . . We shall go to Winnington some time next week to
receive company, but literally that is the only circumstance
that induces us to quit Alderley, which is so much more
delightful in many ways. I have considerable pleasure in
the rapid progress that is tending towards making Winnington wholly uninhabitable. The plaything has lost its charm ;
it is no longer new, and so now, like a child with a gilt
cuckoo, I enjoy pulling it to pieces, as the only satisfaction
it can give me.

I delight in the account of your Christmas pleasures.
Long may you continue to enjoy the society of friends with
all the warmth and enthusiasm of youth, attended by the
calmness and right feeling of maturer age ! The Fanshawes
must have had great delight in spending this, but I must not
say the last, Christmas with you. I really see no reason why

my lord and you should not reach the end of a century in the full enjoyment of your faculties and your friends. We shall give up beautiful Winnington on March 25. . . . Mr. Baring has considerable property in America, where he has resided many years, and the vicinity to Liverpool is the inducement to settle here, that he may have ready communication with America. . . . It is not so much what we gain by rent received, as what we shall save in giving up the establishment, which will be many hundreds, and much comfort; and we shall now set about making Alderley comfortable and habitable, and I shall gain so many hours more in the years which were devoted to consideration about moving backwards and forwards, and the accounts of the establishment and farm, and many etceteras which will now be done away with. The one year's saving will almost furnish Alderley. How busy I shall be for the next two months! I wish all the books especially were translated to their new abode, and my dear geraniums that are in such excellent health, there is no house ready for them; but I must not begin to think of all my troubles. I must only meditate on the happiness of having one house, one garden, one farm, and one set of servants the less!

M. J. S. to Louisa.

April 1817.

. . . I want to get a decent person—a man, I mean—with some education, to take charge of the boys while we are in London. They are really got beyond the women, and the habit of getting the better is very hurtful. Their enterprising spirit is not to be supposed. I am afraid I shall make you shudder when I tell you they got upon the scaffolding of the laundry three nights ago, when raised above the windows considerably; run round and down again, on the opposite side, before they were missed. Luckily no accident happened, but such boys should have *employment* found for them. . . . I wish I could write shorthand, the time taken up in the usual way of writing deprives you of many a sentence. My cold mends, but

I have a disposition to cough when I am eloquent. We have two balls for to-night; and the opera and play to choose between to-morrow; the Duke of Gloucester's private box for 'King John' from Sir E. Antrobus. I liked 'Don Giovanni' better the second than the first time, and I never saw the opera-house so full as on Saturday. There were 800 half-guineas taken at the door, besides tickets. We dine to-day with the Majendies. Rianette and Lucy dined and went with the Egertons to the play on Thursday, in Sir E. Antrobus's box, to see Miss O'Neil and Kemble in 'The Stranger,' and Tom Thumb. They met Lord Wilton, Walter D., and Sir Edmund at dinner, and came home in high spirits with all their amusements, having first cried their eyes out, and then laughed a pain into their sides. To Lucy's great surprise, Watty laughed heartily at Tom Thumb and Liston. E. D. would have scorned to be amused by such buffoonery, but Mr. Watty was himself notwithstanding, and sported opinions of various and discordant bearings, as usual; for instance, admiring the entrance to our house, which Lucy answered as a joke, till she found he meant to support the assertion as a fact. God preserve me from living with people who would eternally oblige me to consider whether they mean what they say! and whether, if they do, I should set them down amongst the silly, or the mad, or the perverse, or the capricious—probably the last is most frequently the truth. . . . Only think of Sir J. L. taking the nurserymaid to the opera in his box with Lady L., where she sat in front, dressed like any lady. I wonder he was not afraid of accompanying Don Giovanni to the fiery regions below! We hear nothing about the drawing-room. I hope it will be next week, for we want the materials of our court dresses very much. Adieu.

M. J. S. to Sir J. T. S.

Sheffield Place: April 1817.

My lord's recovery is wonderful. I am happy to have seen him, and I am sure it has given him pleasure. . . .

I had a delightful walk yesterday to the rocks and all round the millpond. I should have been sorry to have had any companion unless you could have joined me. . . . The sun shone bright yesterday morning on Sylph Place, and on the rose trees on the margin of the water in a state of perfect wildness. The sweetbrier from which you gathered a spray to present Louisa in the spring of 1796 is still there; the ivy-leaved snapdragon still lingers at the foot of the sundial; and nothing is changed except that many of the fine old trees are gone, and those that remain are sufficient to remind one of those that are gone, and imagination fills the places with their forms. I shall be very glad to return to you all, though I am truly happy to have been, and to stay long enough to look about a little. I think I shall certainly be with you before five to-morrow.

Yours ever, M. J. S.

M. J. S. to Mrs. E. Stanley.

Privy Gardens: April 21, 1817.

. . . You will have heard that all danger is over for the present. I wish I could have sent you my thoughts from S. P. . . . His affection for me has always been uniform and strong, and I could have no doubt of his pleasure in seeing me. . . . At no London period was I ever more bothered, or more sincerely wished myself in the country again, and the sudden preparation for court oversets all one's faculties completely. . . . Edward Penrhyn has just been here, and only now discovers his hair must be powdered. Mr. Egerton is to present him and Sir John. Lady Chichester presents the girls and me on Wednesday. We hear dreadful accounts of the squeezing to be expected. Lucy likes the thought of going very much, Rianette confesses alarm; but I believe I am the most nervous of the three. The account of the manner in which people are driven forward before the queen is quite absurd, and Sir John sets up his back very much at the degradation on his side, and want of dignity on the other, and I expect he will either come down on all-fours before the Prince, or not bend at all, for he performed very ill last night at a rehearsal. But it is twelve, and no Coat from the Taylor's yet.

M. J. S. to Moomie.

Audley Square: May 7, 1817.

Dear Moomie,—I should not think of buying you for a chicken, and you are as much of a chicken as either of the two you sent last—tough-jointed, middle-aged pullets, and nothing better. Very glad you have only four of them.

Poor Sir John is suffering for his loyalty. The levée must have tired him, by standing a long time, though he did not feel it at the time, and dined out the same day. I was not at all tired by the drawing-room.

The home young ladies have set their hearts upon a family dinner party to-day of all who are now in London, including the Bishop. Louisa is beginning to recover from the effects of the railroad.

Yours truly,
M. J. STANLEY.

M. J. S. to Mrs. E. Stanley.

Privy Gardens, London.

A true John and Jenny Bull always find the love of England increased by contact with Foreigners in foreign countries, and so do I feel an increase of respect for country gentlemen (who read) after seeing a tableful of politicians and wits of the first magnitude, some of whom profess and acknowledge never to have read Southey's works, and others not to know what Lord Byron published last, though they believe they read it, and others making an excellent story of the three Lake Poets. . . .

The same sort of opinions, equally founded on truth and good judgment, but extremely brilliant, were given upon Southey's 'Life of Nelson;' but as twenty-four hours have intervened since I wrote the above, the thread of my ideas is broken and the flow of my criticism checked.

We dined at the Abercrombies on Saturday, and met Messrs. Lyttleton, Calcraft, Plunkett, Lord Fitzharris, Colonel Abercrombie, and Mr. and Mrs. Ramsden. Lyttelton is a great talker, and very clever, but he and James Abercrombie were the persons to offend me when politics were discussed, since party spirit showed as pre-eminent and as disagreeable as in any Tory. Plunkett spoke very little, however the dinner was altogether above par, and worth giving up my opera for, which I did. We met Sir H. and Lady Davy both at the Fanshawes', but conversation took too much a political turn there, and Sir George Beaumont and Cat. had not a word to say. . . . Morritt's Tory principles gave one no pleasure to hear, and Sir Humphry combated them but feebly. Lady Davy observed he was very slippery in his politics, for some of the Ministerial People had excellent Cooks and perverted his principles. She was bilious, and could not partake of the good things, so she kept her political principles pure.

M. J. S. to Louisa.

1817.

The evening of our Ball went off as well as I could possibly have wished. There was not a single disappointment, rub, or ruffle from beginning to end. There were a sufficient number, and not too many. The house and the girls looked uncommonly well; there were beaux in plenty. Dandies enough not to be shabby, and not enough to make the Ball detestable, as was the case at Mrs. Dawkins's, who seems to have placed her glory in having none but Almack's men, animals in stays, and having craws and puffed bosoms like a lady. I was so well pleased that, though I scarce ever sat down from the early morning of Friday, viz. four o'clock, I did not feel tired. Everybody looked pleased and amused; the dancing went on with spirit, the music was good, the floor was well chalked, the lights burned well, and the ladies all got partners. . . . Rianette and Lucy took it by turns not to dance, that they might attend to the company. . . .

M. J. S. to Mrs. E. Stanley.

Privy Gardens : June 1817.

If we have a fine day on the eighteenth, our River will be beautiful. The Prince and Duke of Wellington are to embark at Whitehall Stairs, land at Waterloo Bridge, walk over it, and return to Whitehall. We must have a Déjeuné and Party in the garden.

.   .   .   .   .   .

All and everything conspired in the air above, the earth below, and the waters which flowed under Waterloo Bridge, to make it the most glorious, beautiful, and gratifying spectacle that ever was exhibited. We had a party of about one hundred. I never saw a number of people so pleased and delighted. We had a Boat with an awning and four Oars to take the party on the water, and it took three trips with different company. They went under the bridge and rowed about before the Prince moved and any confusion began. It is impossible to conceive a more beautiful or exhilarating sight. Donald was in his glory on the bridge, having command of four guns. He and a Captain Swabey, of the Artillery, a very agreeable man with an unextracted ball in his knee, came afterwards to our stairs, for we used our own gate and had temporary steps hung outside. Sir H. Torrens brought each of the girls a medal struck in honour of the day, with the Prince's head on one side, and Waterloo and Wellington on the other. . . . We dined at Sir R. Glyn's and went to Vauxhall that night—a night made on purpose, for weather. We saw Madame Sacchi and the fireworks, and had our own party of beaux to take care of us. I never saw anything more beautiful and singular than the appearance of Sacchi at the top of the rope, very high in the air, when after a grand display of fireworks around her, the smoke disperses, and she is seen descending. We are now on the point of going to Richmond on such a summer's day as I had almost forgot could be. We have a concert and Almack's ball for to-night, but shall cut them both.

D D

M. J. S. to Mrs. Edward Stanley.

June 1817.

Oh uncle! take your pencil and place Lady Davy with a large French bonnet, and her hair in papillotes (because she was very late and lazy on Saturday night) on a plank, composing her petticoats, and darting, heels forward, into Swallow Street Chapel through a window, having climbed from the street to the top of the iron railing on which the board was laid, being received inside the chapel by Wilberforce, her hands seized and shaken by him, with the address, ' Madam, whoever you are, I honour your energy and spirit.' By the bye, I am spoiling my story. She went first and introduced the Saint by the same entrance, who found rather more difficulty in the operation, as there was a height of ten or twelve feet on the other side to climb down. I never had a greater dramatic treat than she gave us in the description of her exploit, and the criticism of his sermon. I wish I had her memory and talent for narrating. . . . All London has been mad about this man.[1] Lady Davy says his gesticulation is vehement, his sketch grandly conceived, but imperfectly filled up; he is often eloquent, and tho' he preached for an hour and a half, the time did not appear too long, but she was most entertaining in the account of her calling for Lady Elgin to assist her into the church from amidst the crowd who were pressing against the doors by hundreds, and her joy that Sir Humphry was not present, as he never entered into these spirited enterprises, was very apt to reason with her on the subject, and, besides, his conjugal affection would have been affected by the danger she ran in crossing the spikes, and it would have made no difference to her, only that a matrimonial squabble in the street would not have been edifying.

Rianette said that our party last night was like an expiring light, which sometimes blazes with increased lustre

[1] Dr. Chalmers.

a moment before entire extinction, and after it appeared quite gone. Our dinner was very agreeable, the conversation various and well kept up. C. Leycester was able to hear a good deal after the first beginning; which he said puzzled him a little, not knowing in which quarter to fix his attention—Congo, polarization of light, mechanics, the insurrection in Brazil, and a few more subjects, I believe, being started in different parts of the table, not exactly at the same moment, but sufficient to distract his attention at first. Edward Penrhyn was all ears, eyes, and attention. . . . At last, at half past eleven, nearly everyone had departed, Dosy Leigh took Charlotte and Lucy to Mrs. Blackburne's, when Rogers entered, and a few minutes after Douglas. It was so late I did not think anyone else would come, and was prepared to go, as Mrs. Hutchinson waited, making an apology to the gentlemen. We had hardly got downstairs, when a knock at the door announced Lady Guilford and Lady Charlotte Lindsay, and we remounted the stairs before they had seen us. We found Rogers, Douglas, and Hugh Rose had drawn round the fire and the young ladies, and were preparing to tell ghost stories. Lady C. L. had just time to ask if we had heard of Lady Davy and Wilberforce being pulled in at a window to hear Chalmers preach, when Lady Davy herself entered to give her own history, and then followed the scene I have described, Rogers and Lady Charlotte occasionally putting in a sparkling sentence which animated the discourse, or rather the harangue. Kitty, the girls, and Rose were in convulsions of laughter. I never saw her in such Glory. I was sorry Mr. Douglas had slipped away before she began. He had been talking to Louisa and told her that it was supposed Lord Byron meant Rogers as one of the men who are described in the Poem of Darkness, dying of fright at each other's ugliness when they met over an expiring fire which suddenly blazed up and showed their countenances. . . . I went at last to Mrs. Blackburne's. We had an excellent concert; fine performers and good music; but were insulted by the presence of Charlotte in a green silk Spencer, green

silk boots, and trowsers to the ankle much below the petticoat. . . .

A friend of Donald's, a Captain Greatly, is just come
from St. Helena, where he has been for some months,
indeed I believe he went out in the *Northumberland*. He
says Warden does not speak a word of French or Buonaparte a word of English.

M. J. S. to Mrs. E. Stanley.

Sheffield Place: June 24, 1817.

It is surprising to see the change in my lord's appearance since I was last here, and his mind is just as active
and clear as ever. He rides out and walks about the house
as usual, but cannot bear much clatter or a number of
people about him at once. . . .

You have, of course, seen Mr. Edgworth's death in the
papers. Dr. Holland told me he had seen a letter from him
written very lately to a friend in town, speaking of his approaching end as certain and near, with the same composure
and firmness as of a journey he was about to undertake.
The object of the letter was to inquire about the publication
of some new tales of his daughter's, anxious to hear how
they were liked if come out, and expressing in the most
affectionate terms the comfort he had received from her
society and attentions during the whole of her life. It was
what Dr. H. called a ' splendid ' letter.

. . . If you have got my letter you will know that we had
no Talma, but that we had Sir Humphry. The conversation
at dinner turned on the desire all Men have to seek Truth,
and you may imagine much that was entertaining might
be said in arguing the point. Ugo Foscolo[1] began the debate,
and maintained that every one wished to know the truth,
although they might wish to conceal it when known, even
from themselves.

---

[1] Italian politician and man of letters. Born at Zante 1778, died in England
1827. His remains were taken forty-four years later to Florence and buried
in the Church of Santa Croce amidst national mourning.

Lady Davy thought 'qu'il n'y avoit point de bonheur que dans les illusions.' Sir Humphry would not enter into the question at all, but grumbled out a sulky dissent occasionally on whatever was advanced. Another question arose from Lady Davy's declaring she liked to see remarkable people; her seeing Madame Piozzi at Bath was the source of this. Sir H. 'had no curiosity,' and he somehow got very near abuse of clever women, and somehow, to my great alarm (but I stopped in time), I found myself in speaking to him on the point of instancing Corinne as the kind of woman who could not be happy in the domestic circle. He led me to it so naturally that I can't think how I escaped saying it, and he made a marked distinction betwixt clever women, that is women of talent, and sensible women.

Serena to M. J. S.

1817.

I am most thankful to God for such a happy close of life, surrounded by blessings and comforts of every kind, and though losing memory, yet my spirits, my state of mind, my sleep &c., all most comfortable, and, as my gaieties are innocent, I hope my friends will not be scandalised by hearing that poor Mrs. H. died one morn after having had a very agreeable party only a few days before. I seriously do think, please God, this may be the case, as I do not think the cheerful life I lead prevents my recollecting that I am to die, and that last Twelfth Day was my entrance into my 80th year. What I most regret is that I, who love writing and talking, suffer from both if I indulge any time. I really can only add blessings to you all.

From your affectionate,

S. HOLROYD.

[In June 1817, Catharine Fanshawe sent her old friend Serena Holroyd the well known enigma on the letter H composed, as she told her, by herself.

Enigma.

'Twas in heaven pronounced, and 'twas muttered in hell,
And Echo caught faintly the sound as it fell ;
On the confines of Earth 'twas permitted to rest,
And the depths of the Ocean its presence confest.
'Twill be found in the Sphere when 'tis riven asunder,
Be seen in the lightning and heard in the thunder.
'Twas allotted to man with his earliest breath ;
Attends at his birth and assists him in death ;
Presides o'er his happiness, honour and health ;
Is the prop of his house, and the end of his wealth.
In the heaps of the miser 'tis hoarded with care,
But is sure to be lost on his prodigal heir.
It begins every hope, every wish it must bound ;
With the Husbandman toils, and with monarchs is crown'd.
Without it the Soldier, the Seaman, may roam ;
But woe to the wretch who expels it from home !
In the whispers of Conscience its voice will be found ;
Nor e'er in the whirlwind of passion be drowned.
'Twill not soften the heart, but tho' deaf be the ear,
It will make it acutely and instantly hear.
Yet in shade let it dwell, like a delicate flower,
Ah ! Breathe on it softly—it dies in an hour !

        Published in 'The Sun' as by Lord Byron.

On finding the Enigma had been attributed to Lord Byron Miss Fanshawe wrote to Mrs. Holroyd as follows :—

'Apropos of Venice and of my Lord Byron and of the letter H, I do give it under my hand and seal this 12th day of February 1819, that to the best of my belief the enigma of the letter H was composed, not by the Right Honble. George Lord Byron, but by me.

                 CATH. MARIA FANSHAWE.'

Serena gave the original MS. to her friend, Mr. E. Mangin, (author of 'Piozziana') who added the following memorandum :

'The above very pretty enigma, Mrs. Holroyd says, was written by her friend Miss Fanshawe, and I wrote to the editor of the Bath and Cheltenham paper stating that the enigma on the letter H was not by Lord Byron &c.'

By kind permission of his grandson, E. A. Mangin, of Hutton Conyers, Ripon, this extract from his grandfather's scrap book is given.]

Serena to M. J. S.

1817.

Yesterday, dearest Maria, I went at 12 o'clock to the Town Hall on a committee. Does it not sound consequential? I reckon myself so perfectly unfit for any thing now that requires a head, that if Mrs. H. Bowdler had not smuggled me, unknown to myself, into this business I should not even like the name of it. It is a school for girls on the plan of Lancaster and Bell, and indeed it is wonderful the rapid progress of mere babies in this new establishment. Some only taught three months can read and work. Mrs. Lockhart passed five days with me last week and spoke of you very prettily. She was at Clifton and I invited her, and had a few exotics for company—Madame D'Arblay, Mrs. Piozzi, Bishop Horne's daughter, 'the little Sally Horne,' as lovely as ever though the mother of seven children. All musical. When I look back on my life past and recollect the total retirement I lived in for many years when much younger, and now so very much the reverse, I think it was badly managed, as it ought then to have been what it now is, and in the last stage of my life live more soberly. Yet as I never go to the public rooms or to card parties I think my life may be trifling, but still not very censurable. I do like cheerful, innocent amusement, doing as I go along a little good and being kind to all the world. Tell me if you and Sir John will give me absolution for such a course.

M. J. S. to Mrs. E. Stanley.

Penrhos : 1817.

I have availed myself of a fine day to see the sublimest scenery I have ever contemplated, never having visited the Giant's Causeway or Staffa. . . . To the South Stack we went in the Trinity House boat with Captain Evans immediately after breakfast. . . .

Lose no time in telling me if you have been in the Parliament House Caves and approached the South Stack by water. I hope not. I suppose you mean to come this summer. I can take no denial of that. They say the birds are more numerous and a finer sight then. But when I saw the mothers with their infant train basking on the ledge, I, poor old me, I must confess, felt more interested in the sight of the pairs who were enjoying the happiest season of their lives preparing for their nests. You might see hundreds of the beautiful white gulls in couples perched side by side on the pinnacles of inaccessible crags or on small ridges of rock. . . .

My sympathy with the spring birds was a little enlivened by my occupation of yesterday evening, when I got hold of a packet of my old man's letters written in 1796, some at the very time he was courting, some from Sheff Place during the summer. Oh! the pity we should not always be young. Yet I think I have but little reason to regret at the end of twenty years that they are past and gone, except that it is more delightful to enjoy the perfect happiness which mutual affection can bestow, thinking of nothing beyond the present moment, than to sit on a ledge of rocks with a parcel of half-fledged little creatures anxious lest they have not strength of wing to venture by themselves from their hitherto safe abode.

Good-night.

LAST GLIMPSES.

SERENA.

Lord Sheffield to J. T. S.

December 1, 1819.

Within a short time we have had the most melancholy accounts of my poor sister at Bath, but I had a letter from her two days ago by which it appears she is in the most comfortable state of composure, full of good sense and seems to be taking leave of us. It is written as well as at any period of her life. . . . The Maria had better write a few lines to her, only mentioning that she hears she is very weak.

Ever truly yours,
SHEFFIELD.

M. J. S. to Serena.

Penrhos: December 5, 1819.

I was much grieved, dear little aunt, to find from your letters that you are at last obliged to acknowledge that you feel rather more than twenty years old. I hope quiet and care will again restore you to the full enjoyment of society on a larger scale than you can at present bear; but if not, what a blessing it is still to preserve all the faculties of your mind and the power of feeling affection as vivid as ever; and to experience that happy composure and peace of mind which has hitherto made your path through life as easy and happy as human nature can expect. Nobody but you, I think, ever went on making new friends in advanced life, who became as much attached as those of an older date; and to young people your society has always been as agreeable as that of a person of their own age. I regret very much that

my girls have not had an opportunity of seeing and knowing
and loving you since they have come to an age fully to feel
for you as they would have done if you had met. . . . I
expect to find our boys in Cheshire when we get there, as
their holidays begin on the 8th. We have every reason to
be satisfied with their conduct. We mean to take them from
Eton next year. . . . Sir John is quite well and you will have
seen his name in the papers in his capacities of foreman of
Grand Jury and Chairman of Quarter Sessions. I will not
frighten you by any politics. My lord calls me a ' Poissarde.'
Certainly he and we do not agree about the Manchester
business, though we see as well as he does how much bad
disposition there is in the country, and how necessary it is
to be firm and vigorous in opposing the progress of that evil
spirit. But we would have it legally and constitutionally
opposed, so as to leave no shadow of right to the side of the
Radicals.

Ever affectionately yours,

M. J. STANLEY.

Serena to M. J. S.

Bath : December 13, 1819.

. . . . I make a very wide distinction between party
politicians and men who wish for a Revolution and to over-
turn the country, its Constitution and laws. I was sure that
Sir John's good sense would make the distinction and come
forward at such a point of national danger, and I saw with
great satisfaction his spirited address to the country. . . .
I am convinced that a great deal of the lawless state of the
country may be owing to the country gentlemen of violent
and ambitious tempers ; that they let their dependants hear
how cheap they hold what, after all, supports us in the very
best established country that ever existed, for where to find
a faultless one in this world will be so difficult, that I believe
it is wise to be content with the best. Their want of wisdom
has nearly caused our ruin, nor are we yet safe, though I hope
the spirit of the nation is not quite lost. Nor are your Radical
friends in danger of being oppressed—I wish they were ; not

Sir F. Burdett and all his party, yet no one more strongly feels the necessity of supporting the popular party than Sir F. when not opposing all the laws of the country and its religion. . . . As I am steady, ye may say obstinate, in these opinions, if you write again I beg you may not answer them but leave me in my errors. I grow daily, dear Maria, weaker and weaker, but I have many blessings. I can read to myself at night for three hours with as much ease and pleasure as I did thirty years ago, and my sight is perfect. I never tire. How few at near eighty-one can do the same. I expect a flying visit of a few hours from Sir William Clinton to-morrow. My brother continues well and is really all affection to me. If I wished it, would come to me, but it would greatly distress me. I wish not now to see anyone I love too well. I will now conclude with my most affectionate blessing to you all, which will only end with the life of your affectionate

S. M. HOLROYD.

[Serena died at 3 Queen's Parade, Bath, January 15, 1820.]

Lady Sheffield to M. J. S.

Sheffield Place: January 19, 1820.

I hope you were prepared for the melancholy event of poor Mrs. Holroyd's death. She ardently prayed to be released, and her situation was such that no friend could wish otherwise. She was to the last perfectly composed, so much so that those in the room hardly knew when she expired without a sigh or a groan. Nothing could be finer than the state of her mind during the whole of her illness, and I cannot express it better than in the words of my friend Lady Cath. Bathurst, who happened to be at Bath and attended by Dr. Gibbs, who was poor Mrs. Holroyd's physician. She says : ' He seemed quite impressed with her exalted resignation and dignified composure, and these were his own expressions, and he is no talker. She wishes the termination soon to take place, and, by what Mr. Spry has told us to-day, it will soon be over : it is a comfort that she appears to suffer very little.   She will be much regretted here by a great many of the best society of the place.'

She left tokens of remembrance to all her friends, and legacies to her servants, and she directs that she may be buried in her Parish Church, Walcot, Bath, and have an Epitaph to her memory at Fletching.

[Madame Piozzi addressed the following letter to Edward Mangin :—]

Mrs. Holroyd, the friend of Gibbon and the much loved sister of Lord Sheffield, died at an advanced age, and was one of the most amiable of her sex.   She possessed, with a temperament of great sensibility, the utmost suavity of disposition, the soundest possible understanding, and, as may be supposed from her rank in life, highly polished manners. In her final illness she was attended by Sir George Gibbes, who told me that her sweetness of disposition was unimpaired to the last, and her religious resignation such that, while he could scarcely refrain from tears, she smiled with hope and said, 'Dear Sir, I almost dread your professional efforts in my favour, for I *would* not recover, and long to flit away.'

[Among the memoranda preserved by Mr. Mangin is the following :—]

Proposed by John Duncan, Esquire, as an epitaph on Mrs. Sarah Martha Holroyd (Serena), age eighty-one :

> ' Here pious Holroyd lies, whose modest mind
> By genius fired, by liberal arts refined,
> O'er fashion's heights long urged its heavenward way
> And bade the gay be good, the good be gay.'

LAST GLIMPSES.

LORD SHEFFIELD.

Lord Sheffield to J. T. S.

My dear Sir John,—There is so much difficulty in
obtaining apartments at Christchurch that, immediately
on receiving your letter this day, I wrote a most amiable
letter to the Dean, requesting that your sons might have
apartments there. I think you judge well not to send
them sooner than two years hence, when they will be nineteen years old, but I should wish them to be there some
time before George departs. He returned again to Oxford
last Friday, having been two days in town displaying his
purple and gold at Carlton House, attending the University address, when the young noblemen were separately
presented and kissed hands. We expect George on the
13th. I should like much to see your boys here at the same
time; but at this season of the year they would think of
nothing but shooting, in a country where there is so much
game, and mayhap might shoot one another. When George
goes out here I do not allow the gamekeeper even to carry a
gun . . . in summer your boys would amuse themselves
much better.

I am glad to find you have met with a tutor to your
mind. It is a strange circumstance that oratory is no part
of the education of young men in this country, especially of
those who may become of the Legislature. Whether of
the Legislature or not, it is a talent which should be cultivated. A certain facility of speaking is highly satisfactory
to the individual, and is highly advantageous at a county or
any meeting, assizes or quarter sessions. It is observable

that unless the talent is cultivated when young, it is not, in a general way, ever acquired. Pitt, the Grenvilles &c., began at nine years old, and they always had a great facility. This talent is neglected both at Eton and Oxford. Your Lady might be of great service to your boys in that respect. When she was a small brat she recited all the best speeches in Shakespeare extremely well. Gibbon [1] used to lament that she was not a boy, saying she would maintain a contest well with Charles Fox. I have often felt, and deeply lamented, that no attempt had ever been made in any degree to assist me in that matter, and, alas! I was nearly forty years old before it occurred to me to make the least attempt at speaking. I am disturbed by the latter part of the enclosed letter of Lord Sidmouth. Our conjoint struggle should have some weight. Can you suggest anything more to be done? It is a bad thing to lie down and die.

Lord Sheffield to M. J. S.

Portland Place: April 22, 1820.

A nice little fellow, much grown [W. O. Stanley], arrived at half past eight last night. It is to be regretted there is no better destination for him than the Guards, but that seems to be the only, ergo the best—but there is no hurry. Revolving these subjects in my mind it had already occurred to me that the diplomatic line is by far the best for Edward, in which his talents will not be thrown away, in which he may pass his time most agreeably, and fit himself

---

[1] Gibbon took a warm interest in the education of M. J. H., and in the year 1783 wrote to Lady Sheffield: 'I have not forgotten our schemes to finish in this school of freedom and equality the education of the future Baroness of Roscommon. I am convinced that she has attained the age in which it would be the most beneficial. Your daughter deserves a special and superior guide. We have cast our eyes on a lady who by etc., etc., appears not unworthy. She lives next door to us (Deyverdun and myself), and our eyes and ears (two pair) would be continually open. . . . If you listen seriously to this idea, I will take every proper step. If you cannot resolve, accept this badinage as a proof of love and solicitude.'

In September 1783 Lord Sheffield had been created Baron Sheffield of Roscommon, with remainder to his daughters.

for the first offices of the State. Even supposing the Man's apotheosis, it would be desirable to have Edward's abilities in train for high situations. Therefore from this time forward let the object be diplomacy.

[With reference to a remark from M. J. S. that she could not perceive that chaperons were still necessary for her sons, Lord S. continues :—]

. . . Notwithstanding your sarcasm, I shall always make use of a dry nurse whenever I can. Therefore I have sent John to take places for William and Ash, and to regale himself in the gallery and hold himself in readiness to bring them home at night. Do you approve of the provident spirits of the Cato St. conspirators in furnishing themselves with a sack to bring away the heads of his Majesty's ministers? If you mean to speculate for the advantage of your sons, it may be better not to display before them on every occasion the most virulent invectives against the Government, and admiration of Buonaparte. . . . I have somehow got it into my head that Maria Josepha and Louisa Dorothea are the most wrong-headed personages of my acquaintance, and so

Ever yours, S.

Lord Sheffield to M. J. S.

1820.

I was summoned immediately on the King's death to attend the Privy Council, but I do not propose to budge till the last week in March. . . . As for your hateful Whiggism, worse than Poissardes—I cannot bear the abuse of that term, so perverted from its origin and so different from what it was when I considered myself a Whig, which the three last generations at least of the family had strenuously been. . . . But Whiggism is now rendered so contemptible by the temper that has been exhibited, that it is not likely to recover any degree of estimation, for which I am sorry. Johnson used to say that the Devil was the first Whig, and Pitt said Whiggism was the pre-existing state of

Jacobinism. In short, resistance to authority is captivating
and rapidly infectious, and the principles of the Radicals are
more to be abhorred than any of which we have tradition.
We shall now be told that the several bills in progress are
unnecessary, but in my opinion they are hardly strong
enough, and they should all be permanent. Ministers are
far too apt to allow the spirit of certain measures to be
frittered away; but I suppose on this occasion they were
anxious to have the support of quibblers, and as large a
majority as possible. I have no objection to a certain
amount of reform in the representation, except that when
reformers begin they never know when to stop. The
landed interest has not sufficient sway in the House of
Commons. We have run wild after commerce and manu-
factures. We have diverted the capital of the country from
much better pursuits into various channels of infinitely less
importance, and we now severely feel the consequences of
it. Nothing can be worse than inflicting representatives
on great manufacturing places, such as Manchester and
Birmingham. They are liable to disturbance sufficient
without the irritation and disturbance of elections, and I
know this by experience. Coventry, then supposed to contain 25,000 inhabitants, was perfectly idle and tumultuous
during eighteen days of one of my elections, and a month
and two days on another. In consequence of which I
brought out the bill which limited the duration of elections.

A foolish cry against the Corn Laws has been mixed
with the late extravagant claims, and also with a cry in
favour of a property tax. If we are to have an insurrection,
I should like it best in opposition to an inquisitorial property
tax. However, if we could have a property tax without
the odious inquisition and with a proper discrimination, I
should applaud it; but certainly land should not be included,
which already pays so enormously to land tax, poor tax,
tythes, county rates, highway assessments, and, during
the war, on account of the army of reserve, militia families,
bounties on volunteering with the Line &c; no share of
which is paid by personal property, and the very extra-

ordinary measure should never be forgotten of offering to
sale the old land tax, the whole of which should still be
considered as a burden upon the land, whether redeemed or
not.

At the same time it should be observed that the owners
and occupiers of land pay all other taxes in common with
the rest of the community.

Those best acquainted with the affairs of the farmers in
this part of the world, say they are on the brink of bank-
ruptcy, and that their situation is deplorable. . . . I enclose
'God save the King' in Greek, translated by a Greek whom
I met at Waldershare. Can your boys construe it? . . .
We had a letter from Lord Guilford dated Turin. . . . Since
the death of poor Fred Douglas he has repeatedly expressed
his regret that George was not of age, that he might have
brought him into Parliament for Banbury. He will be in
another House time enough, notwithstanding my apparent
health.

Ever the very dear Ria's
SHEFFIELD.

Lord Sheffield to M. J. S.

Portland Place: 1821.

Your boys may be stowed in this house . . . and I have
been told that the peers have esquires to attend upon them,
and that might be a good way of attending the ceremonial.
I have not the slightest notion of attending the coronation. Not only because the robes &c. would cost 350
guineas; but also on account of the fatigue of being up the
greater part of the night. However, the summons to
the peers is very peremptory. They must have a certificate
from a medical attendant, and then they must have the
King's licence to be absent. . . . I am afraid my lady and
her boy and girl differ in opinion from me in regard to the
necessity of seeing the coronation. . . . I shall desire an
audience of the D. of York, and request an ensigncy in the
Guards for my grandson, William O. Stanley, which I learn
will put his chance upon a much better footing.

E E

General Clinton to Sir J. T. S.

1821.

You cannot imagine how well my Lord got through his dinner on Saturday. . . . After dinner Lord Sheffield got William Mellish close to him, and from half after eight till near eleven he kept up a constant conversation on finance, politics, and agricultural subjects. He put me in mind of old times, and that night he seemed almost the same man he was twenty years ago.

Lord Sheffield to Sir J. T. S.

Portland Place: May 23, 1821.

I am glad to hear you are forthwith to appear among us within a week. . . . We shall have full opportunity of discussing Scarlett's Bill; it differs little from the plan I suggested two years ago. I am not disposed to object to any limitations or restrictions of expense, but I have told him the attempt to fix a maximum according to the assessment of last year, against which some specious arguments may be urged, will embarrass the Bill, and perhaps render it very unpopular. I am glad none of you regret the migration from Winnington. I always thought the Old Nest the best.

Yours truly,

SHEFFIELD.

[*Memo.*—Received May 25. He died May 30 aged 84 and more.—J. T. S.]

Miss Ann Firth to M. J. S.

1821.

My dear Lady,—You would hear by the letter you received yesterday of the death of Lord Sheffield. The end was very easy. He did not complain of any pain. He was quite sensible to the last, and knew everyone, but avoided taking any notice of them particularly, not saying a word like taking leave of the family. I have seen Lady Sheffield, both yesterday and to-day. She was watching by his bed to the last, of which he was sensible, saying when once she was moving as if to get up, 'Don't leave me, darling.' Lady Louisa Clinton went there in the evening. He spoke to her as he did to us all. He had settled all his worldly affairs, and had nothing of that sort on his mind. On Tuesday morning I heard he was very ill, and came here immediately. You would only hear this day of the great change that had taken place, therefore, if you had thought of coming to town, it would have still been next to impossible he should be alive. I hope there will be good accounts of you to-morrow.

I am your ladyship's much obliged and affectionate,

A. FIRTH.

[Lou Clinton, Lady Louisa's daughter, writing to her aunt, M. J. S., at the same time, says :—]

In the morning he asked if mamma had written to you ; but neither then nor any other time did he say anything about wishing anybody to be there except the Bishop of Lincoln.[1] He knew him directly, and spoke to him for some time. Mrs. Firth was there, and though at first, when told, he said he could not see her then, some time afterwards he said he 'must see the dear Huff,' and again mentioned her.

[1] The Hon. George Pelham.

LAST GLIMPSES.

ACCESSION OF GEORGE IV. AND HIS ARRIVAL IN HOLYHEAD HARBOUR;
WITH REMINISCENCES OF THE COURT OF BRUNSWICK BY J. T. S.

W. O. Stanley to Rianette.

Eton College: Thursday, 1820.

Have you heard how gracious the present King George
IV. was? He wrote to Keate to desire we might be allowed
to see the late King buried, and to see him lying in state
after the other people were excluded, so that we might get
in without an immense crowd, but however, I got in in the
morning through it all; it was a very fine sight indeed. The
room was hung in black all over, and lighted with candles.
We went to the funeral last night, and we had to wait in the
chapel from six till half past eleven, and I was most
preciously squeezed and tired. The procession was very
grand and very full, and the middle part of the chapel up
which they went was lined with soldiers, every other holding
a torch. Directly the body came into church the choir
struck up, which was very fine; the whole of the music,
particularly the anthem, was magnificent. I found a good
many people I knew there. Edward Penrhyn was there
with Neave, and I dined with them, but was obliged to go
back the same night about twelve to be in time for chapel.

Your affectionate brother,

W. O. S.

Louisa Stanley's Diary.

Penrhos: 1821.

August 3.—His Majesty is expected to-morrow. The
town is full.

August 4.—No King yet. I hope he will not come in while we are in church.

August 5.—The 'Courier' has a bad account of the Queen. She is very ill. Mr. Owen Williams sailed in his *Gazelle* to meet the King and carry the first account. . . . A triumphal arch is erected on the pier, and does not look amiss.

August 6.—Just as we were dressed for dinner, a sudden cry of 'A flag on the signal station!' We sat down to dine with orders to the children over head to make a clatter when they saw the red flag go up. The second course was not removed when a thundering row above announced the red flag. Fancying the fleet nearer than it was, we set off with all speed to the pier, and lingered in the light-house until dark. The fleet was then nine miles off, and we were forced to return home. The ships anchored about half past twelve in the bay, and the town illuminated.

August 7.—Edward woke Bella and me with the disappointing intelligence that the King did not mean to stay many hours. The ships looked beautiful in the bay, we went to the pier in boats, and into the light-house, which commanded a view of all around.

About twelve his Majesty shewed himself to the surrounding boats. We were close to the royal yacht. He looked in good spirits. An order was sent to have the royal barge prepared, and the captains in full dress, as the King would land immediately. The scene was magnificent. The royal barge approached the shore amid a general discharge of artillery. Every ship manned her yards, and was decorated with innumerable flags. The King came up the steps with a firm and active step, and was received by papa at the head of the other commissioners of the pier. Papa knelt and kissed the hand held out by his Majesty, who made a speech in a low voice and agitated manner; the substance of it was his satisfaction at visiting a country, the name of which he had so long borne. Papa requested leave to read the address, to which the King replied by a bow. He afterwards walked to the carriage of the Marquis of Anglesey, which was waiting, amid the acclamations of the crowd He proceeded to Plâs Newydd to stay that night. A ball took place in the evening, to which we all went.

August 8.—At four his Majesty appeared, proceeded to his barge and returned on board his yacht. The wind contrary, and consequently Holyhead harbour had the honour of containing the royal yacht another night.

August 9.—The weather still unfavourable. The fi news was that an express had arrived and been conveyed to the King with all speed, and that he had been in close conference with Lord Sidmouth, Lord Londonderry, Mr. Vansittart &c.

It was not long before we heard the contents. The death of the Queen! Every one was impatient to learn what the King would do. That he would sail next day and enter Dublin as privately as possible was all we learnt, and we returned home dissatisfied on the whole, having spent all day in the lighthouse, not seeing much and the day cold.

August 10.—The vessels in their old stations.

August 13.—The King, wishing to enter Dublin incog., went at once with his suite in the steam boat and was safe in Phœnix Park before the Irish had any idea he was not coming royally with the rest of the ships. When they left Holyhead the Royal Standard was flying, which annoyed us very much, as his Majesty was not on board; but they say it was taken down half way over.

[Extract from memoranda by Sir J. Stanley on the occasion of George IV.'s visit to Holyhead, which revived the impressions of his boyhood at the Court of Brunswick :—]

And where was I, who had seen the young Caroline in her fourteenth year, when her coffin lay in its state? At the very moment close to her husband's yacht, with its flag of England half-mast high. . . . I first furnished him with a newspaper which gave the account of the Queen's illness, when his yacht was entering the Bay of Holyhead. There are sometimes strange connections of moments in our life. . . . The King's visit to Holyhead and the Court of Brunswick in 1782. How different the two pictures and what a chasm between the two was in me, between the flags half-mast high and the pale blue gown. I did do something as a tribute paid to the memory of the poor Caroline. Bonfires were prepared for lighting on every height round Holyhead, in honour of *her* husband's arrival, the night of the day the news was received of her death. I stopped the lighting of them, telling those who were in attendance on his Majesty that I was sure he would not approve such an appearance of rejoicing so immediately after he had heard of the event. The answer was 'Certainly not,' and all my hills and all my neighbours' hills were dark, and the town, which had been a blaze of illumination the night before, was dark !

The yacht was moored close to the pier, and it was near noon. The post had come early in the morning, though it was known to all that the Queen was dead. There was no one but myself on the pier, and I seated myself on the steps near the lighthouse. Lord Anglesey, and a gentleman he was talking to, were the only persons on her quarter deck at first, but they were soon joined by two or three others, and a sailor, bringing with him a bag, out of which he pulled several signal flags. I then saw them one by one tied to a rope, and raised up to the mizzen point or topgallant mast point. All this seemed done in a dead silence, not a word said on board reaching my ear, and the sea was too smooth to cause even a ripple. A minute or two passed, and then all at once the flag of the yacht, of the two frigates, and all the vessels in the bay, and in a few minutes also of all the vessels in the harbour and those which were flying in different places on the shore, were lowered half-mast high. No minute guns were fired, no crowd gathered on the pier, not a soul more joined Lord Anglesey's party on the quarterdeck. The Queen of England was dead, was the story told by the mute lowering of flags and pennants in more than a hundred places. . . . What were the real feelings of the King who at the time was on his sofa in his cabin will never

be known. . . . He was not happy at Holyhead, nor during
the remainder of his tour.   He came forth to see his subjects
—he shunned them; he was pleased with nothing he saw
nor with anything that was done to please him. . . . Returning from Ireland a storm drove him into Milford Haven.
He refused to see anything there, and flew away without
stopping to the centre of Oxfordshire, where at Chapel
House he stayed to rest himself.   While those few days
were passing, the Queen's remains were on their way from
her husband's dominions to her first, and which was to be
her last, quiet home.   One eye was over both the passing
and the past.

M. J. S. to Lady Louisa Clinton.

. . . I have indulged myself in idleness supreme, and
told the story to nobody, while every pen in the house was
worn to the stumps, and every other brain racked to invent
a little variety in the accounts they had to serve up for the
amusement of divers friends.   But now I think it seems an
age since we had any direct communication, and I must talk
to you a little.   How very glad I am that your Lou should
have had such a treat—which I have waited half a century
to see, and which, when seen, has so far outreached my
expectations, and which could hardly have been seen anywhere to greater advantage.   I mean the royal salute from
the squadron in the bay, and the manning of the yards.   It
was also my first visit to a frigate, as well as the rest of the
party, and Lou may wander about the world far and wide
without a better opportunity of seeing two as fine vessels as
the *Liffy* and *Active*—and such delightful captains also—
Sir James Gordon, with his wooden leg, the exact model
of an open hearted, good humoured, jolly English tar; Captain Duncan, an admirer of Napoleon's genius, daring to say
so, and winning my heart by playing Napoleon's March as
he passed Bertrand coming from St. Helena.   Captain Adam
and his ' Royal Sovereign ' were very delightful; Sir Michael
Seymour and his one arm, a dear old sailor, and we longed

much to have seen a great deal more of all. Sir John and
I were in imminent danger of becoming Courtiers and Tories
for full half an hour. What an ass a king is when he for-
feits general popularity—it is so easy to gain it. The King's
address, his bow, the appearance of feeling which he knows
how to put on, and did put on, when he landed and spoke to
Sir John, made fools of us both, and if the old fellow had
continued to behave tolerably, . . . if he had asked any
questions with the show of interest in the pier and harbour
during the five days he remained, if &c. &c., I don't know
what would have become of our Whiggism.

But I did not mean to talk of royalty, but of dear Lou.

. . . Think, and answer upon full consideration, if it is not
possible for you to come to Alderley with your girls by the
middle of September and then stay with us during the
month of October—having my own room for your retreat
whenever there was too much noise or bustle below . . .
Indeed, if you made it your constant abode and received
company only when you liked, with the donkey-cart, the
garden chair, and pony, the bath-chair, and a number of
damsels ever ready to conduct you in it about the grounds
and to everything about and near that would most please you,
why should you hesitate? You cannot still feel apprehensions of not living a week or two longer, and it would give
us so much pleasure if you would try to live a month or two
with us.

LAST GLIMPSES.

COMING OF AGE REJOICINGS IN WALES, *November* 13, 1823.[1]

Rev. Ed. Stanley to E. J. S. and W. O. S.

Alderley Rectory: November 11, 1823.

My dear Edward and William,—Lucy will I hope have received in charge a couple of telescopes, which I beg you to accept as hints that an uncle has not forgotten a day so interesting to his nephews. I wish indeed they could enable you to look through time as well as space, that you might form some idea of your minds and bodies when thrice the present period of your lives has elapsed. If, however, they afford you as clear an insight into as many of the queer sciences of this world as mine has done for me during the twenty years I have had it in possession, I flatter myself that they will not prove quite unacceptable.

From your affectionate Uncle,

EDWARD STANLEY.

Extract from their sister Maud's Diary.

Penrhos: November 1823.

November 12.—As busy as can be making ever-green ornaments for the Tenants' Hall. . . One feels as if something great were going to happen, and it *is* an unusual thing to have twins come of age!

13*th.*—The great day has come, to which we have been looking forward as the horizon of every object in view. I can scarce believe it, but so it is. . . . . Every birthday has been always a time of joy, consequently this greatest of all birthdays must be peculiarly joyful.

[1] 'We mean to treat the Welsh with the birthday, as Edward could not have come to Cheshire. So we thought it as well to put off the joint celebration to the Christening anniversary.'—M. J. S.

The sun never shone brighter, the battery was covered with flags, as also the signal station and the vessels in harbour, besides numerous other flags on the pier, and tower; and a number of cottages put little flags on their chimneys, so that the country looked very gay. At twelve the firing commenced: eight guns from the Penrhyn field gave the signal; then the battery fired twenty-one guns, then Mr. Brown's guns opposite the pier fired twenty-one, then Captain Evans's; then the signal station on the mountain, and again from the battery. A fine noise!

Spencer sent all his coaches up in procession, dressed out with flags—three coaches with four horses each. They drove in front of the house, had some ale, and drove off hurrahing and firing their muskets. At half past three we went to see the tenants at dinner—about 150—those from a distance had come by the steam-boat. After dinner there were toasts and speeches. Papa made one or two and William a very nice one, clear and without hesitation. When this was finished it was dark and bonfires were lighted. The country looked beautiful; about ninety bonfires were seen all round; our own large one was then lighted and rockets sent up. We then went in a carriage to Holyhead to see the illuminations. Every cottage, even the poorest, had candles in the windows. Not a single house was unilluminated, and done so prettily, little transparencies with devices to the heir of Penrhos. . . . It gave me an inward delight and pleasure; everybody did their best from their hearts. There was a dinner at Spencer's for the Holyhead inhabitants. There were two bullocks cut up and given to the poor; six barrels of ale were put in the town for the people.

14*th*.—A dinner for gentlemen and tradespeople; they dined in the Tenants' Hall, about eighty in number. We were in the gallery and heard the speeches. There were two long tables quite full. The gentlemen were quite sober, and went away between nine and ten.

15*th*.—A dinner for Holyhead tenants. It really is an exceeding pleasure to have had all go off so well. Not a single blight to it. . . . It is over; but we shall have it again at Alderley!

LAST GLIMPSES.

Mrs. E. Stanley to M. J. S.

(Quoting a letter from Miss Tunno, a brilliant member of their society.)

You and Sir John seem to have superseded all other people and ideas in her head. What she says of you puts me so in mind of some of my own Privy Garden feelings that I must transcribe it for you if you will not betray me, or she will not speak of you with freedom to me again.

'What is uppermost in the mind will come out first and therefore Sir John and Lady S.—"Well, what of them?" say you! Nothing but what you know, I dare say—but until yesterday morning *I* never saw them together alone, never saw Lady S. talk to Sir John—saw him listen and heard him reply. The vivid flash of lightning and the long majestic peal that follows are not more different in their effects to the senses, than the rapid and deliberate manner in which the ideas and utterance of each so strikingly distinguish them and astonish an observer. How they can have travelled with such apparent harmony and paces so unequal is somewhat astonishing, but the counter-balancing powers of velocity and gravity regulate with perfection the heavenly bodies, and why should not the same laws succeed with us mortals? I was not a little amused, or rather interested, to hear Lady Stanley's attack upon Sir John for his slowness and *un*Londonlike feeling, and to see the humility with which he acknowledged it all, and confessed his inability to move either his ideas or himself with the quickness of Londoners or of her ladyship; and yet methinks not one particle of deference was wanting on the part of the Lady towards her Lord, nor on his part any deficiency of a proper consciousness of superiority. Whether in Kensington Gardens or at Richmond, I yet hope to benefit by some of Sir John's discussions, and though I *love* Lady S. and like to fly with her when I can, I shall enjoy the deep and well considered thoughts of the former—ponder as he may.'

APPENDIX.

P. 10.

Thomas Deane, of the Park House Estate in Alderley, born 1610, belonged to the family of Deane, bearing the arms of Archbishop Dene, who settled in Cheshire in the reign of Elizabeth.

His heir was his niece Sarah Deane, who married William Stanley of Astle, upon whom he settled all his property in Alderley, including the Park House.

On his tomb is a Latin inscription setting forth that Thomas Deane de Park, gentleman, died in 1694, that he was a 'lover of his God, his Church, his Country, and his King, and of all good deeds; the giver of the endowment of the school in Alderley Churchyard, and also a bright example of uprightness and usefulness in life, of courteousness and frankness in his manners, and of the greatest charity to the poor and generosity to his relations.' ('The Book of Dene, Deane, Adeane.')

William Stanley of Astle, afterwards De Park, left Astle to occupy the Park House on the death of Thomas Deane de Park, 1695.

J. T. S.

P. 110.

[Many years after, Sir John Stanley received the following letter:]

To His Excellency Lord Stanley who once visited Iceland, per the Danish Consul Mr. W. C. Good.

Copenhagen.

My Lord,—According to a letter sent me from the Danish Governor Thorsteinson in Iceland, I take the obedient liberty to incommodate your Lordship with a few lines. The said Governor has begged me to write your Lordship and if it is possible to procure him a copy of your Lordship's excellent 3 paintings of the Geyser in Iceland to which your Lordship have the plate. He would fain possess them, but he can't otherwise get them but by incommodating your Lordship. The clearing of your Lordship's expenses for this incommodation will be done by the Danish Consul in Hull, Mr. W. C. Good, who will then deliver the paintings to Capt. Neilson of the Danish Skonnert 'Patrioben,' now lying for some days in Hull.

I hope that your Lordship will excuse my confidence and I remain your most obedient and devoted Servant,

NICHOLAS LANGE.

Merchant from Beikavig in Iceland and now in Copenhagen.

P. 112.

In 1765 Mr. Holroyd, afterwards Lord Sheffield, travelled abroad with Major Richard Ridley, brother of Sir Matthew Ridley, 2nd Bart., and Theophilus Bolton, who died of consumption at Genoa.

Major Ridley served in Germany during the Seven Years War. He and Lord Sheffield were painted together in a picture which is now at Sheffield Place.

P. 142.

Extract from ' Morning Chronicle,' Sept. 25, 1797.

MRS. NESBITT.—This celebrated woman has become the topic of universal conversation from the mention which Citizen Noel makes of her Transactions in Germany, and she is likely to suffer a great deal of impertinent slander on account of the allusion to her name. It certainly is no discredit to the sex that an accomplished woman is capable of playing a part so conspicuous and interesting to the state of nations as that which Mrs. Nesbitt has lately performed. . . . An intelligent woman in the decline of years, possessing the charms of conversation, unrestrained by prudery and endowed with elegant talents, improved by know-ledge of the world, drew around her a select circle of friends, and made her retirement at Norwood desirable to the Politician and the Scholar from its intellectual and unembarrassed Politics. We abhor the idea of pursuing political hostilities into private life : we sincerely believe that Mr. Rose cultivated the acquain-tance of Mrs. Nesbitt from the attraction of her mind, and he introduced his young family to her house that they might form their manners under so perfect a model. Such has been the situation of Mrs. Nesbitt for the last twenty years. With an independent fortune of between 2,000*l.* and 3,000*l.* a year, debarred in a greater degree from the female world by the early events of her history, surrounded by men of the first distinction, it was no wonder that a woman so endowed and so successful should be induced to turn her talents to political intrigue. Her marriage *à la main gauche* with a German Prince introduced her to the best society at the Court of Germany, and in all the diplomatic circles she was considered as a woman of infinite address and of profound discernment. . . . The connections which she formed in the Empire and in Switzerland, her knowledge of the languages, the symmetry of her person, which made it easy for her to assume the male habit, and the confidence reposed in her by Ministers, pointed her out as a proper agent, and on the 5th August she left England, and has resided ever since in various parts of the Continent. It is not easy to develope the course she has pursued, but until it shall be declared infamous for Courts to employ secret agents, it surely cannot be imputed to her as a crime that her accomplishments entitled her to the appointment. . . . Mrs. Nesbitt has had to combat through life with the prejudice which her first connection excited, and the woman whom the dreadful pen of Junius consigned to an immortality of disgrace could only rise superior to the memorial by extraordinary exertions. Yet this she has effected. . . . Notwithstanding the recorded anecdote of her marriage with Mr. Nesbitt and the miscellany of her life, she has acquired an elevation in life which she has preserved with Dignity because she has acted in good fortune with moderation. She has used her influence with the great in favour of the unfortunate, and many deserving men owe their present situations in public life to the patronage of this lady. We do not know that she was employed abroad. As a woman of easy fortune she could choose her place of residence, and was too independent to assign motives for her conduct. This, however, is obvious that, known as she is to all the diplomatic circle of Europe, the accusation of M. Noel will be implicitly believed, and the British Court will stand convicted of the charge of undermining a Government with which they professed openly to treat upon candid terms. . . . Mrs. Nesbitt's well known Talents, her connection here, her residence at the Hague, will be used as arguments of her agency, and though this clever woman may have merely retired to the Continent from motives not difficult to explain, her journeys to Pyrmont and Brandenberg, and finally her route to Switzerland will subject the British Court to suspicion that they were not unconcerned spectators of the Royalist Conspiracy.

P. 304.

[Mrs. Nisbett died abroad at the age of ninety, and her house at Norwood was sold and converted into the ' Park Hotel.']

Memorandum of Sir J. T. S. on revisiting Norwood.

After a passing away of fifty-six years, it was not without pleasure that I found myself in the haunt of my early days, with almost everything within its fences unchanged, but for the growth of trees. The wild common had, however, vanished. It was parcelled out in fields and gardens, and covered for the greater part with houses. My pleasure was indeed tempered with remembrances of the friend with whom in the same place I had spent many days of bright sunshine of my life. The woods, the fields, the garden, formerly so well known to me, were so little changed that Time, as to them, seemed to have had his wings clipped, or been lying down asleep.

But where were all I had beheld when my former I existed? The owner and the visitors of the place? If the woods asked, I could only answer in the Echo's words, ' Where are they?' And then the house, no longer the quiet home of one, but an hotel; open to all comers, and though many of the rooms I had wandered over were the same, all the well remembered books and pictures and furniture, which had been in them, had been removed and scattered. My eyes had fallen on new pictures or vacancy, where I had been accustomed to see full length portraits by Gainsborough of Lord Bristol (died 1779) and Mulgrave; and portraits of my schoolfellow, Augustus Hervey, and of Mrs. Nesbitt herself in the beauty of her youth. The clock was gone that Admiral Byng had sent to Lord Bristol, a few days before he was shot, with the words, ' May Time serve you better than he has done me;' and I missed the great bell which had been brought away from the Moro Castle by Lord B—— when the sailors of his ship stormed it, and placed by him over the Norwood stables.

TABLE OF FOUR GENERATIONS OF THE FAMILIES OF STANLEY AND HOLROYD

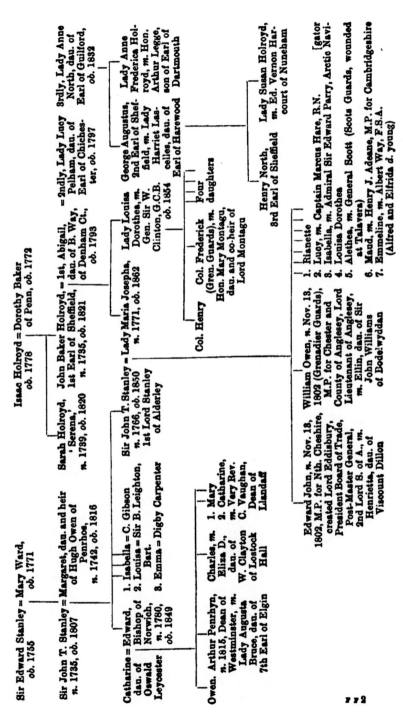

INDEX AND BIOGRAPHICAL DETAILS.

PRINTED BY
SPOTTISWOODE AND CO., NEW-STREET SQUARE
LONDON

CPSIA information can be obtained at www.ICGtesting.com
Printed in the USA
BVOW041100070312

284640BV00009B/50/P

9 781163 122013